Leith-Built Ships, Vol. III

LEITH-BUILT SHIPS

VOLUME 3

HENRY ROBB LTD.
(1945–1965)

R O NEISH

Whittles Publishing

Published by
Whittles Publishing Ltd,
Dunbeath,
Caithness, KW6 6EG,
Scotland, UK
www.whittlespublishing.com

© 2022 R.O. Neish

ISBN 978-184995-507-2

By the same author:

Leith-Built Ships Volume I
They Once Were Shipbuilders
ISBN 978-184995-443-3

Leith-Built Ships Volume II
Leith Shipyards 1918-1939
ISBN 978-184995-481-5

Bustler Class Rescue Tugs
In War and Peace
ISBN 978-184995-504-1

CONTENTS

FOREWORD

One of my earliest childhood memories is of my grandfather, the foreman loftsman at Henry Robb's shipyard, taking me on a visit to his drawing loft at the yard around 1949. The vast size of the room has stayed in my memory, together with the deafening and continuous sound of riveting on the adjacent slipways. As a Leith boy, I had always been fascinated by the docks and the shipyard, so I had eagerly looked forward to Ron's history of Leith shipbuilding. I enjoyed his first two books, but this volume is of particular interest, covering my grandfather's time at Robb's and my own life in Leith, both as a boy and later at Leith Nautical College when I saw the launch of SS *Aaro* for Ellerman's Wilson Line.

As in many other occupations such as miners and farmers, shipyard workers often followed their fathers into the job. My grandfather was no exception, with his father a Clyde shipwright and his father also a shipwright – who built the first RN steam frigate and later worked on warships for the tsar in St Petersburg. However, I did not follow this tradition but went to sea instead.

My enthusiasm for ships and the sea was further increased in 1951; when the dramatic attempted rescue of SS *Flying Enterprise* by the tug *Turmoil* captured the headlines around the world, I could proudly say to my school friends, 'My grandpa built that tug.' Maybe a slight exaggeration!

There are many good books on British shipbuilding, and Ron Neish's series is a major addition, with his excellent telling of Leith's shipbuilding history. I am already looking forward to the fourth volume, bringing us to the conclusion of this fascinating story.

Capt Peter Wallace RN (retd)

April 2021, Plymouth

ABBREVIATIONS

Shipbuilding has developed its own language, with thousands of words which have been coined over time to explain the particulars of working on the build of a vessel or when working on the actual vessel. Some are only used in boatbuilding while some are specific to steel shipbuilding; others are specific to both segments of what is a vast and complex industry.

The list below expands the abbreviations used in this series, and at the end of the book you will find a glossary of shipbuilding and nautical terms.

ABV	armed boarding vessel
aux	auxiliary motor
bhp	brake horsepower
CS	cable ship
DAMS	defensively armed merchant ship
DEMS	defensively equipped merchant ship
DEV	diesel-electric vessel
DWT	deadweight tons
FV	fishing vessel
grt	gross registered tonnage
HMAS	His Majesty's Australian ship
HMNZT	His Majesty's New Zealand transport
HMS	His Majesty's ship
HMT	His Majesty's trawler
ihp	indicated horsepower
LBP	length between perpendiculars (see Glossary, under AP)
LOA	length overall; the maximum length of the vessel
LWL	length at waterline

MT	motor tug
M/T	measurement ton (see Glossary, under Ton)
MV	motor vessel
nhp	nominal horsepower
ON	official number
PS	paddle steamer
PSS	paddle steamship
PTB	patrol boat
RFA	royal fleet auxiliary
rhp	rated horsepower
RMS	Royal Mail ship
RNLI	Royal National Lifeboat Institute
scr	screw-propelled; the vessel has a shaft driving a propeller (as against paddle-wheel propulsion)
shp	shaft horsepower
SMS	Seiner Majestät Schiff (His Majesty's ship)
SS	steamship
ST	steam tug
SWPS	stern-wheel paddle steamer
SY	steam yacht
THV	Trinity House vessel
TM	Thames measurement
TS	twin screws
TSM	twin-screw motor
TSMV	twin-screw motor vessel
TSMY	twin-screw motor yacht
TSS	twin-screw steamer
TSSY	twin-screw steam yacht
U-boat	Unterseeboot (under-sea boat), identified by UB and its number
USS	United States ship
W/T	weight ton (see Glossary, under Ton)

PREFACE

As I have indicated in previous volumes in this series on the ships built at Leith, shipbuilding was a tradition. It was something that got under your skin – but as a great many people never wished to work in this environment, they found it harsh at times. I however took to it like a duck to water. I started out on my working life as an apprentice loftsman. Part of the trade of the journeyman loftsman was to have a thorough understanding of shipbuilding from start to finish – so is it any wonder that ships and the sea quickly got under my skin?

Shipbuilding in its purest form is an art, and it is skilled craftsmen who produce that art. Whilst science has a huge part to play, it has nothing to do with the emotion of building a ship. In my experience there are few, if any, industries that could compare with shipbuilding for job satisfaction – pretty strange, you might think, for work that is dirty and dangerous, with no health & safety to speak of, and lacking facilities to help make the men's day any easier; working outside in all weathers, as the shipbuilders in Leith did, was considered normal. And because you were hired for one ship at a time, the better and faster you worked the sooner you could expect to be out of a job.

I was very lucky to serve my time as a loftsman in the shipyard that was Henry Robb Limited at Leith. When I started my apprenticeship the loftsmen, all very skilled craftsmen, were (in no particular order): Peter Rennie, Jim Russell, Willie Weir, Ali Holland and John Conafray, along with the foreman, Bill Straun. Each of them left many positives with me, but a special mention must go to Jim Russell, retired foreman loftsman. It was Jim who supplied me with the Shipyard Build Book, a full list of ships built at the Henry Robb Shipyard from Ship No 1 to the last ship built, No 535. I must also mark the contributions made by the last naval architect to work in the Henry Robb Shipyard, Robert Rowbottom, who has been unstinting in his encouragement and information.

This, then, is the continuing story of the ships built at the Leith shipyards. The first two volumes tell the story from circa 1850 to the start of the Second World War. This volume covers the time when the one remaining shipyard was that of Henry Robb, Shipbuilders & Engineers Ltd, from 1945 up until the boom years of the mid-1960s.

✷ ✷ ✷

To the many contributors to my website on the Leith shipyards – it would be impossible to mention everyone – thanks to you all.

Any opinion given is entirely my own, along with any mistakes, omissions or errors. I welcome corrections to the histories and can be contacted through the publisher.

<insert The Loftsman logo from Illustrations file, second item>

From British Shipbuilding Yards by Norman L. Middlemiss, 1995, here are some of the many, often mysteriously named, crafts and skills required in building and repairing ships:

Anglesmiths, Blacksmiths, Boatbuilders, Boilermakers, Brass Finishers, Bumpers Up, Burners, Cabinet Makers, Caulkers, Chargehands, Countersinkers, Cranemen, Draughtsmen, Drillers, Electricians, Engineers, Estimators, Fettlers, Fitters, Foremen, Frame Turners, French Polishers, Furnacemen, Holders Up, Iron Saw Men, Joiners, Labourers, Loftsmen, Machinists, Managers, Millwrights, Painters, Pattern Makers, Planers, Platers, Plumbers, Redleaders, Riggers, Riveters, Sailmakers, Sawyers, Scarphers, Stagers, Sheet Metal Men, Shipwrights, Storemen, Toolsmiths, Turners, Welders, Winchmen.

Volume III – the Context

With the end of the conflict that came to be known as the Second World War, many of Britain's men and women were coming back to a changing country, its change accelerated by the new government and the rise of the unions. The country was almost bankrupt, and people were tired of war and its consequences. The daily loss of life had left barely a family untouched, and some had of course been hit much harder than others. The shipyards of the whole country were looking forward to a bonanza time by replacing ships lost and repairing those damaged by the world events.

Yet in shipyards change still happened slowly, and to the upper management of the time almost any change was seen as a negative; they did not view the future with much confidence. Nationalisation, along with government interference, was seen by them as a restriction on free enterprise, making the task of profiting from shipbuilding more difficult. The clamour of the unions for more power and involvement was described by upper management as 'dangerous', and they countered it with the argument that the unions wanted a bigger share of business without taking on any of the risk associated with it. At the time, upper management at the Leith shipyard were dead set against any reduction in hours worked over the week. Still, even with the working week reduced, the shipyard continued to produce ships – a great many ships, – due to fleets seeking to replace their war losses.

Shipyards by their very nature and location become part of the social fabric and psyche of the local community. The yards always include people, and to this end I have included some personal stories from those who built or sailed or served on the ships built at Leith. You will see many of their tales, and the comments sent to my personal website, preserved here.

It is perhaps surprising that as a great shipbuilding nation Britain went from producing just over 80 per cent of all the world's commercial ships in 1893 to producing no commercial ships just 100 years later. It is not my intention to go into in any great detail why this may

A busy shipyard around 1946/7, all the berths have a ship in build. The arrow shows the start of the mould loft, which ran the full length of the building, with the tinsmiths' shop bolted onto the end closest to the sea. This was the old original Ramage & Ferguson loft where some of the finest ships ever to take to sea were laid down. (From the Loftsman Collection.)

have been so, although I do occasionally offer some personal insight and comment. Simply, my aim is to highlight the many fine ships built at Leith.

I have included descriptions of as many ships as possible, but constraints on space, time and research will inevitably mean that some are left out. So in Volume I there is a full list of all ships built at the Ramage & Ferguson shipyard from 1878 to its last ship, built in 1931. Volume II lists all the ships built at the Henry Robb yard from its inception in 1918 up to the start of the Second World War in 1939. And in this book, Volume III, are listed all the ships built at the Henry Robb Shipyard from the end of the Second World War up to 1965. Meanwhile, the ships built during the war will be covered in my forthcoming book, under the working title: Leith Shipyards at War.

ONE
THE BOOM YEARS, 1945–1950

With the end of the war in Europe and, a few months later, the victory over Japan, the Allied countries went about rearranging the map of the world. Nothing was to be the same – or, as they told the returning servicemen and servicewomen, 'This was going to be a land fit for heroes.'

Shipping fleets had of course been hit hard, and the need for replenishment began a real boom time for the shipyards of the British Isles. The yards had maintained a core of shipbuilders working to capacity – as shipbuilding was essential to the war effort, these craftsmen had been exempt from the callup – but full order books now meant the need to employ more men. This, despite the fact that conditions in the actual shipyards were still very basic; in fact, they could be described as downright primitive. But with materials a little more difficult to source and prices rising, any talk of new tools and/or changes to working conditions were put aside.

During the ten years from the end of the Second World War the Leith shipyards built a total of 70 ships, along with some 29 barges and lighters of various sizes and types.

Averaging seven ships per year, this was a busy time for the Henry Robb Shipyard. Full overtime was offered, and the majority of the men could be kept somewhat happy with an increased pay packet. As, however, all wages were paid in cash direct to each man at the end of the week, many wives never knew how much their husbands earned. Indeed, some womenfolk took to standing outside the shipyard gates at closing time on a Friday to make damn sure they got some money to keep the family going before the wage earner made for the nearest pub or bookmaker to fritter away his hard-earned cash. For the vast majority of working men there was no collaboration with banks or even a bank account.

The men were allowed one week's annual trades holiday, and extra time for Victoria Day and New Year – but they worked on Christmas Day. With a tradesman earning approximately 2 shillings per hour (£5 per week), it's clear why overtime was so important. The men were earning as much as possible while it lasted, 'make hay while the sun shines' being the working man's motto for the times. Most shipbuilders worked a standard 48-hour week, including Saturday mornings, giving them time to get home, change, grab a few beers and get to the

MV *Corncrake* under way (photo by kind permission of P&O Heritage).

football. In these post-war years the crowds at matches all over the country reached record levels.

It turned out that they were right to think that way, because radical new techniques, such as all-welded structures, were starting to be used in ship construction, and this meant a gradual but irrevocable loss of jobs; where it had taken four or five riveters to fit a plate it would now take only one welder to do the same job. Some of the riveters could be retrained as welders and some as caulkers/burners, but inevitably other men, surplus to requirements, would be laid off.

Although when the end of the war in Europe was announced there were still some warships under construction, the building of other non-military vessels – which had been on the stocks in 1939 and hastily cancelled – was quickly resumed. In addition, HMS *Carnarvon Bay* and HMS *Padstow Bay*, Bay class frigates originally seen as the ultimate stage in the development of the class, were now arranged primarily as air defence and picket ships, there to protect the larger capital ships from the very potent force of any future air attacks.

The keel had also been laid for the diesel cargo ship *Corncrake*, a typical coaster of her time, launched in December 1945, together with her sister ship *Redstart*; both vessels were based on the successful pre-war coaster designs, with the required tweaks and changes to their lines, taking in new equipment and deck arrangements as well as their owners' preferences. These ships were launched down the ways during the first peacetime spring of the 1940s – peace in the UK, at least – even though it was part of one of the most terrible decades in the history of humanity.

MV *Corncrake*, Ship No 351 (ON 180856), was the first ship of a two-ship order from the General Steam Navigation Company Ltd. A single-screw diesel cargo vessel of 629 tons, her principal dimensions were given as: length overall of 183 feet 6 inches, with a length between perpendiculars of 180 feet. She had a beam of 32 feet 10 inches and a moulded depth of 20 feet 5 inches. She was built for the coastal trade around the British Isles, and launched on 20 December 1945 into the peacetime waters of the River Forth. MV *Corncrake*

MV *Redstart*, from the P&O Archive Collection.

was employed on the profitable Liverpool–London trade route until 1967, when she was sold. Interestingly, this vessel was powered by a German engine, a 6-cylinder diesel engine built by Maschinenbau Kiel A.G. Since the majority of other Leith-built ships of this time would have had a British Polar engine, it must be assumed that the engine was one of those repatriated as part of the war costs awarded to the victorious Allied armies, this payment having taken many forms. She had a service speed of 10 knots, with a cargo capacity of 56,600 cubic feet. After service with the General Steam Navigation Company (part of the P&O Shipping Group) she was one of the small coasters making her way across the North Atlantic (although she had only the infamous weather of this route to contend with, and no U-boats). Purchased by H.W.C. Gillett Ltd, St John's, Newfoundland, and renamed *Twillingate* in 1967, she worked for that Canadian shipping company until 1988 before being sold on again to Panamanian shipping interests. *Corncrake* kept the same name and was eventually deleted from Lloyd's Register in 1999: a useful working life of more than 50 years.

Her sister ship MV *Redstart*, Ship No 352 (ON 180872), launched in March 1946, was the same size and ordered by the same owners. She did, however, have a different engine: a 5-cylinder diesel engine built and supplied by Newbury Diesel Co. Ltd, giving her a service speed of 10 knots. She was sold out of the General Steam Navigation Company in 1967 to Cyprus and renamed *Kapta Mathios*, then further renamed *Spyros G* in 1969, still under the same ownership. She sprung a leak east of Malta while voyaging from Piraeus to Tripoli with a cargo of bagged cement, and sank the following day, 8 February 1977.

The keels of two other cargo ships had been laid while the war was still ongoing, and these were launched in the winter months of 1945. *Kanna* and *Katui* were two standard-type cargo vessels for delivery to one of the Leith yard's best customers – the famous Union Steam Ship Company of New Zealand, to whom they were duly delivered.

MV *Kanna* (photo from Oceania shipping forum).

MV *Kanna*, Ship No 353 (ON 157665), had originally been for an order from the Admiralty for a supply ship for the South-east Asia theatre of operations, but with the end of the war in the Pacific she was taken over by the Union Steamship Company (USS Co.) of New Zealand. *Kanna* originated from a wartime design known as B-type China coasters, and she was to work the coast of New Zealand for many years, primarily the east coast of the South Island, from Wellington down to Dunedin.

She was sold to Panama in 1967 and went through a few name changes before grounding in heavy weather in Borneo in 1984. She was badly damaged and went for scrap that year; the end of another fine ship built in the Leith shipyards of Henry Robb.

The principal dimensions of *Kanna* were given as follows: length B.P. 210 feet with a beam of 36 feet 6 inches and a moulded depth of 21 feet 8 inches. She was powered by a 2SA 5-cylinder diesel engine to her single screw, built and supplied by J.G. Kincaid & Co. Ltd, Greenock. *Kanna* was launched in October of 1945.

Her sister ship, MV *Katui*, Ship No 354 (ON 172871), was launched the following month, November 1945. She was also broken up for scrap in 1984.

With the cancellation of the warship orders still on the books, the shipyard had to go out and get commercial orders to replace them – no problem at the time, because most of the remaining shipping lines required replacements for the huge merchant losses suffered. In fact, for a good few years after the end of the war the shipyards in the British Isles were working to capacity, and some shipping lines were in danger of missing out on new builds if they did not act fast enough.

So it was no surprise that the huge Ellerman's Wilson Line approached the Leith yard with one of the largest multiple ship orders it had ever received; this six-ship order was very welcome for a yard with eight berths to fill, and it ensured continuity of employment at a time when many of the temporary workers – male and female – were at risk of dismissal to make room for returning tradesmen. It was complemented by a further order from the USS Co. of New Zealand for another two large traditional ships, based on a successful wartime design cargo vessel.

All six Ellerman ships were launched from the Leith yard between August 1946 and November 1947, four of them going to the Wilson Line and the other two ships to be managed by the Papayanni Line, part of the large Ellerman's Wilson concern.

As tradition demanded, the four ships going to Wilson all had names ending in the letter O, while the two earmarked for Papayanni had names ending in 'ian'. The first ship was the very elegant SS *Tinto*, Ship No 355 (ON 181292), at 1,795 grt with a length of 280 feet, and she was successfully launched in August 1946. *Tinto* was powered by a triple-expansion steam engine T3-cylinder plus a low-pressure turbine, driving her single screw. The engine was built and supplied by Central Marine Engineering Works, West Hartlepool.

This classic structure-amidships vessel was wrecked one nautical mile off Rio Hainia in May 1972, and was so severely damaged that she was broken up in Santo Domingo in 1973.

Incidentally, there was an exceptionally fine builder's model of *Tinto* in a glass case in the mould loft when I was there – one I spent many hours looking at. (I wish I knew what happened to most of the great models we had in the loft and the drawing offices.)

SS *Tinto* was one of the first commercial ships to be built and launched from the yard just after the end of the Second World War.

The next launch took place in November 1946; *Tinto's* identical sister, sent down the ways into the water that month, was named SS *Truro*, Ship No 356 (ON 181297) – and went to the breakers' yard in Karachi in 1972, the year her sister ship hit the rocks. *Truro's* triple-expansion steam engine had been built and supplied by Central Marine Engineering Works, West Hartlepool.

SS *Bravo*, Ship No 357 (ON 181306), was next to hit the cold water, in February 1947. She had the same triple-expansion engine as the previous two steam ships.

She was followed by the first of the ships going to the Ellerman/Papayanni Line, TSMV *Darinian*, Ship No 359 (ON 181107). At 1,533 grt with a length of 255 feet she was slightly smaller than the previous three ships built for the company. She was also powered by a diesel engine, a 2SA 2 × 6-cylinder, driving her twin screws. Her engine was built and supplied by British Polar Engines Ltd, Glasgow.

All were very fine-looking traditional ships, with accommodation amidships – much of which would not have looked out of place in a much higher class of passenger liner, such was the attention to detail paid by the joiners' shop. A natural pride in their work was a tradition with the shipbuilders of Leith.

The other Wilson Line ship, SS *Silvio*, Ship No 358 (ON 181321), was launched in July 1947. Her triple-expansion steam engine was built and supplied by Central Marine Engineering Works, West Hartlepool. Then the final ship of the multiple order followed in the November. Named TSMV *Palmelian*, Ship No 360 (ON 182415), and managed, again, by the Papayanni Line, she was identical to her sister, TSMV *Darinian*.

Squeezed in between the builds of the larger cargo ships for the Ellerman's Wilson Line were a couple of tugs for yet another regular customer of the Henry Robb Shipyard, the Manchester Ship Canal. Its links with the yard went way back to the days of Cran & Somerville and their precedent for fine tugs.

As Ships No 370 and 371 respectively, MSC *Onset* (ON 169075), was launched in August 1947, followed by her sister ship, MSC *Onward* (ON 182597), from the same slipway the following month. Both were twin-screw diesel tugs, giving them the high manoeuvrability required for the confines of the canal.

As the tugs were being built the yard was active in the construction of another large order for half a dozen dumb barges for the Anglo-Iranian Oil Company. Unlike barges of today,

Left: MV *Darinian* crossing
the bar and heading out to sea
(photograph by Rui Amoria).

Right: MSC *Onset*, Ship No 370, at
work on the Manchester Ship Canal,
with a tow line aft of her charge to
keep its stern in the correct location.

Left: This view from the main
deck of *Kaitangata* shows
the mood of the seas at times
around the waters of the Tasman Sea and off the coast of New Zealand.

Right: MV *Konui* in the Wellington floating dock for some maintenance
work in 1969 (from the G. Ferguson collection).

these had a fair bit of shape to them and involved a lot of work for the steelworkers (also known as the Black Squad) in the yard. The barges were all built on the slips to the eastern side of the shipyard – closer to the Leith docks side, in fact. The barges were numbered in the traditional way, as Ships 364 to 369.

More barges followed towards the end of this decade, with an order for the Beira Boating Company, numbered Ships 383 to 388. In addition came orders for a pontoon and a couple of unnamed single-screw grab dredgers of 150 grt each.

Two traditional wartime-designed and identical colliers were next to be constructed at the yard, bound again for New Zealand: MV *Kaitangata*, Ship No 361 (ON 172886), and her sister ship, MV *Konui*, Ship No 362 (ON 172887). Both were 2,485 grt, with a length of

290 feet, and launched in January and May 1948, respectively. These were very solid, sturdy ships, built to cope with conditions in the coastal and river waters off New Zealand.

This order from the USS Co. Ltd was quickly followed by one for a further three ships, in what was a real boom few years for the shipyard. In fact, from the launch of *Kaitangata*, Ship No 361, in January 1948 to the launch of the dredger *Wanganui*, Ship No 395, in January 1950, the shipyard built and launched some 20 ships along with 15 barges or pontoons. (Thirty-five vessels in a two-year spell was amazing – especially when you compare it with the one ship per year during the final couple of years the yard was open).

On that list were some fine ships, including the two ordered by the British India Steam Navigation Company Ltd (BI) for the trade between Africa and the Arabian peninsula, and on to the Indian subcontinent.

The first ship was the twin-screw passenger/cargo vessel TSMV *Mombasa*, Ship No 379 (ON 183181), launched in February 1950. Her primary dimensions were given as follows: length B.P. 250 feet, with a beam of 43 feet and moulded depth of 19 feet. She had a gross registered tonnage of 2,213 and she was powered by 2 × 5-cylinder 2 SCSA diesels, producing 1,600 bhp, built by British Polar Engines Ltd, Glasgow. Her recorded speed on trials over the measured mile was 13.5 knots, with her service speed given as 12 knots.

Both she and her sister ship, MSV *Mtwara*, sailed the Mombasa–Mtwara service via Zanzibar, Dar-es-Salaam, Kilwa and Lindi, a round trip of ten days. *Mombasa* carried Sir Edward Twining, governor of Tanganyika, on her inaugural voyage to the port of Mtwara, and was the first commercial ship to visit the recently completed deep-water wharf when she arrived on 15 September 1953. She carried 8 first-class passengers, 16 second-class passengers and 250 deck passengers. In addition, she had a refrigerated capacity of 2,000 square feet.

After eight years with BI, during which she carried over 200,000 passengers and more than a quarter-million tons of cargo, *Mombasa* was withdrawn from service and laid up at Port Reitz, Mombasa, before being sold to Crescent Shipping Lines of Karachi, becoming *Kareem* on 18 October 1961. She was broken up in Karachi in 1968, with the ship's bell being presented to her last British India captain.

> I sailed as 5E/O on the Mombasa from July 1951 until July 1952. The ship was well known on the East African coast and was my first working ship in my career with the BI. Mitchell-Hedges the well known explorer and multi-millionaires res made a trip with us from Mombasa to Kilwa to explore the area and establish that civilization as we know it was began there. His exploits went on to become a series of adventure films – namely, the Indiana Jones series. The Mombasa was one of the happiest ships that I ever sailed on.
>
> John C. Robertson

The twin-screw passenger/cargo ship TSMV *Mtwara*, Ship No 393 (ON 184374), named after the town, was the second ship in the BI order to be built at the Leith shipyards of Henry Robb, and she was launched on a fine August day in 1950.

Mombasa seen here at anchor in 1950 (photo kindly supplied by P&O Heritage Collection).

Her principal dimensions were: length overall 298 feet with a length between perpendiculars of 280 feet, a beam moulded of 46 feet and a moulded depth of 27 feet 6 inches. Larger, at some 2,629 grt, than her sister ship, *Mombasa*, she cost £449,500 to build and was powered by 2 × 5-cylinder 2 SCSA Polar diesels, built by J.G. Kincaid of Greenock, Scotland, producing 4,000 bhp. She easily attained a trial speed of 16.75 knots over the measured mile in the Firth of Forth, while her service speed was 14 knots.

With the capacity to carry 26 first-class passengers, 40 second-class passengers and – wait for it – 350 deck passengers, she also had a refrigerated capacity of 2,000 square feet, and she operated on the coasts from Karachi/Mechran and the lower Persian Gulf. *Mtwara* was only in service with BI, however, for around two years before being sold to shipping interests in Saigon and, renamed Ville de Haiphong, intended for service in French Indo-China.[1] In fact, she was sold on again to Chile in 1956, renamed *Navarino*, where she traded south along the Chilean coast from Valparaiso, and then was re-engined in 1965 with 2 × 9-cylinder 4 SCSA MAN diesels, giving her a bit more power at 4,065 bhp.

Mtwara was then sold to the Chilean Navy for use as a training ship in 1978.

‘Navarino’, former ‘Mtwara’, ‘Ville de Haiphong’, was purchased by the Chilean Navy in 1978 to serve as an accommodation and services ship. She was sunk in an artillery and torpedo exercise in November 1981. Despite countless shell hits and severe torpedo

---

1 Now Vietnam, Laos and Cambodia.

Left: This nice view of *Mtwara* at sea is from the P&O Heritage Collection and has been kindly supplied by them.

Right: MV *Puriri* swinging round to move herself away from the berth on the River Greymouth in New Zealand. A river well known for its treacherous bar, where the rushing river waters meet the sea.

damage, she managed to stay afloat for hours before going to the bottom in the Strait of Magellan waters. Fine and gallant vessel!

Walter Wunderlich

The loss of the MV *Puriri* during the Second World War when she struck a mine led to a replacement being ordered. The second MV *Puriri*, Ship 363, was built for the Anchor Steamship Company of New Zealand.

MV *Grebe*, Ship No 374 (ON 181934), a modern coaster built from the original designs for such ships, was launched in March 1948. This was followed by the three-ship order from the USS Co. of New Zealand, all twin-screw cargo vessels. The first ship of these, TSMV *Kaitawa*, Ship No 375 (ON 172888), was lost at sea in 1966.

The loss of MV *Kaitawa* remains the worst peacetime maritime disaster to happen to New Zealand. On passage from Westport to Whangarei with a cargo of coal she was caught in a bad storm on 23 May 1966, and foundered only 5 miles from Cape Reinga,[2] with the loss of all hands.

Her sister ship, TSMV *Kaiapoi*, Ship No 376 (ON 172889), was launched five months after *Kaitawa*, in March 1949; both were 2,485 grt, with a length of 290 feet.

The final ship of this order was launched as the single-screw MV *Kamona*, Ship No 377 (ON 177210), and slightly smaller at 1,785 grt with a length of 235 feet. She was launched in May 1949.

With the build and launch of MSC *Grab Hopper No 1*, Ship No 378 (ON 182601), in January 1949 the year had started as busy as it finished, and there were another two tugs on order from the Manchester Ship Canal: MSC *Panther*, Ship No 381 (ON 182608), and MSC *Puma*, Ship No 382 (ON 182609). Both launched in February 1950; they were very similar to the previous two tugs ordered and with the same tonnage of 154 grt. Both were twin-screw, diesel-powered.

---

2 The northernmost tip of the North Island.

The grab dredger *Wanganui* working at Omaru, 1964 (from the Otago Daily Times).

In total, nine ships, along with an assortment of barges and pontoons, were built and launched in 1950; the Leith yard was keeping every slipway busy. And for the first five years of the 1950s this would continue, with many interesting ships built from a full order book.

There was a long line of work ships built in the Leith shipyards; although they were built for a specific task, they were used for so much more. The first ship to be launched in January 1950 was a fine example of many the Henry Robb yard produced. This was the single-screw diesel grab hopper dredger *Wanganui*, Ship No 395 (ON 172890). A grab dredger was a very complex and specialised type of vessel, with hopper tanks that opened from the bottom of the shell so that the sludge and mud could be dumped directly down into deep water in a convenient place.[3] *Wanganui* was an order from the harbour board of the same name – a small town in the south-west of the North Island of New Zealand – and she was based there on the Wanganui River, keeping it clean for shipping.

Trevor Gibson, her skipper, tells many a fine tale of times on board, including the shipment of cargo – and sometimes live cargo, at that. With a hopper capacity of 250 tons, her given dimensions were as follows: length of 107 feet 6 inches B.P. with a beam of 27 feet and a moulded depth of 10 feet 6 inches on a 252 grt. She was powered by a British Polar engine type M4, 4-cylinder 360 bhp at 350 rpm, giving her a service speed of 8.5 knots. She last dredged in 1988.

As told by the skipper of *Wanganui*, Trevor Gibson:

During my many years working on the Wanganui, there are so many stories to tell, but some that I do recall are told here in a chronological order. So going back to 1964 I remember being sent to South Beach to rig a breaches [sic] buoy in case it was required to get the crew off the Wanganui which had grounded on the beach after a steering mishap?? 29th July 1964. Once the tide had gone out there was no danger and the crew were able to get down by ladder. During the day wires were run out from the ship to the south mole for an attempt to re-float her on the mid night tide.

That night at 23.30 I was out at the mole end to connect a mooring line messenger from the Totoki, Captain Ted Charles passed by helicopter flown by Mike Alexander in the first night flight by helicopter flown in New Zealand. The towline snagged on a pile and could not be freed, we eventually managed to float the Wanganui and she was none the worse for her adventure.

Later that year I was appointed relieving Dredge Master, a position I was to hold permanently on account of Captain L.E.C. Dyer's health.

---

3 In that era little, if any, thought was given to the effect of the dump on the ecosystem below.

Then in 1968 I was appointed permanent Master of the Wanganui, taking out up to 6 loads of spoil per 8-hour day depending on the weather, if the bar was not workable then spoil was dumped in the river abeam of the lower groyne and the checker board.

I remember taking the Port Doctor out to the Russian ship Tula to bring a sick crew woman ashore with poisoning; the ship was en-route to Lyttelton from Russia with a cargo of potash.

As seen in the Wanganui Museum (photo by Trevor Gibson, ex-skipper).

The Wanganui was used in many roles and I was at the helm when we were used as a tug to turn the Tanea (oil tanker) and the Russian potash ships. I also remember getting caught on an outgoing tide and becoming high and dry for 10 hours on the edge of the turning circle.

She was a grand old working girl, and I am proud to have been associated with her for so many productive years; this is a model of Wanganui in a bottle, with all the parts made from driftwood collected over a period of time on the river; on and off, the model took me around 4 years to make.

Some other trips included many battles against the weather, again in 1968, we were heading for Oamaru to dredge the harbour entrance of shingle build-up, and then onto Lyttelton for survey and then back to Wanganui: 24 hrs wharf to wharf on a trip that averaged 30 to 36 hours, but on this occasion all went with us.

Unlike one trip that took 24 hours just to get round Cape Campbell, we lost all lighting, with no radio contact and the crew quarters awash and the chain locker flooded, we put into Picton to effect repairs, another time heading south it took 12 hours to sail 10 miles to get under the lee of Cape Campbell.

In 1970, while dredging at Wellington for 3 months at various sites, including the ro-ro berth and the breastwork, where I had a narrow escape from being crushed. After working the wharf from both ends, the sounding plan would not match up in the middle, I was so busy counting rows of piles, when the crane slewing caught me and took me between the crane and a ventilator, rolling me through and getting squeezed, then having to put the dredge alongside the wharf and radioing Beacon Hill to call for an ambulance all at the same time.

The hospital gave me some pain killers and said to return the next day for x-rays and strapping up. It took me 3 hours to get out of my bunk and get dressed. Once mobile and back at the Taranaki St breastwork we measured the wharf not once but three times. It was 90 feet short of what was on the plan.

The engineers knew but failed to tell anyone else which in the interim had caused many headaches, for the 3 watches that done the soundings. It was not only the water that was 'Blue'.

Then in 1975 we were moved down to Milford Sound, dredging channels into Deepwater Basin, and Freshwater Basin where the tourist launches berthed. Living on board and working 6 days, getting home for 3 days every 3 weeks.

We done all the tourist trips in this awe-inspiring part of beautiful New Zealand, up to the top of Bowen waterfall from where the water was taken for the Milford Hotel power station, drawing our stores from the hotel and living on the best of everything. Flying into Milford Sound was a treat in itself, berthing alongside the ex-Northern Steamships Co. Koatanui which was a freezer vessel for the Cray fishermen and the deer hunters.

Dredging up a non-existent power cable to the hotel which shut the power off for 3 days, while repairs took place, a section of the cable was presented to me prior to departure for services, rendered by the electrical dept MOW Milford Sound.

A couple of surveys at Nelson were next, where we picked up a lot of engine parts surplus to Anchor Dormans requirements, ex-*Puriri* which had the same engines as the Wanganui British Polar engines.

Then we took the Pilot launch Karere up to Waitotara to tow the Totara back to port after an engine breakdown. The tow took just around 7 hours at 2.5 knots.

Then we were Grab Dredging on the bar, when it was said it could not be done, and trying out a Warman pump on the bar, this worked but adaptation would have been too expensive at the time.

The Wanganui carried out a myriad of different tasks on and around the river including core sampling of the riverbed, basin and bar for engineering reports.

We even towed an experimental submersible sledge for bar dredging, which was not successful as it kept capsizing (It was an idea of a local diving contractor).

It is believed now that she has gone to be broken up for her scrap metal value; a few years ago, I was approached by someone who I took to be a salvage guy who wanted me to tell him approx how much scrap steel she contained. I could not bring myself to send him the answer; if a salvage company wants that type of information, then they can work this out for themselves.

The old grab dredger *Wanganui* rusting away at Great Barrier Island, New Zealand, around 2010.

Wanganui in dry dock at Lyttelton, New Zealand (photo from G. Ferguson collection).

Tony Robb:

I remember the dredge with affection, my father (Fred Robb) used to, on odd occasions, supply water to her … and I saw her many times in action, when as a young fellow, I used to fish off the wharf.

Another two modern diesel coasters were then commissioned for the General Steam Nav. Co. Ltd, the largest company of its type in the British Isles. MV *Hirondelle*, Ship No 396 (ON 183267), was first launched in June 1950, with her sister ship MV *Swift*, Ship No 397 (ON 184292), in October the same year. At the same time, an order for three more ships from the USS Co. of New Zealand was being fulfilled. The launch of MV *Kawatiri*, Ship No 399 (ON 179928), on 6 October 1950, was the first of the trio. Her sister ship, MV *Kokiri*, Ship No 400 (ON 179931), would not be launched until September 1951.

TSMV *Kawatiri*, one of the AC class colliers built to a wartime design, very tough and sturdy ships that really looked the part, was to be registered in Wellington, New Zealand. Her two shafts were driven by two 5-cylinder, 2-stroke British Polar M45M engines of 1,450 bhp (total) to give her a service speed of 9.5 knots. With a registered tonnage of 2,484 her dimensions were: length overall 305 feet 4 inches with a beam of 43 feet and a moulded depth of 19 feet 6 inches. She was to give good service to the USS Co. Ltd of N.Z. for many years before being sold to Panama and renamed *Kawati* in 1972. She was then sold on once more in 1979, to be renamed *Hati Senang*, the third ship of this name for the company. She served it well for almost 20 years before being sold on, primarily used to carry coal around the New Zealand coast. She was under the Panamanian flag being managed by a Singapore company for another six or seven years before being sold on again to sail under the Malaysian flag, for nine further years, before being scrapped to make razor blades in 1987.

By this time, the originally-named *Kawatiri* had faced the stormy seas of South-east Asia for around 37 years, providing good service to her owners. When you consider that most

Left: MV *Kawatiri*, loading coal at Greymouth, the South Island, New Zealand.

Right: *Kawatiri* crew: top Garry King, deck boy; middle, Andy Cook; bottom, Scouse and Norm (photos, Garry King).

ships had a useful working life of circa 25 years, this was a pretty good return – and shows just how well these ships were put together. (Although it has to be said that once she had been sold on from USS Co. Ltd she did not appear to receive the best of attention and maintenance.)

This tough little collier made a big impression on the men who sailed on her; below you will find some of their stories:

Deck boy on MV *Kawatiri*, as told by Garry King:

I joined the Kawatiri 1962 at the age of 15 years at Port of Lyttelton as first trip deck boy. Very exciting an nervous time and remember first day met the Bosun who was a Geordie and I couldn't understand a word he said. After a few days everything fell into place and I understood him and he was a good seaman. We sailed to Westport and did the coal run to Auckland and Whangarei for 2 trips. Then on to Tauranga, to load with a cargo of paper for Australia. We sailed to Brisbane, Adelaide, Sydney, Coffs Harbour and back to Brisbane. Remember having power poles from Coffs Harbour and we had a A.B. fell down the hold when adjusting the beams. He spent some time in hospital. I sailed with him again in the SS Waihemo. We sailed back to Wellington, Lyttelton, Dunedin, Bluff and back to Dunedin where we were all paid off for the ship to go on survey It was a great start for me and I went on to next a small coaster and finished my boys time on the TransPacific Waihemo.

MV *Kawatiri* story, as told by Sandy Balfour:

She was a grand little ship and although built as a collier we carried an assortment of other cargoes (steel, gypsum, timber, newsprint and a variety of general cargo) on inter-colonial trades between New Zealand and Australian, more or less tramping here there and everywhere. The scary moment he refers to occurred while we were on passage from Busselton in Western Australia to Dunedin N.Z. deep laden with a full cargo of jarrah hardwood with just a few tons of pig iron underneath it in the bottom of the lower holds.

We were running before a high following sea down in the Roaring Forties and I had just come off watch at midnight when a massive sea broke over the port side inundating the foredeck, followed by a deep rumble as the pig iron shifted and the vessel took a severe port list. I think the helmsman had come off course a bit, and had we taken another sea in quick succession like the first one I doubt I would we writing this now. Fortunately this didn't happen, and after the engineers had shifted some

Upper left: Running before a heavy following sea.

Left: At Westport, loading coal (photo Sandy Balfour).

Lower left: MV *Kawatiri* (photo Sandy Balfour).

Right: Taking a noon sighting (photo Sandy Balfour).

15

water ballast we eventually returned to an even keel – but yes, it was one of those occasions at sea which you don't forget.

Captain Roger Tindall was master on a number of USS Co. ships, among them a fair few that had been built at Leith, including *Navua* and *Kawatiri*. He was captain of *Kawatiri* when she was the last ship to trade coal into the river at Greymouth; the following is a quote from him regarding his experience of trading down the west coast of New Zealand.

A captain's story: Time on the colliers of the USS Co. of New Zealand:

It was the very best experience a young Master could have to start off on the colliers running down the West coast of N.Z. and running bar/river harbours, as those class of colliers had nothing, just Monkey Is. and steering magnetic compass. An old D/F set. Wire sounder on the poop. Not even clear view screens. There was nothing like pile driving a collier down the coast from North Cape to Greymouth in high winds and rain seeing very little. Then on D.R. making in towards the land with only about a mile visibility with wheelhouse windows open in driving rain and eyes peeled, ears listening and nostrils smelling, looking for a familiar land mark or breakwater if you were lucky.

Those times sure as hell honed your skills, and made you prudent. I carried those experiences with me throughout my career even when on a vessel with everything that opened and shut like New Zealand Pacific. This over a period honed an acute sixth sense for knowing when things were not right. In later years that sixth sense gave me a feeling in my water time and time again to go up onto the bridge or take action elsewhere to avert troubles. Also the idea of pilotage exemptions for N.Z., Aus and Pacific Island ports gave you confidence to be able to handle your vessel in all kinds of situations.

A great many of the seafarers from New Zealand, held their ships close to the heart and never shied from telling stories about these tough, tight-crewed ships.

More comments on their time on *Kawatiri*:

John Pothan:

I sailed with her twice as 4th engineer in 1966 and 1967. Once we were on our way back with a full load of steel. For the New Plymouth Power Station. Cyclone Dinah meet up with us in the Tasman, we had a few days without hot meals and as an engineer we were meant to check the steering gear on each watch, I hasten to say this was not done for a few days.

Brian G. Ross:

I sailed as 3rd Engineer from April 1962 until April 1963. Garry King must have been with me just before we did the Survey at Port Chalmers. What a great little ship she was.

I recall an anxious moment, sailing from Bunbury WA across the Australia Bight to Bluff. We had a huge following sea. The ship was rolling bad when suddenly she rolled way over, gave a shudder and stayed there. I immediately started the ballast pumps to trim her level and she slowly responded. We later found that the ingots of pig iron in her hold had slid to one side causing her go out of trim. Man, that was a bit scary. I still have a movie of her loading paper at Tauranga and sailing to Melbourne, Adelaide and Edithburgh.

TWO
THE BOOM CONTINUES – OR SO THEY THOUGHT! 1950–1955

While all orders into the Leith shipyards were very welcome, the largest orders for multiple ships had a slightly different effect on the mould loft and to a lesser degree the steelwork drawing office. This arose from the fact that when two vessels are the same or near identical then the ship's lines only need to be done the once, so all the lofting is done at the same time, and the same templates can be used for one or more ships. This means a reduction in the workload of the loftsmen – although at a busy time this is good for the company in reducing costs and allowing the loft to work on other orders.

It is a real balancing act to be able to keep all departments of a shipyard busy at the same time. Fortunately for the Leith workers of the time, the Henry Robb yard specialised in mostly one-off ships, meaning that unlike some of the other larger yards to the west Robb's had very little by way of slab-sided shells. In other words, each bit of steel was a one-off, with only its opposite hand being of use, so that any shell plate could only be used once on the port side, with its opposite-hand plate going to the starboard side. This type of build meant it was not really in the best interests of the yard to look at building in a more repetitive production-line-type environment employed in other industries, such as the aircraft and automotive industries – so not so much in the way of tooling or jigs and fixtures was required. However, the use of shell jigs was, of course, employed in shipbuilding from an early age of steel building.

Each new build was just that, and most of the Leith-built ships had lots of shape in them, often complex in development which took more time (unlike, as said before, some of the larger types built with an eye on maximising profit, with much the same shape for up to, perhaps, half the vessel's build length). In the mould loft, accuracy was priority number one, as any small deviation in the loft would be replicated in the yard resulting in a poor fit and thus the dreaded rework, which every shipyard could do without. The threat of rework, which increased the build cost of a ship dramatically, was yet another reason for men being trained to the highest standard possible.

Following a hopper barge for the Leith shipping company of Christian Salvesen – required for its whaling station works on South Georgia – and some more small sugar barges of around 50 grt (keeping the platers and riveters busy), the final ship of the New Zealand-bound three-

MV *Waimata* in Wellington (photo is from L. Buttersfield's
own collection – reproduced here with thanks).

ship order that had been commissioned in the previous decade was launched in June 1951.
She was the largest, to be called MV *Waimate*, Ship No 398 (ON 179930); although she had
been originally laid down as *Kurutai*, her name changed during the build. At 3,506 grt and a
length of 325 feet she was a good-size ship for the yard, and her principal dimensions were
given as follows: length overall at 354 feet 8 inches, with a length B.P. of 325 feet; she had a
beam of 50 feet moulded and a moulded depth of 33 feet 9 inches. She was powered by a
British Polar engine, giving her a service speed of 10.5 knots.

She went on to serve the USS Co. Ltd for around 20 years until the advent of containerisation
(which the traditional derrick cargo ships could not compete with), meant that she was sold
on, first in 1972, to a company in the Philippines, and then again in 1977, when she was
renamed *Sky Luck*.

Under this somewhat colourful name she arrived in Hong Kong harbour with 3,000
Vietnamese refugees on board, after a voyage from Singapore. This journey, which should
have taken around 5 days took about 27, and on arrival the authorities refused her landing
permission. This left her no option but to sit around at anchor for about four months.
Conditions must have got pretty bad during this time, and one night the ship mysteriously
drifted to shore and ran aground, at which point the majority of the stranded passengers
proceeded to disappear. Later investigation was to show that *Sky Luck*'s anchor cable had

Left: As the ship *Sky Luck*, aground on the rocks at Lamma, Hong Kong
Right: MV *Waimata* in better days.

been cut; the ship was impounded and demolition was ordered. In 1981, she was broken up at Lamma, the very place where she had run aground.

> I served on the Union Steamship Co. MV Waimata as a very young deck boy, my first time at sea, back in 1955. After leaving the coast of New Zealand, our first port of call was Singapore. Looking back at this time I still remember the marvellous sense of discovery of a strange land and its people, and the thrill of being at sea. For me this was the first of many doorways through which I went finding adventure and great opportunities in life.
>
> Regards
>
> Capt. Ian Telke

The next builds were two beautiful ships for the Ellerman's Wilson Line, part of the company's expansion plans for its fleet at this time of growth in shipbuilding and the transport of goods across oceans in peacetime. Both ships had accommodation, quite luxurious, for 12 passengers, and in an age when jet travel was still in its infancy, for those passengers who could afford it this was the only way to travel.

MV *Cavallo*, Ship No 406 (ON 185099), was launched on 19 July 1951 and was the first one down the ways into the waters of the Firth of Forth in November that year. Her standard of accommodation, including the passenger lounge, dining lounge and cabin fittings, would not have looked out of place in a high-class hotel – the joiners at Henry Robb turned out some very fine work indeed. *Cavallo* was powered by a diesel engine 2 × 8-cylinder, producing 3,040 bhp, driving her single screw. Her details were as follows: tonnage 2,340 gross, 1,251 net: dimensions 296.5 × 48.6 × 15.9 feet. Her engine was built and supplied by British Polar Engines Ltd, Glasgow.

She was used to transport goods and cargo both to Canada and on the shorter routes to Scandinavia, before being sold in July 1971, along with *Trentino*, to the Maldive Islands and renamed *Maldive Venture*. She was then sold for scrap to the Metal Scrap Trade Corporation of India, arriving in Calcutta on 23 August 1980 for demolition.

Tales from the Ship

A galley boy at sea, as told by Chris Bond:

I only have a couple of pictures taken during my Cavallo Days. I only had a small Kodak Brownie and film / processing was expensive when you were only earning £12 per month with no days off until you paid off, I still loved my time at sea though.

My working time was mainly peeling potatoes (by hand) for 47 crew and 12 passengers and cleaning the galley after each meal. We worked from 0600 to 2000 including overtime with a 2 hour break in the afternoon and on the way back to the UK we worked most nights until 2200 painting the ship ready for the arrival into West India Docks London, where the shore management would do an inspection.

We had a really good Captain named Fred Briggs and during the 12 months I spent on her she was a very happy ship. The normal route for Cavallo was Mediterranean, Malta, Tripoli, Cyprus, Syria, Lebanon etc. and the trips were 6 to 7 weeks long. We took over from another Ellerman's Wilson ship at one point and did a couple of trips to Scandinavia.

We carried 12 passengers, mostly elderly people who not only had the money for the fare but could go away for 7 weeks at a time.

Apart from the episode in Sweden with the dockside crane collision I can't recall any other momentous events; it was mostly routine.

Stuart Johnston had the following to say about his time on *Cavallo*:

My proudest moment on Cavallo was at the wheel as cadet going under Tower Bridge once and berthing at wharf immediately after the bridge on the south side of the river. Even though I was carrying out the river pilots' instructions it was still a bit nerve racking.

Great little ship, all my trips were down to the med on the NAAFI run Malta, Cyprus with baked beans and Mars bars! Malta was always an attraction for the crew with Strait Street, aka 'the gut', being very popular. I remember one trip when on deck duty one morning local police chief came aboard to see the captain as he had a number of the crew in the local jail. Captain advised him that he would send down his officers to sort things out only to be advised, 'they are your officers, Captain!' Happy days.

MV *Trentino* was launched in April 1952, an exact replica of her sister ship Cavallo, along with the same power plant. These were known as shelter deck ships; most Ellerman boats were.

The following information is from the last naval architect at the Henry Robb Shipyard:

MV *Trentino*, Ship No 407, under way in ballast.

Ship No 407, MV Trentino, Ellerman's Wilson Line

Dims:	290' BP × 48.5' × 19.75/28.25'
Draught:	19.5'
Dead Weight:	2,986 tons
Service Speed:	13 knots
Type of Vessel:	general cargo, open shelter deck Class VII, 12 passengers
BHP:	3,040
Speed on Trial:	14.7 knots

This was the first ship I saw launched at the yard, on 30 January 1952. The below photo shows her in April, on speed trials, on the Burntisland measured mile. (These were the days before deck cranes and heavy lift Thomson derricks.)

One method of increasing the cubic capacity without an increase in tonnage of a cargo ship, was to build a complete superstructure from bow to stern. The shelter deck was continuous and unbroken at the ship's side and was opened at the middle line in accordance with tonnage regulations. Openings in the tween-deck bulkheads were also required by the rules. These openings had to have temporary closing plates and the tween-deck space was considered open to the sea and not measured for tonnage.

These ships were not as safe as those in which the bulkheads extended to the weather deck, and new tonnage measurement regulations were brought in later which made the shelter deck intact. but the load draught had to remain 2 inches below the second deck.

In [each S class vessel there is a] triangle painted on the ship's side at the load line. The draught must not exceed this, otherwise tonnage would be measured to the shelter deck. The old-fashioned tonnage openings no longer existed in the shelter deck and intact buoyancy was maintained.

Some ships were classified as open and closed shelter deck.

R. Rowbottom.

Some more barges were built, then the motor tug *Hewitt*, Ship No 412, was ordered by the Ribble Nav & Preston Dock, for work in the Preston dock, a very busy inland port at that time. She was the first of six tugs all built around 1952 and 1953.

MV *Trentino* doing the measured mile on speed trials in the Firth of Forth.

At the same time, there was an event occurring in the shipyard that would capture the attention of the world for two dramatic weeks – and at a time when the only live medium for news was the radio.

The salvage tug *Turmoil* was one of eight Bustler class tugs built for the Admiralty. This was the first fleet of tugs with diesel engines, designed for sea towing, salvage and rescue work; they were not suitable for harbour work.

The Leith-built tugs were amongst some of the finest built anywhere and it was always good for the men who built them to hear of their many exploits worldwide. The story of the former tug *Turmoil* is told here from various sources, including my own and those of Peter Wallace.

The story of *Flying Enterprise* and *Turmoil*:

High drama on the *Flying Enterprise* by James Donahue:

The World War II Liberty Ship Flying Enterprise was lost after it got caught in a late December hurricane in the mid-Atlantic in 1951.

The ship took on an ominous 30 degree list after the cargo shifted in the rolling seas. Then a crack developed amidships across the main deck and 12 feet down each side of the hull and the engine room flooded.

That happened on Christmas week. It took over two weeks for the Flying Enterprise to sink, however. In the meantime, the world was captivated by the news stories telling of the dramatic attempts to save the ship and tow it to safety.

The drama involved a brave captain and second sailor who remained aboard the stricken vessel until almost the last moment. They literally jumped from the smokestack to safety after the tow line parted the ship sank under their feet on 10 January 1952.

When it foundered the Flying Enterprise was just 42 miles away from Falmouth.

That captain's name was Henrik Kurt Carlsen. The man with him was Kenneth Dancy, the mate from the tug Turmoil who jumped to the deck of the Flying Enterprise while attempting to attach a tow line. Once aboard the sinking vessel, Dancy couldn't easily get back, so he rode out the drama with Carlsen.

The final voyage of the Flying Enterprise began on 21 December at Hamburg, Germany. It was bound for the United States with a cargo of 1,300 tons of pig iron and 900 tons of coffee. Also aboard were ten passengers. The ship was owned by Isbrandtsen Shipping Co. of New York.

The storm caught the vessel about 400 miles west of Lands End on Christmas night. The pounding seas and gale continued for several days. One large sea caused the ship to roll hard to port, and it failed to right itself. The cargo shifted. At about that time the crack was discovered on the weather deck.

An SOS was answered by several ships and the passengers and crew were removed by lifeboats to the US Navy troopship General AW Greely and the SS Southland on 29 December. The seas were still too high for the lifeboats to pull alongside the stricken ship so everyone had to jump into the sea before boarding the boats.

Captain Carlsen chose to remain with the ship to await the arrival of a tug.

The salvage tug Turmoil reached the Flying Enterprise on 3 January. But there was a problem. With only Captain Carlsen aboard the listing ship, it was impossible to connect a tow line. After several attempts, Dancy made his daring jump from the tug on to the deck of the foundering ship and brought with him a rope attached to a tow line.

By now the Flying Enterprise was listing by about 60 degrees, but the storm was abated and the Turmoil began the long tow back toward the English Channel. By now, due to drift, the estimated location of the ship was about 300 miles from Falmouth.

The listing hulk was a difficult tow. Because it was heeled over, the ship sheered from one quarter to the other. The two vessels were travelling at a speed of only about three knots in a long Atlantic swell.

Then on 8 January the weather deteriorated. Another gale developed when the Flying Enterprise was only 60 miles from safety. The tug was forced to heave to, with its bow into the storm. And the sinking ship was now riding deeper in the water and rolling to about 80 degrees. The tow line parted on 9 January.

When the ship began showing signs of breaking up, Captain Carlsen and Dancy were forced to jump from the ship's funnel into the sea, where they were picked up by the Turmoil. The date was 10 January.

From the deck of the tug they watched the Flying Enterprise sink. They said her bow rose into the air, held for a few moments, and then in a classic ship-sinking picture, slid beneath the sea.

Left: Turmoil stands off *Flying Enterprise*.
Right: Flying Enterprise.

Captain Carlsen received a hero's welcome when he came ashore at Falmouth. He later was awarded the Lloyd's Silver Medal for meritorious service in recognition for his attempts to save his ship. Captain Carlsen rejected the inevitable Hollywood contract and modestly disappeared from public view, however his next command was the Flying Enterprise II.

The order for *Hewitt* was followed by a four-ship order from the Manchester Ship Canal Company. (NB at this time the ship numbers really jumped around, because a ship would often be launched out of number sequence but in line with the yard's build process).

MSC *Quarry*, Ship No 413, was launched in December 1951, followed by her identical sister ship, MSC *Quest*, Ship No 414, in November 1952. MSC *Ranger*, Ship No 415, was launched in January1952, with the final ship of the order, MSC *Rover*, Ship No 416, in February1953. *Rover* was another of the new breed of tug on the canal, the twin-screw tugs being slightly more powerful than the previous vessels built for the company in the Leith shipyards of Henry Robb. She was of traditional design with a straight stem and an elliptical stern, built to tow the large ships up and down the canal like a mother duck looking after her ducklings.

All four ships were actually the same size, with the same type of engine from Crossley Brothers in Manchester. This was all part of the Manchester Ship Canal Company's expansion and renewal of its fleet of tugs for the ever-growing trade bringing goods right into the heart of Manchester – a city of around a million inhabitants, 28 miles from the sea. In fact, the records of ships kept in this country are, of course, no problem to find, but many thanks must go to the Manchester Ship Canal Co. Ltd for its help with records of the many tugs built in Leith for the company. The order was yet another example of how so many different industries relied on the shipbuilding industry; it was reckoned that for every job in the yard another nine jobs were created outside the yards themselves, working on some part or other of the ship.

Arusha, Ship No 417, was the last of the six tugs all built around the same time, an order from the famous British India Steam Navigation Company Ltd (a subsidiary of the huge P&O group), with the requirement of a steam tug.

MSC *Rover* with a ship under tow on the Manchester Ship Canal.

Arusha was ordered for work on the East African coast, where the larger cargo ships were unable to navigate, towing barges and lighters up the rivers. Along with general tug-towing work, she remained on this coast for five years before being sold to the Falmouth Towing Company (another part of the P&O group) and renamed *St Mawes*. She was powered by a triple-expansion steam engine, producing 800 ihp, built by White's Marine Engines Ltd, Newcastle upon Tyne. Her principal dimensions were given as: length overall 121 feet 1 inch with a beam of 32 feet and a moulded depth of 23 feet; at 346 grt she was a large tug. With a service speed of 10.5 knots, she exceeded her speed at trials to give 12.5 knots – way over her contract speed.

Arusha was to work in UK waters for the next 28 years, only broken up in 1984.

The steam-powered tug *Arusha* (kind thanks to the P&O Heritage collection). Note the open bridge and wheelhouse.

This is a great photo of *Wareatea* (A.C. Green collection).

Wareatea, Ship No 418, was built for the firm of William Hollyman & Sons Pty Ltd, and destined for a working life down under. She was launched in May 1952, a steel single-screw cargo vessel (refrigerated), powered by an 8-cylinder 2 SCSA oil engine by British Polar Engines Ltd of Glasgow. Her principal dimensions were: length overall 254 feet (length B.P. 240 feet) with a beam of 37 feet and a moulded depth of 20 feet. Her gross registered tonnage was given as 1,430.

After nearly 20 years on the Adelaide–Hobart run, then replaced by a ro-ro, she was sold to Concordia Shipping of Singapore and renamed *Bonahope* in 1971. She was sold once again to Oriental Navigation Co. S.A. of Singapore in 1972. Her history is somewhat cloudy after this, and her Singapore registry was closed in 1984, then her Lloyd's Register entry was deleted in 1992.

More barges and pontoons built between the launchings kept the yard busy. One of two twin-screw diesel tugs built for the quaintly named Crown Agents for the Colonies (old empire traditions clung on even up to the mid-1950s), MT *Fourah*, Ship No 422, was launched in September 1952, after her sister ship, MT *Farren*, Ship No 423, launched in the June. Both tugs had the same dimensions, both were registered at 306 grt, and both were for service at Freetown in Sierra Leone.

After that, two more pontoons were to be built before MV *Karumu*, another order from the Union Steamship Company of New Zealand, went down the ways into the Forth. *Karumu* was a single-screw diesel cargo ship with dimensions given as follows: length B.P. 250 feet, with a beam of 41 feet 6 inches and a moulded depth of 25 feet 3 inches. Her tonnage was given as 1,988 grt and she was powered by a Clarke Sulzer 5-cylinder oil engine 2S SA 1,500 bhp, built by George Clarke, Sunderland, England. Her service speed was 11 knots. She was launched in January 1952.

MV *Karumu* (copyright B. McNeil, photo shown here by courtesy of G. Ferguson).

Karumu was sold out of the USS Co. with the advent of containerisation, and was renamed *King Luck* in 1972, operating under this name until 1979 when renamed *Tsin Yuen*. She was broken up in 1984.

The first of a two-ship order from Henry & McGregor Ltd was next to launch, as MV *Marwick Head* in August 1952. She was a 1,786 grt diesel cargo vessel.

This completed the launchings for 1952.

Dunnet Head, Ship No 429 (ON 184042), was the first ship ready for launching in 1953, in March, the second order from the local Leith Shipping Company of A.F. Henry & MacGregor Ltd, and to be registered at Leith. She was a single-screw cargo ship of 749 grt and her given dimensions were: length overall 192 feet 10 inches (length B.P. 180 feet) with a beam of 31 feet 2 inches; her moulded depth was 15 feet. She was powered by a diesel oil 2SA 8-cylinder engine built and supplied by British Polar Engines Ltd, Glasgow. She was sold on in 1966 to Bouchard Navigation Ltd, Quebec, where she was renamed *Conrad Marie*. She was deleted from Lloyd's Register in 1992.

In April 1953, the launch was ready for a large cargo vessel ordered by the Rodney S.S. Co. Ltd, London. She was to be named MV *Longfellow*, Ship No 428 (ON 185918), and a large vessel for the yard to work, on at 3,948 grt. Her given dimensions were as follows: length overall 356 feet 7 inches (length B.P. 335 feet), with a beam of 50 feet 2 inches and a moulded depth of 26 feet 6 inches. Her single screw was powered by a diesel oil 2SA 5-cylinder engine, supplied and built by Sulzer Brothers Ltd, Winterthur, Switzerland.

She worked for the Rodney Steam Ship Company until 1960, when her ownership was transferred to the somewhat mysterious Chine Shipping Co. Ltd, London. She was renamed *Bushwood* in 1961, the year she was bought by Wm. France, Fenwick & Co. Ltd, London. She was then sold again, in 1971, to a Panama company and renamed *Mistral*. She would be renamed once more in 1977, to *Malea* while flying the Panama flag, before being broken up in 1981.

The Leith shipyards of Henry Robb were to build a total of three cement carriers for work in New Zealand, the first of them *Golden Bay* (I), Ship No 430, a twin-screw diesel that had a drive with 'electromagnetic couplings' in the drive line. She was ordered by Associated Portland Cement in 1953, a pretty special ship for her time, and was to work in New Zealand for many years before being replaced by another *Golden Bay* (this one built by the Caledon Shipyard, at the time part of the company then known as Robb Caledon, after Henry Robb had taken over the Dundee yard). She had the following dimensions: length B.P. 230 feet, with a beam of 42 feet and a moulded depth of 18 feet.

The following is taken from a story in The Dominion newspaper on the last voyage of the original *Golden Bay*:

> The veteran cement carrier Golden Bay, the first of her kind in New Zealand waters, sailed from Wellington last night for Nelson on her last coastal voyage.
>
> During her 20 years of service between Tarakohe and Wellington she has carried thousands of tons of cement. She is to be laid up pending sale.
>
> Not many coasters attract much attention when they take up their humdrum duties. But in March 1955, however, the Golden Bay figured largely in the news as a vessel of a new type and design.
>
> She was built at Leith (Scotland) by Henry Robb on August 27, 1953, and ran her trials on May 27th, 1954. Before coming to New Zealand her novel equipment had a thorough testing on the British coast over a period of several months.

The design of the 1659-ton Golden Bay presented several difficult problems to the owners, shipbuilders, and engineers. Such items as stability, trim and strength were of the usual kind, but she introduced something unusual in the loading and discharging arrangements for bulk cement.

The power required for this bulk handling equipment is far greater than that required to propel the vessel. She was also designed to carry coal as an alternative cargo to supply the cement works at Tarakohe from Greymouth or Westport.

Two large holds, separated by a centre-line bulkhead, are arranged over the entire mid-ship body. Forward of the cargo holds is situated in the large machinery space where the cargo handling equipment is installed – all electrically driven. Motors control the operation of travelling crawler conveyers in each of the fore and aft holds. These conveyers also incorporated inclined and transverse scrapers, one to each hold, and are arranged to travel the full length of the compartment. A DC variable speed motor powers each of the four longitudinal dragline scraper conveyers, which are fed by cross scrapers of the crawler feed.

The Golden Bay is 245 feet long and she is powered by two British Polar four-cylinder diesel engines driving twin screws, which give a speed of 12.14 knots on trials.

Golden Bay was also the first vessel to be fitted with electromagnetic couplings/alternators, which facilitate the use of the propelling machinery for discharging the cargo while she is in port.

She arrived at Wellington in April 1955 after a 61-day voyage of 13,500 miles out from Britain – via the Suez Canal, Aden, Colombo, Singapore and Townsville. On the passage she averaged better than 10 knots under the command of Captain C.V. Ostenfeld, of Nelson.

Living accommodation is at the after end of the ship and consists of two-berth cabins for the crew.

She brought a cargo of bagged cement which was discharged at Wellington.

Left: *Golden Bay*.
Right: The launch of *Golden Bay* (I), Ship No 430, from the Leith shipyards of Henry Robb.

Golden Bay (I) was to work the coast of New Zealand until 1981 and she was to have many adventures some of which have been sent to me by engineer Tony Skilton who served on all 4 of the cement carriers built in Scotland for New Zealand three of them at the Leith Shipyards of Henry Robb and the replacement for the original Golden Bay (Same name) which was built in the Dundee yard of Robb Caledon.

The Diesel Electric Vessel Golden Bay (I) was to be sold on in 1976 to be renamed to Ryujin Maru and she was broken up in China in 1981.

The following pages, including photographs, are presented with the kind help of engineer Tony Skilton who happened to stumble over some old photographs in the Fletcher Challenge Trust Archives and, with the kind help of Dorothy there, sent us some of the old photographs and stories of the original *Golden Bay* (I). All photographs below are shown by permission of the Fletcher Challenge Trust Archives, Auckland, New Zealand.

Upper left: *Golden Bay* sea trials in the Firth of Forth 1954 (Fletcher Challenge Trust Archives).

Upper right: Coal-discharging trials, North East England 1954 (Fletcher Challenge Trust Archives).

Left: Loading airside connections, *Golden Bay* (I) (Fletcher Challenge Trust Archives).

Left: *Golden Bay* (I) loading bulk cement at Tarakohe 1955 (Fletcher Challenge Trust Archives).
Right: Deck cargo on *Golden Bay* (I) (photo from the Fletcher Challenge Trust Archive). This is a great old photograph and just shows how practical the Kiwis were back in the day.

The ship spent many months in the UK, carrying out coal and cement handling trials, thus giving the equipment a thorough workout before she became the first ever bulk cargo self-discharging ship in the southern hemisphere, when she arrived in Wellington in April 1955. Although *Golden Bay* (I) could handle the granulated coal, the biggest problem was re-sealing the hatches after each load and before loading the bulk cement. In the end, the problem was resolved by permanently sealing the hatches and using her only for cement cargoes (as told by Tony Skilton).

The air slide loading system was a first for New Zealand – the cement fell into the tops of the ship's air slides, where it was kept aerated by compressed air from the shoreside air connections. The ship's internal air slides then distributed the cement in the top of the holds to get an even loading throughout. (NB the slides were riveted to the deck, while the slide housing was welded.)

In the days before the Cook Strait ferries, if you wanted to take your car across to the South Island, you just slung it onto the deck of your own ship. (The car in the photo is believed to be Neil Ostenfeld's Austin A55 – he was still driving it when the new Golden Bay arrived in 1979. When the car broke down, he would ring the engine room and one of us would have to go and fix the blimmin' thing. The caravan was on the next trip!)

Golden Bay (I) enters Wanganui River 1957 (photo from Fletcher Challenge Trust Archives).

The photo is of *Golden Bay* entering Wanganui, followed by the steam tug Taioma, then a small trawler. The date was 16 February 1957, and the information

31

Left: *Golden Bay* (I) lining up to cross the bar at Raglan 1967 (Fletcher Challenge Trust Archive photograph).

Upper right: *Golden Bay* nears the end of a voyage; approaching Fiordland Deep Cove near the southern tip of New Zealand in 1967 (Fletcher Challenge Trust Archive photograph).

Right: Starboard cement hold looking forward (photo courtesy of Fletcher Challenge Trust).

states that *Taioma* had come up from Wellington to try and pull a ship off the beach. However, *Taioma* ended up with a wire around her propeller, and *Golden Bay* (I) had to take her in tow. Whatever, the crowds of people on the shoreline indicate that something out of the ordinary is happening. The small trawler astern of *Taioma* was there to steady her as she was towed by *Golden Bay* (I) over the sand bar entrance and through the breakwaters into Wanganui.

Story as told by Barry I. Bitossi:

DEV Golden Bay Crew Story: a short tribute to Bill Spinx & Frank Giddon, 1st and 2nd Stewards

It should be mentioned that after her trials and being handed over to the company, a crew was mustered and travelled to the U.K. to bring the ship back to New Zealand.

Among that crew were Bill Spinx and Frank Giddon. Bill was chief steward and Frank was the second. Both of these men remained in the ship for as long as they were able to work and to the best of my knowledge both of these men's careers in the Golden Bay spanned at least 25 years. The Golden Bay may very well have been 'Diesel Electric' but Bill Spinx ran the ship like clockwork. Bill's 'party piece' was that he was able to strip the tablecloth from a table in the saloon from under the setting without moving any one item from where it was originally placed. (I have never been able to master this trick.)

I was second cook in the Golden Bay and as such shared a cabin with Frank Giddon.

Over many years Frank's eyesight became so bad that he perfected the art of 'working by numbers'. For example, (1) place teapot in sink under the hot water spout, (2) turn on hot water spout tap, (3) count to ten. (4) close teapot lid and deliver tea. The crew's meals were delivered from the galley to the crew's mess by way of a 'dumb waiter' (the mess was directly below the galley). Meals for the saloon were collected by Frank from the galley door. Frank knew how many paces it was from the saloon to the galley and as long as he was not distracted the meals found their way to the correct table.

And a word about Len Fox (engineer)

I do not remember whether Len was Chief or 2nd Engineer during his time in the Golden Bay and that doesn't matter. What does matter is that as a lad and still at school Len and his brothers became very good friends of mine. Len became a ship's engineer and went off to sail the great oceans of the world and on his returns told us tales of his adventures in faraway places.

Len's tales had a lot to do with myself later becoming a ship's cook and we eventually became shipmates in the Golden Bay.

Len kept an old motor cycle inside the Silo Compound at Wellington and after the last meal was served we would race off back to the Hutt Valley for a night with our respective families and friends.

Getting back to the ship in time to get breakfast going I would get the first train from the Hutt Valley which left our station at 5:30 in the morning. This train always had to wait for a signal to proceed through the marshalling yards. The signal was opposite the silos and as it approached I got ready to bail out of the 'goods compartment door', across the tracks and back on board the ship.

Len has now passed away but before he left us he gave me a water colour of the Golden Bay entering Wellington Harbour with a full load of cement. I would like to share that painting with all or anyone to whom may have an interest.

Painting of DEV *Golden Bay* by L. Fox (shown here by permission).

First cargo into Wanganui 1955 (photo courtesy of Tony Skilton).

Upper left: *Golden Bay* approaching Wellington 1959 (photo courtesy of Tony Skilton).

Left: *Golden Bay* in Wellington in the late 1950s (photo courtesy of Tony Skilton).

Lower left: *Ligar Bay* and *Golden Bay* in Wellington April 1969 (photo courtesy of Tony Skilton).

While the build of the cement carrier *Golden Bay* was going on, an interesting small order was being fulfilled for Priestman Bros Ltd. This was for three grab hopper dredges, all the same size – although the first of them would be of traditional riveted construction and the other two welded.

This was a sure sign that welding was now being accepted as a viable means of construction in the shipyards. Apart from the huge savings in labour and cost, this would in theory produce more profit for the shipyard. A skilled riveting squad numbered perhaps four men while one welder could, again in theory, do more work at a lower cost. It was also relatively easy to train someone to weld. So, although it would be a few years yet before an all-welded ship would be built at Leith, this was the beginning.

The build of TSMV *Auby*, along with a couple of large sugar barges, would complete the shipbuilding at the yard in 1953. Launched in the September, *Auby*, Ship No 434 (ON 196214), was another order from the Sarawak Steamship Co. for a specially designed diesel cargo/passenger ship for service in the tropics. She was a twin-screw vessel at 1,733 grt, with the following dimensions: length overall 228 feet 6 inches (length B.P. of 212 feet), with a beam of 44 feet and a moulded depth of 21 feet. Interestingly she was also built as per the company's practice with 50 per cent of her hull steel structure electrically welded; the butts of the shell were welded and the seams were riveted.

She was propelled by twin screws, each of which were driven by a Ruston type 7VEBXM, 4-stroke cycle supercharged, non-reversing diesel engine, built and supplied by Ruston & Hornsby Ltd, Lincoln. She would be registered in Singapore.

By 1963, the Sarawak Steamship Company's trade with Sarawak was facing intense competition, exacerbated by the confrontation between Indonesia and Malaysia. The following year nine more companies were competing for the same cargoes. Consequently, Sarawak Steamship sold its vessels, *Rajah Brooke*, *Bentong* and *Bruas* to the Straits Steamship Company, retaining *Rejang* and *Auby*. Straits Steamship then took over the trades from Singapore to Kuching, Sarikei, Binatang[4] and Sibu. *Rejang* was retained on the Kuching Rejang river ports service and *Auby* was chartered to the Ministry of Transport during the period of the Malaya/Indonesia confrontation, acting as a troopship and ferrying some 31,000 troops. Then, in 1985, her name was changed to *Ruby* and she was registered in Male, Maldives. She was eventually broken up at Gadani Beach in 1988.

Her forward section provided accommodation for the captain along with the deck and engineering officers as well as for the first-class passengers, with the remainder of the crew housed in the poop and on the upper and main decks. In addition, space was provided for 100 unberthed passengers.

The following story is told by Derek Longly:

MV *Auby*

This interesting little vessel was constructed in 1954 by Henry Robb Shipbuilders of

---

4 Now Bintangor.

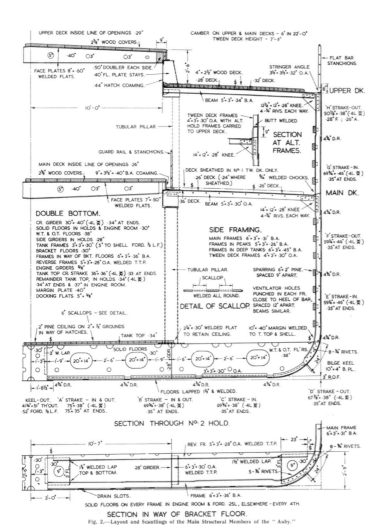

Fig. 2.—Layout and Scantlings of the Main Structural Members of the "Auby."

Section drawing showing the principal steelwork through No 2 hold and in way of the bracket floor.

Left: MV *Auby*.

Right: MV *Auby* with her distinctive look at the quayside.

Leith. She had a tonnage of 1,713 gross and was diesel driven. There was provision on board for a small number of passengers, their cabins being situated within the rather massive looking forward superstructure. Here too were the cabins for the ship's officers and their mess, which I believe they shared with any passengers. There was also I think an open air veranda immediately aft of the bridge, provided with a bar hatch and this, apart from the aforementioned officer's mess, was the only public space, as such, on board. In the event of inclement weather this area could be enclosed with canvas screens.

Voyage on MV *Auby*, 1964

In December 1964 I travelled on the ship on a voyage of nearly a thousand miles distance, from Singapore to Brunei City in North Borneo amongst a number of troops who were on board, comprising Malay police officers, soldiers from the Ghurkha Regiment, a large group of Australian Army special services personnel and a very small contingent of just seven from the Royal Air Force. So far as I can recall there was no additional life saving equipment provided on the ship to allow for the greatly increased number of souls over the normal who were on board her for this voyage, with her capacity at that time being a total of 396 persons.

Whilst cabin class passengers travelling on the ship might have anticipated a comfortable voyage, the accommodation provided for the troops was quite primitive, being but temporary sleeping berths stacked three or more high in the ship's two holds. Eating facilities were simply trestle tables affixed to the hatch covers, on either side of each of which was a long bench to sit on. Awnings were slung above those hatch covers in order to give some shade to the area beneath. Even more primitive were the ablutions. These consisted of a tap supplying cold water, which was used to fill enamel basins supplied for washing purposes, with this task being carried out squatting on deck. The toilets, meanwhile, were merely two rows of wooden cubicles constructed at the sides of the ship.

To keep the troops occupied during the voyage their accompanying officers held daily kit inspections and parades. They also ensured the men were detailed to undertake plenty of 'spud bashing', ie peeling and preparing potatoes for their meals. When not required to be in uniform or on duty, the main leisure activity for the Australian soldiers in particular, was to find some suitable piece of open deck, and then spend long periods lying stretched out under the tropical sun when it shone in order to either acquire or, in most cases, maintain, a sun tan. In those days no-one thought to warn them about the dangers of skin cancer, and many thought a tan to be good for your health!

Perhaps fortunately for them the weather during the voyage was less than pleasant for much of the time. We had a enjoyably calm first afternoon and night at sea but for the following three days the ship was tossed about by the North East Monsoon with periods of heavy rain and violent thunderstorms. The fourth day however when we were off the coast of Brunei was beautifully calm and sunny. The voyage up the Brunei River was superb passing along the jungle clad shore to either side and with small 'kampongs' the stilt borne wooden huts of the native population visible from time to time.

When the ship reached Brunei City those of us headed for Labuan Island transferred by way of a narrow plank laid between the main deck of the Auby onto the roof of the bridge of a small Army landing craft aboard which we made the final part of the voyage.

MV *Auby* made a big impression (not all good) on all who sailed on her, including some of the following men:

David Mills:

I sailed on the Auby in May 1965. I was REME Attached to 40 Light Regt Royal Artillery from Singapore to Kuching.

The accommodation for the troops was hideous so I found myself a little spot in the superstructure where it was cool and less pungent.

The showers were like cages hanging over the sides as were the toilets. One side of the ship had a perpetual brown stain for obvious reasons. 300 men per day performing their daily rituals was not a pretty sight.

The food was criminal and served alternately to port and starboard groups under a huge awning on the top deck.

We returned on her later after a year of active service fighting the communist terrorists and Indonesian army.

Stephen Swayne:

On about 18 March 1965 my Dad was in a large 3 RAR Australian Army truck convoy from Terendak Garrison near Malacca to Singapore and then went by Auby to Borneo. They disembarked at the port of Kuching on Borneo island and proceeded to the 3 RAR base near Bau by truck.

James Hutchinson:

Was a passenger on a trip from Sibu to Singapore via Kuching in 1966. I was travelling to Penang for R & R. I belonged to 205 Signal squadron.

James Mattinson:

I was in Sibu from 1961 to 1963 working as a Shipping Assistant with The Borneo Co. Ltd.

I knew all the ships mentioned, including Auby and Rejang. I was friendly with David 'Dave' Austin from the day he made his first trip 'up the Rejang'. I knew Capt John Martin less well then but became much closer when we were both based in Port Swettenham (later Port Kelang) in Malaysia. At that time John was a partner in the Port Swettenham Pilots Association. Soon after the Association was nationalised by the Malaysian government John took retirement and if memory serves moved to Perth, W. Australia.

One of the reasons Auby and Rejang were kept in service after the merger with Straits Steamship was they were paid a subsidy by the government to continue to provide a 'deck passenger' capacity between Sarawak's 5 Divisions in those days.

If memory serves both 'Rejang' and 'Auby' were licensed to each carry a max of 120 deck passengers.

Derek Longly:

I sailed aboard the Auby in February 1964 from Singapore to Brunei when she was being used as a troopship. Accommodation was very basic. On board were members of the Australian army, Malaysian police, some Gurkhas and just seven of us from the Royal Air Force. We had a rough trip until the last day but it was made up for by the beauty of the scenery as we sailed up the Brunei River. On arrival we had to transfer by way of a narrow plank onto the top of the bridge of an army landing craft to continue the voyage onward to Port Victoria, on Labuan Island.

Below is a selection of photographs from D. Longly, taken when he voyaged on *Auby* to supply troops to Brunei during troubled times in the region in 1964.

Left: Singapore Road.
Right: MV *Auby* en route.

Above: MV *Auby* with flags flying.
Upper right: Spud-bashing on MV *Auby*.
Lower right: Brunei from the deck of MV *Auby*.

Left: Brunei.
Right: Rendezvous with LCT LK4074 Antwerp of the RCA off Brunei.

Left: Landing ship to Labuan.
Right: Dockside, Port Victoria.

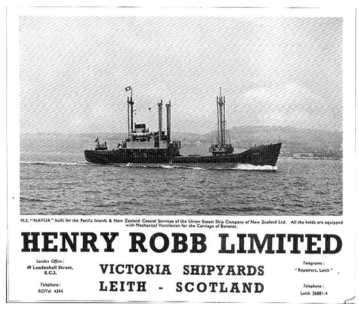

M.S. "NAVUA" built for the Pacific Islands & New Zealand Coastal Services of the Union Steam Ship Company of New Zealand Ltd. All the holds are equipped with Mechanical Ventilation for the Carriage of Bananas.

HENRY ROBB LIMITED

London Office:
49 Leadenhall Street,
E.C.3.

Telephone:
ROYal 4364

VICTORIA SHIPYARDS
LEITH - SCOTLAND

Telegrams:
"Repairers, Leith"

Telephone:
Leith 36881-4

Left: Henry Robb advert.

Below: Classic lines of SS *Cicero*.

The next year at Robbs, 1954, began with the building of four barges for the Middle East, all ordered by the Beira Engineering Co. Ltd (these would be built at the same time as the larger ships). The order was given the contract numbers as follows: Ship No 451 launched in February; Ship No 452 launched in March; Ship No 453 launched in April; Ship No 454 launched in May.

1954 was a big year for more orders from the Ellerman Line Group, beginning with three steam-powered ships. These would be fine-looking ships, with the traditional superstructure amidships and holds fore and aft.

The first, launched in March 1954 and completed in the June, was to be named SS *Cicero*, Ship No 437 (ON 185180). Her built dimensions were given as: length overall 309 feet

8 inches (length B. P. 290 feet) with a beam moulded of 48 feet 6 inches and a moulded depth of 27 feet. She was powered by a triple-expansion 3-cylinder steam engine, with LP turbine producing 2460 ihp to her single screw. Her engine was supplied and built by Swan Hunter & Wigham Richardson, Wallsend. She had a service speed of 13 knots. Her tonnage was given as 2,499 grt.

Cicero would be a Wilson Line ship, primarily for use out of her home port of Hull. Along with her sister ship, SS *Rollo*, she was the last of the steamers sailing with Ellerman's Wilson Line, when they were sold in 1970. She had space for 12 passengers in what was, for the time, high-class accommodation; her dining room had leather-upholstered chairs, and crockery and cutlery monogrammed with the company's initials. She was strengthened for ice navigation and was state of the art: mostly welded construction, and with her hull and double bottoms prefabricated before being erected on the berth.

On 6 September 1964 *Cicero* arrived at Gothenburg from Hull with a fire in a cargo hold containing alcohol; this was extinguished by the local fire services. She then served for 16 years with the fleet, before being sold to the Maldives Islands in September 1970 and renamed *Maldive Builder*. As such, she was sold for scrap, leaving Karachi on 29 June 1977 and arriving at Gadani Beach on the 30th for demolition.

Rollo was ready for launching in October 1954. She was Ship No 438 (ON 185184), identical to *Cicero* (see above for their dimensions). *Rollo* served for 16 years with the fleet, before being sold to Avon Shipping & Trading Co. Ltd, Male, the Maldives. She was renamed *Ocean Empress* in 1970, and followed her sister ship to be broken up at Gadani Beach just four months after, in October 1977.

The following is a great little story from one of the ex-crew of Rollo:

SS *Rollo* Football Team, Alan Vickers:

I sailed on the Rollo in 1957. At this time she had a football team that was registered in an amateur league in Gothenburg. A local sportsman arranged the matches to coincide with the vessel's time in port. I played a couple of matches and the local teams used to be amused when at half time we lit our fags and opened a case of Hull Brewery Export beer. I believe the ship won the league shield one year.

Left: SS *Cicero* during her sea trials carried out in the Firth of Forth.
Right: SS *Rollo*.

Stuart Johnston:

as cadet, I did one trip on Rollo to Gothenburg. She lived up to her name as with a beam south easterly gale all the way to the Skaggerak/Kattegat(?) she rolled like I never experienced. a fellow cadet had warned me beforehand that he reckoned she would roll on a damp patch of grass! Other than that she was a nice ship.

Paul Lee:

I sailed on SS Rollo in the early 1970s as a Cadet Officer. She was a beautiful ship and carried 12 passengers down the Med, on a 6 to 8 week voyage.

I sailed on her on her last trip down the Med until she was sold and run to the Maldives.

The builds for the Ellerman Lines were quickly followed by a welcome order from the local Leith shipping company, Currie Line, for MV *Zealand*, Ship No 440 (ON 186643), for routes from Leith to Denmark. She was on the stocks at the same time as *Cicero* and *Rollo* were in build.

Yet another fine-looking vessel, *Zealand* was designed for cargo with room for 12 first-class passengers – offering a certain standard of accommodation with a very high-class interior finish. *Zealand*'s dimensions were: length overall 291 feet 11 inches (length B.P, 270 feet) with a moulded beam of 45 feet and a moulded depth of 25 feet 6 inches. She was powered by a diesel oil 2SA 2 × 7-cylinder engine driving her single screw, with a grt of 2,030. Her engine was supplied and built by British Polar Engines Ltd, Glasgow. She was launched in November 1954 and registered at Leith. Although it has been said that she tended to roll somewhat in rough seas, she was used both on the Leith–Denmark run with cargo and passengers, and later London–Lisbon.

Left: SS *Rollo*.

Upper right: MV *Zealand*.

Lower right: MV *Zealand* slow ahead, with another smoking vessel passing behind her on the port side.

The main switchboard of
MV *Zealand* (photograph
by Tony Featherston).

Life on MV *Zealand*, as told by Tony Featherston Electrical Engineer:

I sailed on her from 1958 to 1960, responsible for the functioning of everything electrical with the exception of radio, which was handled by a Marconi man.

At that time she sailed from London docks to Lisbon carrying a mixed cargo and up to 12 passengers. She was an easy ship to work and good people to work with.

Here are a few unconnected and light hearted memories of incidents during those days:

An engineer wanted to shut down one of the diesel generators (there were 3 of them) for diesel maintenance, but forgot that a new one must be brought up to balance and share load before shutting down the running one. On the main switchboard he tripped the breaker and, except for some emergency power, shut down the entire ship. I spent a happy hour getting everything running again. I heard later that the Chief Engineer 'spoke' to him.

She was a DC (direct current) ship and so there was some difficulty when the stewardess (we only had one) asked me to help a passenger whose shaver would not work. By the time I got to his cabin there was smoke in the air. I suggested to the stewardess that she should get him a razor that had a blade. That kind works on any ship.

Left: MV *Zealand* rolling along on another voyage over the North Sea.

Right: A view into the engine room of MV *Zealand* (photograph by Tony Featherston).

We were inspected one day in port by a superintendent who wanted to see one of the life boats in the water. The mechanical engineers were busy in the engine room so the Chief Engineer persuaded me to go into a lowered life boat to help him.

Fine, we pushed off to do a circle round the dock, except that half way round the engine stopped and would not restart. It was very embarrassing. It must have been funny to watch, so perhaps we passed the inspection.

We sometimes carried buses to Portugal. They were deck cargo and not locked so we were able to enter them. I think I am one of the few people who can claim to have ridden on a bus on the Bay of Biscay.

We also, on at least two occasions, carried dogs. The Third Mate and I took them for walks round the decks for exercise. Even in fairly rough weather they seemed quite happy and surefooted perhaps because they each had four sea legs. Come to think of it, there cannot be many people who have both taken a ride on a bus and walked a dog on the Bay of Biscay.

It was a dark and stormy night when the steering gear broke. In fact it was daytime and calm, but let's be dramatic. I was involved because the problem might have been electrical, but it turned out to be a broken coupling. The steering gear could still be operated manually by ropes connected to winches on the deck, so we were able to limp along until the problem was fixed. No doubt other shipping was warned to keep out of our way.

The Zealand had a swimming pool. Well, OK! It was a canvas sheet attached to a wooden frame. It could only be used in port and was only large enough to hold five people so laps were about four strokes, but it was good on a hot day.

Left: Looking aft on MV *Zealand*.
Above: SS *Teano* on sea trials
in the Firth of Forth.

I well remember the day of the big flood. A pump for waste water I was working on would run but would not pump water. The fourth engineer decided that a pipe from the pump was clogged, so he disconnected it at a bend near its sea outlet to clean it.

Unfortunately we were rolling heavily at the time, which the Zealand did at every opportunity, and the outlet went under water. As a result we took on more water than we had previously been pumping. He and two other men struggled each time the outlet came up to refit the pipe before the flood came in again. They were totally soaked. I told him afterwards that at least it was sea water and not waste water, but he did not seem to appreciate it.

It was not always rough and I remember going on deck at night under moonlight and seeing us sailing across a sea that looked like glass.

Strange how such memories come back when presented with a picture. Hard to imagine that over fifty years have gone by since I sailed on her.

The third, and last-launched, ship of the Ellerman Line order was SS *Teano*, Ship No 439 (ON 186675). She was slightly smaller than the first two, although still powered by a steam plant. Her tonnage was given as 1,580 grt with principal dimensions: length overall 277 feet 2 inches (length B.P. 260 feet) with a moulded beam of 43 feet and a moulded depth of 24 feet. She was powered by a triple-expansion 3-cylinder steam engine with LP turbine driving her single screw. Her engine was built and supplied by Swan Hunter & Wigham Richardson, Wallsend. She was all-riveted construction with nice lines and classic counter stern. She too had accommodation for 12 passengers.

Teano served the Wilson Line for 13 years before being first sold on. She was sold again a couple more times until fire broke out on board and left her classed as a total constructive loss (in other words, she would cost too much to repair) in 1976. She was another ship destined to be broken up at the ship graveyard of Gadani Beach, Pakistan, this time in 1977.

Left: SS *Teano* under way, looking just as a real ship should.
Right: *Lake Lothing* on her trial runs in the Firth of Forth.

Comment from one of her ex-crew is shown below:

David Cornes:

I served on her as Third Mate from May to October 1960 on the trade between London and Oslo. She was unique in my seagoing experience in not being large enough to carry a radio operator and thus radio contact was maintained by Radio Telephone operated by the Mates – in my case with no certification or training. I enjoyed my time in her and was sorry to leave, although I then joined another Robb ship the Aaro where I remained for 2 1/2 years on the London ~ Copenhagen trade. As a Londoner in a Hull company I was a natural for the London based ships – this suited everyone!

Beginning with the launch of *Teano*, only four ships were built and launched in 1955, including MV *Navua*, Ship No 442. She was one of a two-ship order for the USS Co., the other ship being the twin-screw MV *Kaitoa*, Ship No 423, launched in May 1956. The tug *John Herbert*, Ship No 444, named after a famous son of the city of Preston, and the dredger *Lake Lothing* completed a somewhat disappointing year of shipbuilding.

This fine working grab dredger had been ordered by the British Transport Commission. British Railways (Eastern Division) as an addition to its dredging fleet. She was launched in April 1955.

The General Arrangement of the grab dredger *Lake Lothing* showed her to be of the single-deck type with a raised quarter deck, her main machinery located aft. Her hopper is amidships with a crane aft and another crane forward.

Alongside were more barges and another diesel grab dredger called *Gannet*, Ship No 447, built for the Crown Agents. It was a year of change, causing worry for the men of the shipyard as they needed more orders coming in to secure their jobs. This, along with the increased use of welding in the construction of ships at Leith, produced plenty of scope for industrial unrest.

The 1955 order book might have been smaller than that of any year since the end of the Second World War, but there was a lot of hope for the future: that order books could be filled; that the shipyard could grow; that it could operate sustainably in a very increasingly competitive market into which the so-called inferior foreign shipyards were now encroaching (and, it was widely feared, eventually take over from the British shipbuilding industry).

None of this deterred the firm's decision that the way forward was to go public, turning the company into a limited liability company with its shares traded on the stock market. As of 1955, the Henry Robb Shipyard was no longer a family-run outfit, but one now responsible for reporting each year to its investors – whose chief interest was of course profit. And without the guiding hand of old Henry Robb, this traditionalist shipyard was stepping into this future with no great improvement to working conditions – profits would be reinvested into making conditions more tolerable, and in new plant and machinery, only when absolutely necessary.

Nevertheless, it is perhaps fitting that the fine ships ordered by the Ellerman's Wilson Line were amongst those that ended the decade 1945–1955, just as *Tinto* had begun it. And orders for the following year were much brighter; a couple of large ships for the yard were on the way.

THREE
EXPANSION PLANS 1955–1960

With the onset of electric welding in shipbuilding it was not long before the sounds of the shipyard changed. Where once had been the incessant noise of hydraulic and hand-held hammers riveting away for eight hours and more a day, this new sound was more akin to swarms of angry wasps. The noise was never really silenced, either, as the riveting was replaced by the sound of the caulking gun used to gouge out steel to allow the welding of the plates once the first run had been placed. (The caulker had always been used to close the plates once riveted, and so produce a watertight seal, but in the fifties the transition from riveted seams and frames to welding meant that by the mid-1960s nearly all ships being built at Leith were of all-welded construction).

And even if the noise had abated by a minimal amount, workers now also had to contend with stinking and dangerous welding fumes.

Shipbuilders being by nature rather superstitious still looked on welding as being perhaps not the answer, especially as since the Second World War many vessels that had been built very quickly to wartime standards and all-welded construction appeared to simply break in two on the high seas. One fix was to rivet the last of the shell strakes, the sheer strake, to the main deck of the ship; this was then reduced over time to form only two or three shell plates either side of the ship; these would act as an arrestor should the welding break and start to split all the way around the ship as previously.

When a ship was completed and handed over to her new owners she carried a set of drawings times four along with a proviso from the Leith Shipbuilders that included a very succinct message. No shipbuilder would ever guarantee that a ship could not or would not sink (except perhaps one, and everyone knows the Titanic story). When the Trim and Stability books were handed over to the owners there was always the caveat that they were 'Given in good faith but not guaranteed'.

1956 turned out to be a productive year for the Leith shipyard, with its slips (even though fewer than the nine in play during the 1920s and 1930s) full of ships in various stages of completion. The year began with the build and launch of the lovely-looking vessel MV *Flaminian*, Ship No 445 (ON 187124), which was launched in February 1956. She was another order from the Ellerman Line to be operated under the umbrella of Ellerman/Papayanni Lines Ltd. Her principal dimensions were given as follows: length overall 351 feet 4 inches (length B.P. 325 feet), with a moulded beam of 50 feet and a moulded depth of 33 feet 9 inches, her tonnage was shown as 3,100 grt. She was powered by an 8-cylinder Sulzer 8SAD60 by George Clark and N.E. Marine (Sunderland) Ltd, producing 3,400 bhp to her single screw, giving her a service speed of 13.5 knots.

She was one of the larger ships ordered from the group to be built at the Leith shipyards of Henry Robb, and yet another ship that looked like a ship, with her graceful lines and raised focs'le and poop decks. She was also fitted out for refrigerated cargo (26,550 square feet of space) and was primarily used on the Papayanni Lines' Mediterranean routes, often to be found bringing back a cargo of oranges from Israel. *Flaminian* was with the line for around 18 years before being transferred to Ellerman City Lines and renamed *City of Izmir*. There she remained for a year, before being sold on to Maldives shipping interests and renamed again, *Climax Pearl*.

She was to sail out of the Maldives for another nine years before going to the ship graveyard of Gadani Beach, Pakistan, to end up as scrap metal in 1984. This graceful old ship thus had a working life of around 28 years.

This photograph of the forward main deck of Flaminian shows some of her riveted construction, along with her soft nose in place, facing onto what was known as the Black Shed. The welding cables on the deck show that by this time (circa 1956), some of the construction was welded, although the majority was still riveted. Her foc'sle side shell in place helped turn her into the graceful old ship that she was.

The story below from Frank (one of the crew) tells about the time when Flaminian was in collision just outside Gibraltar:

MV *Flaminian*

I was an AB aboard Flaminian, and spent about four weeks in Gib while a new temp bow was fitted.

The dry-dock photo (below) was taken by myself at Gibraltar after a collision in Algeciras bay.

The collision occurred at about 0600, 12/09/65 which happened to be my 21st birthday. We were bound for Gib, and the skipper wanted to arrive at full daylight. The wheel man and the lookout were aft getting in the logline, so the skipper instructed the mate to alter course and go round the bay to bring us to the pilot at full daylight.

French tanker, 'Florella' I think, the name, was steaming west out of the Med, and the mate decided to pass across her stern after she had passed on our portside.

The Flaminian was on auto pilot and the mate was not familiar with its operation. according to the story we heard the mate clicked the small control lever on the auto pilot thinking it would put FIVE degrees of rudder on, unfortunately any movement

A nice bow-on view of the riveted shell of MV *Flaminian* just before her
launch – you don't see seams like that today on a welded ship!

Left: The fine-looking MV *Flaminian*.

Right: Forward deck of MV *Flaminian* (the Loftsman Collection).

Left: *Flaminian* under construction with her soft nose in place; some of her forward shell plating is still to be faired in place, to complete her bow.

Right: *Flaminian* takes to the water like a graceful swan, the Leith dock tugs in attendance.

Below: *Flaminian* at a dead stop after her launch, now with the tugs moving in, to take her to her fitting-out bay.

Above: MV *Flaminian* in dry dock at Gibraltar, showing the extent of her damaged bow.

Right: MV *Flaminian* after her collision with her bow ripped open, just off Gibraltar.

Below: *Flaminian* with a tug at her stern.

of the lever and the rudder kept turning until the lever was moved in the opposite direction.

The mate's action resulted in the vessel turning hard-a-port and at about 13 knots almost overtaking the other vessel. We impacted the tanker just aft of her bridge housing, ripped out her port lifeboat and port bridge wing.

It was only as we pulled off her that she exploded, streaming burning crude oil for about a mile along the Strait of Gibraltar. Having picked up a quantity of burning crude the forepeak (what was left of it) and No1 hold of the Flaminian was on fire.

With the help of a deep-sea tug we extinguished the fire and were allowed alongside at Gibraltar that afternoon. the tanker got her fires out, word was they grounded her, not sure but did hear there were NO casualties aboard her.

Our only casualty was the bosun's pet budgie which had ingested the thick oil smoke and fell off its perch.

Some comments on this ship can be seen below from ex-crew:

Les Dennett:

Flaminian was my first ship after leaving training school at Gravesend. I joined her as a deck boy and my first foreign port was Gibraltar … boson was Charlie guy I think … fond memories of her.

Darren Yorgensen:

My dad Les Yorgensen also sailed on her. He was a carpenter but passed away on 19th August 2010.

Dave Gregory:

I sailed with Brett on SS Corinthian Feb 63 on the Italian run and again, this time on MV Arcadian April to August 65 on the Great Lakes, Canada/USA from German ports. I was apprentice at the time. I remember him as a smashing bloke, very easy to work with. We usually paired up on cargo work. Saw him after he left Ellermans, didn't he become a quantity surveyor? Sorry to hear he passed away far too soon.

Glenn Furnice:

My Father (Brett Furnice) he was possibly First mate at the time of that voyage. He sadly passed away too young about 10yrs ago and I recently found a newspaper cutting he had kept referring to the collision while sorting through personal stuff after our Mother passed away. I remember him describing the details of the collision which match the story by Frank and said he was glad he was not on duty at the time thus exempt from any involvement in the incident. He would have been about 26yrs old at the time,

Michael Main:

It's a while since we all sailed together! Actually I was on the Bridge (as a coffee-making cadet, I have to add) at the time of the collision with 'Floreal'. An interesting experience, and a brilliant few weeks in dry-dock in Gibraltar afterwards! I was also a first-tripper in 'Patrician' (50 years next year) as Cliff says when she sank 4 miles South of Tarifa and the only survivor from the Bridge on that occasion. I was last on board 'Flaminian' in Colombo after she had been sold to the Maldives and the brass was still gleaming. She was a lovely ship in which I sailed for two happy years and also in her sister, 'Florian', for about the same length of time, a few years later. Both were beautiful yacht-like ships and always a nice crowd, happy ships both, as most ships were, under the Papayanni or City Line House Flags. Great days!

C.M. May:

The tanker she collided with was the French motor tanker Floreal- built 1958- of 29,541 dwt and owned by Soc des Tpts Maritimes Petroliers, Rouen, France.

Sold in 1968 to a succession of owners, and was not scrapped until as late as 1993!

Cliff Foden:

Just like to add to Frank's comments above. I was 3rd mate on Flaminian on this trip and remember the French tanker being the 'Floreal'. Don't know anything about the circumstances leading up to the collision but I know that the 'Flaminian' did not have an autopilot. The only Ellerman and Papayanni vessel with an autopilot was the 'Arcadian'.

Can't remember any of the rest of our crew (sorry Frank, getting on a bit now) except for a cadet – Michael Main, who, I believe was also on another E & P ship which collided with a liberty ship and sank in the straits of Gibraltar a year or so earlier.

The single-screw diesel grab dredger *Samuel Armstrong*, Ship No 441 (ON 185842), continued the list of one-off special ships built by the yard, which now had quite a name for building difficult types of dredgers and large ocean-going tugs amongst its fine repertoire of ship types.

The dredger *Samuel Armstrong* takes to the water at Leith on her launch from the Henry Robb Shipyard.

With her Henry Robb flag flying proudly at the top of her mainmast, and a little of the sliding ways floating around her it was, as ever, a proud boast from the yard that they never had to use chains or weights during a launching to slow their ships down as they entered the water – something that always had to be done when launching into a river or other such restricted areas where shipyards generally seemed to be sited.

Samuel Armstrong was an order from the Ipswich Dock Commission and her principal dimensions were given as follows: length overall 136 feet 4 inches (length B.P. 128 feet) with a beam of 28 feet 6 inches and a moulded depth of 12 feet 6 inches; she was powered by an 8-cylinder diesel oil 2SA engine supplied and built by Crossley Brothers Ltd, Manchester. She was launched at Leith in

Samuel Armstrong going into the water 8 March 1956

August 1955, with a gross registered tonnage of 346. She was subsequently owned by Western Towage & Salvage Co., Ipswich, in 2002, still registered in her home port of Ipswich.

The twin-screw motor vessel TSMV *Kaitoa*, Ship No 443, was another order from the New Zealanders. She was launched in May 1956, along with the first of a two-ship order for harbour tugs from the Preston Dock Commission, which was to be named after another famous son of Preston, *Frank Jamieson* – sister ship to *John Herbert* (which had launched the previous year and been sold to the quaintly named Sinbad Shipping Company of Dubai, to be renamed *Sinbad Glory* in 1981).

Frank Jaimeson was another modern twin-screw diesel-powered tug with a Crossley Brothers Ltd, Manchester, 2SA 2 × 5-cylinder diesel engine driving her twin screws to give her all the manoeuvrability required in the tight confines of dock work, guiding and shepherding much larger vessels to their berths.

The 2,583 grt *Kaitoa*, seen here as an Independent Airlines (Malaysia) of Labuan ship, renamed *Hati-Baik*, was a complete one-off design by the shipyard and only spent some 15 years trading as a New Zealand vessel before being sold off due to the advent of containerisation in the shipping world. She was eventually scrapped in Singapore in 1992.

Kaitoa was followed into the water just a couple of weeks later by the smaller MV *Navua*, Ship No 442. At 1,952 grt, she was launched in late May 1956, as part of the three-ship order for the USS Co. of New Zealand. MV *Kaimai*, Ship No 448, was part of the same order, launched in August 1956, and coming in at 2,007 grt.

She was followed on the building berth by MV *Tennyson*, Ship No 449, ordered by the Chine Line shipping company. With a length of 335 feet and at 3,894 grt, she was the largest ship built at the yard to date.

Ship No 450 was the grab dredger *Lake Lothing* (ON 186997), ordered by the Docks and Inland Waterways Board. She was being built at the same time as another order of dumb barges for the Beira Boating Company, along with the small grab dredger *Annahda*, Ship No 455.

TSMV *Kaitoa*.

The first of a large order from the USS Co. was completed by the end of 1956 and launched as MV *Kumalla*, Ship No 456 (ON 196754), in November – the end of a good first year for the new Henry Robb plc. She would be registered in Melbourne and was specially designed for the carriage of

MV *Kumalla* as *Avondale*. She was a very handsome vessel (photo G. Ferguson collection).

57

pyritic ores from the port of Strahan, on the west coast of Tasmania, to Melbourne. *Kumalla* was a sister to MV *Konini*, built at the same time.

All the ships built at Leith had a lasting effect on the men who sailed in them, and some of their comments can be seen below.

Ian McKechnie:

I stood by the building of her Nov 1965. It was during trials that it was discovered the wrong propeller had been fitted as she didn't make her service speed. The correct propeller was to be shipped out on the next ship in build at the time. We left Leith and sailed north about Scotland to Swansea for a cargo of tin plate at a speed of about 8 knots. We then sailed South about Cape Town and docked in Melbourne after 63 days, average speed 8.6 knots. Wind on the nose all the way which was strange as normally the weather would have been up our stern. Clipper ships used to sail the voyage faster !!!

Michael Ayland:

As the Cobargo she starred in the 1978 Australian film 'McGee and the Lady' about a Captain who was about to lose his ship to a finance company. Worth a watch but was moored quayside in every shot.

Jim Walden:

I joined the Kumalla as a bucko April 1957. I was in the first crew on her maiden voyage to Strahan. I done my two years ordinary seaman's time.

Kevin Harrison:

I sailed in the Kumalla in 1971 as A/B she was a great little ship and a good job on deck as well. I remember the mate very well he was a true gentleman his name was Wally Stewart. We traded between N.S.W. ports and Tasmanian ports.

MV *Konini*, Ship No 457 (ON 196288), was the second ship of the USS Co. Ltd to carry the name. Slightly bigger than the twin sister ships built at the same time (*Kumalla* and *Koonya*) she would be the first ship ready to launch in 1956, in February.

Konini was a sturdy little cargo ship with two holds, one of 100 feet and one of 40 feet, complete with steel MacGregor-type hatches. With a service speed of 10 knots, she was a trim little vessel of 1,946 grt, and her principal dimensions were given as follows: length overall 267 feet 3 inches (length B.P. 250 feet) with a moulded beam of 41 feet 6 inches and a moulded depth of 25 feet 3 inches. She was powered by a 2-cycle single-acting 5-cylinder Clark Sulzer diesel engine, built by George Clark Ltd, Sunderland, driving power to her single screw to give her a service speed of 10 knots. Her tonnage was given as 2,007 grt.

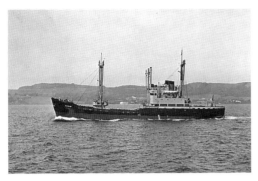 

Left: MV *Konini*, another in the long line of ships to operate from New Zealand's ports and to test herself against some of the worst weather that the long coastline could throw at a ship.

Right: Departing Westport, New Zealand. MV *Konini* under way and this photograph shows that fully laden she did not have much freeboard left amidship, but she was a sturdy little ship that took to the water like a duck. (Photo is from G. Ferguson collection and shown here with permission.)

She remained in the USS Co. Ltd fleet until sold to Hethking Steamships Pty Ltd, Sydney, renamed *Cobargo* and sailed under the Australian flag. She was sold in 1971, to Singapore shipping interests and renamed *King Tower*. Between 1978 and 1985 she was sold on another four times, frequently visiting New Zealand under flags of convenience, in order to transport bags of cement. She was broken up in 1986 after a useful working life of 30 years; with the advent of containerisation, little profit was to be found in running such ships.

The next ship was very interesting; she was an order for a shipping line that had started out in Leith, growing over time to become the largest line in the British Isles, the General Steam Navigation Co. Ltd of London.

MV *Sandpiper* was allocated the shipyard number 458. She was a neat little vessel, built at a time when many ships were now in the region of 30,000 and 40,000 grt, with some talk of ships even reaching the unheard-of size of 100,000 grt. But although the large ships might grab the headlines it was the smaller ships that kept the country going. They were also much better-looking vessels than the huge slab-sided ships now being thrown together in the larger shipyards.

MV *Sandpiper* on her trials in the Firth of Forth; she was a handsome ship, with a raking sheerline.

Her structural steelwork was prefabricated and partially welded as was now the practice in the Henry Robb Shipyard, her double bottom, oil tanks and machinery seatings all being electric welded.

Sandpiper was launched in May 1957; her gross registered tonnage was given as 916 with four holds for cargo, No 3 hold

Left: The officers' dining saloon was tastefully decorated with the added effect of a focal point being two opaque glass panels set in the partition that separates the pantry from the dining room. One of the panels is the coat of arms of the port of Leith, while the other has the crest of the General Steam Navigation Co. Ltd.

Right: The Leith coat of arms on the left, and the crest of the General Steam Navigation Co. on the right.

refrigerated. She was well fitted out, as most of the Leith-built ships were, with the officers' mess arranged at the fore end of the house on the shelter deck. At the after end of this house on the starboard side was the crew's mess. She was perhaps unusual in the fact that her colour scheme and upholstery had been selected by the wife of the chairman and managing director of the General Steam Navigation Co. Ltd.

MV *Thackeray*, Ship No 459 (ON 187727), was another of the larger ships for the Henry Robb yard. She was launched in February 1958. *Thackeray*, part of a three-ship order for Chine Lines, was the largest, and she, along with her sister ship, MV *Macaulay*, were builds that would keep the yard going at full employment for some time.

The dimensions of *Thackeray* were given as follows: length overall 369 feet (length B.P. 345 feet) with a beam of 54 feet and a moulded depth of 29 feet. Her tonnage was given as 4,650 grt. She was powered by a 2SA 6-cylinder diesel engine driving her single screw; her engine was built and supplied by Sulzer Brothers Ltd, Winterthur.

Thackeray was a typical design at a time when ships were beginning to be prized for functionality; by maximising space and therefore cargo capacity, the hope of the ship managers and owners was for larger profits. She had a somewhat bland look above the water, but with her bridge and engine room aft she had a far shorter shaft length and more space for the cargo. She was employed by Chine Lines for nine years, and in 1966 was lengthened to give her even more cargo capacity. This altered her dimensions to approximately 416 feet in length with her gross tonnage going up to 5,279 tons and DW to 7,640 tons.

She was renamed *Sherwood* in 1968, sold on again in 1974, renamed *Nisyros Era*, and was last seen damaged and laid up in 1991 at the Great Bitter Lakes in the middle of the Suez Canal. She was deleted from Lloyd's Register in 1999.

Upper left: Construction of the stern unit of MV *Thackeray* Ship No 459, built on blocks using her aft watertight bulkhead as a level and building up from there, very similar to the way the bow would be constructed. (Image from my own collection.)

Left: MV *Thackeray* seen here as the re-named Sherwood and looking like she could do with some paint! (Photo supplied by Alan – no surname given.)

Lower left: RFA *Typhoon* (photo by Mike Fishwick from RFA *Plymouth*).

A small dredging pontoon was then built for use in Nigeria. As Ship No 466, she was named *Minnow*. Along with Ship No 469 (at 80 grt), this was a ramp-ended pontoon for the Crown Agents of the Colonies.

HMS *Typhoon*, Ship No 460 (ON 301095), was an order from the Admiralty for a replacement class of tug. This powerful, modern, ocean-going rescue tug was a one-off vessel that turned out to be a more than capable replacement for the ageing wartime Bustler class vessels. Her machinery arrangement was like that of the Bustler tugs – two diesel engines geared to a single shaft – and at her conception it seemed likely she would be the forerunner of a whole class of similar vessels – an opportunity unfortunately lost, due to interference by Whitehall and government.

As it happens, it was found that when her engine, originally for use in a submarine, was run at full revolutions her after bulkhead vibrated to such an extent that if it had been left as it was the whole aft end of the tug might have oscillated itself to bits. The fix was simple: never run the engine at full revs.

Her principal dimensions were given as follows: length overall of 198 feet 8 inches (length B.P. 180 feet) with a beam of 38 feet 6 inches and a moulded depth of 18 feet. She was powered by a Vickers Armstrong (ASRI) × 2 BMP 2750 engine supplied and built at Barrow, and her propulsion was through a single controllable-pitch propeller. With a service speed of 16 knots her gross tonnage was given as 1,034 grt. She was launched at Leith in October 1958 and commissioned in June 1960.

Typhoon spent her early career working out of the busy naval base of Singapore, before returning to the UK. Originally an RFA (Royal Fleet Auxiliary) vessel, she was fitted for firefighting, salvage and ocean rescue work, with a heavy mainmast and derrick attached. She later transferred to the RMAS (Royal Maritime Auxiliary Service) and during her career was stationed at naval bases covering Singapore, Plymouth, Portsmouth and Portland.

On 28 December 1979, while sailing from Plymouth, *Typhoon* was involved in the rescue of a Spanish butane tanker, MV *Butaseis*, which was on fire and drifting towards the coast at Brixham, Devon. The crew had abandoned ship. A naval fire party and members of the Devon Fire Service eventually extinguished the blaze, and Butaseis was towed into Plymouth.

Typhoon's next major involvement was the Falklands War when on 4 April 1982 she sailed from Portland with a RMAS crew. She would be awarded a Falkland Islands 1982 Battle Honour. The following month, on 27 May 1982 at South Georgia, she was used (in part) to move elements of the army's 5th Brigade to the ferry *Norland*. Then on 8 June 1982 *Typhoon* had the sad task of towing RFA *Sir Galahad* from Port Stanley to sea, to be sunk as a war grave.

Typhoon spent a few more years down in the inhospitable waters of the South Atlantic before being brought back to Portsmouth for a welcome refit. She was then laid up during 1989 and offered for sale. First purchased for demolition by a Spanish company, she was then resold to Maltese interests and renamed *P. Typhoon*. Under this name she operated out of Valletta harbour for a few years more until, in 1992, she was converted into a trawler.

She was renamed again, *Somalian Glory*, and at the start of the new year of 1993 she was attacked by pirates, arriving in three boats. They fired at her with automatic weapons, but there were no reported injuries.

After a working life of more than 40 years, she was deleted from Lloyd's Register in 2002. The following are a few stories and comments on this fine ship:

RFA *Typhoon*, a short tale as told by J. Harrison:

The merchant seaman life was totally different from that of the Royal Navy and although discipline was maintained, it seemed like a pleasure cruise for me, our frequent trips in and out of the River Foyle were memorable, the skipper lowering a boat for us to spend a great night either north or south of the border depending on the price of beer and fags.

The high sheerlines of the powerful tug *Typhoon*.

I remember lending a couple of quid to one of the seaman and when I was eventually recalled to Pompey [Portsmouth] thought I'd seen the last of it, imagine my surprise (and that of the seaman) when I was on an old minesweeper waiting for a tow from Chatham to Pompey dockyard when who should turn up but the old Typhoon to tow us, the tow was very quickly attached and although the two of us could shout to each other, I never got my two quid.

Enjoyed the time though, sorry nothing eventful happened; I would have looked forward to another few months on Typhoon though. It seemed to have a very interesting last few years before finally being scrapped. Thanks for the memories.

Bob Blease:

After the Falklands she was transferred from Portland to Greenock on the Clyde before her disposal.

Peter Lee:

AB/QM in 1977, while the Typhoon was based in Plymouth, great ship to work on, excellent sea boat, great crew, worked in the RN, MN, RFA before joining RMAS.

Stephen Sutcliffe:

I sailed on Typhoon a number of times while stationed with the RNPTA unit at HMS Terror in Singapore. She was our regular operations ship for target operations in the Far East. The longest trip we did was to sail down to Australia during one of the ANZUC exercises.

John Knubley:

She had a vibration problem with the 3-bladed propeller and her relatively high speed Admiralty Standard range twin diesels (I believe they were submarine engines) on her trials which almost shook her back end off. She lay in Leith before it was decided to take her and restrict the engine speed to 900 rpm. At the time it was said that she should have been fitted with a 4 bladed prop.

Ted Tonner:

Did she not have trouble with the after engine room bulkhead? whilst serving my time as an apprentice shipwright, she seemed to lie up in Leith for quite a while I think the bulkhead was vibrating too much if my memory serves me correctly.

Paul Derbyshire:

Happy memories of this boat in the Falklands, it was tied up next to Sir Tristam and my father Jack Cranny had me on board a few times a great friendly crew and a fantastic boat.

Gary White:

Hi I sailed on Typhoon to the Falklands and the bit you have about refitting in Portsmouth is wrong. When she came back from down South her variable pitch prop needed the seals replacing as she was leaking oil, this took place at the same time as the Mary Rose was being moved. After this event we returned to Portland and then had an eight month refit in Devonport returning to Portland in 1993.

The final picture of Typhoon with the gangway out was actually taken on the night she sailed from Devonport to Portland, the two people on the gangway was actually the Chief Vittling officer R Court and 2nd Engineer Woody Woodruff.

Jim Harrison:

As a RN radio op, I was seconded to the Typhoon in the 60s, we were towing targets for the NATO fleet, can't remember the skipper's name but if any shells got too close he would lose the tow, I would send a radio report and we would head for Derry up the Foyle, weekends I would jump off near a town with a railway station up the Clyde and Monday morning he would come back down river and pick me back up after I had enjoyed a weekend down south with my family. I also got four pence a day extra for 'Hard Layers', even though I was in a bunk which made a change from hammocks, enjoyed the experience, great time great memories.

A three-ship order from the USS Co. of New Zealand was to follow, with the launch of MV *Koonya*, Ship No 461 (ON 196981), in October 1957. She was the second ship in the USS Co of New Zealand to carry this name. This *Koonya* and *Kumalla* were sister ships, identical except for a different hatch arrangement. *Koonya*'s principal dimensions were: length overall 253 feet 2 inches (length B.P. 235 feet) with a beam moulded of 45 feet and a moulded depth of 15 feet 3 inches. She was powered by an 8-cylinder diesel oil engine 2SA driving her single shaft, built and supplied by British Polar Engines Ltd, Glasgow.

She was registered at Hobart, Tasmania, with a gross registered tonnage of 1,946. She provided good service for the USS Co. of New Zealand Ltd (Hobart) for many years before being offloaded due to the advancement of containerisation. She was sold to Guan Guan Shipping Pte Ltd, Singapore, in 1971 and renamed *King Star*. 1975 found her under the same name but with a different owner, the King Line Pte Ltd of Singapore, where she worked for a further ten years before being broken up in 1985.

The launch of any ship attracted a large crowd and the launch of MV *Koonya* was no different. The following images were sent to me by Robert Rowbottom who worked on so many of the Leith-built ships as a draughtsman and later as naval architect.

Upper left: MV *Koonya* launch ready

Lower left: MV *Koonya* from the
stern just before her launch

Upper right: MV *Koonya* successfully
launched and floating in the basin ready
to be collected by the shepherding tugs.

MV *Koonya* under way somewhere in the Bass Strait.

Left: MV *Malatian* with a full cargo, slow ahead, inching her way into port.
Right: MV *Malatian* (photograph from Andrew Grant).

The first ship built and launched in April 1958 was MV *Malatian*, Ship No 462 (ON 187120). She was another order from the Ellerman's Wilson Group; she was to be managed by the Papayanni Line.

Malatian was the first of two sister ships, the other being MV *Catanian*. They were forerunners of the future S-type ships to be built for the same Ellerman Group, a cargo ship design that would eventually become the norm for vessels of this type, built for the run from the UK to Portugal and the Mediterranean.

Malatian's principal dimensions were given as follows: length overall 269 feet 11 inches (length B.P. 250 feet) with a beam of 42 feet 6 inches moulded, and a moulded depth of

Left: *Malatian*

Right: MV *Malatian* at Leixes outer harbour in 1959. Just visible in the background is the Portuguese naval school vessel NRP *Sagres* (2), which as Rickmer Rickmers is now anchored at Hamburg port as a museum vessel. (From a photo by Rui Amaro.)

15 feet. She was registered at 1,420 grt and powered by a 7-cylinder diesel oil engine 2SA Sulzer producing an output of 2,100 bhp to her single shaft. Her engine was built and supplied by George Clark & North Eastern Marine (Sunderland) Ltd.

Malatian was to serve with the fleet until sold in 1971 to the Maldives Shipping Co. Ltd, when she was renamed *Maldive Victory*. In February 1981, inbound from Singapore to Male, she struck a reef while entering the harbour and sank there in shallow water.

After investigation she was declared a total constructive loss, so was scrapped.

From Andrew Grant:

I served as First Mate on the Malatian from 25/09/64 to 08/02/65 taking cargoes to and from Medi. ports. I served with Captain R.L. Pedley and Captain R. Whittle. She was managed by Ellerman and Papayanni Lines.

MV *Catanian*, Ship No 463 (ON 187197), sister ship to *Malatian* – the same size and also under Papayanni Line management – was next to hit the water. She was launched from the Henry Robb yard in August 1958.

She was to serve with the fleet until sold in 1972, to Pacific Ocean Lines Ltd, Male, and renamed *Ocean Glory*. She was sold on a few times more, but retained that name until finally in 1987, she ended up in the ship graveyard of Gadani Beach, where she was broken up.

MV *Catanian* in her white paint livery (photo credit unknown).

Bob Hughes said:

My late father was second engineer on the Catanian in the severe winter of 1962/63. I remember visiting her twice and she was a nice smart little ship. I remember the 3rd engineer shared a cabin with his pet hamster. This led me to acquiring my first hamster. Somewhere in my mother's house there

Left: MV *Pateena* dockside.

Right: MV *Pateena* (Ship No 464), seen here entering Sydney Harbour 1970 (photograph from L. Butterfield's collection).

will be a menu of the Christmas meal on the ship 1962. It had a beautiful hand painted illustration of the Catanian, the colours coming from the paint locker.

1958 was proving to be a busy time at the shipyard, with further launches including another dredging pontoon of 80 grt for the Crown Agents. She was Ship No 466.

Ship No 464 was the second of a three-ship order from the USS Co., to be named MV *Pateena* (ON 152409). She was sister ship to MV *Poolta* (Ship No 465) and her dimensions are given as follows: length overall 268 feet 6 inches, with her moulded beam shown as 43 feet and her moulded depth as 17 feet 6 inches. Her single screw was to be powered by a engine unit similar to those used on the two previous Ellerman vessels. She had a 5-cylinder oil Sulzer diesel engine 2SA producing some 1,500 bhp, built and supplied by G. Clark & N.E. Marine Ltd, Sunderland, to give her a service speed of 10 knots. At 2,099 grt, she was a good-size ship for a coaster, and she was launched in November of 1958.

Pateena, a fine-looking little ship – unpretentious, a working ship and built very well – was destined for the Australian branch of the USS Co., and for the trans-Tasman route from New South Wales down to Tasmania. However, these traditional routes, old and new, were slowly changing because of the new ro-ro vessels – those with the long open deck and the box-like bridge structure stuck on the after end. So it was that, within a couple of years of being built, this type of ship on this type of run was almost obsolete, such was the pace of change in shipping.

Still, *Pateena* was to serve with the USS Co. Ltd, for 17 years before being sold on to Maldives Shipping Ltd in 1976, a company that knew a good ship when it saw it! She was renamed *Maldive Republic* and served the company well for a further seven years, before inevitably ending up at the shipyard graveyard of Gadani Beach.

As told by L. Butterfield:

To emphasis the fact that the skill levels of workmanship in the Leith Shipyards of Henry Robb were amongst the very best in the industry.

Myself I sailed on later vessels of USS Co., built by Henry Robb and they were all extremely well finished off accommodation wise – a higher finish than Alexander Stephens of Linthouse. The Caledon built 'N' class of Union Company were similarly finished off like Henry Robbs vessels. Today 'Golden Bay' visits the Port of Napier where I live and is a fine vessel also from Robb.

As a youngster living in Lyttelton my favourite coaster was the MV Kopara of Richardson and Co., Napier a solid / sturdy little vessel which lasted many years, also built by Henry Robb.

Kevin Harrison:

Hi, I also sailed on M.V. Pateena in 1965, we were mostly on the Port Huon (Tasmania) to Sydney (N.S.W.) run with palletised paper pulp. She was a good ship to sail on as well. Harry Mork was the bosun and the third mate was a good bloke too, had a couple of runs ashore with him but his name escapes me at this time of life. What a great ship, as were all of Union Company ships I sailed on in Australia.

The final ship from this three-ship order for the USS Co. of New Zealand was to be MV *Poolta*, Ship No 465 (ON 196990). *Poolta* was built and launched in 1959, just before the world transformed for ever with the advent of the swinging sixties. The shipping industry too was changing; cargo ships were not immune, superseded as they were by ro-ro and container vessels.

Built for the Tasmania–New South Wales run, *Poolta* was to work on this route for almost ten years before it was decided she would be more profitable converted to carry newsprint, which it seems was very much in demand. Her conversion was carried out in Hong Kong, where she was lengthened to 329 feet and, with an increase in tonnage to 2,889 grt, she was also fitted with stabilisers (which would have come from the company of Brown Bros. in Edinburgh, Scotland – just up the road from the shipyard in Leith – as it had a monopoly on the design and build of them).

Left: MV *Poolta* was the sister ship of MV Pateena, ordered by the USS Co. Ltd. She had the same dimensions and tonnage as her sister ship.
Right: *Poolta* after her stretch job.

The following was kindly sent to me by Ann Copelin (Benson), whose brother, Bill, was captain of *Poolta* (along with a fair few other Leith-built ships) in a remarkable career at sea, before he sadly passed away at an early age.

The first story touches on the 'stretch amidships' that *Poolta* underwent and which seemed to be a success as far as more cargo-carrying capacity goes, although it has to be said that her appearance was not quite as neat as she looked before being stretched – by 60 feet, around a fifth of her original length.

Excerpt from Hong Kong Star daily paper 1972.

When the New Zealand freighter Poolta came here she was 250 feet long and 2,200 tons. When she leaves the Tai-koo dockyard slip, she'll be 310 feet long and her cargo-carrying capacity will be increased by nearly 1,000 tons. Workmen at the dock are 'jumboising' the Poolta by inserting a 60-foot section just in front of her bridge. She is owned by the Union Steamship Co. of New Zealand and usually operates between Sydney, Hobart and Melbourne.

Poolta worked for the USS Co. Ltd, until 1976, when she was sold on – the first of many sales and many new names. (See below for Dave Rowden's story from the Ships Nostalgia website). As it says, this fine little Leith-built ship was eventually broken up for razor blades or whatever in the summer of 1999. It was a remarkable working lifespan for a ship that had spent so long at sea, braving all that Mother Nature could put her way.

Dave Rowden:

I sailed on the Poolta in 1965 as 3rd Mate, at which time she was engaged on a general cargo service Newcastle-Port Kembla-Hobart. In 1968 she was lengthened by about 18 metres and had derricks replaced by cranes at Taikoo DY in HK. She was sold to Bulkships 76-81, then onto Hetherington Kinsbury 81-84. Sold overseas in 1984 to a variety of owners in a variety of locations under a variety of names;

1984 – Tonga – named Kali

1988 – Sharjah – named Ali

1989 – Dubai – named Mahan

1990 – Dubai – named Sublime

1992 – Dubai – named Blue Pearl

1993-1994 – under arrest in Bombay

1995 – renamed by same owners Ocean Success

1999 – sold for breaking up at Alang, arriving 2 June 1999

So this great little ship, which was a pleasure to sail on, lived up to her final name, and lasted 40 years.

To continue the story of this fine little ship, I am indebted to Rodney Giddens for the following story of her delivery voyage from Leith to New Zealand:

Poolta unloading cargo.

Poolta, the delivery voyage remembered, by Rodney Giddens:

When I applied for a year's leave of absence from my work in the head office of the Union Steam Ship Company to have a look at England and Europe the management decided that I should return on the delivery voyage of the Poolta which was under construction at Robb's yard at Leith near Edinburgh. It was just as well they made that decision as my financial position by sailing date was such that I would have had to remain in Scotland.

That is how I came to be crew messman, or 'Peggy' as the position was called by all on board. Nothing to do with my gender but a hangover from the days when peg leg sailors did that work.

My knowledge of shipboard life was restricted to the voyage to England from New Zealand as a passenger on the SS Australis so my first impression of the Poolta was that it was a tad on the small size. The scuppers in the well deck area were about 18 inches above the water line when loaded.

From Leith, Poolta went to Fowey in Cornwall for a full cargo of bulk china clay which was loaded by upending loaded railway wagons over the hatch. The dust created was terrible, like talcum powder, slippery and went everywhere which made a job for me keeping the crews mess clean. The scrumpy in the pubs at 6 pence a handle took its toll and I never managed more than one shillings worth.

Onwards to Gibraltar for bunkering, then via the Suez Canal to Colombo for more fuel. No shore leave at either of those places.

The crew's food was plated up in the galley and passed to me to hand out or keep warm for those on watch. In my early days I had several messages coming down to me from on high. 'Master's compliments, but would you please stop burning the toast!' It seems there was a vent near the bridge that conducted the smoke from the toaster onto the bridge.

While transiting the canal the vessel in front of us was a new ship for the New Zealand coastal trade. I remember a green hull with yellow stripe, so I guess it was a Northern Steam Ship Company vessel. Anyway, part-way through the canal, a small tug boat that was proceeding in the opposite direction turned sharply and struck the midship section of the NZ ship in front and bounced off. Just before impact the crew appeared on deck, dived in and swam for the shore. The now abandoned tug missed our ship and the convoy continued on its way.

The monotony of shipboard life on the long haul from Colombo to Perth was broken one day when a warship appeared over the horizon and headed straight for us

MV *Poolta*, arriving in Sydney, passes under the famous
harbour bridge all decked out in her finest.

at high speed. We wondered if war had been declared but it just took up station 200 yards away for a while. One of the ABs said to me, 'Watch what happens on that ship.' He went aft and dipped our ensign, and on the warship a tiny figure appeared on deck and ran very fast all the long way to the stern to return the salute.

The ABs were a great bunch, a few weirdos but not too extreme. One very hot day, Chad, an AB, asked if I would step out on deck for a photo. A quick brush of the hair and out onto the deck and wham! A bucket full of water got me from the deck above. For a long time I had a picture of me dripping wet, still with the foolish smile for the camera on my face. The cook was quite skilled and treated us to baked ice cream desert at one meal. On another occasion the cook, having made a potent brew from raisins and bread yeast for himself he got very drunk. He called me into the galley and accused me of being a head office spy. Nothing I could say had any effect other than to make him madder and madder till he was chasing me round the galley with a large chef's knife that he was going to fillet me with (his words), until I was rescued by the Bosun. The bosun was a very large, and as I learned later a very nice, Yorkshire man. He confidentially said to me on my first day on board, 'Peggy, don't ever serve me any vegetables, I eat only flesh.' My hair stood on end and I wondered just what I had let myself in for.

Somewhere on the voyage one of my thumbs became infected and the Mate declared he would have to lance my finger. Such an excuse to broach the medicinal brandy was not to be wasted so by the time my finger was lanced I felt no pain at all. The next week my time was spent on deck duties to keep my hands out of the washing up water. Perth meant a few hours ashore at last. Approaching Bass Strait the crew covered the hatches with tarpaulins and sealed off all the deck vents as we were expecting rough weather. My admiration for what I considered to be a fine little ship increased. Looking forward from the superstructure most of the forward part would be submerged and then as the ship rose the water poured off on each side and the hatches etc would appear above the water again.

The china clay was to be unloaded in Burnie, Tasmania. Before that could happen the ship was declared black by the local unions as in their opinion Aussies should have been sent to Scotland to bring the vessel out. For our safety we were told not to go ashore so the locals came on board and there was quite scrap for a while. The next day one of our motormen announced he would see about this, put on his best suit and hat and went down town. On his return he announced he had a drink in every pub and it was safe to go ashore. What he did we never discovered but when he jumped ship a few days later for a vessel going offshore the rumour was he was wanted for murder in Melbourne.

As unloading finally got under way it was dreadfully slow (compared to the loading), as a small single grab was used. More dust.

In ballast on the way to Sydney there was a big following sea and the master decided that was the time for me to have a go on the wheel. I tied a few knots in the wake that day! I seem to recall the voyage took about 7 or 8 weeks. From my point of view everything on the Poolta functioned very well and there were no breakdowns or problems that reached my ears. Before I retired I was employed in visiting overseas ships to grant health clearances in Tauranga, New Zealand. How today's seamen would envy the comfort and working conditions that we enjoyed on the Poolta.

Rodney Giddens continues, with another interesting observation:

Some time prior to the handing over I visited Robb's yard and was shown around. There I saw in action what was reputed to be the last two men riveting ship's plates in Scotland. Red hot rivets, brazier etc. Then I was taken to see what had replaced them – an automatic welder propelling itself along the join in two plates welding as it went and no one in attendance at all.

HENRY ROBB LIMITED

M.V. "Catanian" (1,600 tons d.w.), built for the Ellerman Lines Limited of London

BUILDERS OF HIGH-CLASS PASSENGER
AND CARGO SHIPS, ALSO ALL TYPES
OF SPECIAL SERVICE CRAFT

MACHINERY INSTALLED BY ENGINEERING DEPARTMENT

VICTORIA SHIPYARDS
LEITH, SCOTLAND

London Office—49 LEADENHALL STREET, E.C.3.   Telegrams—" REPAIRERS, LEITH."
Telephone—ROYAL 4364.   Telephone—LEITH 36881-4.

Above: The welding shop circa 1955 in what was later to be known as the Black Shed. You can see some double-bottom units under construction, slowly moving away from a plate-by-plate construction sequence on the berth, to building in assembled units taking less labour and in theory less time with more profit. (From my own collection.)

Left: Advert from the 1960s when the yard was pretty busy, just before the management made the decision to take over/merge with the Caledon Dundee shipyard.

Poolta was to be the last of the ships built for the USS Co. of New Zealand. This may have been down to the fact that the yard could not build large enough ro-ros for its customers, or they may have just been too costly to be built in Leith. I do not know, but the loss of Henry Robb's most prodigious customer was without doubt a blow – though perhaps not so keenly felt immediately, as the yard was still booming with full order books.

FOUR
HENRY ROBB SHIPBUILDERS
1960 – 1965

In between the builds for New Zealand, there came another interesting ship, one that was to be seen around Leith docks for many years. She was the motor tug *Craigleith*, Ship No 467.

Craigleith was an order from the Leith Dock Commission (as it was called at the time), a traditional tug design for her day, with nice lines and a lot of timber used in her wheelhouse and surrounds – so she looked like a tug. Launched in 1958, she was ordered at a time when Leith was a busy port, still tidal, and Craigleith was intended for use alongside the other tugs of the Leith Dock Commission. In fact, she was one of the few ships ordered by the board that was built in Leith – a case of local interests not always being served.

She was designed and built with a combined rudder and Kort nozzle; this type of steering arrangement was also put to particularly good use in much larger and more powerful tugs built a good few years later.

I used to pass this old tug every morning on the way to the yard. By that time the docks had a lock gate built, which meant no tide could affect the movement of ships within; but to enter the docks the ships now had to pay more, in order to pass through the new lock gates. I often wonder if this had anything to do with the decline in ship dockings at Leith.

Left: *Craigleith* at her base in Leith docks.

Right: *Craigleith* on her trials in the Firth of Forth, her Henry Robb flag flying proudly at the top of the foremast.

Craigleith was later sold on by the (then) Forth Ports Authority, ending up in Canada – where a lot of ex-Henry Robb ships seemed to end their working days – and after a very respectable working life of 46 years she was finally broken up for scrap in 1984.

More on the tug *Craigleith* from Capt J. Kemp:

She was sold to Frank Pearce tugs in Poole Dorset. I was mate for the trip home; we got to bass rock and had to return to Leith due to the engine water pumps leaking. I remember whilst leaving Leith every ship there blowing their horns. At Poole, she was renamed Pullwell Lima; I sailed on her many times towing stuff to breakers yard, one time towing a cable ship called Bullfinch from Plymouth to Blyth.[5] The tug was sold to a couple of guys in Canada and was refitted at Poole. Last I heard of her was in the Lloyd's list as in the Azores with main engine head problems. Some 6 months after this we were at Poole yard and held by customs. We had been watched during the refit of the tug at Poole. She had picked up a ton of drugs somewhere in Asia and made it across the Pacific and was sized by customs. Her main engine was way ahead of its time being 8 cylinder Crossley; it stood 4 feet high had 800 horse power driving prop in quartz nozzle.

The ship under construction at this particular time of change at the Leith shipyard was the second of the large ships to be built at the yard. MV *Macaulay* was sister ship to MV *Thackeray*, and was launched in December1958, for the Chine Line.

'Large' means that these ships were among the biggest ever built at the Henry Robb yard; remember the company went for quality as opposed to quantity, and also the yard was just not big enough then. When the company got around to planning to increase the length of the stocks to allow it to quote for larger ships, it was already too late. But that's another story …

Macaulay had the same spec and size as *Thackeray*, and similarly was built for the purpose of moving bulk cargo. She served the Chine Line group for a number of years before being sold on and renamed *Jevington*. In between times she was lengthened to an overall length of 126.2 metres – up from 111.6 metres – and her gross tonnage increased to 5,330 with a dead weight of 7,640. She was scrapped in 1984.

David Mullins:

I sailed on the Macaulay in 1962 as Bosun. At that time I was the youngest bosun on a deep sea ship in the UK. During a voyage to Boca Grande in 1962 we were caught by a S. Atlantic hurricane which damaged the ship.

Ship No 469 was a ramp-ended pontoon for the Crown Agents, while Ship No 470 was another order for the same agency, this was for a twin-screw grab dredger to be named *Marabou*, launched in February 1959.

---

5 Near Newcastle.

Left: MV *Macaulay*, Ship No 468 (ON 300870), at the quayside (photo credit unknown).

Right: MV *Macaulay* renamed *Jevington* (not to be confused with a later Leith-built ship known originally as *Garrison Point* and also renamed *Jevington*). Here she is at Sunderland south dock loading coal for Hamburg in 1980. (Photo from I. Blenkinsop, 2nd mate.)

Left: The more modern look of Ellerman's Wilson Line: MV *Aaro*. Ship

Right: MV *Aaro* with a full cargo under way.

Construction had also begun for the build of three nice vessels for the Ellerman's Wilson Line. The first of the three was the smallest, though still a fair-sized, ship at 2,600 grt, and was named MV *Aaro*, Ship No 471 (ON 301625). Her principal dimensions were: length overall 330 feet 3 inches (length B.P. 300 feet) with a beam moulded of 48 feet 6 inches and a moulded depth of 19 feet 9 inches. She was powered by a 7-cylinder 2SA Sulzer diesel oil engine producing some 3,500 nhp to her single shaft. Her engine was built and supplied by Fairfield Shipbuilding & Engineering Co. Ltd, Govan. Her service speed was 13.5 knots.

No 471. MV *Aaro*, looking every inch the refrigerated cargo ship, or 'reefer' as they were known (picture sent to me by George Carr).

She was a fast, modern design, with her bridge set further aft than previous ships for the line, but she still had an after hold. Launched in August 1959, she was completed five months later and handed over to her owners in late January 1960.

Aaro was one of a new breed of dry cargo ships ordered by the Ellerman's Wilson Line, to be operated by the Wilson Line primarily on the London–Copenhagen route (see the third mate's story below). She was first registered at Hull, England.

Aaro was to serve the Wilson Line until 1972 when she was sold together with a few other ships, as the Ellerman Group was restructuring. She was bought by the Maldive Islands (like *Pateena* – many Henry Robb ships ended up working for interests connected to this group of Indian Ocean islands) and was renamed, first *Maldive Trust* in 1972, then *Islami* in 1981, then *Maldive Faith* in 1983 before her final name of *Northern Star* in 1984. Not long after that, she was sadly on her way to the ship graveyard of Gadani Beach.

This wooden model is of the single-screw motor vessel *Aaro*. The model is built to a scale of 1:48 and was made in the joiners' shop of Henry Robb Ltd.

Some stories of life on board MV *Aaro*:

Brian Ayre:

I served on her as Third Mate in 1961/62 on the London ~ Copenhagen trade. General cargo out, bacon, beer and furniture home. She used to unload at hays Wharf in the Pool of London and then shift to Millwall dock to load. In Copenhagen she used to unload at Nord Toldboden near the Little Mermaid and then shift to Christiansbrygge to load. She was a fine ship.

Unknown:

I sailed with Wilson Line as cadet. The happiest ship by far was the Aaro. Beautiful lines, modern, comfortable, with a great crew. Sailed from Hull to Denmark and back with bacon in mind. In contrast to the usual dark green hulls that I was used to, the colour scheme was light, modern and added to the beauty to her neat lines. Alas, two trips was my lot, and Wilsons moved me on.

Mike (no surname given):

I travelled on this ship from London to Copenhagen and back with my parents in around 1963. It took, I think, twelve passengers. I was the thirteenth, so had the pilot's cabin. I was about 11 years old. On the way back we experienced a cracking good gale. It was such that no other passengers made it to dinner – it was just the captain and me!

One of the officers was Mr Simpson, who tried (with limited success) to teach me chess.

I remember that part of the cargo was enormous sacks of feathers, presumably for making eiderdowns? Also, I remember seeing the London stevedores unloading pallets of Tuborg beer: every pallet that came off would have bottles taken from it, the necks broken off, and downed on the spot. Not hard to see why containers became so attractive.

I also remember, as the earlier writer noted, that the ship moved from one dock to another while in Copenhagen. My parents and I had been away from the ship, and we returned by taxi to see the stern of the Aaro disappearing into the distance. We then spent some time chasing round Copenhagen to find it again.

A great trip, well remembered, and it kindled a life-long love of the sea and sea-faring in me (albeit in yachts rather than merchant ships).

Dick Cross:

This ship was the reason I went to sea. As an 11-year-old in 1966 I looked into the engine room from the boat deck, saw the biggest imaginable engine possible. Life story and Chief's Ticket later I still have fond memories. Particularly of her larger lookalike Rapallo, which I sailed on as Cadet and Junior Engineer.

M.L. Eno:

I served as Third and Second Officer on Aaro during the mid-late 60s, plying between Riverside Quay/Albert Dock in Hull and Copenhagen, Odense and Aarhus. Captain Jardine was Master and Henry Blagdon, Chief Officer. She was an immensely happy ship; my time on which I will always treasure. Speeds of 16+ knots were often achieved. With twelve fare-paying passengers, the food was always superb and 'tab nabs' the best of the best. It was a singular honour to sail under Captain Jardine, a fine man and sailor. God bless all those who sailed on her!

Stuart Johnston:

I sailed on the Aaro as cadet on what I think was her second ever trip from the Mill-wall dock in London with if I recollect a large consignment of Triumph Herald cars. when we offloaded in Copenhagen near the Little Mermaid. … once on the dock it was discovered that all the batteries had been nicked by the dockers in London. So much for the cargo watch we had to do during loading unloading! Came back to London and was so pleased to be on the helm as we passed under Tower Bridge and docked on a wharf on the south side of the Thames. I think the cargo was Tuborg beer and bacon. Aaro was the best ship I sailed on what with up to date radar and Decca navigator systems. Lovely ship.

Darren Yorgensen:

Yes my dad sailed on her too; he was called Les Yorgensen and he was the ship's chippy, sadly he has passed away now August 19th 2010.

Howard Eastwood:

I sailed on this ship in 1970/71; 5th Engineer, my first ship, the 2nd Engineer was called Eddie Frame and the 3rd Engineer John Filby. The Captain was Freddie Firth. We sailed from Hull on a 10-day voyage to Copenhagen and Arrhus, it was a nice ship,

Peter Wallace:

I saw her launched while I was at Leith Nautical college. Long ago!!

 This was a very productive time in the shipyard, as the following story by draughtsman John Knubley shows:

John Knubley, draughtsman at Henry Robb: My Story at Happy Henrys

I successfully sat an entrance test to become an Apprentice Ship Draughtsman and started in the Ship Drawing Office along with Stewart Liddle in July 1959.

 Our First year of our time was served as Office Boy. My direct boss was Bob Tait the Assistant Chief Draughtsman with John B Caine Chief Ship Draughtsman. Being the Office Boy meant running errands and not getting caught going to the shops as there were no Tea Breaks in the D.O., taking out Drawing Prints to the Yard, to foremen such as George Ewing in the loft, Bob Storie in the Joiners Shop, Barrel Cook in the Sheet Metal Shop, the Carpenters, Plating, Welding, Engine Shops and anyone else who needed Drawings.

 George Ewing took great delight in giving the apprentices the run around until he was killed in an unfortunate accident in the shipyard. He was followed as foreman lofts-man by Bill Strawn ex Burntisland Shipyard. I was given a small drawing board in the corner of the office on which to start some drawing work in between all my other tasks.

 We were encouraged to get to know the yard and take a look at the ships being built. My first Drawing started with redrawing some simple plans such as a Towing Arrangement for the Charles Hearn and practicing the use of Drawing pens and printing with ink on Linen. As the skill developed I moved on to more difficult work and at the end of my first year I was given a full size board in the middle of the D.O. where we could be kept an eye on by all the Draughtsmen.

 Robbs Drawing Office took up the top floor of the office block and was divided up into 4 offices. The Ship DO took up almost half of the top floor including the Electrical DO under Bob Inglis, the Engine DO under John Rennie and Estimating with John Orr and the Technical Department under Jim Hill. The Ship DO was in 3 sections, Outfitting under Bob Tait, Steelwork under George Woodburn and Hull Pipework covered by David Mason.

 The First Ship I saw launched was the MV Aaro for Ellerman's Wilson Line (a Handsome Ship).

 We were required to go to Night School 3 nights per week to study Naval Architecture al Leith Nautical with the same John Orr as our lecturer and Bristol Tech, and subsequently Napier Tech for Mechanics and Maths, eventually we were allowed Day Release which saved 2 nights schooling.

 Ship No 460 the Admiralty Tug Typhoon was still in the Victoria dock. She had vibration problems believe were caused by the mismatch of her Admiralty High

Diesels to a 3 blade controllable pitch Propeller, the cure was not to run the Diesels over 800 rpm.

I progressed through my apprenticeship starting with outfitting plans, then getting more complicated drawings to do as my skills improved, moving on to Steelwork drawings such as the Fore End of the Tribeni (Robbs' first Bulbous Bow) and deck plans for the Ellerman S Class ships. In the final year of my apprenticeship going into Estimating to do such things as Launch Calculations and plans for the Ligar Bay and went on down her for the launch, the preparation of Trim and Stability Books, assisting in and monitoring Inclining Experiments to confirm the ship's stability and any required other technical information for the ships at that time.

At that time 10th-scale lofting was being introduced and PERT, Critical Path Planning, was being introduced to the yard.

On Completion of my Apprenticeship I returned to the Ship D.O. to my own board at the side of the drawing office to draft Outfitting Plans, Mast and Rigging details including ship nos. 486 & 7, Accommodation Quarter Scale General Arrangements for the S Class vessels before moving on to Ship 500, to be called the RFA Engadine. I produced the Eighth Scale (drawn at one eighth of an inch to the foot) General Arrangement drawing which established the overall layout and profile of the ship then on to the quarter scale Deck General Arrangements, Masts and Rigging Details. Each of these took up the full length of my 12-foot-long Drawing Board.

It was a good skive to go down to watch a launch then return to the D.O. to view and comment on the Launch Party from the height of the office. There was some excitement at the launch of the Survey Vessel Tribeni when she took a steep list to port after she left the end of the Slipways (40 tons of concrete in her bottom cured the Stability Problem).

The end of my 8 years at Robbs came after we were locked out of work for 8 weeks, following our return to work a number of us started to look for employment out with shipbuilding which at that time was seen to be a dying industry in the UK, and I moved on to further my career in a number of Draughting Jobs before joining RDL North Sea as an engineer and subsequently a Contract Engineer which was my entry into Project Management in the North Sea Oil Industry.

I asked John further about the lockout, and he informed me that this was due to the draughtsmen in the union going on strike to support other draughtsmen at Swan Hunters on the Tyne in 1966. Interesting, as in the future this would never be replicated with support going the other way.

John was the union corresponding member at the time of the strike and the union paid us our net wages for the strike period.

The Employers retaliated in March April of 1966 by locking us out, at the start of the lockout we were not stopped from going in to work but could only finish the jobs we were working on so that did not last long.

The union paid us 80 per cent of our net wage for the 8 weeks period of the Lockout.

It was about that time there was talk of some of the Loftsmen going to Peru.

Three or four of the loftsmen from Leith did go to Peru to work; this exodus provided enough specialised skill for them to open a couple of shipyards over there. When I was in the yard it was spoken about, but nothing much was mentioned about the guys heading off on what must have been a great adventure for the time.

MV *Rapallo*, Ship No 472 (ON 301633), was next to be launched, in December 1959, just one day before the start of a new decade. This classic-looking diesel cargo vessel took her name from a town in the north of Italy, on what is known as the Italian Riviera. A larger vessel than *Aaro* at 3,402 grt, she was to be registered in Hull and managed by the Wilson Line. She was part of a three-ship order, and along with her sister ship *Arcadian* (Papayanni Line) *Rapallo* was one of the finest-looking of all the ships built for the Ellerman Line. Her dimensions were given as follows: length overall (length B.P. 340 feet) 365 feet 10 inches, with a moulded beam of 54 feet and a moulded depth of 31 feet. She was powered by a diesel oil 2SA 7-cylinder Sulzer engine producing around 3500 bhp to her single screw, to give her a service speed of 15 knots. Her engine was built and supplied by George Clark & North Eastern Marine (Sunderland) Ltd.

Some of her condensed history is shown below in information supplied to me by Stuart Johnston.

As built she was fitted with refrigerating machinery.

On 21 November 1961, while lying at buoys at Istanbul, she was struck and damaged by the Italian motor vessel San Marco and the Turkish steamer Mehmet. Both of these vessels were out of control in high winds.

During July 1968 she was on hand when the T. and J. Harrison ship Tactician suffered an explosion and fire in her engine room. She took Tactician under tow and delivered her 650 miles to Ponta Delgada, San Miguel Island.[6]

On 1 June 1972 she was sold to Mossgiel Steam Ship Co. Ltd, Glasgow (Ellerman and Papayanni Lines Ltd, Liverpool, managers). She was transferred to Ellerman Lines Ltd (Ellerman City Liners, managers) London. She was renamed City of Limassol in 1975 and sold to Beirut owners two years later. The new owners renamed her Beiteddine on 1 June 1977.

She was sold to Spanish ship breakers and arrived at Aviles on 14 July 1986 where demolition commenced.

---

6 In the Azores.

The following is a great tale from John Wilson, who sailed on *Rapallo*:

The classic-looking Ellerman Lines MV *Rapallo*.

She was one of Ellerman's Wilson Lines out of Hull. Many of the seamen called the Wilsons 'Green Parrots' – I never did find out why. The hull was green, but why parrot?

She was my favourite ship and I joined her as Deck Boy/Peggy in King George dock in Hull, after seeing her name and destination on the board at the pool in Posterngate.

My first glimpse of her caused a bit of trepidation because I saw a seagull swim by in the dock and I could have sworn she rolled in its wake.

Going aboard I discovered that I had my very own cabin located in her counter, starboard of the screw. My very own porthole too. I wondered how many men had also called this cabin home and what stories they could tell.

I took great pride in that cabin and soon had the brass dogs gleaming and the tile deck as white as snow. Later in the trip I was asked how I managed to get the deck so white and I told the seaman that I had used carbolic …I didn't though. I'd used a strong mix of Tepol and detergent. … his efforts with carbolic lifted his tiles.

She was going to Canada and was carrying sandbags as ballast. I was told that her only cargo was a small steel box that had been welded to the bottom of No 3 hold, the contents of which were unknown only that it was worth 3 million pounds.

We set sail from Hull and the plan was to round Scotland and take the great circle route. Her best speed would give us landfall in 9 days except hurricane Celia had other plans. The 'old man' decided that sitting in the lee of the Hebrides was no answer so we set off for Northern Ireland and maybe a better chance to cross. Still no go so it was down the Irish Sea to see if there was any improvement to the South. There wasn't and that box we were carrying needed to get to Canada so … batten down the hatches, deadlights and string a wire lifeline from the stanchions around the deck.

'Rapallo' was only my second trip to sea and to see even the grizzly old hands wearing lifejackets made me wonder if this second trip was my last.

Chaos in the messroom …soup in cups with cold sandwiches … One old salt saying 'And you B****rd' each time a big green one came aboard and smashed against the portholes. He even called me that because I filled the sink too high and she took a roll sending greasy water with bits of carrot and gunk along the draining board, hit the rise at the end and propelled a gallon or so all over his head…

Sleeping caused a few problems because each time her stern lifted out the water the spinning screw would give you a good shaking. That was ok but when she 'missed a step' I learned first hand about Newton's laws of gravity. She'd catch the second wave under her forepeak and that would jolt her stern down which included my bunk.

I'd be left in mid-air and should she happen to take a roll to port my bunk would end up 4 or 5 feet to the left so by the time I came back down again my bunk was not there only the hard deck. I crashed onto the deck 3 or 4 times before having the sense to lash myself in. I think people pay up to 5 quid these days for rides like that at the Annual Hull Fair.

Rapallo looking just right.

I don't remember for what reason but I had to go focsle. I think it was to get something or other off Chippy, not a long stand or a skyhook because I'd already done one trip so was smart enough. I still had my Vindi beret but a blast of wind snatched it off my head and deposited it on the crest of a wave on the port quarter Odd you know as I watched it disappear in a trough and then reappear further away before sinking out of sight forever that I couldn't think of a fitter place to have lost it … a tremendous storm in the North Atlantic a piece of Vindi back at sea.

Always I enjoyed seeing men walking up or down the deck with a slant, first / this way then \ that and often at an angle so acute that you could actually walk along the base of the bulkheads. Knowing I looked the same to them made me feel like a real seaman. Nice how that roll stayed with you for a long time after coming ashore off each trip.

Do you remember experimenting by giving a leap into the air just as she started to dip into a trough … how quickly the deck would fall away under you. Being careful not to overdo it or you'd likely break your leg or worse when you eventually

MV *Rapallo* in Gibraltar (photo belongs to Stuart Smith. Copyright Mike Lennon, Hants).

landed. That bucket you were carrying feeling like it was full of lead and then full of feathers.

Getting whatever it was off Chippy I made my way back and one of those big green B****rds got me and swept me off my feet. I grabbed the lifeline and held on for dear life, I was shaken like a leaf in a wind storm straining to hold the line cutting my hand on a jag in the wire. I remember to this day how curiously warm the water felt … death passing me by …

Getting back, one lucky lad.

I had my turns on the wheel and really enjoyed it but it was basically hard a port, hard a starboard to keep her going anywhere near the right course.

Crib of course was always full steam ahead in the messroom and that most thinkingest of games, Chess. I spent many hours watching the moves and started to get the hang of it. Harry was the champ and I've never met anyone like him before or since … He was a 'Gentleman Sailor', always clean as a whistle even his shoes. He could work as hard as anyone but never attracted any sort of dirt on his clothes nor ruffle the creases in his Wrangler jeans. By the end of the trip I was champ, being unbeatable. Harry wasn't too pleased I'd taken his title and the very last game we played he was within 3 moves of beating me when 'Rapallo' took a roll and scattered the pieces here there and everywhere. Harry wanted to re-set the pieces and finish the game and I told him No … 'Oh, you B****rd,' he said.

Sam Gee was E.D.H., and we became great friends. He had a radio and the wire led from his porthole to the cross trees on the mizzen. I snapped that wire on numerous occasions … on purpose … during the trip with raising and lowering the aft derricks while he worked up forrard. He ended up shinnying up the mizzen to attach his Christmas tree aerial on the truck. 16 days out I heard a woman singing on his radio and whether it had anything to do with all the rolling and pitching we'd been doing I don't know but I thought it was the sweetest sound I'd ever heard. Sam was to become manager of the New York Hotel in Hull, married with a child, and then moved back down south in England and I lost contact with him. I do remember that his mother had a house called 'The Compass Rose'

A day before landfall the Bosun said it was good enough for us to do some work on deck. A very likeable fellow and he used to wear one of those baseball caps except this one was made out of thin p.v.c. and he was bald underneath it. Well the job he gave us was chipping the gunwales … I was chipping the upper and he the lower. chip, chip, chip, silence, clunk … you got it, the head flew off my hammer and landed perfectly in the middle of his hat … Now he had padding, I'd say, about the size of a goose egg. Later in the day he asked me to help him bring in the log line so I got steam to the winch. I don't know what went wrong to this day but just as it was coming aboard he got his arm in a bight so I shut down the winch except it didn't stop and he was dragged screaming down the poop. The winch stopped after it had given him one good turn. He said, 'I'll never work with you again you B****rd,' and he never did.

Rapallo from astern ((photo belongs to Stuart Smith, photographer unknown.)

I woke up in the morning and Rapallo was in calm waters which felt strange after over 2 weeks of being thrown about. I liked how green the water looked and looking up saw millions of pine trees on the shore … Canada … Beautiful.

I walked forrard to see if any damage had been done during the storm and noticed some bent stanchions but more surprising was a little fish on the deck. All black with small lime green luminous spots on its body. I picked it up and threw it back overboard and just as it left my fingers I could have kicked myself because I may have discovered a new species that could have been put in a bottle of formaldehyde and identified ashore. Years later I heard of a guy who found a blind fish in a cave and had it named after himself, 'Smith', so there could have been a fish called 'Wilson' – my claim to fame gone forever.

We picked up the pilot in the St Lawrence and I was sent to raise the courtesy flag the Maple Leaf. Now when I was at the Vindi one of the instructors showed us how to roll the flag up hoist it tweak the halyard and Bob's yer uncle. I hoisted it, tweaked, and it unfurled beautifully … upside down. The old man glared at me from the bridge and I'm sure I saw steam coming from his ears. Trying to lower it caused more problems because it was still windy and the flag got caught up in the blocks on the mast and started to get covered in grease. The old man gave a violent jerk of his finger which needed no interpretation so I climbed the mast and got it sorted out giving a very low and apologetic bow to the pilot from the cross tree.

We tied up in Montreal and that box was unloaded and I got some time ashore. I was never (well not often) one to just visit the local dive because I liked to see how the other half lived. I took a ride on the then highest mobile staircase in the world atop of the Prudential Building. Went to feed squirrels on Mount Royal and got some denims from a famous place where it seemed most of the seamen visited though I don't remember its name now.

Remember all the ships names painted on the quayside. Did you ever see one saying 'Rapa …' Well that's as far as I got before the Mate caught me and said any more of it and he'd have me scrubbing the entire dockside clean.

I was told I would be leaving the ship and did so quite a few times as it was my job to be swung overboard at the end of a boom in a bonus's chair to tie up and let go as we went through the locks on the Seaway. Making a mad jump for the Jacobs ladder as she got under way. A couple of times the gap was too wide so I ended up walking to the next lock.

Toronto, Hamilton, Detroit, Milwaukee and then Chicago. I really liked Chicago and went ashore to see if I could spot any bullet holes left by Al Capone. Being from Hull, which is flat and industrial, I was amazed to see two round skyscrapers the first 25 storeys of each being a car park. Below the buildings was an outdoor ice skating rink and I was fascinated watching a young girl dressed all in light blue, figure skating round the ice as though she was born on it. I wonder if she ever got an Olympic gold medal later in life because she certainly was good enough.

I stopped at a cafe to experience my first American hamburger and along came a cop and sat next to me. Of course he was of Irish descent and was called O'Malley. A really nice guy and he showed me his gun taking out the bullets first and when he'd done swaggered off down the street twirling his night stick. Impressive or what to a young lad. I didn't have a hat so stopped in a store and bought one just like O'Malley's … you know, they looked like threepenny bits. It was 2 sizes too big for me and kind of flopped around my ears. That was the second hat I lost overboard 'cos that's what the old man told me to do with it.

The Chicago dockers were on strike so we all worked the cargo. Cases and cases of cherries … of course a pallet of them slipped and were damaged so … you can only eat so many cherries, you know. $40 was my take from the work and up to that point was the most money I had ever had in my life.

It was a great trip back to the U.K. and we passed Wilson's 'Rialto' and I thought the crew aboard her must have been mad to join her the way she was being tossed around … then I suppose we looked the same to them.

I was to end up spending a night on 'Rialto' in Le Havre because she looked a lot like 'Rapallo' to me, especially after an evening on French plonk – but that's another story.

The sister ship to *Rapallo* was destined for one of the other divisions of the huge Ellerman Group; she was to be registered in Liverpool and managed by the Ellerman & Papayanni Lines Ltd, Liverpool. In the tradition of the line she would take a name ending in 'ian', and accordingly became MV *Arcadian*, Ship No 473 (ON 301349). Her specifications and dimensions matched those of her sister ship, with the exception that her engine – while being the same specification – would be supplied and built by Fairfield Shipbuilding & Engineering Co. Ltd, Govan. (At what was an exceptionally busy time for marine engine builders around the UK, engines would be sourced from whoever could supply them to fit in with the builder's construction timeframe.)

MV *Arcadian* (photograph from Andrew Grant).

These beautiful vessels, with luxurious interiors – very popular with crew, as well – had a passenger-carrying capacity of 12.

Arcadian crossed the North Atlantic several times on trips to the Canadian Great Lakes up the St Lawrence Seaway. Then she was used on the Mediterranean fruit runs, becoming a well-known sight around the ports; distinctive with her classic shape. She sailed as a Papayanni Line vessel until 1974 when, as part of a reorganisation of Ellerman's Wilson Lines, she was absorbed into the Ellerman City Line and (along with all the other ships) was renamed according to that company's convention, to become *City of Famagusta*.

MV *Arcadian* renamed City of Famagusta at Avonmouth, 1967 (the late Richard Parsons, Arcadian).

By the late 1970s Ellerman Group was again reorganising in line with the advent of containerisation, and the company sold many ships deemed surplus to requirement. As a result, 1977 saw her sold to Lebanon shipping interests, and she was renamed again, this time *Batroun*, and operated for another nine years before she was eventually sold to Pakistani shipbreakers and ended up at Gadani Beach in December 1986, where she was broken up.

From one of her crew:

Built 1960. Beautiful ship. On charter to Head Line of Belfast. Four trips up the St Lawrence Seaway to the Great Lakes. The Ellerman vessels were all built by Henry Robb of Leith and had a distinctive silhouette. I sailed on this ship again, as third mate, from Dec 1970 – May 1971 (to the Med). It was the last Ellerman vessel I sailed on. It was later renamed City of Famagusta (I think) and I saw it in Antwerp 1976. At this time all the Papayanni ships were absorbed into Ellerman City Line and renamed according to that company's convention.

In the days before the advent of jet airline travel over the vast Atlantic Ocean, all kinds of cargo would be shipped overseas – including the less mundane. For example, *Arcadian* was tasked with the job of taking live mammals over the sea. An amazing story has come to light

Left: MV *Arcadian* at the fitting-out quay used before the dock gate system was put in to create the Western Basin. Just behind her stern you can see what turned into the shipyard apprentice training centre, with the large black sheds behind used as welding and unit build sheds. (Photograph sent to me by Phil Wilson.)

Right: Beluga whale (photo from Wikipedia).

of a voyage she undertook in June 1965, when she was tasked with carrying an exceedingly rare cargo of four beluga whales from Quebec, Canada, to the port of Immingham in England in June 1965.

The whales had been caught the previous winter in the lower reaches of the St Lawrence River. They were to be transported in two massive 200,000-gallon tanks constructed on the deck of the ship specifically for the purpose of transporting this unusual cargo to Marineland Zoo in Cleethorpes, England.

The animals were loaded at Quebec, along with two handlers to keep an eye on their welfare during the ten-day trip across the North Atlantic. About five days into the voyage *Arcadian* was caught in a fierce North Atlantic storm, and from newspaper accounts from the time the ship was battered by heavy seas, and one of the huge tanks with two of the whales in it was smashed by sea water. (The report only says that the whales were lost, not how!) The weather was so bad that the captain hove to while running repairs were carried out. A day or so later another of the whales died although, again, the report does not indicate how this might have happened.

The ship managed to dock a day earlier than planned and it is believed that one of the whales survived the journey and was taken by road to the zoo. She was a 12-foot female who they christened Mama, but sad to say she only survived another two months and died at the Marineland Zoo on 26 August 1965.

Below are some further comments on *Arcadian*:

John Nichols:

I sailed with Capt Mathieson in about 1964 when I was 2/mate on Florian. He was a fine seaman and we all thought he modelled himself on Peter Finch in Battle of the River Plate. He was a gentleman but a stickler for protocol and behaviour.

Tim Oyston:

Just did the one trip straight from sea training college Gravesend 1974, sailing from Hull down the Med transporting tractors from International Harvesters returning with fruit from Israel.

Tom Conway:

I sailed on the Arcadian from maiden voyage as an engineer, for approx two years. Captain Kilby and Chief Engineer Watson. Great ship.

Maureen Hallam:

Angus Matheson was my father, he passed away in 1991. He always said that the Arcadian was his favourite.

Built for the port of Blyth, the grab dredger *Cresswell*, Ship No 474 (ON 301257), was another in the long list of speciality ships built at the Leith shipyards of Henry Robb. Built not for its looks but to do a specific job, the dredger was just one of the types of ship that were a lot more complex than they looked. This one had a complicated hopper system to enable the ship to dump its load of silt mud and, of course, sea water. Strange as it might seem, the hopper would open up at the bottom of the ship while at sea.

The principal dimensions of *Cresswell* were given as: length overall 135 feet 6 inches (length B.P. 128 feet 6 inches) with a beam of 28 feet 6 inches moulded, and a moulded depth of 12 feet. Her registered tonnage was 374 grt. She was powered by a direct reversing 8-cylinder 2SA Crossley diesel oil engine, built and supplied by Crossley Brothers Ltd, Manchester.

The following pictures were sent to me by Dave Judge, who worked on *Cresswell* as a diver, along with his father, Norman, who was skipper at the time.

Above: The dredger *Cresswell*.
Right: *Cresswell* heading south to Lowestoft (by J. King).

The story of this humble old workhorse is brought right up to date by the man who purchased her last, and when he could not find a buyer for her, sent her to be scrapped.

As told by John King:

I started my career in shipbuilding as an apprentice draughtsman at J. Bolson & Son Ltd, Poole in 1965.

One of the ships we built in that time was a low air draught tanker 'Banco' which was a sister of the Robb built vessel 'Astro'.

Scrapping the 'Cresswell' was quite a sad experience. I bought her for £12,000 lying at the McNulty yard in South Shields 1992. We steamed her down to Lowestoft, averaging over 10 knots, which is pretty much her original speed. She never missed a beat.

I tried to sell her on as a going concern, but the direct reversing main engine frightened every one off. She was cut up at the old Brooke Marine yard.

Sad to think that we no longer build and operate these humble little ships, maybe just one of the many follies of an island nation!

Below are some comments from ex-crew of *Cresswell*.

Cresswell on her trials in the Firth of Forth.

Mike Cutchie:

I worked on the Cresswell as a student in the summer holidays 1964–66.

One became reasonably expert in using the high-pressure hose to keep the decks clean.

The grab/crane was driven for many years by Norman Penrose, ex Blyth Spartans wing-half.

The abrupt rising sensation when the hopper doors were opened out at sea to dump the silt was quite unforgettable.

Raymond Daniels:

I joined Blyth Harbour in 1978 as apprentice fitter, the Cresswell was there and working, she was used for clearing out silt and mud in spaces between jetties and anywhere the

Cresswell wheelhouse All Stop (by J. King).

other suction dredger Crofton could not get, I always remember the engine room was kept very clean, all painted white and the brass polished, I can remember the Priestman crane which I helped change in the early 80s, I can still name some of the crew, she would use a bucket grab to fill her hold then sail out 4 mile to dump then back to do this several times each day, I can still picture her rocking back and forth with the slewing of the crane.

Ship No 475 was next, a twin-screw diesel tug ordered by the Preston Dock Commission at a time when Preston was a major inland port in the north-west industrial heartland that included Manchester. Named as MT *Charles Hearn* (ON 186360), she was launched in September 1959, and this hardy tug at 139 grt was to go on to have a remarkably long working life.

Her dimensions were given as follows: length overall 86 feet 3 inches with a beam moulded of 23 feet, and a moulded depth of 12 feet. She was powered by twin diesel M5-cylinder 2SA engines, producing around 740 bhp, giving her a service speed of 10 knots. Her engines were built and supplied by Crossley Brothers Ltd of Manchester. She worked the Preston docks until 1967 when she was sold to John Howard & Co. (Northern) Ltd, London, renamed *Kinkhow* in 1968. She was renamed once again in 1968, *Odesseus*. She would be British-owned until 1979 when she was sold to Middle Eastern shipping interests to be renamed *Radha* in 1991, flying various flags of convenience.

In 1994 she took on another new name: *Norman*. Then in 2006 she was registered in Freetown, Sierra Leone, and underwent even more name changes, beginning with *Admiral IV* in 2006 and ending with her last known name, *Hero 2*, in 2009 while registered in Zanzibar. Last heard of, she was still in service but under an unknown flag.

Ship No 476 was to be a rock-tipping barge for the firm of Cosray, to be named *Cosray 23*, followed by Ship No 477, another rock-tipping barge, *Cosray 24*. Both launched in April 1960.

FIVE
BIGGER SHIPS TO BUILD

The cement carrier diesel-electric vessel *John Wilson*, Ship No 478 (ON 315702), launched in January 1961. She was another specialised and complex working ship whose principal dimensions were given as: length overall 267 feet 4 inches (length B.P. 246 feet); her moulded beam was 42 feet, and her moulded depth 18 feet 6 inches. She was a single-screw vessel, her engine built and supplied by Bellis & Morcom Ltd, Birmingham. (For more details on her engines see the story below from one of her engineers.) Her registered tonnage was 1,675 grt.

She was ordered as a follow-on vessel to the first ship (*Golden Bay*) by the Wilsons (N.Z.) Portland Cement Ltd, a company owned by Golden Bay Cement. *John Wilson* originally traded from the Portland Cement Works to Auckland and Tauranga, and had a lot of specialised machinery on her for the loading and discharge of bulk cement. In 1974 she became part of the Wellington-based fleet of the Tarakohe Shipping Company, and served alongside *Ligar Bay*, distributing bulk cement from Tarakohe.

A fine-looking vessel, she had been built to do a particular job, and by all accounts she did this very successfully for 20 years or so.

John Wilson departing Wellington empty for Tarakoha in the early 1970s (photo from Tony Skilton).

John Wilson from the new *Golden Bay* (built at the Dundee Caledon yard of the new amalgamated company of Robb Caledon, as Henry Robb Shipyard was then known). This photo shows John's port side as she turned around to depart, with a great cloud of oily engine smoke trailing from the funnel. Tarakohe was the port for the Golden Bay Cement Works in Golden Bay, at the top of the South Island of New Zealand.

All the Golden Bay ships from 1954 to 1979 were financed by Blue Circle Cement, London, the major shareholder in Golden Bay until 1989, when the company was sold to Fletcher Challenge Ltd, New Zealand's largest construction company.

As told by Tony Skilton:

The Dear old 'John',

One of the most comfortable cement ships on the coast – the others all had a great propensity to roll, even in the dry dock.

The John was transferred from Wilson's Cement (which was owned by Golden Bay anyway), to the Wellington-based Golden Bay operation in August 1974, at which time she had carried 2,725,051 tonnes of cement, had steamed 299,212 nautical miles, and the running hours on the three main engines were 26,744/28,508/and 28,598 respectively.

By July 1984, operating from Tarakohe to Dunedin (Clyde Dam), Picton, Wellington, Wanganui, New Plymouth and Raglan, she had carried an additional 993,120 tonnes, steamed another 189,819 miles, and racked up another 19,700 (average) hours on each main engine.

I joined it as 4th engineer in 1975, and left it as C/E in 1982, to go back to the GB on the Aussie run.

The ship was cut up at the Auckland viaduct in 1985, after Golden Bay had proved her new propeller was functioning OK. The scrapping of the 'John' didn't start until the GB's new propeller had proven itself as reliable.

Here [Fig 133] is a photo of the John Wilson being broken up at the viaduct in Auckland in 1985; and I have many more taken as she was being broken up – and she caught fire, when the coating inside the chain locker went up as well!

Somehow, I managed to live in 5 different cabins on this old girl. 4/E, 3/E 2/E cabin when it was down below in the port fwd corner of the Poop Deck, then 2/E cabin after it was shifted up top on the Boat Deck, port side, aft of the C/E's cabin, then finally, in 1982, I popped across from the Golden Bay and had a short stint as C/E.

The following photographs showing *John Wilson* at sea are from Tony Skilton. He does say that she was a very well built and comfortable ship – definitely the most gentle in a seaway of all the cement ships he sailed on.

Left: Water on deck

Right: *John Wilson* at sea, June 1975

Below: *John Wilson* approaching White Island with the volcano very active (December 1984)

Golden Bay being towed by John Wilson.

The *John Wilson* tows the new *Golden Bay*:

In August 1984, on the way from Brisbane back to Nelson, a blade snapped off Golden Bay's cp propeller when it was put astern to test the gear. As a result, the 'John Wilson' was filled up with cement and fuel and became the 'company tug', doing an excellent job of towing us from Nelson to Wellington. Golden Bay assisted the John Wilson in getting the tow up to 6 knots using the Pleuger 'active rudder' propeller, then, slowly, the 'John' managed to find another 2 knots from somewhere inside those ancient, struggling Bellis & Morcom generators. The tow wire came from the Mt Robert ski field chair lift out of Nelson, and at the forward end was connected to a bridle that passed completely around the John Wilson's accommodation block, while the aft end was shackled to Golden Bay's anchor chain, which was then let out about half way.

Being at sea without the main engines running was a bit strange – you could hear every noise in the hull – noises you normally wouldn't hear because of the engine and propeller noise.

After arrival in Wellington the crews of both ships were paid a healthy bonus for successfully completing an 'evolution out of the ordinary'.

The *John Wilson* and her engines by Tony Skilton:

Regarding the John Wilson – she had unusual engines – most engineers I talk to have never heard of them. She had 3 × 5-cylinder Bellis & Morcombe diesel generating sets (used during WWII for powering searchlights I believe, but were first developed as bloody steam engines! And they looked it too!), and was single screw, with the propulsion motor being a double-wound set of windings all in the one motor casing

97

Left: Three 250 turbochargers on *John Wilson*.

Below: Main propulsion control panel.

(effectively, she had two propulsion motors, one behind the other, but on the same shaft). She was a very well-built and comfortable ship – definitely the most gentle in a seaway of all the cement ships I have sailed on.

The following is the deconstruction of a ship – perhaps better known as the breaking up of a fine old vessel. It is the unfortunate end for most things made by humans once they become too expensive to keep or they no longer are seen as profitable for their owners. We cannot keep them all, and change is inevitable.

One quiet and peaceful night at sea, I was on watch, and the motorman proceeded to wash down the main engines with detergent & water, which had to be done on a frequent basis as these ancient machines spewed forth amazing quantities of the lube oil/kerosene mixture that was used to hand lubricate the engine rocker gear.

In 1985 *John Wilson* was cut up alongside the viaduct in Auckland. The photos show the sad demise of a ship that had character plus, was a very comfortable sea boat in all weathers, had numerous unusual quirks (it wasn't unknown for the old Arkus autopilot to wait until the officer of the watch had gone to the bathroom, then throw a wobbly and engage in an abrupt turn to starboard all on its own. John Wilson did this again when towing Golden Bay to Wellington, right off Karori Light!)

Taken from the wharf whilst standing beside the cargo pump on the left, looking aft. The port half of the hatchtop has been cut away from No 2 Hold, then the engine room, and the starboard side of the poop deck, steering flat, and part of the crew accommodation.

The 600-volt propulsion generators had only a small drip shield above each armature – the rest of the machine was totally exposed – armature/brush holders/conductor rings – the lot. The motorman was happily washing down the centre engine, then for some reason turned towards the No.1 Gen'r whilst forgetting where his salt water washdown hose was pointing.

It went straight into the No.2 gen'r! There was a huge flash as the machine short circuited to the bed plate, and all I could see was this huge, oversized apparition of the motorman silhouetted in the fwd bulkhead (straight above the numbers written on the rubbish skip). I was sitting right beside the excitation and telegraph panel, from out of which came a huge 'bang'. Removing a generator from the propul-

This view is into the forward cement hold. The light blue shading is the original coat of paint applied in Henry Robb's shipyard at Leith in 1960. The tunnel in the centre is where the motorman would open and close the feed gates to allow the cement to flow into the longitudinal archimedes screw in the bottom of the tunnel. The rotating screw would then move the cement aft into the cargo pump room, where it would pass into the Fuller Kenyon cement pumps and be blown ashore by huge volumes of compressed air. The aft hold had an identical arrangement except that the cement would be screwed forward into the pump room before being transported ashore.

Left: *John Wilson* with her foc'sle head gone.

Right: The chain locker on fire. The wreckers were told to just let it

sion loop had to be done manually, and I'm blowed if I know how I did it that night, my heart was beating so fast. The motorman survived, and so did I.

Whenever I look at this photo I will always remember Frank Harkness, aka 'Gunsmoke', or 'the Gunman'.

A sad end to a fine ship. After the upperworks and hull side plating had been cut off, the remaining 'canoe' was towed around to the slipway in Freeman's Bay, dragged up and sectioned before being carted off to Pacific Steel in Otahuhu.

I have on my deck at home two Bellis & Morcom pistons, nicely cleaned and powder-coated, and the valve cutouts in the crowns make them extremely comfortable to sit in. Strangers sometimes give them a solid kick, not really believing what they are seeing. They only kick them once!

Tony Skilton

The next two orders on the books were for two more rock-tipping barges, both of 80 grt, requested by the Leith Dock Commission, which had plans to enclose the docks to turn the port into the largest non-tidal docks in Scotland.

This took care of Ship Nos 479 and 480: the barges were named *LDC No 5* and *LDC No 6*.

Ship No 481 was to be the river and estuary tanker *Toro* (ON 302771), an all-welded steel ship, the lead in an order of three ordered by the Union Lighterage Co. Ltd. This was a company that had used the Leith shipyard many times in the past.

Toro was a new type of design, which was to utilise the new build methods now coming on stream. The advent of welded ships meant that the shipbuilders would now build vessels first in unit form then weld all the units together in sequence on the building berth. The size of the unit built would be determined by the lifting capacity in the shipyard. Henry Robb had cranes with a lifting capacity of 20–30 tons, so units would be fabricated to suit.

Toro's principal dimensions were given as follows: length overall 171 feet 3 inches (length B.P. 162 feet 6 inches) with a moulded beam of 33 feet and a moulded depth of 10 feet 6 inches. Her registered tonnage was 512 grt, and the vessel was registered in the port of London. She was powered by an 8-cylinder 4SA diesel engine producing around 660 bhp to her single shaft, her engine built and supplied by Klockner-Humboldt-Deutz A.G., Köln-Deutz.

She was launched in June 1961 and completed that October. In 1972 she had a change of name, to *Bradford*, and was last heard of in 2012. She was subsequently deleted from Lloyd's Register, when her existence was in doubt.

It is worth noting here that while the advent of all-welded ships was certainly a boom for the shipbuilders it did contribute in a very large way to many of the demarcation troubles that the shipyards would have both then and in the

John Wilson at Otago.

future. The shipwrights who had traditionally held sway in the yards as the principal builders of ships were now being edged out and overtaken by the platers and welders; most of the shipwright's work would now only be carried out on the berths, with very little contribution to the fabrication of the units carried out undercover in the fabrication shops.

While the small oil tanker *Toro* was under construction the yard was busy building two pretty large ships on order from the famous British India Steam Navigation Company Ltd, (the BI Line, later to become part of the huge P&O group).

First, MV *Hebe*, Ship No 482 (ON 304252), was launched in March 1962 and completed in June 1962. She was to be chartered out to the Admiralty on a 19-year bareboat charter, so was painted naval grey and renamed RFA *Hebe* (A406). Her principal dimensions were given as: length overall 379 feet 3 inches (length B.P. 350 feet) with a moulded beam of 55 feet, and a moulded depth of 31 feet. She was powered by a 5-cylinder 2SA Sulzer diesel engine producing around 5,500 bhp to her single shaft. Her engine was built and supplied by Swan Hunter & Wigham Richardson, Wallsend. Her service speed was 15 knots, although she far exceeded this on her sea trials, when she attained a speed of 17.5 knots over the measured mile in the Forth. She had accommodation for 57 officers and men. Her tonnage was given as 4,823 grt and she was registered in the port of London.

Hebe started her service as a store ship for the RFA in 1962 and was used as a fleet stores ship; with her large hold and a cargo capacity of 7,103 cubic metres (250,850 cubic feet), including 113 cubic metres (4,000 cubic feet) insulated, she was ideal for the purpose. As it turned out, though, *Hebe* was not to be the luckiest ship built in Leith. She was involved in a couple of incidents that resulted in the loss of life, the last of which was the end of the ship as a seagoing vessel.

In the December of her first year and not eight months after being launched she was involved in an incident at Chatham Dockyard when the small harbour tug, *TID 97*, was sunk in Basin 3 while berthing her. Three of the crew were killed. A couple of years later she was involved in a mercy mission when along with HMS *Owen* she helped rescue 140 refugees, including 126 British subjects, from Zanzibar after a revolutionary coup there. Those rescued were landed at Mombasa.

In 1971, her management transferred to P&O General Cargo Division, then in 1973 her ownership moved to the Peninsular and Oriental Steam Navigation Company, so she became a P&O vessel for the rest of her working time with the Ministry of Defence.

She was to continue her work as a store ship until 30 November 1978, when she was severely damaged by fire at Gibraltar. Her superstructure was so severely damaged that repairs were considered uneconomical. The charter with the Ministry of Defence was cancelled and she was returned to P&O. One member of the crew was killed in this devastating fire. In 1979, she was sold to Good Luck Navegante S.A. (Good Faith Shipping Co. S.A., managers) Panama, and renamed *Good Guardian*.

In 1979, she arrived under tow at Piraeus for repair, and by 1981 she had been sold to Poseidon Shipping Co. S.A., Panama, and renamed *Guardian*. Two years later she arrived at Casablanca and was subsequently reported under arrest. In 1987 she was sold again, this

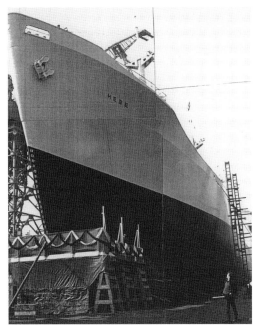

Left: *Hebe* ready for launch in the summer of 1962 with a young draughtsman admiring the fine shape of this vessel. Taken with a small camera, the images have had to be pasted together to show the full size of the ship.

Right: *Hebe* takes to the water, 18th June 1962

Above: *Bacchus*, the sister ship of *Hebe*, on her trials in the Firth of Forth. They were both fine looking vessels.

Left: *Hebe* now launched awaits the tugs to bring her back for fitting out.

RFA *Hebe* in this P&O photograph.

Above: *Hebe* portside view.

Upper right: *Hebe* A406 in 1972 (photo credit David Gerrard at www.rfanostalgia.org).

Lower right: *Hebe* (photo by F.R. Sherlock).

time for $159,000, to Cyprus shipbreakers and renamed *Wafa* before arriving at Famagusta, Cyprus, for demolition the same year.

So ended the chequered career of *Hebe*, Ship No 482.

As told by Mike Day:

A photo of RFA *Hebe* entering Malta, year not known. No deck cargo or chacons and fairly light forward. I was on her in 1970 when she was going to Singapore via the

Cape. An interesting run for such a small ship. Then did a nice run round the Med after we had refitted in the Isle of Dogs.

A break from the fleetwork of the front line ships, supposedly to help me with the cargo work requirements of 1st Mates. No comment!!

Hebe (photograph from Barry Dixon).

Dave Cameron remembers her:

I remember in 1974 she was rigged to carry mexiflaoats for the RCT. We unloaded stores off the island of Maseriah in Oman and then joined her again at Salalah. Instead of watching the evening film on the back deck, we used to gather with a drink and watch the to and fro of rockets from the hills and the airstrip each night.

The sister ship to *Hebe* was next to be launched and completed in October and November 1962 respectively, with the name MV *Bacchus*, Ship No 483 (ON 304368). She had the same specification in size and the same tonnage registered, at 4,823 grt. As she was to be chartered out to the Admiralty on a 19-year bareboat charter, she was painted naval grey and renamed RFA *Bacchus* (A404). She spent most of her time in Mediterranean waters.

Bacchus was to have a luckier time than *Hebe*. *Bacchus*'s management and ownership changed to match *Hebe*'s, and then in 1977 *Bacchus* was damaged in a collision with *Frontier* on leaving Limassol, Cyprus. However, she continued her work as a store ship until she saw out her full 19-year charter with the Admiralty and was handed back to her then owners, P&O, in 1981 – and was immediately sold on to Lion Shipping Co. Pte Ltd. (Lian Soon Agencies Pte Ltd, Managers) Singapore, and renamed *Cherry Lanka*. She was sold to Goodluck Corporation, Pakistan, for demolition in 1985, which commenced at Gadani Beach on 1 January 1986.

RFA *Bacchus*.

Hebe and *Bacchus* together (photo credit unknown, supplied by Mike Day)

Both *Hebe* and *Bacchus* were popular little ships, with small crews – by RFA standards, that is – even the chief officer took a watch!

Hebe and *Bacchus* berthed in Chatham. This was an unusual event, naturally enough, when they were regularly running to Singapore via various naval, army and RAF bases either through the Med or via the Cape.

> I am so pleased that someone is recording information about such a great little yard.
>
> I have a very unusual photo of Hebe and Bacchus in Chatham together. Very unusual as they were both engaged on round trips to Singapore for the whole of their career. After the Suez closed they did alternate round trips around the Med bases and then around the Cape to Singapore. They were an interesting break from Fleet ships but in all honesty I was pleased to get back to the real RFA.
>
> They both replaced two old Fort ships which had done the Singapore run from the fifties. When the Suez was closed (I was on Hebe in 1970) they were the smallest ships going around the Cape of Good Hope.
>
> Best regards, Mike Day

There followed the second small river and estuary tanker, *Uno*, Ship No 484 (ON 304409), a sister ship of *Toro*, with the same specifications, except her tonnage was shown as 530 grt. She was launched in December 1962, making two launches during this month.

The following year was a barren year for ship launches, although throughout the 1960s many other developments were ongoing throughout the 1960s, with the new ways of shipbuilding requiring new sheds for the fabrication of units, and further sheds needed to mark and burn out plates after they had gone through the new paint process machines. All plates would now come from the new steel stockyard which had taken the place of the old Cran shipyard to the west of the site. A further three slipways were filled in and levelled, to make way for the new shipyard layout.

Although welding could be seen as a huge step forward (for some) in shipbuilding, the real leap forward involved the loft. Previously the lines for the ships had been laid off full size, and full-size templates produced. Now the loft would take on more of the look of a ship drawing office, with very long stable tables replacing the full-size lines, which would now be produced in one-tenth scale. All the steelwork required for the ship could hence be drawn out in ink onto quality long-lasting film, and the drawing fed into the new magic eye machine. The Hancosine burning machine cut out the required shape and marked the plate at the same time – all from the ink drawings produced very accurately by the loft.

The savings in time and labour were enormous. Full-size templates would still be provided for plates with shape, or in the use of batten forms, to allow the plater to mark the plates that would not be going into the burning machine.

It is interesting to note that in all the time that the Henry Robb Shipyard was in operation there were only four foremen loftsmen. Going back to when the shipyard had access to a loft, the management had appointed a certain William Wallace as head loftsman. The following story is from his grandson, Peter.

William John Wallace, shipwright and shipyard manager

Willie was born and went to school in Paisley, where in 1902 he won a prize for General Excellence, Special Woodwork. Thus his skills in carpentry were recognised from an early age, and he followed both his father and grandfather, to become an apprentice shipwright in one of the lower Clyde shipyards in about 1903.

In 1910, probably on completion of his seven-year indenture, he moved to Dublin to be with Mary, his fiancée. There he worked at the Dublin Dockyard Company Ltd at Pembroke, on the River Dodder, where the company had three floating and graving docks, and built a smaller range of ships, such as coasters, small warships and lightships. Among the ships Willie and Dan would have built were the Irish lightships Penguin and Petrel and also HMCS Galiano, a fishery protection vessel and notable as the only Canadian warship lost in the First World War. It is interesting to note that in 1915 low wages and poor conditions caused a general lockout and a strike in Dublin. At the time dockyard labourers earned just three shillings[7] per week.

Willie and Mary, living in Dublin, had four children, but these were unsettled times in Ireland, culminating in the Easter Rising of 1916. At one point, his son, Dan, remembered being hurried down a side street away from sounds of gunfire, and 'being much affected by the sight of a dead horse'. However, much worse was to come.

In 1918, a virulent strain of 'Spanish' influenza swept around the world, infecting approximately one-fifth of the world's population. Between 30 and 100 million people lost their lives, making this event the most devastating pandemic in recorded world history and with a far higher death toll than the Great War. One of the fatalities was Mary, on 11 November – Armistice Day.

This devastating loss left Willie with his 17-year-old brother and four children, aged 7, 5, 3 and just six months. Far from home and relations, in 1919 he decided to return home to the Clyde.

The family later moved to Leith in the 1920s, when Willie started work in the drawing loft of Henry Robb Ltd.

---

7 Equivalent to less than £20 in 2022.

For most of the 20th century Robb's were the largest shipbuilders on the River Forth. When I was young, Willie, my grandfather, took me into the shipyard and showed me this vast room where the 'lines' of ships' frames and plates were drawn on the floor at full scale. From these, wooden templates were constructed and used for the actual fabrication of the ship. I also saw them hot riveting the hulls before welding became the standard method of construction. I think this would have been around 1949.

During the Second World War, he served in the City of Edinburgh Home Guard, rising to Major.

For the remainder of his working life he continued at Robb's, mainly in the drawing loft, and retired as Manager about 1951. He would have been involved in the planning of virtually every ship built there during his time at the yard. Probably the most famous of these was the Turmoil, a powerful tug built for the Admiralty in 1943. She captured the world headlines for a fortnight in 1952 while trying to save the Flying Enterprise, a cargo ship listing heavily in the Atlantic.

Willie died in Leith, not far from Robb's shipyard, in 1957.

As well as reciting poetry, particularly at Burns Suppers, Willie wrote a considerable number of poems, some serious, some humorous, some patriotic, some topical, such as that below bemoaning the lack of a pay rise at Robb's:

It sure is a racket, our skinny pay-packet,
will somebody please put us wise?
We're promised some money, and that isn't funny,
but WHEN are we getting that rise?
The management ponders, and one often wonders,
are they really so deaf to our cries?
We're getting quite weary, our blinkers are bleary,
with looking around for that rise.
It's awfully boring, how prices are soaring,
they're just about reaching the skies.
They'll go up still higher, the fat's in the fire,
We really could do with that rise.
The Stone has been stolen, the thief's head is swollen,[8]
He's come up to Robb's in disguise,
and being no novice, he's burgled the office,
and scampered away with our rise.

Until his retirement in 1951 William would have been involved in the steelwork of every ship built at Henry Robb Shipyard during his time at the yard.

---

8 On Christmas Day 1950 four Scottish students, inspired by nationalist sentiment, stole the Stone of Destiny/ Stone of Scone from the Coronation Chair in Westminster Abbey. About four months later it was recovered from Arbroath Abbey. So this poem was presumably written at about that time.

Grab Dredger No 1. As you can see, this type of dredger was built for unremitting hard work, and they were complex ships to build, a type that the Leith shipyards of Henry Robb specialised in building. (Photo supplied by Don O'Connor.)

There was only one launch in 1963: Ship No 485, a large twin-screw grab dredger from the Commissioners of the Port of Calcutta. She was to be named *Grab Dredger No 1*. At 1,309 grt, she was a large, complex vessel to build, and had a length between perpendiculars of 210 feet with a moulded beam of 45 feet, and a moulded depth of 17 feet 9 inches. She was powered by a 9-cylinder diesel engine, built and supplied by Mirrlees of Stockport, England. Her service speed was given as 10 knots. She provided good service for many years in and around the port of Calcutta, and was only scrapped in 2014. She was deleted from Lloyd's Register in 2000.

Most ships built need to have a delivery crew appointed, either by the owners or the shipyard, depending on the original build contract. The following is the story of one of these delivery voyages undertaken on *Grab Dredger No 1*.

As told by Don O'Connor, 'Dreaded Dredger No. 1'

I was sailing with P&O as second engineer on Orcades but decided to retire and go to Australia for a sea change and thought a run job might be the way to get there free of cost

So applied to Pedder & Mylcrest to take this vessel to Calcutta and got the post without any problems (I wonder why!) Arrived at Henry Robbs yard 12th December 1963 and we departed Leith 16th December 1963. The Crew consisted of Capt. and mate (5hrs on/off) – Chief engineer Bill Fraser the works manager +myself + a fellow from a local Leith garage, quartermaster +6 ABs and a cook. We had quite an eventful voyage as you can imagine on a vessel built for calm waters going on a long deep-sea

The ship's builder's plate, which the shipbreakers in India offered to sell to me; it took some while for me to convince them that the cost of posting the plate was more than it was worth.

The tanker *Hamble* under way.

trip. I did keep a diary but won't bore you with any details, but we did not arrive in Calcutta until 7 Feb 1964 – We had no refrigeration /no f/w. showers/no air con/ etc, etc – quite different from the *Orcades*!

Twin screw 9 cyl Mirrlees, made about 10 knots with following sea but only averaged about 5 knots. We encountered quite bad seas for much of the trip, and this caused quite a lot of problems with the aux cooling pumps and we only got into the Bay of Biscay before the turnbuckles securing the hoppers broke loose and only the forecastle and engine room were the floating parts of ship.

I did finally arrive in Melbourne and settled down, got married, and have 3 sons and 4 grandsons.

The next two orders under construction, beginning late 1963, came from the Shell Mex & B.P. Co. Ltd, for two coastal petroleum products tankers. Ship No 486 was the first of the vessels, launched in April 1964, and named *Hamble* (ON 305976). Her dimensions and specifications were the same as her sister ship, *Killingholme*, Ship No 487. These were given as follows: length overall 214 feet 10 inches (length B.P. 201 feet) with a beam moulded of 36 feet 11 inches, and a moulded depth of 15 feet 6 inches. They were each powered by a single 6-cylinder oil diesel engine 2SA producing around 1230 bhp to single shaft, with engines built and supplied by British Polar Engines Ltd, Glasgow. Original tonnage as built was given as 1,182 grt.

Hamble seems to have been renamed *Shell Refiner* for a short time. She served the Shell company well for 17 years before being sold to (Metro Oil) Sarnia, Ontario, Canada, and she was renamed *Metro Star*. It is here when her history gets interesting.

During the winter of 1981–82, *Metro Star* was lengthened by 18.2 metres, and her deck was raised by about 1 metre, at the Marystown Shipyard in Newfoundland. The new midship addition added two more cargo tanks to her existing five. It is not known whether she was just lengthened or if she received an entirely new midsection. Some of her service history is shown below.

Then, on 31 October 1982, *Metro Star* ran aground at St Augustine, Quebec City, and started taking on water. She was subsequently beached to avoid sinking, fortunately without the loss of any of her gasoline or diesel oil cargo. Her fleetmate, *Metro Sun*, later came alongside and offloaded *Metro Star*'s cargo.

On 4 November 1982 she was refloated (it is not known which tugs were involved with her salvage) and on 10 November she was returned to Shediac, New Brunswick, by the salvors

As *Metro Star* and looking pretty beat up.

Killingholme, seen under her
new name, BP *Scorcher*.

Ligar Bay departing Wellington in 1974
for Tarakohe, for another load of cement.

at Pictou, Nova Scotia. She was later towed to Halifax, Nova Scotia, where subsequent inspections resulted her being declared a total constructive loss.

But her owners decided to repair her all the same, since they had invested heavily in her refit only eight months earlier. So the repairs began, in February 1983, at the Halifax shipyard of Irving's Shipbuilders, Nova Scotia. In the same year, Lloyd's of London records her owner as Shediac Tanker Corporation of Sarnia, Ontario, Canada; but her history after this gets a wee bit murky, with different owners and a couple of name changes including *Erin T* then *Marine Supplier* out of Panama. It was then stated by Lloyd's that *Marine Supplier* was most likely owned and managed from Nigeria. There has been no further news since 2005, but she may well still be around.

Her identical sister ship, *Killingholme*, Ship No 487 (ON 306044), was also launched in 1964. She was renamed *BP Scorcher* in 1975 before ending up as another Nigerian ship, *Nigerian Star*, and was last heard of in 1983. By 2013 Lloyd's had doubted her existence – although she could still be in service under another name and a flag of convenience.

DEV *Ligar Bay*, Ship No 488 (ON 316442), was the third self-discharging cement carrier built for the New Zealand market. She was ordered by the Tarakohe Shipping Co. Ltd for the New Zealand coastal service, shipping bulk cement. Her principal dimensions were given as follows: length overall 226 feet 7 inches with a beam moulded of 38 feet, and a moulded depth of 16 feet; her given tonnage as launched was 1,330 grt. She was powered by two 8-cylinder diesel 4SA engines with electric motors to produce around 1,734 bhp to her two shafts, giving her a service speed of 11 knots. Her engines were built and supplied by the English Electric Company Ltd, Newton-le-Willows.

This twin-screw cement carrier, although similar looking to her predecessor vessels, *Golden Bay* and *John Wilson*, was by all accounts nowhere near as good a sea-keeping vessel as them. (See the accompanying story from one of her engineers, Tony Skilton.)

Ligar Bay taking on some
sea under way.

Ligar Bay, the rolliest and
most violent ship of them all.

Ligar Bay's regular ports of call were Wellington, Wanganui, New Plymouth, Raglan and Picton, with cement loaded at Tarakohe in Golden Bay. Ligar Bay was transferred back to the parent company, Blue Circle Industries Ltd of London, in 1979. She continued to run cement and drill mud on the coasts of the British Isles for another six years, before being replaced by *Golden Bay II*, built by the Caledon Dundee shipyard.

She was also used by the North Sea drilling rigs before being sold on to West Indies Cement Carriers and working around the Caribbean islands for a couple of years prior to another sale, this time to Seaward Shipping & Dredging Lt. of the Cayman Islands, and trading from Puerto Rico and Venezuela to Antigua. She was then used as a storage vessel in Antigua until eventually being purchased by an Antiguan owner. She was blown ashore in 1989 by a hurricane and not refloated until 1992. *Ligar Bay* was grounded again in 1995 by another hurricane, in Parham Harbour, Antigua, and was deleted from Lloyd's Register in 1996.

Tony Skilton – who sailed on all the cement carriers built in Leith and also on the new *Golden Bay II*, built in Dundee – told the following story:

In the mid-1970s, whilst passing through the Terawiti Rip en route to Tarakohe in ballast, she rolled, then snapped back so fast that the top 8 feet of the foremast snapped off, and with the radio aerial, was never seen again!

In the very early '70s whilst entering Wanganui, a hard-a-port helm order was given but the bosun put her to stbd – she ran upon the rocks of the south mole and opened up Nos 1, 2, 3, and 4 stbd ballast tanks. When eventually she was taken back to Wellington with the stbd bulwarks awash (which they were most of the time at sea anyway, both sides), she was gently nursed into the Jubilee floating dock and stayed there for the next 3 months while her bottom was rebuilt.

One trip south from Raglan in 1977, we headed direct to Wellington empty. Copped a real hiding on the way, and the porcelain hand basins in the 3rd & 4th engineer's cabins were shattered with the continual thumping of the waves on the stbd side of our cabins.

We were left with just the pipework sticking up where the basins used to be. The chief steward's (Jack Hasset from the Hutt Valley) cabin, and the 3 engineer's cabins on that side were all soaking wet – the outer bulkhead was deformed from the pounding and the porthole frames let the water in.

Diesel electric propulsion, with two English Electric 8RK Mk1 engines – in nice weather you could shut one engine down and run both props on the remaining generator and still have full manoeuvrability, albeit with much less power available.

Like the rest of the self-discharging Golden Bay ships, once you reached port, one main engine and generator set was kept running, but the output was reconnected to supply the power for the cargo discharge machinery in the pump room. She also had 2 V4 Paxman generators that were a real pain in the butt!

Funny thing – the ship was all Direct Current electrics (as was the original Golden Bay, and the John Wilson) for the propulsion systems and the domestics. When little 14" B&W portable television sets became all the rage, crew members would bring their new TV down, set it up in their cabin, then plug it in. PPPoooff! Sorry.

Alternating current TVs from ashore don't like DC current from ship's systems. The ship had two little motor-generator converter sets on the flat just inside the engine room door – noisy little things – when the ship was on AC shore power, these units were driven by AC power, but the attached generators produced 220V DC for the domestic systems.

I've still got the woven log line from this ship down in my basement – made a very handy and reliable set of rope blocks up, and this log line was perfect for the job.

If we (the engineers) had had a major breakdown to contend with in the pumproom our overalls would become thick with cement. The trick was to get the log line and put it through one sleeve of your overalls and out the other, tie both ends of the line to something on the poop, then throw the overalls overboard to get washed in the wake. One night, Bill Brodie, the mate, stopped and anchored the ship without giving us a call first – the result was a couple of pairs of lost overalls. …

Another little point – after the ship's specifications were drawn up, very late in the piece someone decided to lop 35 feet off the overall length to allow for more clearance when turning in tight spaces – hence the very blunt bow, which would slam into every wave and virtually stop the ship. She was also a pig to steer (been there, done that), as the horsepower was not great, and the single rudder was NOT very close to the props longitudinally, so therefore did not get much water flow over it.

The four photographs (following) are all from the private collection of Emmanuel Makarios, who sailed on *Ligar Bay*.

The following were also sourced by Tony Skilton, with the help of Dorothy, at the Fletcher Challenge Trust Archives, Auckland, New Zealand. They unearthed some more old photographs of ships built at the Leith shipyards of Henry Robb.

With two more tipping barges for the Leith Dock Commission, to help with filling in the new breakwater, this completed the building of ships for 1964. Ship No 489 was named

Left: On the slip at Nelson, where *Ligar Bay* often did her survey, in this photograph taken during the mid-1970s.

Right: *Ligar Bay* berthed at Wellington during the mid to late 1960s.

Left: *Ligar Bay* berthed at Wellington not long after her delivery from the Leith shipyards of Henry Robb.

Right: *Ligar Bay* berthed at Queens Wharf, Wellington, in the early 1970s.

Above: George Allen on the bridge of *Ligar Bay* (Fletcher Challenge Trust Archives).

Right: The starboard English Electric 8RK main engine (Fletcher Challenge Trust Archives).

Left: *Ligar Bay* diesel-electric propulsion control panel, 1964. (Fletcher Challenge Trust Archives). The main prop motor control wheels (shown) were moved by servo motors when the ship was in bridge control – we just sat and watched! (Tony Skilton)

Right: The brand new *Ligar Bay* berthing at New Plymouth 1964 (Fletcher Challenge Trust Archives).

Left: *Ligar Bay* arriving at Deep Cove with a load of cement for the Manapouri Power Project, around 1965. The vessel ahead is the hostel ship Wanganella, which was used as accommodation for the workers building the tailrace tunnel. Wanganella had been launched in 1929 – from the Harland & Wolff Belfast slipway that Titanic had been built on. Wanganella was sent to China for scrapping in the early 1960s, but scrap prices dropped so low that she was then put back on the trans-Tasman run before becoming a hostel ship, as shown. She was finally towed away to be scrapped in 1970. (Tony Skilton) (Fletcher Challenge Trust Archives)

Right: *Ligar Bay* pumping cement into the silo at Deep Cove 1965 (Fletcher Challenge Trust Archives).

George Okihere (photo from John Knubley, taken from a shipbuilding/engineering publication).

LDC No 7, and at 80 grt was launched in May 1964, and *LDC No 8*, Ship No 490, launched in early December 1964.

1965 began with the launch of a tug ordered for work in Nigeria, and the resulting *Abdul Maliki*, Ship No 492, was launched in February to continue the fine pedigree the yard had earned by building tugs. She was quickly followed by her sister ship, *George Ohikere*, Ship No 494, for the same owners, the Nigerian Ports Authority. Both were twin-screw diesel tugs of 154 grt.

One of the two motor tugs ordered by the Nigerian Port Authority, *George Ohikere* was second of the two-ship order launched in March 1965; her hull was fully welded, and she was twin-screwed, powered by twin British Polar engines.

The river and estuary tanker *Astro* was next to launch. She was a sister ship to the previous ship, *Uno*, built for the same owners – the Union Lighterage Co. Ltd. Launched on 28 November 1964, *Astro* was a small practical river tanker at 550 grt, and a little bit longer than her two sister ships. By today's standards of tanker they are of course pretty small, but they were designed to be used around the coast and go upriver to the inland ports which could not be reached by larger vessels, so they were very useful ships for the oil companies.

She was renamed *Blackburn* in 1972 but reverted to *Astro* in 1984, and at the time of writing, at almost 50 years old, is still going – another fitting testament to the quality of workmanship at the Henry Robb yard.

Astro was followed by another special ship, a survey and research vessel, which when built would not have looked out of place as one of today's superyachts (in fact, she was in my opinion one of the nicest-looking ships built at the Leith shipyards of Henry Robb). Named MV *Tribeni*, Ship No 493, her launch was squeezed in between that of the two Nigerian tugs.

Tribeni was an order from the Port Commissioners of Calcutta; her principal dimensions were given as follows: length B.P. 175 feet with a moulded beam of 35 feet, and a moulded depth of 17 feet. She was powered by a 4-cylinder diesel oil engine producing around 1430 ihp to her single shaft. Her engine was built and supplied by Christiansen & Meyer, Hamburg, with her registered tonnage given as 918 grt.

Delightfully, she was launched with a coconut rather than a bottle of champagne, which would have been against the local religion.

It seems that towards the end of her career with the Port Commission *Tribeni* caused a few headaches with the pompous jobsworths who haggled over whether it was worth it in money terms to keep her going for another year. Once it had been agreed by committee, the work was ordered to be carried out by a local Indian shipyard, but the result was poor to the extent that she was of use for only 12 days out of her final year – and at great cost. *Tribeni* was eventually sent to be broken up in 2003, a sad end for such a beautiful ship.

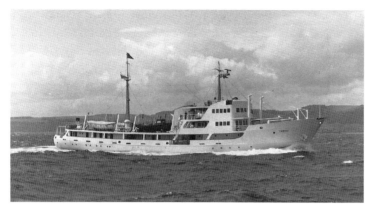

Upper left: The survey ship *Tribeni* on trials in the Firth of Forth (photo from the Loftsman Collection).

Left: In this picture of *Tribeni* on the stocks at the Leith shipyards of Henry Robb, the hull is nearly ready for the bow units to be attached. Note the conditions of working in a shipyard at that time. (Photo from the Loftsman Collection.)

Lower left: The lower bow unit of *Tribeni* being constructed from the forward collision bulkhead to her soft nose. This was the first bulbous-bow ship built at Leith.

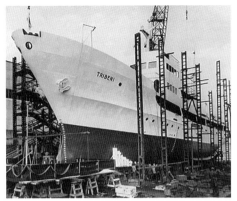

Above: *Tribeni* being readied for launch, looking pretty good with a fresh paint job on her. The shipwrights are working to transfer her from the building keel blocks onto the sliding ways. (This was done with muscle power and long wooden wedges.) Note the (rather faint) sign down by the small bulbous bow; this was not a form of German graffiti, but an ancient sign originating from the Sanskrit. (Photo from the Loftsman Collection)

Right: *Tribeni* is launched into the Western Basin.

In the two decades covered by this book, the Henry Robb yard built 110 ships – from the end of the Second World War to the launch of MV *Salerno* in November 1965. During this time the yard also built and launched some 36 unnamed barges and lighters/pontoons. The next decades would see the advent of one of the most dramatic changes in shipping since the change from sail to steam: containerisation would change the industry for ever, for good or ill.

1965 would also see the shipyard of Henry Robb win its largest ever single order, for a total of seven ships.

SIX
OUTSIDE WORK

The yard was busy after the Second World War, with a great many changes soon to affect shipbuilding, such as the onset of welding, then later one-tenth scale lofting.

While the order books were busy the yard was also capable of taking on so much more, with the tradesmen in the shipyard regarded as premium craftsmen. Many outside firms would also call on the men to carry out all manner of work.

This chapter will feature the outside work, as it was called, that HR carried out well into the 1970s.

The yard worked on everything from new doors for a bank to the new oil tanker terminal built in the Firth of Forth, catering for the North Sea oil boom.

I am indebted to an ex-draughtsman from Henry Robb, John Knubley, who sent me some information to remind me just how much outside work was carried out.

In the days before the Leith Dock Commission (later Forth Ports) built the lock gates at the far end of the basin, turning the docks into a non-tidal area,[9] Henry Robb carried out a large amount of dry docking, repair work and modifications on commercial vessels such as RFA Wave class tankers, and on Fort Class replenishment cargo ships, one of the last to be worked on being RFA *Reliant*, an aviation stores ship.

The Royal Fleet Auxiliary work ran out in the mid-sixties as the old RFA ships were disposed of and new ones were built to replace them. Ships such as Ship No 482, RFA *Hebe*, and Ship No 483, RFA *Bacchus*. Both ships, having been built for British India Steam Navigation, were chartered by the RFA.

Now we go back much further, to a ship that had been built at the yard in the early 1930s; she was back at the yard to be converted from steam to diesel. *Scot II* was also given a new wheelhouse and funnel. It's such a shame that the same vessel is/was laid up as a rusting hulk on the Caledonian Canal at Fort Augustus. She is in desperate need of rescue, although at the time of writing I do not know what has happened to the attempts to save her.

With some of the finest joiners and carpenters in Edinburgh on the books, it was no wonder that the yard was kept busy with outside work. Everything from exhibition stands

9 Good in theory – but who knows how many ships turned away due to the cost of entering through those gates?

to steel stairways and walkways, along with the aforementioned heavy wooden doors for a bank[10] in George Street, Edinburgh. The outside work department had its own manager, Bert Botel, who kept an eye on the work.

Speaking of joiners, it is perhaps a nice way of bringing in the shipyard joiner's story:

I, like many others, left school on the Friday, and started work on the following Monday. My uncle, Peter Jeffrey, who was a left-handed riveter in the old hand squads, got me a start as an apprentice joiner in Robb's. I started with two other lads, Billy Harper and Davy Wood, we were put into the Joiner's store as store boys, until we were 16 and old enough to start our apprenticeships. There was no structured training for the stores, but we just 'Picked it up,' as we went along, learning how to measure screws, and identify general ironmongery, whilst fetching and carrying, collecting time cards daily, and assisting in the plywood stores, or Fairways shed, at the Old Dock, where completed furniture was stored prior to fitting out in the ships.

On reaching my 16th birthday I was put 'On the bench,' with a tradesman, and was given some sandpapering to do. This seemed easy, but at the end of the day my fingers were raw with the abrasion. Some toughening up had to happen quickly! Then the first job – to make my own tool chest, all hand dovetailed, in Californian Pine, with sliding trays and brass lock, completed with chest handles. The paint shop painted it, and sign wrote my initials on the front, I still have it, 61 years later!

Then, after a spell in the Joiner's shop with a journeyman, I was sent out onto a ship, 'On the stocks'. Here marking out took place to determine the position of the wooden bulkheads dividing the accommodation into cabins, and locating welded nuts and hangers for the fixing of furniture and fittings. We were given a leather glove and a stick, and would hold the nut or hanger in position while the welder tacked it. Of course we suffered from welding flashes, and were entitled to a free pint of milk daily. (Early Health & Safety.)

The first ship I worked on in the 'Fitting out' berth at the West Pier, was the BI ship Mombasa, a passenger/cargo vessel plying between Africa and Arabia and India largely for the Muslim Pilgrimage to Mecca. She also had first class passenger cabins, and these were fitted out to a very high standard. I worked with a tradesman fitting out the first class smokeroom, all Sycamore panelling and Walnut French doors and furniture.

I worked on many of the ships built for Australia and New Zealand, remembering particularly the Ligar Bay, a bulk cement carrier. I was also on most of the tugs built at that time for Manchester Shipping Canal. These were excellent training for older apprentices, as the curved shapes of the tugs meant much more detailed fitting.

I did sea trials on another couple of tugs for Bibby Line in West Africa, the Fourah and the Farren. I was appointed 'Key Boy' for these ships, which meant holding all the keys of the ship securely, and allowing access to those requiring it, both at the berth

10 Now just another of the many bars in this well-known street.

and during trials. What we did in effect, was to cut our own skeleton keys for each of the lock suites, and that saved constantly looking up the keyboard. I remember, before the Fourah sailed for Africa, being called out to fix a lock on the binnacle. It was late afternoon, and I was told I could probably book 'Overtime.' (*A big bonus in those days!) To save time, instead of cutting a new key, I altered the wards in the lock, so any key would fit it! This still took time, and I was in the Tug's engine room, using the vice. On coming up to the bridge it was a dark winter's afternoon, and the boat had sailed! No one realizing I was still on board! At eighteen years old, I was starving, and just wanted home for my tea! Robb's sent the small steam pinnace they had, and took me off just off the May Island, much to my relief!

Industrial relations were always very poor in my days at the yard. There was no trust at all between management and workers. Conditions and pay were worse than other industries, even going to the toilet was regulated, you had to drop your brass number check at the entrance turnstile to use the toilet, and if you were more than 7 minutes you lost a quarter of an hour's pay. Timekeeping generally was very strict. A minute late in the morning meant that you lost a quarter of an hour, 16 minutes lost you half an hour, and at 31 minutes late, you were locked out for the day, losing a whole day's pay. For apprentices, at the end of your five years apprenticeship, all these lost minutes were added up, and added to your time at apprentice rates; even though you'd done five years, and were on journeymen's wages!

There were no official tea breaks, but everyone managed an illicit cuppa! The hot water urns for making tea at dinner break were kept padlocked until the hooter sounded for break!

I did however love working there. The work was of the highest standard, and everyone took pride in their craft and the ships we worked on. The men were rough, but kind in many ways, and helped to build our characters in later life, setting standards and moral guidelines, and particularly giving us a Political education, and examples of decent working class living.

I left the yard after my three years in the Army. I returned for one year on return, but then left never to return.

It's sad to see the closure of such a fine yard and the loss of employment for so many men whose community was so dependent on Shipbuilding, the end of an era.

A particularly good point should be made here with no apology, as I have personal experience: a good tradesman from a shipyard could work on any outside work or company, but to bring a good tradesman into the shipyard from outside – well, that was a different matter for many different reasons, not least the fact that nothing on a ship is straight, and it all comes with its own language. I have seen many capable people come into shipbuilding from jobs outside and struggle. This was one of the reasons that each of the trades had the prefix 'ship' in front of it: ship's joiner, ship's carpenter, ship's plumber, ship's engineer and so on. These were all specific and specialised trades.

The 1950s produced some of the stories surrounding the trades and in particular working in the Henry Robb Shipyard, such as this tale:

The Ship's Plumber, Henry Robb

My Apprenticeship 1951–1956: Introduction

In March 1951, I presented myself at the plumbing shop of Henry Robb Shipbuilders at Victoria Pier for my first day of apprenticeship as a ship's plumber. This would last for a period of five years.

For the first time in my life I wore a pair of dark overalls and working steel toecap boots. It was strange to say the least. The previous week I had been wearing a suit, shirt and tie as required of an office worker. What had I let myself in for? I would soon learn. I was going in as a raw lad and would emerge a man. Shipyards were, as I was soon to find out, renowned to sort out men from boys. To quote the old maxim, `if you can`t stand the heat, then get out of the kitchen`. It was not an unfriendly place, and the friends I made there would become friends for life. However that was yet to come.

I was met by the plumbing foreman, Duncan 'Dandy' McLean. For the uninitiated, the Dandy was synonymous with the name McLean through the fictional detective character featured in the Weekly News at that time.

I was immediately assigned to work with an experienced plumber, David Borthwick, within the workshop proper. How disappointed I was, for I was hoping to begin work on the ships straight away.

My workplace was on a mezzanine floor above the main workshop. This was not a pleasant place, for the smoke from the gas fires that heated pipes for bending drifted up to it, despite the presence of large air extractors.

My work here consisted of lead lining the wooden rocket boxes that would contain distress signals, lead window boxes that were fitted beneath the opening windows of wheelhouses, making lead pipe flanges, and lead 4" soil adaptors for W.C.s on board ship.

Although I did not enjoy the working environment of it, I appreciated I was getting a firm grounding in the basics of the trade. I knew that the boys who were assigned to shipboard work in the first instance were denied this learning.

However, after six months I was moved out into the yard proper where I was to work on a seagoing tug boat, the Arusha. This was still on the stocks. Here I became knowledgeable in nautical terms.

It was a language all on its own. Aft – back, for`wd – front, bulwark – side, midships – middle, deckhead – ceiling, bulkhead – wall, companionway – corridor, the list was endless.

After the Second World War the Leith shipyards of Henry Robb Ltd built many off-site constructions, and a pretty novel one for its time was a fire-drill ship representation built next to the fire station at MacDonald Road Fire Station.

One of the most feared disasters at sea is fire breaking out on a ship. Perhaps surprisingly, it can be just as bad if the ship is in dock, and this was one of the reasons that the Edinburgh & South-East Scotland Fire Brigade pushed for a training facility to replicate some of the varied problems of fighting a fire on a ship. After all, if you are close to a port it makes sense to have this type of capability for fighting fires on a ship, just as you would practise firefighting on an aircraft by using an old aeroplane.

Who better to build such a facility than a shipyard? The training facility built by Henry Robb circa 1960 was complete with an engine room and two decks to represent a superstructure above, along with a bridge deck complete with cabins, giving firefighters and Mercantile Marine crews a good basic training in facing such a problem. The MacDonald Road

The fire-drill ship in MacDonald Road, a replicated ship's superstructure to help train firefighters and seafarers to tackle any blaze on a ship in Leith docks or offshore in the Firth of Forth. Its instigator was Frank Rushbrook, who commanded the Edinburgh & South-East of Scotland Fire Brigade from about 1960. (© Kim Traynor, and licensed for reuse under Creative Commons)

Fire Station was not all that far from the shipyard; it is situated just off Leith Walk – and just up the road from Brown Brothers, who were world famous for producing ships' stabilisers and so on. We used to develop the shell plates for them, as each stabiliser had a cutout in the shell from which it could be extended.

All of this was good outside work, which helped keep men employed.

(The French had one even better; they used an old Henry Robb River class frigate to train their firefighters in ship-based firefighting techniques.)

The dummy ship at MacDonald Road is now no longer around, and the land may well be covered in flats, as so much of the area now is.

When the North Sea oil boom started, we thought this would help create a bonanza for Leith. This did not quite materialise, but some work did come the way of Leith.

Robb Caledon was awarded a contract to build the steelwork and supporting structure for what would become known as the Hound Point Terminal for George Wimpey, and it was for ever called the Wimpey Job. This was a good contract to be working on, as it paid more than our hourly rate. While I was just an apprentice, I was paid an extra 5 pence per hour on this job. It meant an extra £2 per week to me, as young lad; very helpful.

The job was laid out in the loft, while templates were made to ensure the accuracy of the work, bevel boards were made to make sure that all the bevels cut in the square section steel were all correct.

The Hound Point terminal in the Firth of Forth minus any oil tankers; seen here at dusk.

The welding had to be done to a high standard too, and any of the welders wishing to work on this job had to be tested and coded before they were allowed anywhere near it.

The walkways were assembled on the quayside – wide open as it was, with ships being outfitted at the time, in winter it was freezing. We had the job of ensuring the steelwork was level and accurate, and 20 minutes was all we would spend out there in the bitter wind before hurrying back up the loft for a heat; when I think back to it, it was brutal.

The following is from Wikipedia:

Hound Point is a marine terminal off a rocky headland of that name on the southern shore of the Firth of Forth, Scotland, just east of the Forth Bridge at South Queensferry. Opened in 1975, it is owned and operated by Ineos as an oil-export terminal for North Sea oil and is the largest such facility in Scotland.

The terminal is made up of two sea-island berths that can load vessels of up to 350,000 DWT and a vapour recovery platform. Crude oil from the Forties pipeline undergoes stabilisation and gas processing and treatment at the Kinneil Terminal at Grangemouth before being pumped to a tank farm at Dalmeny on the southern shore of the Firth. The oil is then pumped to the Hound Point terminal where it is loaded onto tankers.

The name 'Hound Point' derives from a local legend concerning the lord of nearby Barnbougle Castle, currently Lord Rosebery. The legend states that one of the first lords set off to fight in the Crusades, leaving his beloved hunting-hound behind. At the moment the man was killed, the hound began howling uncontrollably, eventually dying of its grief. Ever since, the howling ghost of the hound is said to appear on the Point whenever the present lord is about to die.

Some conversion work was carried out on ships to make them fit for North Sea operation, including much work to facilitate the ships' ability to deploy divers into the cold and murky depths.

I remember working on two of the Vickers ships: the names *Voyager*, *Challenger* and *Explorer* ring a bell, but it was a fair old time ago to recall.

The yard even helped build a new brewery in Edinburgh – a job that everyone wanted to get on to for some strange reason. The McEwan's brewery in Fountainbridge, Edinburgh, was duly completed, along with a MacBridge unit[11] for the dock in Dundee – but that was only constructed just after the Robb Caledon (Dundee division) yard had been forced to close by British Shipbuilders.

---

11 A ship-to-shore bridge that moves up and down with the tides.

LIST OF SHIPS BUILT BY HENRY ROBB SHIPBUILDERS & ENGINEERS LTD 1945–1965

The following is a complete list of the vessels built in the Leith Shipyard of Henry Robb, per the shipyard build list book, from the end of the Second World War right through to 1965.

The list is compiled in the order of vessel number, not by the date of launch. Some vessels on the list were not launched until much later for many reasons, but especially because of priority given to whichever ships were needed the quickest. But in addition, engine delays were a constant source of concern, while employment relations could also put back launch dates.

Note: All dimensions are in imperial feet and inches.

Ship No	Name	Dimensions	Tonnage	Type	Launched (day/month/year)
351	MV Corncrake	180 × 32.10 × 20.5	629	S.S. Diesel Cargo	20/12/1945
352	MV REDSTART	180 × 32.10 × 20.5	629	S.S. Diesel Cargo	05/03/1946
353	MV KANNA	210 × 36.6 × 21.8	925	S.S. Diesel Cargo	23/10/1945
354	MV KATUI	210 × 36.6 × 21.8	925	S.S. Diesel Cargo	21/11/1945
355	SS TINTO	280 × 42 × 25.3	1,795	S.S. Cargo Steamer	27/08/1946
356	SS TRURO	280 × 42 × 25.3	1,795	S.S. Cargo Steamer	11/11/1946
357	SS BRAVO	280 × 42 × 25.3	1,798	S.S. Cargo Steamer	06/02/1947
358	SS SILVIO	280 × 42 × 25.3	1,798	S.S. Cargo Steamer	18/07/1947
359	TSMV DARINIAN	255 × 42 × 25	1,533	T.S. Diesel Cargo	21/05/1947
360	TSMV PALMELIAN	255 × 42 × 25	1,533	T.S. Diesel Cargo	12/11/1947
361	TSMV KAITANGATA	290 × 43 × 19.6	2,485	T.S. Diesel Cargo	27/01/1948
362	TSMV KONUI	290 × 43 × 19.6	2,485	T.S. Diesel Cargo	25/05/1948
363	TSMV PURIRI	200 × 39 × 13	1,248	T.S. Diesel Cargo	22/07/1948
364	-	80 × 19 × 5.3	85	Barge	
365	-	80 × 19 × 5.3	85	Barge	
366	-	80 × 19 × 5.3	85	Barge	
367	-	80 × 19 × 5.3	85	Barge	
368	-	80 × 19 × 5.3	85	Barge	
369	-	80 × 19 × 5.3	85	Barge	
370	MSC ONSET	88 × 24 × 12	154	T.S. Diesel Tug	19/08/1947
371	MSC ONWARD	88 × 24 × 12	154	T.S. Diesel Tug	02/09/1947
372	-	50 × 12 × 4.6	150	S.S. Grab Dredger	

Ship No	Name	Dimensions	Tonnage	Type	Launched (day/month/year)
373	-	50 × 12 × 4.6	150	S.S. Grab Dredger	
374	MV GREBE	220 × 37 × 21.6	933	S.S. Diesel Cargo	25/03/1948
375	TSMV KAITAWA	290 × 43 × 19.6	2,485	T.S. Diesel Cargo	19/10/1948
376	TSMV KAIAPOI	290 × 43 × 19.6	2,485	T.S. Diesel Cargo	16/03/1949
377	MV KAMONA	235 × 45 × 16	1,785	S.S. Diesel Cargo	12/05/1949
378	MSC GRAB HOPPER No 1	142 × 30.6 × 13	479	S.S. Diesel Dredger	12/01/1949
379	TSMV MOMBASA	250 × 43 × 19	2,213	T.S. Passenger & Cargo	29/02/1950
380	MOLE	130 × 28 × 10.6	311	T.S. Steam Grab Hopper Dredger	15/03/1949
381	MSC PANTHER	88 × 24 × 12	154	T.S. Diesel Tug	11/02/1950
382	MSC PUMA	88 × 24 × 12	154	T.S. Diesel Tug	17/02/1950
383	-	75 × 20 × 9.6	105	Barge	
384	-	75 × 20 × 9.6	105	Barge	
385	-	75 × 20 × 9.6	105	Barge	
386	-	75 × 20 × 9.6	105	Barge	
387	-	75 × 20 × 9.6	105	Barge	
388	-	75 × 18 × 7.6	103	Water Carrying barge	
389	TSMV MAMAKU	175 × 36 × 12.9	927	T.S. Diesel Cargo	28/07/1949
390	-	50 × 33.8 × 6	85	Pontoon	
391	KETAM	95 × 25 × 7.6	125	Hopper Grab Dredger	21/06/1949
392	CLAROBEN	81.8 × 20 × 9.6	129	Crude Oil Carrying barge	
393	TSMV MTWARA	280 × 46 × 27.6	2,629	T.S. Passenger & Cargo	20/08/1950
394	JEAN INGELOW	99 × 25 × 7.6	149	S.S. Diesel Grab Hopper Dredger	24/03/1950
395	WANGANUI	107.6 × 27 × 10.6	252	S.S. Diesel Grab Hopper Dredger	18/01/1950
396	MV HIRONDELLE	196 × 35.6 × 20.4	757	S.S. Diesel Cargo	22/06/1950
397	MV SWIFT	196 × 35.6 × 20.4	757	S.S. Diesel Cargo	19/10/1950
398	MV WAIMATE	325 × 50 × 33.9	3,506	S.S. Diesel Cargo	24/06/1951
399	TSMV KAWATIRI	290 × 43 × 19.6	2,484	T.S. Diesel Cargo	06/10/1950
400	TSMV KOKIRI	290 × 43 × 19.6	2,470	T.S. Diesel Cargo	08/09/1951
401	-	57.6 × 8 × 6.6	60	Hopper Barge	
402	-	55 × 17 × 6.6	50	Sugar Barge	
403	-	55 × 17 × 6.6	50	Sugar Barge	
404	-	55 × 17 × 6.6	50	Sugar Barge	
405	-	55 × 17 × 6.6	50	Sugar Barge	
406	MV CAVALLO	290 × 48.6 × 28.3	2,340	S.S. Diesel Cargo & Passenger	17/11/1951
407	MV TRENTINO	290 × 48.6 × 28.3	2,340	S.S. Diesel Cargo & Passenger	09/04/1952
408	-	43.10 × 25 × 6	35	Dredging Pontoon	
409	-	45.6 × 17.6 × 6.6	45	Hopper Barge	
410	-	45.6 × 17.6 × 6.6	45	Hopper Barge	
411	-	53 × 16.4 × 5	50	Irrigation Barge	
412	MT HEWITT	86 × 23 × 12	137	T.S. Diesel Tug	24/04/1951
413	MSC QUARRY	88 × 24 × 12	154	T.S. Diesel Tug	01/12/1951

Ship No	Name	Dimensions	Tonnage	Type	Launched (day/month/year)
414	MSC QUEST	88 × 24 × 12	154	T.S. Diesel Tug	04/11/1952
415	MSC RANGER	88 × 24 × 12	154	T.S. Diesel Tug	29/01/1952
416	MSC ROVER	88 × 24 × 12	154	T.S. Diesel Tug	17/02/1953
417	ARUSHA	112.6 × 32 × 15.3	346	S.S. Steam Tug	17/08/1951
418	MV WAREATEA	240 × 37 × 20	1,430	S.S. Diesel Cargo	09/05/1952
419	-	75 × 20 × 9.6	85	Cargo Lighter	
420	-	75 × 20 × 9.6	85	Cargo Lighter	
421	-	75 × 20 × 9.6	85	Cargo Lighter	
422	MT FOURAH	110 × 30 × 14.6	306	T.S. Diesel Tug	01/09/1953
423	MT FARREN	110 × 30 × 14.6	306	T.S. Diesel Tug	10/06/1952
424	-	40.2 × 26 × 5.11	15	Crane Pontoon	1952
425	-	21 × 15 × 4.3	-	Pontoon	2/12/52
426	MV KARUMA	250 × 41.6 × 25.3	1,952	Diesel Cargo	4/01/52
427	MV MARWICK HEAD	250 × 40 × 22.6	1,786	Diesel Cargo	1952
428	MV LONGFELLOW	335 × 50 × 26.6		Diesel Cargo	14/04/53
429	MV DUNNET HEAD	180 × 31 × 15	748	Diesel Cargo	18/06/53
430	MV GOLDEN BAY	230 × 42 × 18	1,659	T.S. Diesel Cement Cargo	27/08/53
431	-	50 × 12 × 4.6		Grab Hopper Dredger (Riveted)	1952
432	-	50 × 12 × 4.6		Grab Hopper Dredger (Welded)	1952
433	-	50 × 12 × 4.6		Grab Hopper Dredger (Welded)	1952
434	TSM VAUBY	212 × 44 × 21	1,733	T.S. Diesel Cargo & Passenger	24/09/1953
435	-	87 × 17.6 × 4.1	100	Barge	
436	-	87 × 17.6 × 4.1	100	Barge	
437	SS CICERO	290 × 48.6 × 27	2,499	Steamer Cargo/Passenger	30/06/1954
438	SS ROLLO	290 × 48.6 × 27	2,499	Steamer Cargo/Passenger	12/10/1954
439	SS TEANO	260 × 43 × 24	1,580	Steamer Cargo/Passenger	23/02/1955
440	MV ZEALAND	270 × 45 × 25.6	2,030	Diesel Cargo & Passenger	11/11/1954
441	SAMUEL ARMSTRONG	128 × 28.6 × 12.6	364	Diesel Grab Dredger	08/03/1956
442	MV NAVUA	250 × 41.6 × 25.3	1,952	S.S. Diesel Cargo	27/05/1955
443	TSMV KAITOA	290 × 43 × 27	2,583	T.S. Diesel Cargo	10/05/1956
444	JOHN HERBERT	86 × 23 × 12	146	T.S. Diesel Tug	22/06/1955
445	MV FLAMINIAN	325 × 50 × 33.9	3,100	S.S. Diesel Cargo	09/02/1956
446	FRANK JAMIESON	86 × 23 × 12	146	T.S. Diesel Tug	10/08/1956
447	GANNET	95 × 25 × 7.6	250	Diesel Grab Dredger	02/12/1953
448	MV KAIMAI	250 × 41.6 × 25.3	2,007	S.S. Diesel Cargo	08/06/1956
449	MV TENNYSON	335 × 50 × 26.6	3,894	S.S. Diesel Cargo	20/11/1956
450	LAKE LOTHING	156 × 34 × 17	659	Diesel Grab Dredger	05/04/1955
451	-	75 × 20 × 9.6	105	Barge	
452	-	75 × 20 × 9.6	105	Barge	

Ship No	Name	Dimensions	Tonnage	Type	Launched (day/month/year)
453	-	75 × 20 × 9.6	105	Barge	
454	-	75 × 20 × 9.6	105	Barge	
455	ANNAHDA	110 × 29 × 10.6	281	S.S. Diesel Grab Dredger	27/03/1956
456	MV KUMALLA	235 × 45 × 15.3	1,946	S.S. Diesel Cargo	09/11/1956
457	MV KONINI	250 × 41.6 × 25.3	2,007	S.S. Diesel Cargo	15/02/1957
458	MV SANDPIPER	215 × 36.6 × 20.6	916	S.S. Diesel Cargo	01/05/1957
459	MV THACKERAY	345 × 54 × 29	4,650	S.S. Diesel Cargo	12/02/1958
460	HMS TYPHOON	180 × 38.6 × 18	1,034	S.S. Diesel Ocean Salvage Tug	14/10/1958
461	MV KOONYA	235 × 45 × 15.3	1,946	S.S. Diesel Cargo	16/10/1957
462	MV MALATIAN	250 × 42.6 × 15	1,420	S.S. Diesel Cargo	17/04/1958
463	MV CATANIAN	250 × 42.6 × 15	1,420	S.S. Diesel Cargo	28/08/1958
464	MV PATEENA	250 × 43 × 17.6	2,200	S.S. Diesel Cargo	07/11/1958
465	MV POOLTA	250 × 43 × 17.6	2,200	S.S. Diesel Cargo	13/05/1959
466	-		80	Dredging Pontoon	
467	CRAIGLEITH	88 × 25 × 12.6	175	S.S. Diesel Tug	16/05/1958
468	MV MACAULAY	345 × 54 × 29	4,650	S.S. Diesel Cargo	11/12/1958
469	-			Ramp-ended Pontoon	
470	MARABOU	130 × 30.6 × 9	310	T.S. Grab Dredger	13/02/1959
471	MV AARO	300 × 48.6 × 19.9	2,600	S.S. Diesel Cargo	19/08/1959
472	MV RAPALLO	340 × 54 × 31	3,400	S.S. Diesel Cargo	26/04/1960
473	MV ARCADIAN	340 × 54 × 31	3,400	S.S. Diesel Cargo	27/07/1960
474	CRESSWELL	128.6 × 28.6 × 12	374	S.S. Grab Dredger	16/06/1959
475	CHARLES HEARN	86 × 23 × 12	139	T.S. Diesel Tug	16/09/1959
476	COSRAY 23	185 × 50 × 8	573	Rock Barge (Tipping)	15/04/1960
477	COSRAY 24	185 × 50 × 8	573	Rock Barge (Tipping)	28/04/1960
478	JOHN WILSON	246 × 42 × 18.6	1,675	Bulk Cement Carrier	15/04/1961
479	LDC No 5	90 × 15.6 × 6	100	Rock Barge (Tipping)	16/01/1961
480	LDC No 6	90 × 15.6 × 6	100	Rock Barge (Tipping)	03/03/1961
481	TORO	162.6 × 33 × 10.6	512	River & Estuary Tanker	09/10/1961
482	RFA HEBE	350 × 55 × 31	4,823	S.S. Diesel Cargo	18/06/1962
483	RFA BACCHUS	350 × 55 × 31	4,823	S.S. Diesel Cargo	16/11/1962
484	UNO	162.6 × 33 × 10.6	530	River & Estuary Tanker	14/12/1962
485	GRAB DREDGER No 1	210 × 45 × 17.9	1,309	Grab Dredger	13/12/1963
486	HAMBLE	202 × 36.11 × 15.6	1,182	Coastal Tanker	29/04/1964
487	KILLINGHOLME	202 × 36.11 × 15.6	1,182	Coastal Tanker	30/07/1964
488	LIGAR BAY	210 × 38 × 16	1,330	Bulk Cement Carrier	10/10/1964
489	LDC No 7	90 × 18.10 × 17.10	80	Dumping barge	11/05/1964
490	LDC No 8	90 × 18.10 × 17.10	80	Dumping barge	07/12/1964
491	ABDUL MALIKI	85 × 24.3 × 12	154	T.S. Diesel Tug	04/02/1965
492	ASTRO	167.6 × 33 × 11.6	550	River & Estuary Tanker	28/11/1964
493	TRIBENI	175 × 35 × 17	918	T.S. Survey Vessel	30/06/1965
494	GEORGE OHIKERE	85 × 24.3 × 12	154	T.S. Diesel Tug	19/03/1965
495	MV SALERNO	280 × 45.6 × 26	1,559	S.S. Diesel Cargo	24/11/1965

MV *Salerno* heading through the Kiel Canal en route to Stockholm (photo by Rod Baker, who sailed on her).

You will be able to read all about the seven S class ships built from 1965 onwards, along with many more well-known ships, in the fourth book in the series of Leith-built Ships.

ACKNOWLEDGEMENTS

This series of books would not have been possible without the help of many people, some sadly no longer with us; if anyone is missed this is only down to my own forgetfulness and I apologise in advance. There are just too many to fit in here, but you know who you are and you have my thanks.

I have mentioned the loftsmen at the Henry Robb Shipyard, who all helped to instil a sense of pride in ships and in the craft. I must also thank Robert Rowbottom once more, as he helped me more than he could have envisaged. To another ex-Robb draughtsman, John Knubley, who has also been a tremendous source of information.

To all the men of the Leith Shipyard who influenced me in one way or another.

To Bob Sickles, ex-publisher of upstate New York, who encouraged me to pick up my writing again after I had all but given it up.

It would be remiss of me not to mention: ex-Robbs engineer J. Stevenson, who provided me with some initial information; B. Booth, shipwright, for many later photographs; and the archivists at Glasgow University for allowing me access to the wonderful Leith, Hull & Hamburg/Currie Line archive.

To the Scottish Records office for some initial help with information.

I would like to thank the people at the P&O Archive for the use of information and for the many photographs provided to show in the book.

To Barry & Shaun, RFANostalgia, for more time and help than I had ever expected, many thanks go to these guys.

Also, to Chris White of the www.historicalrfa.org website.

To Dr Stephen Gapps and his team at the Australian Maritime Museum.

To Dr William Collier and archivist Kathryn Preston from the oldest ship design house in the world, G.L. Watson Ltd, now based back in Glasgow, who provided help and encouragement, and some wonderful old original photographs.

To Lindsay Butterfield and all the other guys in New Zealand and Australia, who provided help and information – way too many people to list here.

My editor, Anne Hamilton of WriteRight Editing Services at http://www.writerightediting.

co.uk, who took the job on and helped me immensely in the editing/layout parts of my book before sending it to the publishers.

To Dr Keith Whittles and his team for believing in my project, and allowing me to bring this series of books to a wider public.

To Caroline Petherick at https://www.the-wordsmith.co.uk, for providing great direction and guidance in the completion of my book; she has been a pleasure to work with, while helping with some pretty complex and technical type details throughout this book.

To my darling wife Angie who has the patience of a saint, always believing in me and encouraging me to reach for my dreams, to persevere and never give up.

GLOSSARY OF SHIPBUILDING AND NAUTICAL TERMS

ABV	armed boarding vessel
Anchor	A heavy, pick-like device attached to a boat's stem by a warp and chain. Modern anchors are made of steel; common types of anchor are plough, fisherman and Danforth. The chain, which connects the anchor to its warp, is fixed onto the lower anchor end, adding weight and preventing chafing of the warp on rocks or shellfish beds.
AP (After perpendicular)	The distance between the two lines, known as length between perpendiculars or LBP, is divided up by the naval architect to create what is known as frame stations. They will form the grid whereby the naval architect will begin to create the small-scale lines for the ship known as scantling lines (see also under loftsman).
Base line	The design line that all forward and aft measurements are taken, from the AP or the FP. All height measurements are taken from the baseline; in the case of a drop keel these heights will be shown as a minus. These measurements are used to create part of the offset table.
Beam	The maximum width of the ship.
Beam knee	A bracket holding the transverse deck beam to the vertical frames at the side of the hull.
Bilge	The lowest part of the hull interior, under the sole. Water and or fuel tanks are often placed in the bilges to lower the centre of gravity and so help keep the ship upright.
Bilge keel	A longitudinal, external, underwater member used to reduce a ship's tendency to roll and to aid directional stability. In Britain twin bilge keels are often used on small boats moored in estuaries with a large tidal range so the boat stays upright when the mooring dries out. With their much shallower draft, yachts of this type can be sailed in shallow waters. Not as hydrodynamically efficient as a fin keel.
Bilge pump	A pump, either manual or electric, with the inlet set at the lowest point in the bilges, where water will collect when the boat is upright. The inlet is protected by a screen to stop blockages.
Black Squad	The collective name for all the steel-working trades that built a ship.
Block	The foundations set up for traditional shipbuilding. Block construction is a 21st-century shipbuilding method involving prefabrication. See pulley.
Bow	The front and generally sharp end of the hull. It is designed to reduce the resistance of the hull cutting through water and should be tall enough to prevent water from easily washing over the deck of the hull. The bulbous bow designed into some larger ships since the 1920s improves speed and stability.
Bowsprit	On a sailing ship, a spar that extends forward from the foredeck, outboard of the hull proper. Common in square-rigged ships, where they were used to attach the outer or flying jib. In modern sailing boats they are often made of lightweight carbon and are used to attach the luff of lightweight sails such as spinnakers.

Breast hook	The brackets that hold the shape of the soft nose.
Bridge	(in shipbuilding) A means of temporarily connecting two plates together to be faired and welded.
Bulkhead	The internal transverse structure of the hull; the number of bulkheads is determined by the length of the ship under class rules.
Bulwark	The upstanding part of the topsides around the edges of the deck, providing some security when a boat is heeled.
Buttock lines	The intersection of the Moulded Surface with a vertical plane at any given distance from the centreline of the ship. Buttocks are curved in the Sheer View (see View) but straight in the other two main views.
Capstan	A vertical metal or wooden winch secured to the foredeck of a ship, used for hoisting the anchor. Capstans may be manually operated, or powered hydraulically or electrically. A traditional sailor-powered wooden capstan is fitted with removable spoke-like wooden arms which the sailors push round and round, often in time to a sea shanty or chant.
Coffin plate	The plate joining two side plates over the keel of a vessel at the stern, which in plan view creates a shape similar to a coffin lid.
Complement	The full number of people required to operate a ship. Includes officers and crew members; does not include passengers. The number of people assigned to a warship in peacetime may be considerably less than her full complement.
Counter stern	A traditional stern construction with a long overhang and a shorter, upright, end piece. The counter is usually decked over. The stern is rounded when seen in plan view; other shapes of stern, as seen from the side, are transom, elliptical and round.
Cube	The cargo-carrying capacity of a ship, measured in cubic feet. There are two common types:

	Bale Cube (or Bale Capacity)	A measurement of capacity for cargo in bales, on pallets etc., where the cargo does not conform to the shape of the ship. The space available for cargo is measured in cubic feet to the inside of the cargo battens on the frames, and to the underside of the beams.
	Grain Cube (or Grain Capacity)	A measurement of capacity for cargo like grain, which flows to conform to the shape of the ship. The maximum space available for cargo is measured in cubic feet, the measurement being taken to the inside of the shell plating of the ship or to the outside of the frames, and to the top of the beam or underside of the deck plating.

Deadrise	The difference in height between the base line and the point where a straight line through the flat of bottom surface intersects a vertical line through the side of the moulded surface at its widest point.
Deck	The top surface of the hull, which keeps water and weather out of the hull and allows the crew, standing and walking on it, to operate the boat more easily. It stiffens the hull. Temporary frames (or moulds) can be removed and kept for another boat.
Displacement	A measurement of the weight of the vessel, usually used for warships. Merchant ships are usually measured based on the volume of cargo space; see Ton > Tonnage. Displacement is expressed either in long tons of 2,240 lbs, or in metric tonnes of 1,000 kg. Since the two units are very close in size (2,240 lbs = 1,016 kg and 1,000 kg = 2,205 lbs), it is common not to distinguish between them. To preserve secrecy, nations sometimes mis-state a warship's displacement.

	Displacement, light	The weight of the ship excluding cargo, fuel, ballast, stores, passengers and crew, but including water in the boilers to steaming level.

	Displacement, loaded	The weight of the ship including cargo, passengers, fuel, water, stores, dunnage and such other items necessary for use on a voyage, which brings the vessel down to her load draft.
	Deadweight tons (DWT)	A measure of the ship's total carrying capacity. It's the difference between displacement, light and displacement, loaded.
	Cargo deadweight tons	The weight remaining after deducting fuel, water, stores, dunnage, and other such items necessary for use on a voyage, from the deadweight of the vessel.
Deadrise		The difference in height between the base line and the point where the straight line through the Flat of Bottom surface intersects the Flat of Side of the Moulded Surface at its widest point.
Dog		A means of holding down iron or steel plate. The more dogs that are required the more distortion is found in a plate; this is usually due to poor welding sequence, and a sign of rework needed, hence many more man-hours to do a job that has not been dimensionally controlled.
Double bottom		Forms a watertight barrier on the bottom of the ship. It extends from the keel to the tank top, creating another layer of protection should the ship be holed below the tank top. Also used to store ballast water.
Draught		Distance from the bottom of the keel to the waterline. It may alternatively be spelt 'draft'.
Draught, loaded		The depth of water necessary to float a vessel fully loaded.
Drop keel		A retractable or removable fin / centreboard / daggerboard.
Fairing		In shipbuilding, ensuring that material put in place is correctly located
Forward perpendicular (FP)		See After perpendicular.
Frame		In old, heavily built square-rigged ships, the frames were made up of four individual timbers, futtocks, as it was impossible to make the shape from a single piece of wood. The futtock closest to the keel was the ground futtock and the other pieces were called upper futtocks.
Frame lines		The transverse intersections of the Moulded Surface/Line with a vertical plane cut across the vessel, In the Body View (see View) the frame lines are curved, so in this view they show the shape of the vessel. In the Half-Breadth Plan or the Profile View, the Frame lines are straight.
Freeboard		The distance between the waterline and the deck when loaded. Boats using sheltered waters can have low freeboard, but seagoing vessels need high freeboard.
Freeboard, moulded		The difference between the moulded depth and the moulded draft. (It is the height of the side of the vessel which is above the water when she floats at her load waterline.)
Graving dock		Dry dock.
Gunwale		The upper, outside longitudinal structural member of the hull.
Hatch		A lifting or sliding opening into the cabin, or through the deck for loading and unloading cargo.
Heads		Marine toilet. An abbreviation of the term 'catheads', which, up at the bow, were the normal place for toileting in square-rigger days. Always used in the plural. (The designed function of the catheads, timbers set outboard of the hull, was to provide protection for the hull against the friction of the anchor warp.)

Howff	The inner sanctum within some shipyards, usually trade-specific, so the shipwrights in their various groups would have howfs scattered around the shipyard: the platers would have their own howf, as would the welders, and so on.
Hull	The main body of a ship or boat, including her bottom, sides and deck. Some people are surprised to find that in a modern ship of any size the hull, for most of its length, has a flat bottom the full width of the ship. This is, however, essential for stability, because when such a ship heels then on its lower side there is a greater air-filled volume under the water than on the upper side, thus pushing the ship back upright, countering the heel.
Iron fighters	A colloquial west of Scotland / Clyde shipbuilding term for the Black Squad.
Keel	The main central member along the length of the bottom of the ship or boat. It is an important part of the ship's structure, which also has a strong influence on its turning performance and in sailing ships resists the sideways pressure of the wind, enabling the course to be steered.
Keelson	An internal beam fixed to the top of the keel to strengthen the joint of the upper members of the ship to the keel.
Kevlar	A hi-tech and very strong synthetic material, used for cables, bulletproof jackets etc, developed by DuPont in the 1960s.
Knuckle	Where a plate changes angle or direction (creates effectively a fold in a plate); a good way of reducing the amount of welding which is required. This method of platework also reduces distortion when carried out properly.
Length	The distance between the forward-most and aftermost parts of the ship.

	Length overall (LOA)	The maximum length of the ship.
	Length when submerged (LOS)	The maximum length of the submerged hull measured parallel to the designed load waterline.
	Length at waterline (LWL)	The ship's length measured at the waterline.

Lines drawing/plan	A plan showing the three principal views: Sheer or Profile View, Half-Breadth or Plan View, and Body (see View). The Lines/drawing plan is the 2-D representation of the 3-D Moulded Surface of the vessel.
Load waterline	A line created during the initial design phase of a ship; it starts as a reference waterline showing where the ship can be loaded up to. During the ship's life the load waterline may be changed, but the original design reference waterline will always be so.
Lofting	The process used to create life-size drawings of frames so they can be manufactured. Today frames can be cut by a robot directly from a computer programme with extreme accuracy.
Loftsman	The loftsman (loft) was responsible for taking the scaled-down naval architect's scantling lines and producing them full size or one-tenth scale so the ship's form could be made. The loft then took the finished faired offsets from this and developed the shell plating and all the other steelwork involved in building the vessel. Templates were made so that the curved forms could be cut out of steel full size, along with the dimensional control of the build. Today this is all done by CAD (computer-aided design) generating a 3D model from which the ship's production drawings are taken. The role of the loft has been replaced by the designer and the nesting team, the dimensional control team, and quality control and planning.
Luff	The front part of a fore-and-aft sail, attached to either the mast or a stay.
Longitudinals	Stiffening members that run fore and aft on a ship. They can be shell longitudinals or deck longitudinals.
Mast	A vertical pole on a ship which supports sails and/or rigging. If it's a wooden multi-part mast, this term applies specifically to the lowest portion.

Mast step	A socket, often strengthened, to take the downward thrust of the mast and hold its foot in position. In smaller craft, the mast step may be on the keel or on the deck.
Mizzen	In a sailing boat with two or more masts, a permanent mast and sail set aft of the mainmast.
Moulded surface/ Moulded line	The inside surface of the plating of a ship. The moulded surface has no thickness and is fair and smooth. Once the ship is built the plating will usually but not always extend outside the Moulded Surface. The heel of each shell frame on this moulded surface is commonly known as the Moulded Line. The moulded line is the start point for the design of the vessel, consisting of station lines, frame lines, waterlines and buttocks. The points on these intersections create the moulded surface. It should be remembered that this moulded surface is theoretical and is not an actual part of the ship. It is exactly the shape which a finitely thin piece of sheet rubber would take if stretched tightly over the shell frames and main deck beams with no plating in place. (I used this description in an interview once, and they almost fell off their seats – I did use a different word, though, for the rubber sheet.)
Offset table	Used in ship design; contains measurements that give the coordinates for the lines plan (showing the curved lines that indicate the shape of the hull).
Ogee	The line of the shaped plate that forms the 3D line from the main deck to the forecastle deck at the ship's side.
Parallel middle body	The straight sides along the centre part of the ship, also known as the Flat of Side: common in large slab-sided vessels. Not something that any of the Leith-built ships had, as most were complex-shaped ships, with little parallel body.
Planing	When the bow of the ship or boat moving rapidly lifts clear of the water. This is more hydrodynamically efficient, so is designed into speedy vessels.
Port	The left side of the ship when looking forward; so called by the Vikings as this was the side that would go alongside a harbour wall. The opposite side of the vessel to Starboard.
pratique	The licence given to a ship to enter the port on assurance from the captain to the authorities that she is free from contagious disease. The clearance granted is commonly referred to as Free Pratique.
Pulley	A small, part-enclosed wheel used to help redirect the angle of a rope or, in combination with more pulleys set up as a block and tackle, to reduce the power needed to pull the object controlled by the rope.
Rigging (standing)	The common way of attaching wire is to form a small loop at the end which is fixed in place by clamping a soft metal swag over the free ends. (Talurite is a common brand of swagging.) The wire loop is then fastened to a rigging screw, with a bow shackle to the chain plate. In small sailing boats Kevlar rope is sometimes used in place of wire.
Rigging (running)	The ropes or cables used in sailing ships to control the sails. Cables are of two types: Type 7 × 7: a semi-flexible wire used for luff wires in sails, halyards (sometimes plastic-coated) trapeze wires and light halyards. Type 7 × 19, which is used for all halyards, wire sheets, vangs and strops that must run through a pulley.
Scuppers	Gaps in the bulwarks which enable sea or rainwater to flow off the deck.
Shackle	A quick-release metal device used to connect cables to fixings.
Shaft horsepower (SHP)	The amount of mechanical power delivered by the engine to a propeller shaft. In the SI system of units one horsepower is equivalent to 746 watts.
Sheave	A pulley.
Sheer	The generally curved shape of the top of the hull when viewed in profile. The sheer is traditionally lowest amidships, to maximise freeboard at the ends of the hull. Sheer can also be reverse – higher in the middle to maximise space inside – or straight, or a combination of shapes.
Sheet	A rope used to control the position of a sail: e.g. the main sheet controls the position of the mainsail.
Shell	The principal function of the shell is to act as a watertight skin. Also known as the hull.

Skeg	A long, tapering piece of timber fixed to the underside of a keel near the stern in a small boat, especially a kayak or rowing boat, to aid directional stability.
Soft nose	The upper strakes of plate that form the bow of the ship, extending from the solid stem bar to the main deck.
Spar	A length of timber, aluminium, steel or carbon fibre of approximately round or pear-shaped section, used to support sails; types of spar include a mast, boom, gaff, yard, bowsprit, prod, boomkin, pole and dolphin striker.
Spring	The amount of curvature in the keel from bow to stern when viewed side on. The modern trend is to have less spring (known as hogging or sagging) in order to have less disturbance to water flow at higher speeds, thus aiding planing.
Starboard	The right side of the ship when looking forward. The word comes from the Viking, whose ships had a styrbord, steering oar, on that side. The opposite side of the vessel to Port.
Stays	See Rigging (standing).
Steamer	Steam-powered cargo or passenger ship.
Stem	A continuation of the keel upwards at the front of the hull.
Stern	The back of the boat.
Strake	A strip of material running longitudinally along the vessel's side, bilge or bottom. On a steel boat each longitudinal strake of plating has a name, such as Garboard strake, Bilge strake and Sheer strake, with any strakes of plating in between labelled A, B, C etc.
Strong back	A heavy plate used as a fairing aid to keep plates straight and fair, and to assist in the alignment before and during welding.
Swag	See Rigging (standing).
Taff rail	A railing, often ornate, at the extreme stern of a traditional square-rigged ship. In light air conditions an extra sail would be set on a temporary mast from the taff rail.
Tank top	The continuous or covered part of deck either closing off, or forming the tops of, the tanks that occupy the bottom of the ship.
Ton	The unit of measure often used in specifying the size of a ship. There are three completely unrelated definitions for the word; two of them refer to volume (the word was originally 'tun', a large barrel) and the third definition relates to weight.
	Measurement ton (M/T) or Ship ton	Calculated as 40 cubic feet of cargo space. See Cube: Bale Cube. For example, a vessel with a capacity of 10,000 M/T has a bale cubic of 400,000 cubic ft.
	Register ton	A measurement of cargo-carrying capacity in cubic feet. One register ton is equivalent to 100 cubic feet of cargo space.
	Weight ton (W/T)	Calculated as a long ton (2,240 lbs).
	Tonnage	A measurement of the cargo-carrying capacity of merchant vessels. It depends not on weight but on the volume available for carrying cargo. The basic units of measure are the Register Ton, equivalent to 100 cubic feet, and the Measurement Ton, equivalent to 40 cubic feet. The calculation of tonnage is complicated by many technical factors.
	Gross tons	The entire internal cubic capacity of the ship expressed in tons of 100 cubic feet to the ton, except certain spaces which are exempted such as: peak and other tanks for water ballast, open forecastle bridge and poop, access of hatchways, certain light and air spaces, domes of skylights, condenser, anchor gear, steering gear, wheel house, galley and cabin for passengers.
	Net tons	Obtained from the gross tonnage by deducting crew and navigating spaces and making allowances for propulsion machinery.

Transom	A wide, flat or slightly curved, sometimes vertical, board at the rear of the hull, which on small power boats is often designed to carry an outboard motor. Transoms increase width and buoyancy at the stern. On a boat designed to be powered by an outboard, the stern is often the widest point, to provide displacement to carry the heavy outboard and to resist the initial downward thrust of the craft when it's planing.

Views	There are three main views of a ship, as follows:	
	Profile or Sheer View	This view looks at the vessel's Moulded Lines, as from starboard to port. Whereas in this view the Waterlines and the Frame lines are straight, the longitudinal curve of the deck, or Sheer Line, is shown in its true shape as a nice fair curve, giving the alternative name to this view.
	Body Plan/Body View	It is drawn in two parts, both of them relating to the port half of the Moulded Surface. There's no need for the starboard half, as it's a mirror image. ☒ the right-hand part is a view from in front of the vessel, looking aft ☒ the left-hand part is a view from behind the vessel, looking forward. In this view the Frame lines are curved per their true shape, while the Buttocks and Waterlines are straight. My Loftsman logo in the Preface is a simplified version.
	Half-breadth / Plan View	The view looking vertically downwards onto the vessel's Moulded Surface. Again, only the port half of the vessel is drawn. In this view the Waterlines are shown in their true shape, while the Frame Lines and Buttocks are straight.

Warp	A thick rope normally used for holding a vessel in place, either alongside a quay or another vessel, or to a buoy or anchor.
Waterlines	The intersections of the Moulded Surface at a given height on a horizontal plane. For example, the 3-metre waterline is a section cut 3 metres above the base horizontal. ☒ In the Half-breadth View the waterlines are curved ☒ in the Body View they are straight vertical lines ☒ in the Sheer View they are straight horizontal lines.

SOURCES

I have tried to write this book to appeal not only to the ex-shipbuilder or someone from Leith, but with a much broader reach in mind. If you have a love of ships and the sea, then this book is for you.

The sources I have drawn on come from an extremely broad range of informants, with some of the best information direct from the people who were there, not just from dry research in dusty old library archives – although those sources too become particularly important, as we are slowly losing a lot of our great maritime history. This book, the third in a series of four, is my attempt to keep some of that history alive.

First-hand comments that were sent into my original website on the Leith shipyards have been saved where possible and used in the category they were originally placed in.

But as time marches on – and this book focuses on the ships built from 1945 to 1965, in the middle of what became known as the swinging sixties – the first-hand accounts becomes ever scarcer. So I have made much use of the internet; my own original website was a particularly good source of material, which I have used extensively throughout the series.

Where I have found contradictory sources, in order to come to a conclusion I have used my own judgement as a shipbuilder along with the shipyard's original build order books, even though some of the early entries are missing or unclear.

The following are just some of the websites that you may find useful:

www.theloftsman.com
http://www.imo.org
Scottish newspapers
www.archive.scotsman.com (This website will charge you a fee for accessing the records.)

Other Edinburgh newspapers are held on microfilm in

The Edinburgh Room, Edinburgh Central Library, King George IV Bridge, Edinburgh, EH1 1 EG. Email: edinburgh.room@edinburgh.gov.uk

Glasgow newspapers are held by:

It all starts off as steel waiting to be joined, in this case by rivets.

The Mitchell Library, North Street, Glasgow, G3 7DN. Email: archives@cls.glasgow.gov.uk

I have found that the museums and state libraries of Australia, including those in Adelaide, Victoria, New South Wales and Brisbane, have all been a very helpful resource for information.

Museums in New Zealand were once more very helpful and a good source of information

Of course, we should not discount Wikipedia; it just takes a little bit more time, because one does need to check the information shown, but as a starting point and at no cost, you will not find better.

If you have the name or the year built (preferably both) of the ship you're interested in, type it into any one of the internet search engines, and you should be able to find some information.

Look out for Volume IV, the continuing story of the ships built at Leith from 1965 until the shipyard's closure in 1984.

MW00558990

Praise for
An Illegal Immigrant's Journey

An unravelled and ardently persuasive account of Brenda's life story unfolding as she narrates her experiences in this passionate book about her Journey to the land of the free, and the home of the brave, as it is written in this nation's national anthem.

Readers will take a ride on the journey with Brenda, as they encounter the pages of her book, they will observe her resilience, the will to keep going after her goals, and the things that matter to her the most.

All would have not been possible without the intervention of God. With God all things are possible (Matthew 19:26).

—**Rev. Paulina Cole-Hardy** (MBA), Psalmist and author of
Reclaiming My Position: A heroic Message To Young Women

Wow! What can I say—a journey of unparalleled proportion. This is a book that not only takes you on a journey from immigration to legal residency status, but it warns of the pitfalls, traps, unsuccess and ultimately success of the 20-year journey of one woman and her family and all the satellite lives impacted.

What an awesome testimony of fear overcome by courage, of adversity overcome by strength, and of torment overcome by power and authority. This story will not only help those who are seeking legal residency, but it will help all who start with a vision or a goal, yet who cannot see how to traverse the outcome.

This is a story of how, with God's help, and a relationship with the Father changes lives!

—**J.B. Tremont**, author of *He Loves You Not: A Commonsense Guide to What Not to Do in Relationships*

Right now, in the United States, it is so important to really understand the immigrant experience. Each story is so personal and Brenda's book holds nothing back. Such an honest telling of an all too common story will help shape and change how you see everyone in your life. Her story is so clearly conveyed you will appreciate the intensity and hardship of her experiences as you would that of your own family member.

—**Lindsay Friedman**, Librarian, Free Library of Philadelphia.

Brenda writes a compelling story of resilience and perseverance to become an American citizen. Her book captures the reader's attention as she unfolds painful and unfortunate circumstances that would emotionally cripple the average woman. However, for her faith in a mighty God and vision to have a life she knew God called her to, Brenda refused to fall short of the glory she now owns. This book is a must-read. Brenda's story will inspire and encourage you to pursue your dreams, no matter what the cost.

—**Pamela Elaine Nichols** M.H.S., Relationship Coach and author of *Muddy High Heels: 14 Lessons Learned from My Breakdown, Breakup and Breakthrough*

AN

ILLEGAL

IMMIGRANT'S

JOURNEY

How America Became My Destiny

Brenda Amanda Mwaya

Pucchie Creations
PUBLISHING HOUSE

1st Edition 2019

ISBN: 978-1-7334653-0-4 (Paperback)
ISBN: 978-1-7334653-1-1 (Ebook)

Library of Congress Control Number: 2019912631

Book design by DesignForBooks.com

Printed in the U.S.A

CONTENTS

....

Contents

Contents

"This, I believe, is one of the most important sources of America's greatness. We lead the world because, unique among nations, we draw our people—our strength—from every country and every corner of the world. And by doing so we continuously renew and enrich our nation. While other countries cling to the stale past, here in America we breathe life into dreams. We create the future, and the world follows us into tomorrow. Thanks to each wave of new arrivals to this land of opportunity, we're a nation forever young, forever bursting with energy and new ideas, and always on the cutting edge, always leading the world to the next frontier. This quality is vital to our future as a nation. If we ever closed the door to new Americans, our leadership in the world would soon be lost."

—Ronald Reagan,

40th president of the United States

DEDICATION

I would like to dedicate this book, first and foremost to God, my Creator. My life makes sense now. Everything thus far. I couldn't say thank You enough. I pray that this book will attest to the love You have embedded in me as Your own. Don't stop loving me. I depend on You. Help me never to be a casualty of Your Bible verse Hosea 4:6 in everything concerning me.

Thank You God for the provision of my earthly daddy the late Ted Edward Jacob Mwaya—the pioneer and author in my family before me. What a father! What a force. He taught me how to write. I was blessed. Gone too soon but he will never be forgotten.

To my mother the other "iron lady" with a strong will. Thank you for having me. Thank you for your strength. Look at us now. To God be the glory!

To my most wonderful, incredible, gifted, outstanding, God-fearing children M.A, D.R, J.P, and J.J. I bless God for you daily. Thank you for teaching me to be a mother! I do not regret any part of this journey called life. I am now wiser and stronger. I had to go through somethings to get to my purpose and destiny. It is well with my soul!

Lastly but not least, a special thanks to the following psalmists namely Juanita Bynum, Smokie Norful, Benjamin Dube, Sonnie Badu and Whitney Houston who is now deceased, may her soul continue to rest in peace. These five people I have mentioned, God used them individually to minister to me through songs during the most trying years of my life as an illegal immigrant in America for almost 20 years. To each of you, from the bottom of my heart, I am saying thank you! You sang anointed songs that kept my mind away from insanity. God works in mysterious ways, indeed! I believe.

A Cheerful Welcome

So, you now have arrived in the land of Milk and Honey. Welcome to America!

You can now shout it out from the rooftop. Or better yet, from the rooftop of the Empire State Building in New York City. Oh, if you haven't been there yet, take some time off to visit one of the most magnificent, breathtaking, and tallest buildings in America!

You will understand better what I mean when I say, "scream" the words. Scream them out excitedly. Scream to the world out there, "I Made It to America! I have arrived!"

Every day, thousands of visitors flock to the borders of America, The Beautiful.

I am sure you know that this country comes with blessings and curses depending on what greeted you first from the time you landed on American soil, when your passport was successfully stamped "welcome." There, you were also granted a number of days for your visitation. That is if you were a visitor like I was 20 years ago.

To you, I say, WELCOME! Brace yourself for a beautiful ride in the land of the living.

The United States of America is a melting pot of almost every nation, race and culture on the earth. There are not many countries in the world with such a level of cultural richness and prosperity, as America. She is The Mother of The World! I am very sure that this is why I had asked my husband to come with me here together with our children.

We had to come to America!

Here we are, still standing, with many lessons learned over the years and still learning by the day. I, Brenda at 24 years of age made my entrance in New Jersey. I arrived with my husband Keneilwe, thirty, and our two young children, Marvel and Avedi, who were three and one years old at the time of our arrival.

There is no date in our family history as outstanding to us as December 22nd, 1997! It is a date that four people anticipated their destinies. A day that would change every course of my family's life because we finally landed and made it in, on American soil.

....

America, destiny at its best! America, the land of promises. The only promises we foresaw were of nothing but success.

CHECKPOINT NEWARK

I t all started with Checkpoint Newark.
    The United States Citizenship and Immigration Services is a federal agency, as well as a component of Homeland Security. USCIS agency has immigration customs offices positioned at every point of legalized entry-exit border of America. Airports are one of them. The major concern between my husband and I during the trip to America and when we had landed at the airport was no other than the immigration offices there. The whole time we went through the process of checking in, we held our breath and dared not show our fear. Instead we followed suit on everything we were instructed to do on arrival. The flight was full of people just like us visiting America from all over the world and getting off at Newark International airport on that wintry afternoon.

When our flight had landed, we learned that as visitors, we had our own separate entrance into the airport different from the citizens or permanent legal residents of the country. It makes sense. Therefore, we were directed to another area where the immigration officers at the port had directed the visitors to form two single file lines and where they were finally asking each visitor for their passports. The officers then took the passports from us one person or family at a time and stamped them, issuing us time allocated to each traveler to visit the country. The travelers also were given back their individual passports accompanied by an immigration card known as the 1-94 which had the visitor's alien number during the visiting period.

On the card, there was some visible and specific information including an entry date, an entry port and expected date for the visitor to exit the country within the immigration stamp. This allows for the visitor to be able to visit America at another time in the future if need be, if and when the instructions had been followed according to the details on the card.

This card with its alien digits carries a visitor's detailed information of the address where the visitor may be staying while in the United States of America. The I-94 card has to go alongside the visitor's passport from point of entry into the country and during the entire time the visitor is on tour in the country.

At any given time, while a visitor is in the country, for any legal reason, an immigration officer can retrieve detailed information of the alien in question and be able to know much about the visitor's status in the country.

The visitor's stamp is not limited to one function. It also shows as credible evidence that the visitor or passport holder actually left the country via any one of the legalized exit ports of the nation each time they do.

The United States Citizenship and Immigration Services federal agency has a centralized data system that comprises all necessary information on every documented foreigner as well as most of the undocumented foreigners coming into the country from all over the world that are here in America for many different reasons.

The immigration officers at any port or legal entry during a visitor's time of entry can decide to stamp a denial or refusal for any visitor's entry into the country if they suspect something may be wrong with a person's declarations for the reasons of their visit. The I-94 card is one of the many ways the government is able, to keep track of the numbers of visitors in the country.

During entry into the country, there are also times, when the immigration officers can hold a visitor for a number of hours in their offices before allowing and releasing them into the country. They can do this for many different reasons known to them as trained officers. One of them can be if they don't believe that the visitor will truly visit and return to their country of origin after the visit. We felt like we would be called aside to be interviewed for the details of why the whole family was visiting America all at once at that particular time. I guess we had momentarily forgotten that it was the Christmas season and families do travel together for festivities, after all.

DONALD TRUMP & IMMIGRANTS

Fast forward to 20 years later. I am convinced that visiting America with other agendas such as violating a visa in hopes of a pathway to citizenship is not a great plan. I and my spouse had intended to come to America and return before the 6 months were over. Unforeseen circumstances changed everything we had anticipated. There are much better legit ways of becoming an American citizen. And times have tremendously changed immigration wise. President Donald John Trump is now in office and everybody in America, if not the whole world, knows what time it is. It's definitely not time to come to America and walk around the streets as an illegal immigrant, that's for sure!

Besides, the computer data systems concerning American immigration offices are highly intelligent and very well organized. After the terror of 9/11, immigration rules and regulations have changed drastically for the better to protect the country's citizens, the nation as it stands, the world in general and even the country's visitors.

America is one of the most civilized nations on the planet. She is very advanced, and I have no doubt in my mind that she now deals with its daily government and necessary business issues especially concerning immigration at a much higher level than she did two decades ago. All you have to do is watch the daily news. It is all there for everyone to see.

So please someone reading this, spare your friends or family members mental issues by letting them know that coming to America is not like what it used to be, two decades ago or more. If it's you, planning to visit and overstay your welcome, please don't be thinking to come to America like my family and I did. We left our home country on such a whim without a sensible and a tangible plan in place. America is not a place for whimsical shenanigans! If somebody told me that I would be sitting here telling you my story someday, to help someone else out there, I wouldn't have believed it. At first life here seemed like a walk in the park!

On the day of our arrival at Checkpoint Newark, on that beautiful perfect afternoon, my family and I simply got a warm

welcome and entry stamps with six months to stay and visit the country. My husband and I tried our best to contain the joy we both felt in our hearts and on our faces!

Really? The stories about the secret interviews in the secret rooms by the fierce immigration officers was a thing of the past. Just like that. Finally! We were in!

FOR THE LOVE OF AMERICA

Please have a seat, let me take you on my family's ride from Malawi into America during a period of two decades to this day.

I am going to assume that you are reading my story and you are probably an American citizen who is here because six or ten generations ago, someone in your family was an immigrant from somewhere on the world map. Or you could be related to someone who is an immigrant in America. There is also a 99% chance that you have come across a person who is an immigrant, if you have lived in America long enough. Heck, the whole country for all I know is made up of immigrants from somewhere. Perhaps, maybe you, yourself could be an immigrant like me. And if you are an immigrant, especially an illegal immigrant in particular like I used to be or know someone who is an illegal immigrant by the time you are reading this story, I hope you brought your inner wings to fly away with.

Wheew!

You will need those invisible imaginary wings. Use them to fly away within your own imaginary self, whenever life gets tough on the physical grounds of your mind as you read my story because life will get rough. And life did get tough for me and my family from time to time and still does because we are imperfect human beings living in this imperfect world. There is no guarantee that every day will be peachy either, especially when you are an illegal immigrant.

Living life far away from home is one of the toughest things for most people to do. For my family, our home away from home happened to be America. Yes, this is America! If you make it here, I

promise you, that you will make it anywhere else in the world. But for now let's focus on you and your excited self. The legal immigrant you, before you overstay your visit.

You are now so happy that you have finally made it in! Your temporary "home." You think maybe now it is time you can actually sleep at night because just to obtain a visitor's visa B1/B2 was a difficult process in itself.

I know. Personally, I know some people in my country who literally borrowed money several times to use for the visa application alone for each trip to the American Offices in my hometown, Lilongwe, Malawi, just to find themselves going back to their homes empty handed. Simply because the visitor's visa application had been denied for one reason or another. This had happened after many nights of fasting and praying.

I once heard from an Indian connection that there's a place, a sanctuary in India. All people do there is pray for their relatives and friends to get a visa to America! Yes, it's that deep. Coming to America is not a joke. It's a privilege and an honor that most people forget and take for granted once they are in the country.

Yet in my own country, there are people I have known that relied on just their strong belief to be granted a visa, in order to pay back the visitor's visa fees, air ticket to America as well as pocket money once they had made it to America. Imagine? A gamble on life, I say. A sheer real leap of faith, my goodness!

Bravado.

Now if that is not fearlessness, then I don't know what is? Those people are the ones who make it big here in America once they have been finally granted the visitor's visa. They never forget what it took them to get here. Some even keep on trying and have managed to be granted a visitor's visa after the 5th try and application. That's great potential in motion! I personally want to deal and work with such a people in my life. Such people only stop trying when they die.

For the ones that manage to borrow money for their visa and airfare, and what had seemingly appeared to be relentless headaches, the sleepless long nights for a while can momentarily take a sigh of relief until the large sums of unpaid loans start becoming

a reality once again, once they have settled in. The hard reality is always waiting and simmering at the back of their minds about the money needed to be paid back in full from the day they finally acquired a job, so far away from home, in America. One thing that people in our homelands don't understand is the fact that money doesn't grow on trees in America. Nor anywhere else for that matter.

A person usually takes a while to get situated with a job, stay in a job, and a place to live altogether. So, when the annoying phone calls, relentless text messages from their debt collectors, from wherever they call homeland, start ringing, they can almost bring a person into a sudden stroke, anxiety or a deep depression. Sigh! I am shaking my head, because the things that people go through here, to live and manage through life in America, are at times incredulous. I hope that you are not one of the immigrants owing a debt for the purposes of coming to America and now strategically dodging your debtors. But again, if you are. Whew, my heart goes out to you!

What to do? Here you are, finally in America! Take heart, I can relate.

You have been granted entry into the country. You did not experience the secret interviews in the secret rooms by the fierce immigration officers. And now you are thinking, all should be well, right? Well, hardly so. My question to you is do you have a work permit, green card, or any tangible plan to gain citizenship? You probably had no clue to all these questions. Am I right? I know. I was once just like that. Speaking from experience, I realize that with many visitors, entry into America as visitors with plans to overstay their visit has been the beginning of their new problems on a bigger level.

Yes. You heard me right. Most likely, life is harder with this type of a visa, that I Brenda, and my family of four had obtained way back on May 30th, 1997 to be able to come to America by the end of year of 1997. The idea was Christmas in America. Oh what a joyous feeling! On paper, oh yes, a fabulous idea! But that's how naive I was way back then. Infatuation at its best. Infatuation is one of my biggest weakest links. I am so glad I have such a grand imaginative mind. You are saying, "huh?" Well, I don't know where

else I would be if I didn't dream so big and my mind wasn't such a big busy place. You see, everybody needs an imaginative and creative mindset to survive here in America. I know my creative and imaginative mind has kept me afloat in the most difficult trying times of my life right here in the USA. This country I believe is the most exquisite place where imagination along with creativity are allowed and celebrated more than any other place in the world. And there is no other season in the world that imagination, grandiosity and exaggeration comes alive such as Christmas time in America. I am so glad that it was Christmas time that we chose to come here not any other time or seasons of the year. A memorable and an unforgettable time of my family's life and each individual in it. I couldn't declare enough how much I have loved the Christmas season since I was a child.

A SPECTACULAR CHRISTMAS

Something about the gift of giving that does something in the soul of both the giver and the receiver, simultaneously. It's like magic is in the air each Christmas time for me. And yes, we came during the time when the weather fitted the season, too.

My family and I had never seen so much snow on any other Christmas season elsewhere prior to this particular Christmas and even after the many Christmas seasons to come, both in our lives here and in our homeland. We arrived from Lilongwe, Malawi, the warm heart of Africa. Malawi has a subtropical climate under the global equator. Snow in Malawi would be a very bad sign of the times!

We had not known that the weather could even be so cold. Icicles around the gutters of neighborhood houses and on parked cars were a reality not just fiction read in American book stories. And a man's beard easily got frosted if he stood outside long enough in the cold. It was so cold I had experienced frostbite for the first time standing outside in the cold but I don't think that I really cared. We were finally in America! The sight of neighborhood houses where most decorated from inside outside. A sight

like one I once saw in a Christmas movie. It almost seemed like everywhere we went, we were in Christmas town and the music in every store we visited played Christmas songs that were infectious all around the city outpouring into every household we stepped in. This was a dream come true, at least for me it was. Christmas all the way! This was music into my destiny.

OUR AMERICAN CONNECTION

Surely, I would like to state that we were coming to "visit" for at least 6 months. We had our B1/B2 Visitor Visas tucked away in our only most prized possessions at that point in time, our passports and our $190.00 to our family's name. Let's face it. It was a lie my spouse and I were willing to believe. It was a gamble we took on our lives! We would visit the country and remain in the country for a few months and return back home before violating the 6 months of stay. We would be able to do so with the aid of my younger sister Abiti Bula, who had romantically come to America on Valentine's Day of 1997 with her beau, the late Boutrous B. (May God continue to rest his soul in peace).

My soul gets sad each time I think about her beau, gone too soon. He is one of the people I will never forget in my life for contributing to our destination here in America. Prior to this, I knew no one in America. Until Boutrous came into our lives in 1995 through my younger sister, Abiti Bula, then he and her became our American connection. Boutrous will never be forgotten in my family's heart. Nor will my family's legacy ever forget his family's contribution to my family. Gone too soon but never forgotten.

He and my sister were lovers at large by 1996, they were so young and so naive about the real hardships of life as well as American culture on an adult level. They came here to Philadelphia with the mindset that they will get away from everything and everyone so familiar in Malawi, to live life like nobody's business and that they would make it big in America—The Promised Land!

So, that's what everyone thinks.

Their journey landed them on American soil that Valentine's week but sadly ended tragically, three years later. That's another sad story I pray to forget in my heart. Sometimes, I wish that I could go back in time to change some things so that all tragedy is come to extinction. The truth be told, we are an imperfect people living in an imperfect world. To change everything negative into positive is far from possible. It hurts nobody to want to be that change you want to see, though. It starts with one person at a time. One step at a time each day. One must at least try moving forward, towards the mark of impossibilities turning them into probabilities that become possibilities.

This is truly my one wish. If I had another chance at wishing something into reality, it would have been to reverse that tragedy in that one particular life story I had witnessed.

But that's a story ending that I would never wish upon anybody, friend or foe. Sometimes life doesn't really prepare us for what's to come although signs are everywhere for us to take heed. It is very unnerving if one is far away from home and is an illegal immigrant.

THERE ARE NO MONEY TREES IN AMERICA

In most people's mental understanding outside America, pertaining to America, there is this notion that one day they will come here, to America, and make it big right there and then. That's why I am here to educate, uplift and inspire someone out there about coming to America or anyone who is already here through my own American journey. I share about the real-life issues and experiences in my life and family's life once we arrived in America and give my insight which had its rocky background stemming from home, Africa. Only that these family and life issues of what was not right in our household only manifested themselves fully in America. The REAL journey had begun way back home in Kawale 1, Lilongwe, Malawi. That is where we lived.

Kawale 1 is one of the poorest ghettos of Malawi. The inhabitants own their lands through generations. Most of the town has been gentrified in the past twenty years by the newer generation and owners but the many potholes and dirt roads and not so many street lights are still a reminder that the area is a ghetto. A few homes still do not have access to electricity due to poverty. Where my husband and I came from, was not too poor but we were surrounded by a constant sense of poverty among the people and shabby homes all around us.

Our living conditions there were, at least from my perspective, one of the original reasons why the decision to come and visit America was made very easily at first, until we got here.

We came for greener pastures and perhaps to make it big too some years down the lane by working in both America and Malawi every other 6 months until obtaining papers to work in America, legally. Unfortunately, that plan was in vain. It ain't always easy. But if it does happen, there's a process to go through in every success story. I know for sure, because my family's immigration journey to arrive to where we are today, definitely didn't happen overnight.

If you are an immigrant, then the immigration process is one of the biggest ways and keys of opening that immigration door and eventually leading to other major doors that allow the immigrant to make it big—legally—in many aspects of life.

It is often a false reality to think that anyone will land in America and then the next following weeks they will then end up very well established and steadily accomplishing high positions, accumulating wealth or stuff overnight.

You see, we all know that Rome wasn't built in a day! We should all implement that theory with pretty much everything that is not a miracle.

Everyone should and must take that saying to heart, seriously.

Rome wasn't built in a day!

Real unforgettable things which are destined for success and established for centuries to come do not happen overnight unless it is a big jackpot lottery winning. And even that has its own blessings and curses.

Nothing's that easy, period.

For real!

If you don't have your papers here in America, you have a long winding road ahead of you to travel!

I repeat, you won't make it big here overnight. I hate to be the one to tell you this, but it is feasible in a few months maybe or perhaps in a few years, yes you can!

If you should ever make it big here overnight, I suggest you surround yourself with wise influential people in your life to help you keep you rooted and grounded, so you don't lose your way due to quick riches, fame and power. Anything big and tangible obtained in a very short period without proper instructions and wisdom could destroy a person in a heartbeat whether a person has American legal papers or not.

Yes, some may make it big here in America but after how long is really, the question. After giving all and what else, I may ask?

I am glad you answered!

Time and Tears! Let's not forget sweat.

Without a doubt getting on a path to citizenship is essential in making it big or for things to happen in your life, here. You see, this is where the problem was for me in my life and family's life. Especially in my personal life.

My journey took almost twenty years to really arrive to where I am today. I can confidently say that I am now officially a legal permanent resident of America! Yay! Clap hands, somebody! Forget about the first six legal months from entry date on that December 22nd, 1997 to June 21st, 1998, that deemed us as legal visitors for a minute. And yes, the six months fly by so fast if your plans have been forfeited. That was our reality.

FROM LEGAL TO ILLEGAL STATUS

The very next day on June 22nd of 1998, my family and I became illegal immigrants. From that moment until May 23rd, 2017, I was still an illegal immigrant. Everyone in my family that I had entered America with, had each obtained individual legal paths to

citizenship but I was the last one to arrive on board, legally. You are saying What? How? Why?

Come again! Yes, you heard me right. Let me explain.

If a traveler from another country comes to America legally for a visit, work, or education to mention a few examples under a certain specific visa which expired for whatever reason after such time. Then the person ended up remaining in the country, without renewing their status, they then become an automatic illegal immigrant or illegal alien. That status remains so until the individual legally qualifies to change status to be able to live here legally via an immigration process which takes money and a long time.

Most people do not qualify to adjust the status, and eventually become illegal immigrants. You know, that was my situation. I was once an illegal immigrant. Anything to do with immigration used to make my tummy whirl and gave me goosebumps.

I say to you, the illegal immigrant out there, I can truly understand your dilemma. Keep the faith. Take heart.

A day comes when you are legal to stay in the country if you abide by the laws and you continue to eat your humble pie in the meantime. The funny part is that you will look back and laugh at your past and sometimes you will even forget all about being an illegal immigrant and other temporary issues.

Many things in life are a process and you may just need those experiences to get you to the right place at the right time ready and set to do what it is you were created to do. Yes, even in a foreign land! Destiny and purpose are right there with you even in your most dark days far away from home. Take a deep breath. Life does get better. Many of our life's paths and experiences are tailor made to get us to a place of our individual specific destinies. Know that your trials are tailor made for the reason you were born and the destiny of your life even far away from home. It is wrong and unfair to want to walk in another person's life path or compare your life to another person's life during your trials, when each person was born for a specific purpose and more.

I, for example, went through everything in this journey from my home country to a faraway foreign land so that I can get to my destiny which is here in America. I want to share my story to help

a person out there, not to fall into the same troublesome issues knowingly. My family and I, did many things in our journey to America for almost twenty years oblivious to consequences and repercussions because nobody had taught us or warned us of the pitfalls. I have been my own guinea pig. My family altogether, were experimenting along with time.

Walk in your own individual life path with an open mind but if you are in this situation that I was in or know someone who is, you may save you or them from unnecessary headaches by sharing my story with them. Although it stems from an illegal immigrant's point of view it is relatable to many others in everyday life whether they are legal residents of America or not. Most of the general lessons that you will learn from my story, in this journey and from my mistakes or those from the people in my family is that most of the mistakes and costly actions were done in ignorance, stupidity, and naivety. We did this as regular human beings but not because my family or individuals in this phase of a journey were illegal immigrants. Simply that the illegal immigrant status in America magnified our personal issues altogether.

As for me, I needed to be an illegal immigrant in America to find meaning to life and any purposes to why I was born. It was this one process or nothing at all. I know this now twenty years later in a foreign land very far away from my motherland. I now understand that America is my destiny. It had been all along.

I found out that one of my purposes in life is to be a whistle-blower to the world on what works and what doesn't work for the sake of common good. My journey may be different from yours the reader, or the illegal immigrant you, but most of my life's lessons are basic and universal. Keep in mind that no matter what, you are still unique along with your purpose and destiny no matter where you are in the world. Illegal or not!

Nobody could ever be you! You can't avoid every place, every-one and everything you need to get ahead for the sake of your purpose and destiny because you DON'T hold the rightful status to be there. Or my own life story would be unheard of if I believed that I was only supposed to be here with my legal papers ready in

hand. Sometimes life has a way of keeping you from the finish line to the beginning. You will get this later.

Once you find your purpose, even in a foreign land, you must pursue it and share it. That's the main reason everyone was born. Each person has something only they can do from within themselves and they must share it with others for the sake of mankind! It was meant to be shared for the common good.

So, celebrate you and get comfortable being you. Citizen or immigrant! You could never be anyone else! Even if you tried. You would spend your life in vain trying to be someone you were not created to be. Whether you are an illegal immigrant or a legal resident of the country wherever you are, your issues are tailor made to qualify you for the benefit of others. Master to live and separate, then study you as you process your life ahead of you. For now, learn to encourage yourself in your troubles. And remember always that whatever you are going through in America or elsewhere in the world, that too shall pass away, just like what you thought you couldn't get through a day before and here you are, still standing!

Nevertheless, you are still here, living and breathing. After everything you have been through, you are still in your right mind.

Thumbs up to you!

I would like to take a moment and personally congratulate you for making it here this far, you immigrant you!

It's not a thing to be proud of, out rightly or legally because you are here in the country of America illegally by the laws. But the fact remains that against all odds, you still stand. You continue to abide by the rules, you continue to work extra hard and be focused.

I charge you to get a mirror and stand in front of it wherever you are!

Look at thyself, speak to yourself, say," Yay! I am a survivor! I made it this far! I shall live and not die! I can do this.

If only, I take it one day at a time. One step at a time." And say to thyself that "every day is a day closer to my legal papers, my purpose and my destiny. I must not give up!"

A HARD REALITY

Then take another moment. Look up and take a silent moment in honor of those who died in lieu of any process to America, to make it big like you have done so far. Talk to yourself and pat yourself because you didn't faint! You are here, still chasing after the American dream!

I kid you not, it is not easy coming to America! I don't care what you may have seen outside of America in movies about anybody who is living in America! Most of it is cut out to sell, America The Beautiful! I ain't mad, though. It's just that, life here is not always as easy as 1,2,3.

To experience the real America, it's not wise to live far and pass judgement. Everybody's experience here is not uniform although pain is universal and if one lives long enough, it is inescapable! Here in America, one can experience pain easily from many angles, all at once because of lack of much needed transparency in communities. But pain is just as necessary for a healthy outlook on life and growth, generally speaking.

One of the problems and challenging factors that I found out among immigrants to America is that friends and family members who are already here cannot tell the outsider far away the truth about each and every kind of hardship immigrants meet along the way here in America. Besides, if an immigrant tried to tell the outsider, often times the outsider does not believe the immigrant and so the myth goes on. Life is easy and great in America! Lie.

It's harder for first time generation of immigrants to make it in America.

So, if you are a lonely and hopeless immigrant, or an illegal immigrant and you feel some type of a way about your significance in this country far from home, let me remind you that you matter.

You are somebody, papers or without papers. Your illegal immigration status or issues should not stop you from enjoying life to the fullest although it is an obvious hiccup. But for crying out loud, live! Don't get me wrong, the reality that you are an illegal immigrant is very frustrating and defeating most of the time.

Pouting is not going to get you the solution to a legal status change, quicker.

Believe me, I know.

Continuing to view yourself as an illegal immigrant every day, is a sure, quick, easy way to feeling very small about yourself. I have been there way too long.

It feels even worse when you start focusing on how you had received so much honor and respect once in your homestead before all this and here you are feeling numberless, powerless and status-less. Like a nobody, literally.

But I have come to encourage you that whatever illegal immigration status you may find yourself in today, remember this one thing, there's a big cause on why you left everything to start over again so far away from home. You are a hero.

Why don't you cheer up a little and do a chicken dance! Like right about now! Just as if you just don't care! Yes! You deserve it! There's a fighter deep inside of you that you had no idea was there to begin with if hadn't taken a leap of faith to come to America against all odds!

It is hard for anybody to leave stuff behind such as large family member communities, give up familiarity to location, power and authority, in-depth family ties, position, material ownership as well as stability, all given up, for something unseen and intangible so many thousands of miles away. Whew! Faith and Hope indeed. You can do it. And I am absolutely sure that from now forward with each passing day, you will spend here in America, you will unleash more of your potential that could never have had you stayed back in your country. You may have gone through times before without many necessary things at most, at other times with limited resources to bring out the best in you. Once again, take heart.

THERE IS GAIN IN SACRIFICE

You will make it here. You will become all those things you have envisioned yourself to be. Give yourself realistic time to achieve them. You didn't go through all hell to give up now. You are more than a conqueror! I say that with much humility. Knowing everything that I have come to know now. Everything you are going through is a setup for your future. If you pay attention you will find out what you are really made of. You will discover that not much of what you go through is useless.

Everything you go through in life generally is either a demotion for what is hard to learn until you learn then you get promoted to the next level of your life. Once you have acquired everything you needed to, to equip you and qualify you for the next step in life until you arrive at your destiny. The main goal of your life is to get you to your destiny.

Life in all aspects, is a journey and everyone is walking it individually no matter where everyone is in the world.

Even when one is experiencing life as an illegal immigrant. Especially living life as an illegal immigrant is quite a trying lesson in itself.

Often times, the lessons ushered to illegal immigrants are very humbling. For instance, a person who could fight people with their sharp tongue can no longer do so whilst living in America. Simply because they are not at liberty to square points with anyone lest they get in trouble with the law and immigration officers are called in.

If one is here for the purposes of making their life better, which is why most immigrants come to America, then the last thing they want is the police on their back. Being an illegal immigrant humbles you. Trust me, I have been there, done that!

One may never get to hear and know all of the stories of every individual who has ever tried to come to America, or of everyone who has successfully done so after a series of trials.

In my journey thus far, I can guarantee you heartache and pain. I wish it weren't so. I guess I am headed somewhere towards where the sign says Big with Peace in it. I can only hope.

....

I know that making it big in life is according to one's mental perception and measure of what they see or understand their own individual "big" or success to be in their own eyes. Success is not uniform to everyone.

But in my eyes, I have seen success whenever I have witnessed immigrants manage to work like crazy while supporting two households with quality supplies. They fend for their American needs as well as their homes from wherever country they came from. This is something they could have never been able to achieve whilst living in their home country doing professional jobs but earning little money.

Some immigrants when they are here do manage to afford quality education for some of their family members in great schools back home whilst they are managing feasible lifestyles for themselves here in America. To me such a people are heroes!

In hindsight, these are issues that a born American neighbor may never understand the reason why an immigrant coming and living in America is such a big deal and privilege. Especially to an illegal immigrant who on paper doesn't qualify to live here but literally makes it big by diligently performing strenuously day in and day out. Of course, in less popular jobs that may never take off in America. These people, in most cases, work in deplorable conditions without putting up a fight or crying out for proper rights.

To me their stories are a success because they are moving mountains just to make things happen for themselves and their family members near and far! These people build and move the country from underneath without seeking recognition or applause but just for that American mighty dollar for wherever they call home and the American dream altogether. To me that's deep passion.

Success stories against all odds in a foreign country as an illegal immigrant have also prompted me to give you the reader a few comforting lessons, and a few kind words, I myself, have acquired along my journey here in The Land of Milk and Honey! This is indeed where people live in homes with picket fences. Yes.

Picket fences are not a foreign thing in America. They are one of the sure signs, and a deal sealer that you the citizens have made it!

I am sure that some of my experiences and life's lessons are eye opening to others so that you can thrive on the best ideas on how to live life successfully if you can help it and live it, big. I included some of the not so great moments and avoidable mistakes so that you can shy away from whatever worse but similar experiences I went through because of ignorance or stupidity if you should ever find yourself in the same situations.

I felt compelled to share my journey and its experiences on paper because these events have touched my life in a major way and have impacted my life, revolutionizing the way I do things today.

A MAJOR TURNING POINT

This all took time, through many trying experiences, a lot of foolish mistakes but my saving grace arrived when I REALLY discovered the Holy Bible.

That Bible verse of Hosea 4:6 has been the driving force into what I truly am now. How can God's people perish due to lack of knowledge? That was what the Bible says.

I personally did not like the sound of that particular Bible verse, at all. This is knowledge on all things on planet Earth. The right kind of knowledge in life can change one for the better and the opposite is true. This does not leave out knowledge on immigration to America. Or how to live life as an illegal immigrant in a foreign land. The verse meant to have knowledge on everything, all things and all situations! The right kind of necessary knowledge can save a person from perishing! That verse convicted my spirit.

Lack of knowledge in everything can cause a person to perish before their time. Ugh! I had found that verse to be provocative and distasteful to my spirit. I had to do something!

Nope, I was not going to be a casualty or a victim of that Bible verse! I was not going to accept it!

....

I was determined that I would not be one from that group of people who lack knowledge on as many things in life as I can help, in all aspects of life so that I could live my life, successfully! Even as an illegal immigrant far away from home with many odds against me while I waited patiently for my papers.

I had always seen myself as a child of God. I grew up attending Sunday schools of every church that I went to throughout my childhood. I still go to church every week. I am knowledgeable of The Word of God from reading the Bible.

So, when I came across that Bible verse, in the time frame that I was actually really studying the Word of God. I was certainly not going to claim the verse for myself! I was determined to learn what I am responsible for to change my life for the better! I was not going to be one of God's People who would perish due to lack of knowledge, absolutely not!

I began to change the way that I saw myself from inside my heart to the outside of myself. I began to change the way I did things. I knew that doing the same things over and over again that I had done in the past until that moment would amount to nothing except stagnation and insanity. What I needed to do was try anything else that I had never done before to get to a different positive result to help me get out of the funk and towards my future.

My mind. I had to change my mindset and my actions would follow!

I am surprised to say that the shocker was my discovery to the crazy circle that didn't start overnight of repeating the same stuff and expecting a good but different result. It started back home in Africa. It progressed into America where I thought everything would happen for the better, automatically. I had no plans living life in Malawi as a young adult and surprise, surprise, I had no tangible plans living life in America as a young adult either! Even when I finally made it in.

Yet, I expected success. I expected change.

CHANGE OF LOCATION, SAME MINDSET

Change without a plan and a goal in mind is impossible and futile.

How could anything around me change if my mind was still the same? The only thing I and my family managed to change was the location. The mindset was still the same for many years while we lived in America before this realization. I was expecting to profit from something I did nothing about!

It was silly.

I worked but I had no plans about the money I earned except pay bills and nothing else when we got to America. I didn't have goals to set for myself or my family nor did I expect them to really happen if I had thought of them or faintly set them in my heart. I wanted out of Malawi when we were in Malawi and a better education for my children and that was it. I had a simple vision which was incomplete in my mind. Even the usual daily endeavors in Malawi and its hardships didn't appeal to me. I was easily bored and oftentimes depressed.

PEOPLE DIE & LIVES CHANGE

In Malawi, 20 years ago, depression was not a common declaration. It was not a known, acceptable disease as it is here in America. When I look back, I believe that I was depressed for a while. I didn't grieve my father when he died in February of 1993.

My father Ted Edward Jacob was a real man and one who I was proud to call father from the time I was two years old. He had adopted me when he married my mother Linley. I am many things today because of him as my earthly father and household leader. I was a young woman and very clueless to life's real issues by the time my dad died. So, when he passed away, there was a part of me that momentarily died too. My dreams and aspirations had died, momentarily.

A part of me wanted to move on as if nothing had happened.

That's exactly what I had attempted to do at the time. The idea was escape Malawi.

I just wanted to get out of there for some urgent reason. I didn't understand it then. I understand it now. It was America, my destiny was calling!

It seemed that some things had to happen to shape and direct me to my destiny and purpose in spite of the pain I had to go through. Some of the things in life, a person just can't prepare for.

1993 was a horrible year for my family!

When I felt like life couldn't get any worse that same year, there came the month of October. I had almost accomplished my matriculation from one of the most prestigious and renowned High Schools of Pretoria, in the Republic of South Africa. The school is known as Pretoria High School for Girls to this day.

My family had been in South Africa since 1988 until 1993 because my father was a diplomat to The Republic of South Africa representing my motherland, country of Malawi.

My dad's untimely death in February of 1993 left me in an emotional shamble. My mother's younger sister who had a hand in raising me during my childhood, youth and early young adulthood years had also died in October of that same year before I could sit and finish writing my final examinations at high school. I was in total despair. I felt so alone and far away from home in the last pivotal years of high school. My grades were severely affected.

I just wanted to finish the exams altogether and get out of Pretoria back to my family and home, Lilongwe, Malawi.

How could life be so cruel? Two of the most key people in my life had died in February and October of 1993 consecutively. Neither of them was even fifty! They were what held my mother's side of the family together. I thought I was going to lose my mind that year.

I hadn't experienced real sorrow or any hardships in life up until 1993. I did not know how to properly function after that. I was mad at God, The One I understood distinctly that He, alone was responsible for giving every living creature life and He alone, was also The Taker of life. I was perplexed. Why my dad? He was

so young and full of promises. My family's life was just becoming much more pleasant as a whole.

A bright future for a young family of six people namely, Tej, Linley, I Brenda, Abiti Bula, CheChimpele, and TaZie was cut short just like that. It seemed like my dad was the one who had held the right keys and the right channels to take us, his family, higher. It had been that way until the day he died. The leader we had assumed by nature was no longer going to be there forever. "Where was God in that?" I often did ask myself. I had so many unanswered questions.

My mother, with her children, before that February came to an end, briefly returned to Malawi to bury her husband and the father of her kids. We buried my dad in his home district Mangochi, particularly Mbaluku village. After the funeral procession, my mother and all of her children returned to Pretoria, RSA to pack and return home for good except I remained at my high school, North Lodge hostel to finish my high school year.

When I had finally graduated high school in October of the same year, I was very naive in so many ways especially in the way of my thinking. Although, at that time, I hadn't come across the Bible verse of Hosea 4:6. In actual sense, I was living my life under the intense influence of that verse and I was truly a vivid casualty of that Bible verse without even knowing it.

I look back now, and I am convinced that I was perishing due to lack of knowledge. The knowledge to know and accept that people actually do die and everything that God does, He does for a purpose.

My life in 1993 till my matriculation event in October and my departure from Pretoria in November of the same year, was very hard, living away from my family for the first time in my life. I spent those months at the North lodge hostel or dormitory of Pretoria High school for girls feeling very sad until the day I returned to the rest of my family in Lilongwe in November 1993. My mind was on the battlefield with this God I faintly knew. I was discouraged and questioned His Ways and His Existence.

Off course as a very young woman at that time, God to me was truly just a figurehead. Someone I couldn't relate to intimately

except that He was the source of my breath and that when people die, He takes their breath back and out of them. And sometimes, He answers prayers right away, at other times he takes time or may never answer. I was young. Life seemed very hopeless. I had so many questions and no one to answer me. I had no idea that the end of my father's life was going to usher me into my own adulthood, my purpose and my destiny. Even his death was necessary for my growth as hard as this was for me to accept. It took many years to understand and accept it. I will admit that, this acknowledgement has never stopped me from wishing that he was still around to see me now and his contributions in my life. But would I be this person I have become if he were around to do for me all that he did for me as a father, when he lived?

I wonder.

I had absolutely no plans growing up about my future except for a few empty wishes and the wishes, ideas were all about obtaining wealth. But that's how far I got and not real plans on how to get there. No aspirations whatsoever! I had my dad and my mom until in my late teens and I went with them wherever they would go! My dad, the game changer was no more!

All of a sudden, my mother's household lacked for the very first time in our lives. There were no set plans placed in motion for my family even when we had returned home to our land in Malawi. My mom was lost. And she had to become a survivor all at once.

Alas!

The only good thing I looked forward to after finishing my own high school was a man. Another man! I realized today that this was how I grieved my father. From one great man to another one who momentarily held my destiny! You will get it by the time you finish reading this story.

KENEILWE HAD MY FUTURE

His name is Keneilwe. Keneilwe means I have been given in Southern African Tswana dialect. A peculiar young man. His parents The Bokos and my grandmother Naside were neighbors

for a long time before I was even born. They lived on the same side of their street and still do to this day. Their compounds are located in Kawale 1 town within Lilongwe District of central region part of Malawi.

The Bokos and Naside's compounds stood three plots of land away from each other. His family has a large property of land and Keneilwe had lived there since he was a toddler. My grandmother's compound is large too. Our two families have shared the neighborhood as neighbors for over forty years now.

Keneilwe intimately ended up being my first love on this side of heaven on planet Earth! I had never experienced any of the feelings that I felt towards any other living creature before my first encounter with him. And I do love my siblings, my parents and my relatives, I must say.

Before I met him, I had never known that this kind of love ever existed. This man was like no other man! He in return felt the same way. It was incomprehensible. It was destiny in a person! The two of us, an undeniable package. We were supposed to be!

Even our chance meeting was destined. I met him in April of 1992 when my mom and her four children had returned to Malawi for vacation after four years of living in Pretoria, RSA. It was mandatory by Malawian government to expect families of diplomatic services to return to Malawi from whichever country they had just finished serving their government duties after the allocated years. The families either returned to their country of Malawi for good or returned to their country to be sent out to another country to continue representing Malawi.

The latter was the case in my father's situation. He had been promoted to be an ambassador in Vancouver, Canada later on in 1993. Unfortunately, the promotion never took place because my father's sickness took a toll on him from December 1992 until mid-February 1993 when he passed away while in Pretoria.

The trip to Malawi in April 1992, was for my mother and her kid's vacation to Lilongwe, Malawi to bid farewell to our families until we would see them again in the near future whilst in Canada or on another Malawian future vacation. My dad had already been

in Malawi to get commissioned to go to Canada much earlier in 1992.

My mother and her children spent about three weeks-vacation in Malawi.

On April 16th of 1992 Keneilwe and I began to see each other as a young man and young woman. By December of 1992 we were lovers. I even left Pretoria at one point during Christmas season of 1992 and fled to Lilongwe to visit him against my parents' orders. With the help of my younger sister Abiti Bula. That's another story for another day!

My God, it was love like I had never felt. I look back now, I say it was destiny calling. He had our four children embedded in him. I know this now, 25 years later.

At that time in my young adult love season of life, I couldn't survive to live life without that man. I couldn't understand it then. I totally understand it now. We were inseparable! He had my stuff! Boy he had my stuff! Believe me when I say that that man had my stuff! Here I am writing all about it!

And everything that I have been in the last twenty years from Malawi to America as an illegal and then legal immigrant. Without a doubt, he has been one of the propellers of who I have become today. One of reasons why I had to come to America and then later on, I discovered America as my destiny along the way. He, is also one of the pathways, I found my purpose. You will understand this later. I promise you.

In 1993 though, I couldn't have known all this because life in general had become very bleak. I had no idea about my future. America was not yet on anybody's mind. But one thing for sure in that November of 1993 when I returned home to Lilongwe, Malawi from Pretoria, the only thing I looked forward to returning home to Lilongwe was seeing this young man. He was in his 26th year.

I made sure that my ticket to Malawi got me to Lilongwe a day before his birthday. Love is a wonderful thing, I tell you. It makes hard times seem so small and feasible.

I had been with my family for all my life this far that they were everything I knew and loved so much up until 1992. But this

young man who lived a few doors down my grandmother's house, had something I needed to make it through. He had my stuff! I didn't even know it yet at the time.

People sometimes may not understand that we will draw to who or things that have our future. Sometimes we fight people in stopping them from making the worst mistakes of their lives and sometimes the result is futile and sometimes we must indeed intervene to interject!

This one was one that nothing and nobody could stop. It was imperative that I be with that man!

Believe me when I say that life was nonexistent without him. Like a moth to a flame!

But oh, I couldn't even want to imagine life without him! It was impossible! It was like as if I was a fish and he was the pond I needed to dwell in. I couldn't live without him. I couldn't say it enough. He was like my high. I didn't even know by then what's it like to get high on anything. I had such a clean upbringing the only thing I wanted at this point, was this man! I could not explain it. He was like my drug!

Even if I tried, I couldn't control myself. It was the destiny he carried for me inside of him. He didn't even know it! I didn't either! Nobody did but The One Who had both our destiny did! The Creator!

Imagine how powerful the people are, who God causes to help us to carry out or connect us to our individual destinies, without any of us most of the time even knowing what is really going on in one's life. Or within ourselves.

It is because of what this man was carrying in him for me, as a result, it is what had pushed me to become the real person that I have become today. You will understand better as my family's life unravels. I didn't know it then, but he carried my four children in him for starters. It is actually OUR four children. I have to be careful about calling them mine. I suppose that's how the children have motivated me to become all that I could be here in America, still standing by the Grace of God and whatever form of hope God uses to keep a person alive and striving to do well. I will tell you

that for me, He used and still uses my children to push me towards my destiny in a great way for sure!

My children are the reason or the driving force that God uses to inspire me to get to where I am. They are the remnants of their father, my husband.

I don't believe that I would be half of the things that I am if I did not have a child. I don't say that recklessly, not at all. I have respect for people who for whatever reason don't have children. They also have their trials and tribulations, without a doubt. For me what drives me to do better, is who God placed in my life. My children along the 25 years I have been with their father, Keneilwe.

There Is Always HOPE Even When Life Seems Dark

To this day, God uses my children to inspire me to do better, not to give up when things get really rough. And I kid you not, my life has not been a bed of roses. Maybe for a time of two and half years into my marriage, I may have slept in a bed of roses night after night. I know what lovers mean when they say that they felt each other's pain and cried together in times of trouble. I experienced the same with Keneilwe. Our souls were tied together.

This all started the November of 1993, the day I landed back in Kawale 1 Lilongwe, Malawi for good, so I thought. It turned out that exactly nine months after my arrival to Lilongwe from RSA, I gave birth to who I call, the most beautiful female creature God ever entrusted in my care and qualified me to call mother! Marvel is her name. A bountiful daughter of 3.9 kilograms born at a private clinic in area 3 in late August of 1994. Life was good!

This child was loved and pampered by everyone. When I say everyone, I mean the whole block where we came from. Contrary to her pregnancy where my mother had kicked me out of her house as soon as she heard from my younger sister, Abiti Bula, that I was with child.

My mother spoke to me after the baby was born. We all became a family once again, although I had moved on and had moved myself into Keneilwe's household or compound. I was a disgrace to my mother and so to prove the shame I had brought her, she had kicked me out. I had no other place to go. Keneilwe was a young bachelor and the only person I could seek refuge from.

Keneilwe's compound was the only logical place for me to go to. I had no other options. I wasn't working. I eased my way through into his life in the most unconventional way. I hope that God has forgiven my naivety and stupidity. I had no common sense not even wisdom! I did whatever driving force was having me to do. I sold and handled myself for cheap.

I had no shame nor remorse to rethink anything twice. I just did! I didn't even know what self-love or self-value was at that time. I was 21. You just have to forgive me.

In general, I learned this lesson over the years that any person should never latch onto anybody or anything without proper steps put into place or taken into consideration. There is always the right way and the wrong way to doing things. Most people use how they found you to remind you of who you are along the way no matter how much you are trying to change your life for the better. A bad way to start any relationship, I may add. A woman shouldn't throw themselves at anybody pregnant or not. I did. It was a huge mistake the way I handled my early pregnant days and my life altogether in the years that followed. There are always consequences and some-times they do not manifest themselves immediately.

Nevertheless, life progressed and things seemed to take off.

My mother on the other hand had issues with me being a housewife. She was not going to have it. She was a young widow and she feared for me to stay home with no skills nothing to survive on. What if what she had experienced in her own life would happen to me along the years of my housewife days? She often feared.

She had not gone through life sacrificing what she did for her children with her deceased husband when he lived, for their children to amount to nothing. My mother, we call her the other "iron lady." Doing nothing is not living according to her.

CULTURE EXPECTATIONS

After my father's death, in my mother's mindset, It was my time to work for my family and give back to her also, as an older child and to help out with school funds for educating my younger siblings who were in dire straits themselves because my dad's pension was depleted due to government loans and anything else that needed to be paid for, after he was gone and buried. It is traditionally so in African culture for an older child to assume family responsibilities or help out with financial issues of their family.

Another person would say, but why was I made to bother about my siblings or my mother after I had my own baby and a household of my own? Shouldn't I be excused from extended family life responsibilities and issues?

I am so glad you asked!

Yes, my mother had kicked me out of her house during my daughter's pregnancy by February 1994.

My new husband was already five years into his job, making good money at one of the leading banks of Malawi, The National Bank of Malawi and we didn't have to pay for any utility bills on his parents' premises, so he had good money to help others besides his primary family.

This was one of the attractions that drew me closer to him. He was kind and he had a job. Therefore, he would be able to take care of me and our new-found family. He was also generous. I love kind and generous people. They are moved by genuine love and compassion for those around them who are in need.

He always reached out to help those that had less than himself. Whatever we had to do to help my mother and siblings, he and I did together. One of the ways we helped my mother's family was by sending my youngest two siblings Tazieh and Navessa to attend a private preschool in the neighborhood during their early childhood years. Navessa became my adopted sister as soon as her mother, my mother's younger sister, died in October of 1993. In reality, she is my cousin.

For my husband's unborn child, before she was born, it was advisable for her father and I to marry at the city hall legally so that I could qualify and gain medical insurance and benefits under his work umbrella as his immediate family. I needed health insurance to be able to experience better prenatal care and after birth medical care in regards to our unborn child. The only way to qualify for those benefits was for me to become his wife on paper.

So, on one mid-February afternoon of 1994, it was on Wednesday. I met Keneilwe, his friend Abdullah from his job, his friend's girlfriend Torrie downtown at the City Hall in Lilongwe to be our witnesses to the tying of our matrimonial knot. Keneilwe and I had officially become husband and wife that sunny day. There were no fireworks, nor fanfares or alarms going off. Just a Justice of the Peace Officer to swear us in as husband and wife!

Hopefully someday I pray, God knows I secretly desire every day in my heart for real, a white wedding with fanfare going off and a ton of fireworks spewing out joyous sensations leaping up into the sky. A handful of hand bells and a church wedding bell chiming in loudly his name and mine in symphonic and harmonious sounds that bring angelic beings and wedding goers to a standstill in sheer mesmerization! I have never stopped to dream of wedding and things. I underhanded myself. I have lived the consequences.

Know that my busy imaginative mind always keeps me alive and dreaming. Without getting lost, let me take you back to the days after officiating that matrimonial knot.

The first few months of our marriage were a bed of roses. Our first year was immaculate. I don't remember any hardships at all. Keneilwe was a friend, a husband, a father, a provider, a covering, a leader and everything a woman looks for in a man. He and I became one soul. I do believe very much in soul ties. When I say that we felt each other's pain and joy that is an understatement. I could not articulate that enough. Soul ties are real. As a matter of fact, a healthy soul tie with a friend, a parent, a business colleague, a sibling, a child, or a spouse can make so many things very easy in a relationship. It's really beautiful and empowering. Two are better than one; because they have a good reward for their labor than one indeed working alone according to the Bible book in Ecclesiastes

4:9 especially when the two are with one accord doing a mission. I so want that badly again with anyone in any healthy and good relationship out there. Whether it is with my children or neighbor or anyone who has my best interest in their heart. It's such a fantastic feeling that money can't buy!

You will understand why I am still looking for healthy soul ties in my life by the time you read the last page of this book. Everyone who gets things done in life needs loyal people and supportive people who are with them in whatever endeavours they are in agreement with in order to get them done successfully. Physical support, spiritual as well as emotional support are a few of the most important types of support every person needs to execute everyday life issues. And every day should be a day to learn new things to enhance life in general in order to move forward.

Well there's a saying that you cannot teach an old dog new tricks. My newly wedded husband began to spend a little bit more time with his friends at the pub just like he had done in his bachelor days. I guess his buddies had started to miss him. Keneilwe in Malawi was one of the most generous men I had ever met. That was one of his attractions. He was this way with everyone. He was one of the best buyers of beer for his friends and he has quite a great sense of humor when he is happy.

The End Of Marital Bliss

So, the old dog went back to his old tricks. And trouble followed. I don't really know how our soul tie was broken so quickly but things changed. Things got worse especially whenever him and I started focusing on other things except each other. We may have had at least one year or a little over a year maybe of happy times together in our marriage before things really started to fall apart.

A lot of our marital problems stemmed from outside forces that affected his decisions. We were not of one accord. He spent time and money extravagantly on friends and alcohol and no quality time with me or his new family. All this made every story I

heard about him and other women at the tavern appear credible. He was still continuing his bachelor habits.

At times, I would hear stories about his escapades with bar-girls or pub girls or hookers at the tavern well known as Nanjiri a few miles away from Lilongwe where we lived. He made these trips on Saturdays, when he was gone all day.

I didn't want to dwell on it so much towards others on the outside but inwardly, it was affecting me deeply. I believe that I preferred denial because I wasn't ready to face the facts and I wasn't ready to give my mother any satisfaction that truly what she had predicted about the love of my life was coming to pass. She believed that I had made a mistake and she never budged about him until late in my married years. She mellowed a bit towards my husband much later in the years of our marital journey.

I honestly was not ready to deal with any ugly truth about my husband or marriage.

I could be the only woman who thinks this way. But I had no doubt in my mind that once my husband married me, I on my own, with all of my love, would change him. I was really full of myself and I lacked wisdom. I am healed of denial now. Thank God! The old adage says that If anything quacks like a duck, walks like a duck, the chances are that, the thing is quite a duck! I was in over my head.

I began to spend more time at my mother's compound as a way of dealing with my marital issues.

Talk about people who run away from reality because of the pain that reality may cause, I was one of those people. I didn't know how to take the bull by its horns.

I mean part of leaving Malawi was to run away from what was familiar, to start a new life elsewhere, even if it was for a very short time. The main contribution to my problems, or my marital problems wasn't the environment, but the mindset of the people in the marriage and the people in it, really. So, I found a new escapade at the time.

One of the places I sought refuge from was a home within my grandmother's compound, my Aunt Selena's house. Aunt Selena, is a wife to my mother's younger brother. Her and I got along very well.

She was a housewife and did everything daily at her home while my uncle was always on the road within Malawi or in the Republic of South Africa driving heavy goods trucks across the nation of Malawi and beyond, carrying cargo and making money. She had time on her hands and she was always hospitable to me. We had so much in common. We spent a lot of time talking heart to heart about life's issues and marital issues and everything else in between.

Each afternoon after securing my potion of house chores with the help of two younger teenagers who lived with me, I would pick up my baby girl to visit my aunt, just to spend time with her family until it was time for me and my daughter to return to my own compound to await my husband.

Most of the time he would leave work and stop over at the tavern nearby to drink with his buddies. Most nights, he arrived while we had fallen asleep. This type of behavior progressed.

I had become a very sad housewife with not much to look forward to in my young marriage and I had begun to feel valueless. I felt as if I was just a mother to his daughter. And a wife to someone who didn't know exactly what to do with me. I had become just like all of the other wives of the compound where we had settled. Everyone just did the daily mundane things repeating each day throughout the whole year after year. I hated that reality and feeling and feared for what may become of my own future. Everyone did the same things each morning, afternoon and evening year in and year out. I was not happy. Once again there was no excitement in my life anymore! I believe that depression had settled in.

I became voiceless to the point that my nagging about his neglect of me was resulting in heated verbal arguments late in the nights or early in the morning hours when I could see him. I had no wisdom and I didn't know how else to handle my marital issues except that I eventually increased hours in spending more time at my grandmother's compound.

It was so bad that I had even begun to frequent my grandmother's compound on weekends. It is very difficult for me to make friends as I normally don't trust easily therefore I found myself drawn back home to my grandmother's and mother's compound

again and again, more and more! For a married woman, this was an unusual and unacceptable behavior in our culture and am sure for any married woman or person for that matter in any culture.

I even begun taking food to cook for my household to my grandmother's and mother's home to return back to my home in the evening with it already prepared.

My grandmother didn't agree with it and I often received words of rebuke from her. I was in pain, I felt like nobody could understand my pain and therefore nobody could help me or tell me what to do about my life or the kind of trouble I had put myself in. I was in big trouble. Things in my life began to get worse in the fact that I was more at my grandmother's compound than my husband's.

My aunt's house was one of the four openings or doors facing the back side of the biggest house on the premises where my elders lived on their compound. The four doors led to four smaller, sizable but functional houses. My aunt lived in one of the four smaller houses there. Two identical on the right side and two on the left side like a square. No entrance at the back just windows. The other three of the door entrances, led to my grandmother's monthly renters. My aunt lived in one of the blocks of the building with my uncle, her husband and three children at that time. If you stood in my grandmother's bathroom side of the house or my mother's bathroom section, or kitchen and pantry rooms, and the dining room, or my bedroom side of the house and looked out through the windows, you would be able to see what's happening outside the back of my grandmother's and mother's house where my auntie and renters were living in their homes. My auntie didn't rent because she is part of our family through my uncle.

When looking at the houses from a bird's view, the bigger house was also standing slightly taller in stature so that it gave the people in the bigger house an advantage to see outside clearer into the other people's homes especially at night time.

My grandmother's and mother's house encompassed the other half of the whole plot or land. Their house was a long wide rectangular shape. To its left side if you are standing from the front entrance of the gate looking in of the compound, directly towards

it, is the house garage. On the same side of the house has my grand-mother's side of her bedroom and full bathroom. Part of the living room, pretty much half of the living room. The other right side has the three large bedrooms. The middle was a long corridor dividing the large living room, dining, kitchen and pantry, the bathrooms and my bedroom at the far end. The front entrance of the house had a long and beautiful veranda filled with beautiful flowers and green plants my mother took time to raise. Immediately after the veranda there's a red finely pointed brick fence surrounding a very well-manicured green grass around the compound and flower beds leading to a red and high iron gate that leads people in and out of the compound. There's a smaller door within the gate so that people didn't have to open the huge gate each time they walked in and out of the compound. My mother had brought back a lot of classy and expensive things from her years in Pretoria as a diplo-mat's wife. Her house in Kawale 1 was truly another world inside Kawale 1.

The house lacked nothing except my dad in person.

All my mother's children had settled in this new home com-fortably. My mother's idea of our life in Pretoria as diplomat's kids was transferred to Kawale 1 so that her children didn't lack much besides the presence of their father. She had planned and designed her mother's home for her children to continue living a comfort-able life. I have always saluted her for that. I only lived in my bed-room for less than four months and that was it. From the day I arrived from Pretoria on November 25th, 1993 until the day my mother found out that I was with child which was early February 1994.

Even as I frequented my elder's compound back and forth, my whole being was yearning to cleave to my new home but for some strange reason, I couldn't feel completely at home in my new compound belonging to my husband's family a few plots of land down the street. I didn't miss my bedroom. I missed my relatives so much.

Each time, I went to visit my mother's compound, it was not always to see my bedroom, or things I had left behind, grand-mother or mother, although somehow there was always a chance

that I would go inside their house to say hello or sit for a moment before I proceeded through my mother's kitchen door to visit my aunt on the other side. Usually my grandmother and my mother and other family members would always be watching something recorded on a video tape on their VCR such as the famous movie, Coming to America, or music videos by the likes of Yondo sister, or Kanda Bongo man.

As for me, I wasn't one to sit around like that glued to an electronic box in front of me. I still am not like that except occasionally for bonding purposes with my kids. Once or twice a month, I make sure to watch a decent, a funny or a love American movie with them, or something from Bollywood with Shah Rukh Khan in it. He is our favorite Indian movie star. At other times we watch Nollywood which is how I can find myself more than an hour glued to a television set with my children otherwise I prefer Gospel YouTube or talking to people in person. The latter is my best new normal.

I was never a television kind of girl growing up unless it was to watch the Bold and The Beautiful, a pre-recorded show during my high school years at The North Lodge Hostel weekdays every evening before study at Pretoria High School for girls' when I was living in The Republic of South Africa. Even as a child, I preferred to talk to people than watch television.

Naturally, I could talk for a living. I am not eloquent but just talkative. A huge difference, I tell you. Lol!

I truly like to talk to people who may seem like they have something I could learn from. My aunt was a great candidate. She was a happy jovial person and pretty. She was trustworthy, very friendly and is older than I am. She has a few years ahead of me in marriage to my uncle and I felt that I could talk to her about life in general and she had my best interest at heart. My grandmother and my aunt are the two people I could trust with everything I could tell them that is important and private to me when I lived in Africa. In them I found no harsh judgement towards me.

Most of the times whenever I went to my mother and grandmother's compound, it was my aunt I visited and held long conversations with on everything. I could tell her anything, and time

with my aunt flew by so fast because I was also very fond of her. So, my time there with her was not a strange thing to anybody. Anybody who knew me, knew that I frequented my grandmother's compound to see my aunt.

But on this particular Saturday, my grandmother and mother were away for a day in Bunda village a few miles away from Lilongwe. Bunda village is where my grandmother's mother and her other relatives originally came from and some of my great grandmother's relatives still live there.

Bunda village is a remote agricultural place well known for its rich agricultural resources and background.

My mother and grandmother had gone there for an important family occasion. My mother left me a word with my cousins before she left for Bunda Village for me to show Mr. Mountain, my uncle Rey's personal driver, some maize bags allocated for Mangochi where the driver was going that day. Uncle Rey is my mother's distant cousin. His driver, Mr. Mountain was to bring with him the bags of maize set aside for my dad's mom Abiti Vai, who lived in Mangochi District of southern Malawi. My grandmother is now deceased, she passed away end of 2016. May her soul rest in God's eternal peace, gone but never be forgotten.

PHYSICAL ABUSE AND TRAUMA

On that particular day concerning Mangochi, Mr. Mountain was by my elderly parents' compound once again just like he had done several times in the past on his way to Mangochi. He helped out by taking the bags to my grandmother who used the maize as part of her staple food along the many months to follow. My mother did this on a regular basis throughout the years of my childhood even adulthood.

My Uncle Rey was a big boss at a big agricultural company in Kanengo, Lilongwe. That's how my mother had the privilege to use his driver for her personal use. If you come from a Third World country, community and family connections go a mighty long way.

You can understand this easily. In American culture it is called hustling and bustling.

Mr. Mountain was no stranger in my mother's compound. His arrival at the compound was no different to the previous visits he had done in the past.

But on this particular day, that Saturday, I got to see a darker side to my husband, that I had no idea existed before that day. As usual, I and my two-year-old child walked over to my grandmother's compound. I was there once again to visit my aunt and chat away my day with her as I did in the past. She was always seated on her veranda or near it washing her kids' clothes or cooking her household meals on a charcoal stove as we talked about everything.

When I was abruptly interrupted by my young cousins who lived with my grandmother and mother at the time to hurry up into the big house because Mr. Mountain had arrived. They wanted me to instruct and show him exactly which maize bags were allocated by my mother for Mangochi. My mother is known as "Margaret Thatcher" in my whole family and if you knew how the real Margaret Thatcher was(May her soul continue to rest in peace) when she reigned over Great Britain, then you would understand that she was quite a force and not fun to cross politically when she stood as prime minister for her country. She was a strong female leader and character. One of the most unforgettable, and best leaders of our time! I will tell you that. She ruled with an iron fist. So, does my mother in our family. I had no intentions of doing anything more to fall out of favor with her. I directed Mr. Mountain specifically on the bags for Mangochi for my "Gogo" or grandmother Abiti Vai. As soon as Mr. Mountain loaded up the truck with the maize bags, his car sped off to the streets of Lilongwe and was headed for Mangochi.

It just so happens that Keneilwe arrived at my grandmother's and mother's house as soon as Mr. Mountain drove off and he only saw the tail end of the car that had sped away. He also knew that I was at my mother's at the time and hour, so he immediately assumed that the car that had sped away in the distance belonged to a man visiting me or else why did I frequent my mother's home so often? This was his reasoning.

He didn't even give me a chance to answer him or bother to hear my plea. Nor did he register the location either. This was my mother's house. Lo and behold, he started to beat me up. He was so angry and filled with outrageous jealous and envy he beat me up so badly as if he was beating up another man. The tragedy of being heavily intoxicated is that one loses sound judgement. Someone always pays for it. Without a doubt, I paid that day in unforgettable agony. I still have unforgettable shame and traumatic issues that reappear in my heart from time to time about that particular event.

I have visible side effects from that day's events. During the beating, at one point he had held on so tightly to my long braids on top of my head and yanked out some of the braids to the front and top of my head before everyone else who was nearby could pull me away from his manly grip.

I was in shock and I was beside myself with anger.

Oh, the pain was excruciating! It zapped at my scalp like some electric shockwaves through my brain.

I sometimes get goosebumps just to think back on that sad and miserable event. The constant baldness is a daily reminder that love, this type of love I had felt for this man and whatever he claimed that he had felt for me in return was, at times, more like a curse than a blessing. Outrageous in every way and the opposite of what my gut was telling me all along. It was a wrecking ball type of love. One that your mama may not agree with. As a result of that day, everything I had felt towards him changed. The level of respect and my values towards him lowered. I became resentful of him. He became obnoxious to me. I became anxious personally and my personality was of that of a raging lunatic from that point on. He had made it openly known that he had no respect towards my family, or where I came from by freely beating me up in my mother's house. He had reverence for no one there.

I knew that this type of love was dangerous and could cost each of us a lot more than our sleep. I couldn't believe that my husband had the audacity to beat me up anyhow, especially in my own mother's house. That told me clearly how he viewed my family, my elders or me, his wife. My brother CheChimpele was hardly

14 years old. He couldn't defend anybody even if he tried. I had no-one to defend me. What my husband did on that day was outrageous and disrespectful.

Such impact of mental scars on anybody are hard to erase! I believe that those scars crossed the Atlantic Ocean and lingered on in my mindset, deep in my soul and body. This, as I continued with life in Philadelphia no matter what I had tried to do to change the outcome of our lives together.

Here we were in America! New location but the old scars never left or were made to disappear to erase what really took place on the physical and psychological part of the body, oceans away in Africa years earlier.

I had sores on my scalp that eventually healed but my frontal top mid hair never grew back in. Before today, I often had feelings of inadequacy because I was letting my outward looks determine my inner value and had sad feelings of being scarred for life and even suffered nightmares because of it.

I had to consciously talk to my psych to make myself never to think in that way about myself anymore, but to focus once again on my strengths and put my energy in re-discovering my sheer chance at life and realize that I wasn't dead due to that beating. I must celebrate my life because my past helped me build the person I am today even with baldness. I still have a reason to live because of who and what God placed in my life, children. I have work to do. At least I owe my children whatever I can give them with all that my potential can do.

As a solution to my hair days, I have resorted to covering up my baldness with wigs. They were created for the likes of my situation. Such is life.

I can always wear them to hide the bald spots but my wigs have never been on my head because of sheer fashion. No, a thousand times no!

It is due to scarred hair root issues. I just had to put it out there plainly and simply. Meanwhile to his defense, he is convinced that my baldness is due to alopecia. He completely erased the event and moved on with life as if it never happened. But my scars are a constant reminder that the trauma I went through in my mother's

house was real at the hands of the one I loved, my own husband. Sigh!

Trauma never left my memory. And nope, I didn't forget the incident.

I was so traumatized, I was afraid to go to his compound that day. I stayed at my grandmother's and mother's house and compound. I got a backlash from my mother and I didn't like my situation. But I never wanted to prove to my mother that she was right about the man I chose for myself all along. Therefore, I went back to him. An abused person's weakest and deepest thought pattern. The denial that, that awful thing, didn't really happen. The instigator will change if only I just do these things for them a little more and a little bit better!

Lie. You will die trying! Run. Get out now while you are intact.

From that point on, the trust that I had for him to protect me from all harm as the better and stronger half of our matrimonial bliss was gone.

I had a change of heart about what I knew of him on everything. He had a darker side that I didn't like. It was a possessive type of heart and I couldn't dare let any man look at me at any jazz events we went to or we would have to abruptly leave the event unceremoniously for home in a hurry with him almost fist fighting another man who dared to look at me. Or he would beat me up for entertaining a response to anybody who tried to chat with me casually with no meaningful talk.

It became so sickening. I thought it was love at first, but it wasn't. It was insecurity unravelling and manifesting itself before me in a man who I was once deeply in love with and I had no clue on how to deal with it. He didn't hesitate to hit me if he felt like I needed to be put in my place wherever that meant to be at that particular time. He had a certain kind of demeanour that no one could read easily. He comes off to everyone as a quiet and innocent man. But he can put me in a nutshell so quickly with his sharp tongue marking me accordingly to whatever type of a person at that hour he felt I was to him. That also applied to the caliber of

family type I came from whatever it may deem to him at that particular event.

According to him, it was I who needed him not vice versa. This always bothered me because I felt like all my works could never prove to him about the way I felt for him every day I was with him. I also knew that when you love someone the last thing you do is cause them any pain, so I was conflicted in my mind about him. What was this type of love he claimed to have for me? That is, if he ever really loved me! Then every time he was too quick to prophesize about how no man out there could put up with me. I was no good for any man out there, with my fatty ass and this type of person I had become according to him.

I realized eventually as years went by, in regards to him or us, that we could not get functional no matter how hard we both tried. And by me allowing him to paint me any other lesser picture he wanted no matter where we were in our environment, I got to a place where I realized that it was I who had allowed him to paint, at any time on this canvas of description that held up for me!

Less of anything and less of everything no matter how hard I tried inwardly or outwardly to show him that I loved him so, and that I wanted desperately for this marriage to work. I couldn't win against this man unless I changed the picture of me for myself. I had given him permission to emotionally paint me badly every time he had a chance to showcase about me in front of our children as well as strangers.

I did not understand it. I did not like the way it came about each time he felt like he had to square points with me. I always complained to him that I was confused about leadership in our household. I couldn't follow him because I don't think that he ever grasped the meaning of a leader in a household and the role that a leader plays. So, in the end we were both leading and that type of behavior caused havoc in our lives. Two monsters and chaos!

It was as if we both were men at times fighting for individual rights. Then at other times both women looking to be pampered, loved and appreciated for duties performed. We got so confused and unashamed about our dysfunctional behaviors that it didn't matter how we acted towards each other in public or in front of

our children and relatives. It was always a train-wreck waiting to happen. Our kids have been through so much, I hate to admit.

We even got used to beating each other up in public or behind closed doors that the dysfunctional behavior did not interrupt our " love making" or anything normally performed or exchanged by lovers in a normal relationship setting and didn't register to each of us as very abnormal for many years to come until one day, when I said to myself, enough already.

Time For A Change

My people perish due to lack of knowledge. Hosea 4:6. There it was loud and clear all over again in my mind screaming at me!

I hated the feeling of perishing, yet I was not changing anything that I did.

This was after many, many years of trying to do the same dysfunctional things and expecting functional results. Truthfully speaking, the soul always knows. I must have known this much longer way back before the trip to come to America in 1997. But denial is a great pacifier and a time buyer hoping for a miraculous change somehow.

That Hosea 4:6 voice was always there in my heart, but I didn't want to face it all along. I knew that my marital life was really headed for ruin. Whatever we had was not real love. Real love protects. Real love grieves with another who is grieving. Real love feels and shares the pain. I wanted out, but I was also so deeply far gone in love with him or whatever dysfunctional feelings I had towards him. Hey, I always said that he was a father to my children and he loves them. But wasn't I there to be loved long before they came? That is one true fact for sure. I knew I had to get some kind of life to be able to stand on my own just in case things turned south.

On the other hand, I could no longer tell the whole world about how charming my husband was towards me. It wasn't a secret. Bad news has a way of spreading fast like wildfire. In Kawale 1, my mother was evidence of that. Sometimes she would even see unpleasant things without my having to open my mouth about my issues. Some of it she couldn't help to avoid since it happened within her spheres.

Unfortunately, when people live close together in communities, it is very hard not to hear what's happening in the hood. I don't know if she was my saving grace, but God had allowed to use my mother, positively this time around because in the past so much letdown had happened. It was so much that I even lost trust, hope or any type of comfort in her and my younger sister, altogether. I was still very close to my younger sister although she had snitched on me about my pregnancy with Marvel in 1994.

My mom and sister have always been very close to each other too, more than them with me, and they did a lot of backbiting together about me by that time. Please don't get me wrong, I have made peace about it over the years. And you know, it's not as if I had a cap over my marital shenanigans either, therefore involuntarily, I had given open access to those nearer and dearer to me for it to become, sadly a hot topic in their lives at the time. For a change, my mother, had managed to come up with a solution to one of my marital issues in a form of employment.

GOD CAN USE ANYONE
TO ELEVATE YOU

This time around by 1996, my mother had managed to use her connections in securing me a job as a paid intern at one of the prestigious banks of Malawi, The Commercial bank of Malawi in Blantyre in their Corporate Services; It was located opposite one of the most prestigious hotels of Malawi, the Mount Soche Hotel.

I was often commuting between Blantyre and Lilongwe, which caused many difficult trust issues as my spouse and I were separated for the first time since we began to live together. He increased his freelancing in bars and bottle stores for social upkeep of his lifestyle. This is all that he had known to do since he became a working adult. He still wasn't able to graduate from bachelorhood, two years later into the marriage. He didn't seem to want to graduate either. By this season I was with our second child. Oh, what a difficult time it was physically and mentally!

Avedi was our second child, our bright and shining armor. I finally got my wish, a son. He was conceived and born during a very challenging season of our lives. I thought that with his birth, hope will be enhanced, and he will seal our marital fate for good because we had become a complete family with a daughter and a son.

SOUL TIES & AN ELEPHANT IN THE ROOM

Unfortunately, I believe now that whenever a person is sexually tied to someone, in this case, my husband and I, and something are off in one person, my husband and his sexual shenanigans, at the time the inner woman in me knew of it.

But if nothing is said or confessed, by the instigator or cheater, there's an emotional battle of the two people involved in that relationship spiritually as well as within their souls and it doesn't matter what the cause of the arguments or fights is in the relationship, there is no steady peace. That was our situation. The souls were no longer of one accord. I believe this is one of the major factors today contributing to endings of marriages, endings of friendships, rivalries in siblings, and business downfalls. Trust and soul ties to others that shouldn't be in.

There is strength in agreement. Two with one accord is better than one indeed, always. My marriage instead of progressing forward, got worse because I experienced postpartum depression after Avedi's birth and the depression lingered on for a while and my husband and I were not of one accord by any means.

This was all happening during the third year of our union. I was in Blantyre for the internship at the bank and pregnant for the most part of the training and away from my family who were at my home, Lilongwe in the central part of Malawi.

Blantyre is in the southern region of Malawi, about four hours ride. It is also my birth place.

Towards the middle of 1996, I had been transferred permanently as a banking clerk and was located at the Center City branch in Lilongwe a few months before I gave birth to my son.

Before his birth, I was on bedrest from the 7th month. He was born in December of 1996 at The Likuni Hospital Private wing after 18 hours of labor. Many things during his pregnancy and after were very difficult and somewhat miserable in my life. His birth was without a doubt a joyous celebration. He had become another one of a few and favourite things in my life together with his older sister. I was highly blessed but I felt sad and lonely in my heart. I felt that I didn't belong where I was, and I didn't fit in. I couldn't understand why.

Everyone I loved and cared about was with me. I just didn't understand life and what life was beckoning me.

When You Know, You Do Better

I was earning my own pay which I did with it as I pleased. I look back today, and I know that was not how family corporate finances should run. There were many things that were wrongly done by my spouse and I in our family as a family unit but who was there to tell us how a functional family runs? It was two blind people leading each other. Somebody who hasn't been anywhere properly cannot lead someone else! You can only teach anyone what you yourself already know.

By the time my younger sister Abiti Bula was leaving for America with her beau Boutrous B, on the eve of Valentine's day of 1997, I really was very depressed. But I didn't really know how deeply depressed I was then. I was very sad that what I had gone through by this time in my marriage only positioned my marital journey towards a path of failure. The path that my marriage took was not the way I had fantasized it to be. I was often left alone behind at home to care for household affairs and I hardly saw my husband. He often was negligent of his household affairs until late

at night. Weekends were for him and his buddies from morning time. On Sundays he would drink some more. I thought that when he settled down and married me, he would stop with the drunkenness and disappearing acts altogether, but I was wrong.

LOVE, ADDICTIONS & PRIDE

What most people may not know about addictions is that the loved ones or people around the addict are the ones who really suffer the most during the additions and they are the ones who often feel neglected, left out and lost when the addictions take a toll.

He had bouts of aggression whenever he could not understand my ways. I did the same whenever I couldn't understand his ways. In our relationship looking now in hindsight, nobody took blame, or apologized for anything. It was two prideful people working together in a relationship where pride was an enemy by all means. Yet pride was given a podium to rule from and everybody worshipped it and yet expected an amicable relationship and outcome from the works of pride on a daily basis. Impossible and foolish!

It was a train wreck in the making. There were a series of degrading and damaging name calling by both parties every other day. By the time the second child was almost a year old, our marital bliss had seen the dark and uneven temperamental sides to both individuals. I too had managed to splash some hot porridge or water on his arm because I got so frustrated in a heated argument about his disappearing acts. It was just one of the many times he did before our marriage had entered year two. When I look back over our lives I get so disgusted at how dysfunctional we were and yet we believed that we were in love. That was not love. I don't really know how to articulate it, but it was not love. It was far from love. It was not even what Beyonce calls "drunken" love.

After a series of these sad events in our marriage, I was certain that my marriage would be over.

I had heard many rumours of his encounters and engagements with miscellaneous females whilst I was in training for my

job in Blantyre and even when I was back to settle down. It was very hard for me to continue to hear his reasoning each time he tried to defend himself because it was not as if he was put in one imaginable place and then turn around not to be seen in those awkward and compromising places in my absence by different witnesses. Anyhow, these people would turn around and then tell me what they saw him do. This was all happening when he was supposed to be married to me and living together with me at the time these claims were made.

ONE CAN NOT ESCAPE FROM SELF

By early of 1997, I really wanted out of Malawi to go elsewhere in the world where I could just have my husband to myself and kids without anybody else interfering with my family life or marriage. What I had envisioned as a perfect family life was not what I was experiencing in the second or third years of our marriage.

I was so relieved when my sister and her boyfriend had relocated to the United States of America in February of the same year. It was sort of like the same idea. Escaping from a dysfunctional lifestyle to the unknown far away land. Up until that time, there had been no one else in my family circle living in the United States of America. However, my sister's boyfriend's family had roots in Philadelphia. The boyfriend came from one of Malawi's prominent and well educated families. He had a younger sister in Philadelphia by the name of Phoebella.

Phoebella,
A Sister Born In Adversity

Although she was more than 5 years junior to me, she was so mature beyond her years that she took on the heavy mantle of caring for everyone once we arrived in Philadelphia from 1998 until when we could financially fend for ourselves.

She is one of the few special persons here in America, on planet earth I am forever grateful for!

I had never heard of Philadelphia. I only thought of New York City, San Francisco, Los Angeles when I spoke of or thought of anything to do with America. When my dad and my family lived in Pretoria, there was once a comedy and a family television show that showcased a program called Mr. Belvedere. That family lived in Pittsburgh. New York and Pittsburgh were the few North American cities I knew of due to television. I hadn't heard of Philadelphia.

Well, let's just say that I was in for a big surprise! A certain city somewhere in the world had my family and I on its map and agenda for such a pointed time. Philadelphia held my destiny!

When my sister and her boyfriend arrived in Philadelphia that February of 1997, I was still back home, in Malawi. I felt like something had been taken away from my soul once again. They had left a space in my heart of uneasiness. I often wondered when I would be able to see them again. Their presence had become so much part of my household's lifestyle in Lilongwe as well as my whole family life in general! I had gotten so close to my sister especially in the year of 1996.

When they left Malawi, I started having fearful thoughts that it was possible that I may never see them again, especially my sister. I was very anxious each time I thought of America. America was a very far away land. It is not a journey one easily makes haphazardly. It costs so much money to go to America and the whole trip from obtaining a visa, and airfare to acquiring accommodation before arrival, is an emotional roller coaster ride especially if proper reservations haven't been properly set in motion on arrival.

America is huge. A stranger or foreigner can almost feel like an ant on a field of elephants easily trodden and most likely to feel alone and lost far away from their homeland.

There was a time I found out that there were groups of people who I knew way back in my homeland of Malawi who had travelled to America for work or education and had always returned back home after the work project or school course was done.

Then there were ones that I knew of who had travelled to America not for work, or the ones that went to America but didn't hold their citizenship there, that group of travelers didn't come back home to Malawi.

I had no idea then that there was more to the reason why they didn't come back home that was best kept aside from me, at the time. I could blame this discovery on ignorance and or you could call it bliss.

CHANGE IS IMMINENT

Sometimes what you don't know may cause you to feel invincible about things that may look impossible to the ordinary person. That could be a very good thing. Knowing too much can also hinder one with too many factors that can be false and impregnable on paper but very easily doable physically.

Seldom, one just needs the help of ignorance to be able to find out what they are made of to do those things one would not necessary do if they knew what they were up against. It all depends on a personality. Sometimes knowing too much to one, can be the very nemesis standing in one's way to their success and destiny!

In my sister's life and my very own, by 1993, I believe that premature deaths of our beloved father and favorite aunt were a vivid reminder to us to live in the moment and not to be afraid to do what we deem necessary. It had become real that people really die and are gone but not forgotten. To the ones that are dear and close to us, they must be cherished because death is real, and that death is very much part of this journey called life especially when death touches a loved one, first hand.

It was tough living far away from my younger sister when she left for the United States.

Parts of my soul were tied down with my sister's very own soul. I became more aware of this during her absence.

This type of soul tie was a healthy soul tie, because we had shared a lot along the way as we are indeed siblings.

Due to absence, our hearts grew more fond of each other. In our hearts, in our souls, we experienced a deep seated sadness for each other and we became even more closer, although we were thousands of miles apart. We kept closer via telephone calls.

My sister would make phone calls to me at the end of my working hours at my job after bank hours via Commercial Bank of Malawi, City Center Branch in Lilongwe because America was always behind. Malawi is ahead of America by 6 hours in America's summer time.

She was always fond of sharing with me her exciting stories about her new nanny positions every now and again. She would share the details of what she had to do at the job. She was at one time, serving as a live-in nanny and at other times she served as a live-out nanny. I didn't really understand the nature of things in America and how her boyfriend dealt with it while she was gone far away from their apartment to live-in at a job and he was home alone most of each week.

I guess I was still very much chintilentile. That's a chichewa word for backwards. Living in Malawi, for the most part of my life until age 24, I knew that the order of things were that husbands or men worked while women stayed home to fend for their family's household duties. Usually, the ordinary average man and wife live together under the same abode. I had no idea that according to circumstances, a man can at times stay home to fend for the family while a woman worked and can become a breadwinner of the family. I was very much on African traditional timeline.

Meanwhile, the two young lovers were in America, doing and minding their personal issues on American traditional time frame and lifestyle. They were no longer bound to or practicing traditional relationship rules and regulations, I was so accustomed to, in Malawi.

Nevertheless, that didn't solve the void my sister felt living far from home. She still felt a deep sense of loneliness within her. She missed her family, her whole family. She missed me a lot.

When we spoke over the telephone, her stories were very fascinating, exciting but always ended the same way. She had missed everyone she had loved back home. She was yearning to be with her family but returning home was not even an option but keeping on was the only way to go. Keeping on strong in America was very hard for her to do because she also had never been so far away from home either. This was her first time away from home. It was a bold move! But I am so glad she made that move and took it.

It was Destiny in the making, for her and for her extended family.

By the time Valentine's day chimed in, she had signed out of her motherland from Kamuzu international airport together with her beau, who had made things happen for her financially. Her first long trip away from home was a profound one, that seemed to send her off with cheery adios to all the issues that cried of her country with a loud thud.

It was very good that she travelled across the oceans when she was 20 years old and naive. Sometimes being so young makes one feel very invincible. Or else the opposite is a problem. I am glad that she and her boyfriend managed to come to America and withstood enough time together to allow my young family to join her and her beau when we did that December of 1997.

My mind's concept of America in general has always been of grandiosity, prosperity and adventures. I had a hard time comprehending my sister's feelings of loneliness in America. I just couldn't understand her.

How can that be? Everybody wants to go to America to visit if not to live there. What was her problem? I kept asking myself. Yet deeply, I felt compelled to join her someday, if not soon. So that she could no longer feel so lonely. Curiosity begun to run so rampantly deep within me. I couldn't contain or hide the idea of following in her footsteps to that foreign land. Whatever caused her to be sad. I wondered. I just had to find out for myself.

....

There were undeniably many reasons for my wishes to go to a faraway land, anyways to start life afresh somewhere besides home. I longed to keep my sister company as a family member and secretly wished to give my children a great education abroad. I reasoned in my heart that it could all be done. After all, the idea of America got me excited about life altogether, something I hadn't felt in a long time. I began to have hope again in the midst of a dry season of my marital journey.

Clearly by mid of that year, my marital journey had almost deteriorated to the point that my own options of staying in Malawi were dwindling to none. I was very unhappy living life the way it had unfolded.

I was not looking forward to anything besides everyday mundane household and weekly work affairs. I couldn't make it any clearer to my husband that being left behind at home on weekends and seeing him very late at nights during weekdays was no longer ok.

I couldn't be any more obedient to that lifestyle. I had tried with everything I knew within me too, but I was never cut out for that lifestyle. I couldn't fake it anymore. I could not fit in with the majority of housewives I knew in my neighborhood. I was caving in from within me and I just couldn't explain it anymore.

I felt out of place at work. I went into work and I returned home from work really feeling very unsatisfied. I just felt like I didn't belong anywhere. I felt so lost in my own homeland, it just would not make any sense to anyone even if I tried to explain.

I had no spiritual life.

I was a church member at a Biwi Anglican congregation in the nearby neighborhood 30 minutes- walk from Kawale 1 where my family lived. I didn't know that I was a church member who practiced the rituals and routines of church involvement on Sundays, but I had no real relationship or intimacy with God. The One I thought I attended church for.

I did not really celebrate God or maximize Him in powerful substantial ways except simple superficial standardized ceremonies whenever necessary. And at other times, I remembered Him whenever there was a funeral I had attended. I was just going through

the emotions of life but dead in my soul. Now that I look back over my life, I understand why. At that point in time that chapter of my life in my country was closing for a very long season. Everything that was to come was just another step into my future, my Destiny! I know it now.

FRIVOLOUS ISSUES ARE CONNECTED TO YOUR DESTINY

That is why my life got to be a bit uncomfortable to take in when things that shouldn't have been giving me a headache started happening and began to give me a headache from people, things and places I never expected. A series of crazy things were just transpiring all around me that seemed fairly unjust and unexplainable. I couldn't understand much.

There was a hiccup at the place of work earlier before I was an employee at The Commercial Bank of Malawi. I once worked very briefly for KPMG in Lilongwe Old Town. Among the employees, was a guy there, Hastings, who was fascinated by me. I didn't know how deeply until one day out of the blues, a woman married to him wrote me an ink pen letter and left it for the guards there to hand it to me. In the letter she was pleading with me to leave her husband alone. She, out of fear, figured that her husband would leave her because he was very engaging in long talks at his dinner table about this new girl at his job. I believe that I was less than 23 at this time. I will tell you this though, about myself that I have been a little bit catchy to the eyes of a few men along the way. It has never been a big deal to me, so I never make a big deal out of it. But I have caught the eyes of many men out there, without my knowing. My looks are a gift from God not something I revolve my being around consciously.

At that time, I would say that my youthful beauty invoked negativity instead of favour. I had no idea the effect I had on a man without even my doing anything consciously. Am not sure if my own husband had read a letter from my coworker's wife or had

heard about it somehow and he started accusing me of having an affair and had chosen to use the knowledge of my dilemma to his advantage. It was the beginning of his name calling. I have been called every hideous name anybody can fathom!

It just became a vicious circle in my marital affairs. We had a constant situation that nobody could make go away and nobody could go back to any dispute and actually trace back to how, where every animosity had rooted from or why it erupted. Life was simply tastefully chaotic.

We couldn't talk to amend things amicably like most couples do every time there was chaos. We had chaos quite often and we were both often frustrated because we both had raised temperaments which fueled our chaos even more.

When we tried to talk, everything would end in such great confusion each time we tried to patch things over.

Things got to another level of disrespect, dishonor and discomfort so fast. That every day we lived on together, the discomfort grew with each passing day and the gap between us enlarged so much so we gradually became strangers to each other within our home. I was sure we were done. Everything that was unravelling between the two of us loudly and clearly said so.

It didn't take a genius to figure out if he and the men who spent most of their nights after long working hours each day were indeed having affairs or not with the women at the bottle stores since they frequented and preferred to spend their talents and gifts with strange women there than their own wives in their homes. Their escapades there, to these public but very social places filled with women who were professional prostitutes among other things and elsewhere were places for the men to just chill innocently and pass time. But at times to have with the women in motels and hotels the unusual and the forbidden affairs.

The disappearing acts of the men in their homes prompted a lot of women to dread the worst about their men. Not me. I changed my mind on denial. I eventually became bold. I preferred to hold the bull by its horns and I needed to know the truth. I like to feel the waters, surf the waters, ride the rough waves of pain and sometimes get inside those waves of denial and look dead straight

within to see what I could do about whatever I was facing. And then do something outstanding to change the situation if there was something I could do for a better life. Sometimes if there's not a chance to do so, I then look and make a way to create that chance.

I was going to either ride the rough waves or die in them. I was going to ride the fearless waves and float to shore alone if I had to! I was certain he was having an affair. I was no longer sticking around for that. It was time to chart the unfamiliar territory and its waters!

It was not long before I finally got so fed up that on one Saturday night when he didn't come home early enough I just up and decided to pack up some few bags, my two children and my one live-in cousin who always helped us in the house with chores as well as a live-in nanny that we had. And the five of us, left off and we all moved into my grandmother's and mother's house on their compound a few hundred yards away from my husband's family's compound.

THE BOLD STEP
INTO MY DESTINY

This time, I was not even thinking about ever returning to my marriage. The frustration was way too much. I could not see where our lives were headed anymore, the way we lived.

I just *didn't* want to hear or face my husband anymore. I felt awfully betrayed. I felt abused, misused and taken for granted. It was now my time to explore uncharted waters on my own. It was time to go! It was predictable. It was a must. My future depended on it.

My Destiny had been calling all along and I through the eyes of fear and uncertainty couldn't even tell that it was meant to be!

It had to happen.

It was time to run off somewhere, where this type of trouble could no longer find me. Boy was I so wrong living in my own bubble!

I love the spirit of naivety sometimes. With it, one can almost live in a bubble that does not exist except in that person's head. I had no knowledge that this stress free life I had envisioned in my head was far from reality. I hadn't seen anything yet. I was a kid still. But I didn't know that at the time.

In my head, I had believed that it was obvious for everyone around me to see the same exact vision that I had in mind ahead of my new family. I really was expecting my husband to see what I was seeing clearly and collectively. I had no idea that whatever was in front of me obviously would never be able to be seen by another the very same exact way. Not unless the two share the same exact vision or unless the two are one person which would be impossible unless their souls were really tied as one together therefore operating from the common mindset. Even that can be a long shot sometimes. My soul was no longer tied to my husband neatly, so much had contaminated our matrimonial bliss it was no longer us as one but very much two different people on two different agendas and goals in life. In us, in our marriage there were many elephants lurking where there was supposed to be just the two of us.

What I always saw would not always be the same for another to capture, this is also in general with others. I have made peace with that now.

But at that time, I had not matured yet. I had no real in-depth insight to people's behavioral patterns in general let alone their personalities. I don't really think that I cared really so long I got my agenda done. That was the old me. Whew, thank God for deliverance!

Still I had to get my point across in spite of the resistance I received from my spouse. He was not hearing my point on America.

America! What for? What was wrong with Lilongwe, Malawi? I thought I could change my husband once I married him. Sometimes youth comes along with it, a list of ridiculous expectations for, and from others. I was really stupid, immature and naive about people's personalities and what makes them become whatever they become along the way, altogether. I was in for a ride of my life. And each time the issue at hand came to the table for more discussions, he was always putting up a fight. When I finally had succeeded

in sharing with him and showing him my vision, I also diligently expected him to see my vision and run alongside of me with it. The obvious was spit out. Flat out rejection.

He didn't jump for joy, he didn't desire to fathom it or capture it. He didn't embrace it either for himself or for us. Instead, he for many days rejected it and worse off, he, himself had no vision or plans for his own life or where he wanted his young family to head to. It is one of the most frustrating moments in life when a person wants to lead but they themselves have no idea on how to lead others who fall under them. It can throw many people off. It sure did throw me off our marital wagon. Everything begun to seem like a big messy trap. I felt no wrong when I got of that trap the very first time.

The only things that I was certain of at the time when I left him for the first time ever, were a few things that I had maintained. Some of them were my monthly income from my two year employment at The Commercial Bank of Malawi, our two toddler children; Marvel and Avedi and my family from my grandmother's compound nearby.

To my surprise, I thought that I had left my grandmother's and mother's compound for good when I did in 1994. Yet there I was again in 1997. Home sweet Home. My presence there wasn't for a visit or for a vacation. Believe it when I say that my return there was just as uncomfortable as my mother's daily nagging about everything. Dare I forget to mention that my mother expected me to fend for everyone I had brought plus some and pay for my monthly abode and responsibilities in her home whilst I was there until my husband came back to pick me up and his children. It did make sense.

What everyone else around me was thinking at that time was that I would go back to my husband. What they didn't understand was that I was not going back. If I went back, it would mean that I would not be able to plan and prepare for America. So, I knew it in my heart like I know my name today that I was not going back to his compound and he in return didn't come for me or the children. At least for a while. I had left my husband's premises, and that was final. In my heart, I was already charged up for America.

I knew it in my mind that I was headed for America. I knew it like I know my name today, that I was supposed to be in America.

I had no money yet for the airfare nor for the visitor's visa. In my mind America was already a done deal no matter what things looked like at the time. I only thought of America for myself and for my children.

I was going to leave my husband behind and I was alright to come with my children only. My two children were the very reason I was coming to America anyways. I was determined to give them a better life.

My mother tried to talk me into leaving them with her but that was never in my plans or will. Looking back twenty years later now, my children have done much better than I had envisioned. They are not perfect but I am glad I stood up for my ambitions, desires, dreams and plans for them. My mother meant well but I couldn't make it here without my children like she was suggesting to make life easy for me, since I had no idea what to expect here if I arrived with them.

Life at my mother's house while I was waiting to come to America after the first separation from my husband was great on the outside except I was deeply depressed within me. I am good at putting on a great front to everyone around me. There was no denying the obvious longing and anguish that I felt inside. I had missed my husband so much, but he never came for me in the first month and I was sure that he would never come for me as time progressed.

Whenever he wanted to see his children, he asked my cousin or the kids' nanny to bring them over to his parents' compound a few hundred yards away from where my grandmother's compound stood, to see them and spend some quality time with them.

This went on for a month. He got so free with his time even more and his new and found independence propelled him to go all out partying with his buddies late at night clubs, and way outside the perimeters of a supposedly disciplined married man. I began to hear worse rumors of him and his buddies fooling around even more with other women in my absence as time progressed.

A WOMAN SCORNED

D ue to my rebellious nature at that time in my life, I didn't know any better. I had a meeting with my 24 year old self, fully fledged in hormonal outrage and madness and went full force in revenge mode. I didn't know it then but looking back now, I came to understand that I lacked any type of wisdom especially the one that's necessary for marital bliss. I had no respect or principles for my marriage. Whatever dose of it I had was very perverted. I went into my marriage with no idea what I was getting myself into. And when life got rough, I was very sure that I was done with my marriage from that one single episode. That was just a piece of a cake compared to real life's trials everywhere else.

Within myself, I felt done. As a matter of fact, I was very sure that my marriage was over and done with. I turned around and did the unspeakable. The outrageous!

I became the unfaithful adulterous wife I would read about for the very first time in my own life. This was something I never thought that I was capable of doing when it came to the way I had loved this man. I had finally become the ugly things he would call me in our previous heated arguments. I had done a deed that would forever change my life and the way this man saw me.

I didn't understand this man before I committed adultery as years before us unraveled together. I still didn't understand him after the adultery. Many years down the lane, I still don't understand him in our lives altogether.

I am now convinced that he himself doesn't understand himself.

I am pretty sure that he didn't know what he had then in me as his wife even before the adultery took place because he still treated me with the same malice after the adultery. I just haven't quite understood him at all. It had been quite a waste of time to explain my plea to him all along about my nonmarital adventure that fateful day in 1997. All I wanted to do was to stress to him on how much his neglect of me made me feel time after time. I just didn't know what else to do to numb the pain, loneliness and regret that I felt so deep inside of me.

....

Yes, I have never denied that I had committed adultery on that sad day nor will I ever deny committing adultery because there's no point in lying and denying what really took place on the day I cheated on my husband for the first time in our marriage. It was something dark and impulsive I had done during one miserable Saturday at Salima beach lakeside.

It was something I did in my past that I will never be proud of. Ever! Keep in mind that I no longer entertain denial. But at that time in my young mind, I was doing the only thing I thought would help me in a sad and twisted way.

To my defense, it was all in retaliation. This was my carnal solution to appease my nervous system and my justification to the way my husband had been treating me. I chose to do something about it and I had resorted to this one horrible, one-time sexual fling with a tobacco tycoon's son at the beaches of Salima district of Malawi, about 120 kilometres away and 1 hour and 40 minutes ride from Lilongwe. It all happened in the third year of our marital frenzy.

Am I proud of it? Never. This was a part of me that came out of me when wisdom and intellect went into hibernation. At that moment, consequences were an afterthought. I was only thinking about me, myself and I. Most importantly, I was focused on my means to an end. America was on my mind!

THE ADULTERY

I had met this son of a tobacco tycoon at customer services in the bank where I was working as a customer services representative. He was the first multi-millionaire I would ever meet in my life, by 1997 and in a very long time to come.

I knew so because I had handled and updated some of his father's tobacco estate and his own personal savings accounts there at the bank as a customer service banking clerk.

My eyes were focused on the airfare to America. I was going to sleep my way to America. Sad to say. I had no other way and that was the only way at that time. Besides, my husband Keneilwe,

the carefree guy didn't want to leave Malawi for any reason. I had to think with my head not my heart. Shallow hey?

Please don't judge me.

Desperate times usually call for desperate measures. Back then, I was a desperate, neglected young wife who was always in distress. Age does really matter, believe me, I know that now. Big time!

The era of early 20s in my life brought to the surface things in me I had no idea were within me. I didn't like that side of me, at all. I still don't like that side of me even to this day! If I didn't ask for God's Grace to keep me on the right path, on a daily basis, I don't want to think of what I am capable of doing negatively. It's a dysfunctional side. With God, it's easier for me to tame it. I am normally a thinker and I analyze a lot before I jump into anything. But that particular event and treacherous adventure, I did not properly think out before acting on my thoughts and my actions were definitely a cry for attention in a very negative way. It backfired.

I mean, are you surprised? My husband though, was not with it then. He has not been with it over the many years that followed. I don't think that he will ever understand how much I needed him in our first years of marriage as his wife or every day of our marriage. Like water to fish!

For the first time in my life, I came to know and face consequences all at once. I felt very lonely. Consequences are very real and usually in many people's actions only an afterthought. In many ways, it is not a fun thing to go through. For me, consequences have been an inescapable, silent, but a relentless nagging pain.

I obviously had no idea of what kind of consequences I had brought upon my household or my marriage immediately after the sexual event had happened. The action itself was tormenting on me. Even bigger to what it did to my whole relationship in the years to come.

I was often in distress. This time I was really, deeply sad. One of the major problems within me was an identity crisis that I had as a person. I had no idea of who I was first and foremost by myself as a being. I had no idea of what my actions would result into for the decisions I had chosen to take for myself as a person outside

my marriage yet during my marriage. I didn't understand what I had done in relation to others that looked up to me. I had no idea of what I had done to my children on a spiritual level by my adulterous act or the real meaning of who I really was to them as their mother. Or better yet, what else I was creating in this man about me since he had already blacklisted me to others as a horrible unworthy woman by audible horrendous names only fit for a she-dog.

Whatever little trust or respect he may have had left for me at that point in time, as a wife or a mother to his kids went out of the window! Gone.

I deserved it. I felt qualified for every creative horrible names he had cooked up for me. I just accepted whatever I thought that I had earned.

Being so young and foolish, I only focused on scoring points whenever somebody hurt me. I had no idea that this one act would have a terrible ripple effect many years later. I had no idea that, I would spend the rest of my life hearing what a whore I was in the least expected ways or places by someone who chose to stay with me anyhow, although he should have walked away that same night he had discovered all the ugly things about me. The day that he thought of me as unworthy of his affection, love and respect. He had every reason to walk away that night and yet he stayed. But for whom?

Why? Was it really for his children? Our children! Or for me to pay in relentless tears.

It is absolutely baffling when I look back over my life sometimes because whatever causes us to be with people who we think we should be with, when we don't self-examine and reexamine our hearts for the reasons we stay, we can end up causing more damage to those people if we stay put. Which simultaneously ends up hurting everyone concerned if we are not careful. That is usually what happens if the motives are derived from foolishness, self- centeredness, immediate gratification and selfishness with no wisdom whatsoever or a genuine concern for another being!

Along the years, I have come to an understanding and observation that women when it comes to matters of the heart, we deal

with a lot of abuse inflicted by men or those of the opposite sex that confess to love us deeply. For most abused women, sadly some women have kept a costly silence that has led them to their early grave with horrendous stories untold loaded with painful situations inflicted upon them, at the expense of those they thought loved them.

Oftentimes, an abused woman does not see themselves powerful in any way to begin with to rescue themselves out of an abusive bondage.

But the moment a woman seeks refuge in the wrong places by doing the very same evil deed the men do effortlessly to prove something to themselves or others, the repercussions are heavy and costly. The very act of a woman's retaliation becomes a problem and a cause for her to become a laughingstock to her society, community or among her inner cycle, instantly.

The woman in question becomes an abomination unto everybody who renders themselves perfect in their own eyes.

She becomes the notoriety in that township. The unworthy of the slimes. What a hypocritically correct world we live in?!

It is safe to say therefore in my opinion that we have indeed made our societies crazy and contorted about the principles of living this so-called life of integrity with a proper and yet sound principles for all gender, race or entity on how anybody ought to treat another.

It is as if nothing and nobody matters anymore! Don't women count too? It is what it is. Life goes on! I guess. That's the new and favorable confession these days, out there.

What people forget in general is the fact that if a person stays human long enough, as with a sound consciousness, sooner or later, they will come to their senses. That is exactly what took place in my own life. I came to myself immediately after doing the nasty deed.

I returned home feeling remorseful and very dirty immediately and wanted to wash away my sins or whatever was going on in my soul with one hot bath. How stupid was that?! How lame can that be? How childish I felt?!

I was so naive. 24 was quite a number in my lifetime! Nothing I knew at that point could take away the misery I felt from that point on.

And on the day after the shagging, it was as if I had posted a telepathic note on my forehead saying, "I have just finished sleeping with a guy who is not my husband" directed and shot at Keneilwe wherever he was at the time of my Salima beach sexual encounter. It was as if he had seen from afar, which would be the reason why he had immediately raced to my grandmother's and mother's house that evening, which had become my new home. Ugh.

The reality had sunk in. I had become an adulteress!

Hardly an hour after my arrival from that unforgettable sexual escapade. I was just about to get out of the trifling shower, before I was taken in shock due to hearing my husband's voice coming from my grandmother's and mother's kitchen looking for me with anxiety. The way a mother hen acts out when she cannot locate all her chicks. He had finally showed up for me. After how long? A bit over a month. After what seemed like forever! And he seemed frantic. What happened to him? I still wonder to this day!

He had finally come over to plead with me to go back home to him. What? Why?

Dear Lord! If only he had come a day sooner, I thought in my mind. I wouldn't be lost in this mental abyss between my two ears and deeply down my heart.

It truly was as if he had received this telepathic memo without even recognising it at the very same time the infidelity deed had happened. What had registered within him at the time of my sexual shenanigans had obviously pierced his consciousness to the core of surging him to the door of the house where I was, right there and then. He in actual fact though, was oblivious to the real prompting of his urgent need to finding me. It was not just a nudge. It was not a coincidence. It was a soul tie. So, there were remnants to a soul tie after all the commotion in our marriage and his late nights habits when we lived together? Yes. Who was I kidding?

In many ways our souls were still tied to each other although there was still so much noise coming from the other soul ties we had not severed from previous relationships as well as from

ongoing extra marital affairs. Our marriage was crowded by invisible past and present intruders. The noises from them caused our intellect and discernment to fail in gauging any true incentives or whatever was left to gauge to see if there was any love left for each other anymore.

The soul tie was as strong as his vivid intuition. These things in him were the elements that drove him to my door.

It was so sad to see. This was supposed to be a joyous moment. A needed reunion after a month of longing for each other. It was filled with so much excitement but fear within me at the same time.

I had spent many sleepless nights prior to my escapade. Each night that passed by, I had hoped that it would be the night he would come back to me. When he finally came back for me, it was too late. A tarnished dream.

Yet, my heart felt happy to see him, but my mind was conflicted. It was filled with uncertainties and a heaviness about it.

I felt so convicted. I knew it then that from that day onwards things about him and I will never be the same again. I had so many mixed feelings going through my head.

I was confused and torn to his sudden urge to taking me back. In my heart, I was amiss. He had come back to find me a day too late. The timing was off. Life was beginning to get very emotional for me.

My dirty crimson stains declared out loudly my secret state of mind in despair. The clips of me crying and sobbing relentlessly in the car, all the way back home from the afternoon of the sexual one day affair continuously repeated themselves in my head over and over again that night and for the rest of the week.

Even today as I express candidly about that event, the clips go through my mind all over again. I feel sorry for that young confused wife who had no idea on how to navigate through the issues of life when the going got tough. All she knew then was to hide away and cry like a kid in private for her failures. Defeat was a constant word to reckon with.

I knew then that every bad habit or deed has consequences. This one bad action on my part had costly painful consequences,

all due to one day's secret rendezvous with a man I had met openly at my work of employment customer services in public and ended up meeting in secret at a beach hotel far away from home in a non-marital setting, in an unsuspecting bungalow.

A shame, I had become!

I had brought it upon myself all because I didn't know that I had traded my loneliness for that which was worse than loneliness itself.

Shame was defeating. Shame was very uncomfortable. It made me feel less of myself. It made me feel unworthy and very deserving of anything sad and negative that was around me. I had become less of value to myself and worse off to the one man who knew that I was indeed, already so worthless.

And I know that someone out there may say hush to my anxieties on this issue of adultery. Yes, I am aware that people do it all the time and there is nothing new under the sun about adultery issues. Unfortunately, the path I had chosen to take by reacting the way I did caused me great duress. There were many things I could have chosen to do to show distress in my marriage. The worst choice I opted in my actions was the very thing someone chose to believe about me, regardless.

It was wrong of me to retaliate by means of adultery. A thousand times wrong! This was no way, the best way in any case to reason with my abandonment issues or rejection issues I experienced at his hands.

Everything evil that is done in secret always has repercussions and consequences out loudly in public. Some consequences do not even take a long time to manifest themselves in one's life and may not always show out loudly to all others, but they are happening, secretively they are happening.

Some are just a constant nagging, terrible and silent brewing pain that one goes through alone in private. Other consequences are loud and very painful involving the doer of that horrible act and the relations of that perpetrator who committed a negative action. At other times the relations of the ones at the receiving end of the negative action suffer the consequences even in their innocent standing but just because they are connected to the one who

they see suffer or have seen suffering. Usually in life, actions have a ripple effect in most cases.

Chances all the time are that something innocent and free of guilt should not feel negative or uncomfortable when doing it or after doing it.

If it were a good thing when performing it why did it feel uneasy? I knew in my heart that the choice of my actions to retaliate for the pain that I felt in my heart towards my husband was shallow and not justified by what I had decided to do about it. It does not take two wrongs to make anything right.

In fact, two wrongs qualify the matter to dissolve into frustrated nothingness once done.

With the measure of my actions, I had become just as bad as my husband who had always left me behind and unattended to, in contrast to the expectations of a dutiful husband. I had nothing tangible to hold on to my marriage and did not have anything steady to stand on, to build our relationship up again.

It came to two wrong people trying to lead each other to the correct path of everything that builds a positive, strong tangible, faithful and honorable union while we were both sick with wounded souls and an emptiness in our hearts. We both operated from wounded hearts.

We were two blind fools in our hardheads who were confused about what it meant to yearn for true love and how to get it by practicing functional ways to gain it for the sake of sustaining whatever was left for the marriage altogether and for our future together.

My marital life with my husband from that time on would be nothing but a mess filled with each person trying to run a race within the marriage against each other and confuse every innocent being that was a product of that matrimony.

A complete opposite to the meaning of wedding vows that promise protection and the meaning of forever!

So then, this man was supposed to be mine forever but had allowed abandonment to come between us for a season. During that season, he did as he pleased elsewhere. And just like that, in one night, he was right there in my face wanting to have me back

in full throttle. Suddenly, he was ready to go to America with me. What?!

I couldn't believe my ears! This wasn't happening the way it should have been in the first place! According to me, he and I were not supposed to be separated in the first place. He was not supposed to have been abandoning me from the day we got married. He was supposed to love me, cherish me until the day death do us part. I, in return respect him and help him become all that he could become as a man and husband till dust to dust. We would live happily ever after! That was my fantasy. That was my wish. Oh, but if wishes were horses! Then I would ride my life into bliss forever.

Everything that I ever wanted to do in my life, had him in mind. America was my deep seated, desire. He was in that trip and desire too. There was nothing I wanted to do on earth that didn't have him in it. I had unborn kids in me that I secretly knew belonged to him from way back in our early days together when we first met in April of 1992. Everything that had the word better in it for us had a touch of his DNA in it. How could he not see that, at all?!

Never in a million years did I ever think that on one sad day, everything that I had imagined, would be lost and life would not be the same ever again! Simply because I had lost hope in my marriage, spouse, and in myself. And had resorted to adultery while in distress. Right there, I realised that in life one person or one action can change the entire cause of one's life and destiny!

Why couldn't we just have agreed to come to America without all the drama and dilemma in between to begin with? I often wonder.

This new person in me, due to my choice of actions, changed my life's entire attitude and the way I felt about people in general and many things in life.

I was not the same woman anymore. What I had gone through, at his expense had changed me internally, forever! What I had done by my own actions had immensely affected me psychologically and physically forever! I had slept with some man who was also confused about his own young marital life. What a mess! How can the blind lead the blind? To make matters worse, he had

a funky last name with a twist to it. His name literally meant sex me up in chichewa, my native language. I kid you not! What are the chances?

That the man I had decided to cheat on my husband with was "do me" for his surname. Simply pronounced Mkwate.

On the other hand, I had just upgraded myself by picking up another reason to get butchered verbally by my spouse even more. Why did I tell my husband the details of the man I had just cheated on him with? Why?

My personal abuser did so for the many years to come after my confession.

Who is to blame? I say. Myself. No matter what, I should have never confessed everything in detail to my husband that night. It all backfired and once again, I paid the consequences for a very long time to come. Ladies, in short, cross your legs and keep life moving! Life simplified. My partner in that criminal act of adultery was not a Mr. Panadol, or a Mr. Jameson, a Mr. Sharps, or a Mr. Frostbite perhaps. But he was a Mr. "Do-me". My choice was hilariously convicting. If you speak my language you can understand the severity of that word and meaning in this whole shameful act. Sadly prophetic. Ugh!

Did he do me to my own destruction or what? Yes, he did.

It only took one man to change the way I had seen myself as a woman. I don't blame Mr. Do-me. I blame myself. It was I who opened up that door instead of shutting down when he beckoned. What I know now, I wish I knew then.

This young man on his end must have thought that I was one crazy awkward woman he had slept with on that damned day, probably the strangest encounter in his entire life!

The sexual encounter took place in one of the bungalows of Salima's beaches. The surroundings were like paradise whence it was one of the most beautiful beaches of Africa! The actual shenanigans were some of the most awkward, clumsy events in my life, I am ashamed to admit. I honestly didn't expect it nor prepared myself emotionally for it. The sex was a disaster. It wasn't meant to be! I understand that better many years later. He had sex on his mind and I had a casual get to know each other getaway on mine.

Being a woman isn't always easy on the streets out there. Especially if you are a lost woman like I was.

Obviously, I was very new to what casual sexual partners do out there.

That is the reason why the ride back home to Lilongwe after that escapade was a nightmare. It was filled with silent sobs of regret and self- loathing. Mr. Do-me had on several occasions during the ride tried to calm me down but nothing worked. It was a sad mess.

I know without a doubt that he was shocked to see the two people in me that day. He had met the inner childlike representative who felt wounded and sorrowful after the sexual act. And then the other young adult wanting to exhale, who managed to go away with a stranger! What a mess! I had never felt so cheap and so confused about my actions all in one event.

For what? Instead of anything positive, I had gained regret, shame, guilt, misery, and another unhealthy soul tie. More unhealthy soul ties and a low self-esteem, that's what! I had begun to live in a complex world.

Was America worth all this nasty business and my whirlwind of this new lifestyle?

I don't think that I was even anywhere near making any sense of what was happening in my life at that time. It seemed as if all my dreams and wishes came to a halt altogether.

I wanted to come to America but at what cost? I asked myself. I had just sold my soul to a married man. Mr. Do-Me!

We were both married and obviously miserable. Therefore, we shouldn't have been together to begin with. We had no business being there. It was broad daylight adultery! It was dangerous on a deeper spiritual level and we were both handling it with immaturity and disrespect for what we both once believed in and vowed to. No sense of honor or faithfulness to the ones we were supposed to be with. What about the innocent children we both had brought forth in our individual homes from the marital vows we had previously voluntarily entered in? It was a nightmare! I had to bring my American plans to a halt. Because I had lost a sense of integrity,

identity and priority. All the meaningful principles to life at that moment to what I had come to know had become contorted.

There was a noticeable pause in my plans for America because what else was I going to sacrifice for it before it costed me everything else? I had to gather myself. I had resorted to taking a shortcut to a means by consciously picking up a relationship of a day's length that had started off as an obvious set up to a failure from the start, that found refuge in a short, misguided escapade to what seemed like an endless era of sadness and loneliness. A sexual meeting and nothing else meaningful! A fall into a much deeper but bigger void! Whether it was one to continue, by occurring from time to time, or just another empty, sadly random, but sporadic happening. Nothing good was going to come out of it, only severely broken hearts. Just a bunch of nothingness. Meshuga!

What was becoming of me? I was not the person I had hoped to be anymore. As much as I was obsessed with the idea of collecting funds for the airfare to America for me and my two children, oh no, not like this. Not by giving up everything good I knew of myself. A thousand times no.

It was so shallow of me to prostitute myself for an ambition that was self-involving, self-centered and no proper wisdom or insight to go along with it. After that sexual episode, I was more sorrowful about meeting this guy altogether and every motive behind it in regards to going to America.

I thought of myself as a cheap and dirty, worthless woman! Maybe my husband was right about me, after all. That was the sad conviction I resorted to. What had I become?

If not careful in life, an individual is most likely to act upon every enemy's pronounced accusations of them if the words are given ground in that individual's life. I had begun to believe most of the negative things my husband had proclaimed over me in our marriage over some time. I had developed feelings of unworthiness.

Call me weak, but truly spoken words over another or to self, have power to turn things against or turn things in favor of whoever receives them. I for many years, believed every negative word that he had spoken over me.

To add salt to injury, I really felt like a prostitute when the man I had sex with, that night as we parted ways, gave me about 15 thousand of Malawian kwachas, an equivalent of $880.00 by year 1997, "for your trouble," he called it. He kindly put it before he sped off after dropping me off. Ugh!

I never felt so low about my esteem. I guess it would be the crescendo of how I saw myself through the eyes of men. I had spiritually, emotionally and physically demoted myself from an averaged working mother to a prostitute momentarily, on her way to America.

Was America really worth this? It was horrible! I understood on that day, two things about life in general.

The love of money by a human being. And the scale of judgement passed on male and female to a committed crime by society.

Yes, the first lesson was that the drive behind the love of money is truly the root of all evil. I saw this man only as a money pot and my only way out of my homeland.

He was going to be my ticket to America. I didn't see any other way out of my country financially at the time. I literally saw him as a person who held my way out in his hands. I also didn't see myself as a human being who deserved any better, or this guy and I would never have arranged to meet in the first place. We were not even proper friends to begin with.

Normal friends take time to get to know each other as people before even becoming lovers for sex or what not. In this relationship, the sex was on a first time and last time basis. Bottom line, we had no business being together. Period.

The worst thing ever was that I had not counted the cost either on my behalf nor did I fathom the intense guilty consciousness that would plague me throughout most of my married years to Keneilwe. I went with the wind and thought of my whereabouts and actions afterwards when it was too late. Oh boy, how I have paid.

The other lesson I learned at that moment in time in 1997 was that a man can sleep with a woman and not be moved while a woman can sleep with a man, commit the exact dirty act as a man did but feel horrendous for the rest of her life. And the judgement

passed on that woman if and when found out is more severe than the one a man has to endure.

I just wish that I didn't have to go through these harsh lessons in life for me to get to know what I must know to elevate in life for the next level. For a very long time, it had felt yucky to be me. The story of my life.

Nothing else could that man ever do to me after our sexual encounter together make matters worse. I was a mess and when my husband that night pressed to know if I had sex, the foolish representative in me repented it all. With the hopes of mending it all. Meaning that all that was wrong by that time, in our home, would be mended and a reset button would be pressed in motion on zero for another chance at marriage. What a very stupid move on my part. What a bad idea!

This was actually one of the first recognizable and memorable schemes I discovered about my husband's other side. It was a manipulative side to him that became super loud as the years progressed. I hate that side of him. It oftentimes, backfires too.

Not everyone in life is able to handle the truth! That is a fact. Unless one is repenting to a nun or a monk in a convent, monastery, who has no feelings attached to the person confessing the sin or the issue at hand for the confession. Please ladies, use wisdom! If and when caught for the purposes of probable reconciliation. Use caution! Don't you do it! I beseech you, my sisters! Some men take everything they know about you and use it against you at the most unexpected times in the most unforgivable ways. Think. I didn't.

I have lived to regret it to this day!

What would have happened had I refused and denied everything evil that I did on that day? I have often wondered. Would we be happily married and live harmoniously ever after? Or would I live to suffer alone, inwardly and silently in the darkness of my acts? I would never know. We will never know.

What's done is done!

You see a man's ego is hard to come around once bruised by the presence of another man in the picture, sexually and intimately. But this is a story for another time in another book. One thing for sure is that real men do not do well sharing a woman or knowing

who has slept with their belle or is still sleeping with her on the side.

Obviously, I was super naive and clueless. If I could take back time, that sexual endeavor would have never been exploited by me, altogether.

Therefore, there would be no explaining to do on the day my husband was reading through me, like he did that very night of the adultery. Like a kid I just kept spilling out the beans as if I were a robot. It goes to show that not all females can handle adultery or the after effects of it. I was so stupid. Utterly foolish. We live and learn.

Which means that the only trouble that evening would have been for me to convince my man to come to America with me and our children. And why we needed to do so at that very moment in time. It would have been very easy and simple to do! But this is not how all life's stories go. I didn't have a fairy tale moment or ending. Sigh.

As plainly discovered, he at his own time, came to himself and had a change of heart. He was going to join his children and I to America, after all.

America was no longer an option but the only way to go! Nobody was going to stop us now.

I could be wrong too about coming here when it comes to him. He has never been happy, I mean really happy about living here. It has been 20 years now. Nothing has changed. I just don't know anymore. I am blowing air out of my mouth if you can imagine it.

Everything negative that had transpired in our marriage I strongly feel, from the beginning up until that adultery moment was ironically the very propelling force that led us to the United States. At least for me that's my theory. It was what I needed. I needed to come here to America to start life all over again. On a clean slate. I needed to come to America because it was my escape, my destiny and family's too although everything seemed as though it was against us coming here, at the time.

Wait a minute, is there such a thing as a clean slate in a grown person's life who has prolonging and lingering emotional baggage?

Especially if consequences were screaming out loudly from everywhere.

One of the consequences that the adulterous affair did to me was the fact that I eventually developed a phobia of going to my job before we left Malawi. I had nightmares of the tobacco farmer's son walking into the bank again and again playing in my head after the sexual act and seeing myself having to pass out each time he showed up. I did not want to face him after I had seen him naked and gone to bed with him in an unconventional setting and knowing everything that had transpired.

In regard to him, after that episode, I don't know what he felt about me or our one day sexual affair. Frankly speaking, I preferred to erase the entire event from my mind, altogether.

I had suffered anxiety by each day I went to work. I just wanted out of Malawi, so fast.

UNRESOLVED ISSUES LINGER

On the other hand, there was hope and good news, finally! Hubby was going to come with us as a family. I suspected that he was afraid to lose his children. It was not as if we had set a return date in motion once I intended to leave with them. The journey was indefinite. Then I also believed that he wanted to come just to make sure that I was not going to sleep around with any man like I did before. Never mind his women shenanigans. I guess my feelings don't count. You must know that, I have on purpose left out his detailed women shenanigans because it would be very stupid of me to be with him and continuously taunt him on his dark side. If I dwell with him then it is pointless to revive what I have chosen to bury! I wished he saw the same in me.

What a huge mistake for any man to make once they have decided to go with their woman especially if they themselves do not know who they really are in a time of turmoil! And what they want out of their own life and those people around them during those situations when they rise. We made decisions impulsively to come together with our children, while he was secretly still holding

onto my ugly past. He never counted the cost to his emotions or final decisions to join us. He only saw what was around and didn't consider everything on a broader horizon. What I had eventually concluded was that he was not ready to travel far away from home first and foremost. He grew up in his parents' compound and he had been in many parts of Malawi but never wished to go elsewhere outside Malawi although nothing had stopped him. He was not ready to have a functional relationship with me because of the way I was made to join him as man and wife. It was a marriage of obligation. I was pregnant with our daughter by end of 1993 after my father and his mother had passed on into eternity in February and April of 1993 consecutively.

We were both individually grieving influential people in our lives. We had that in common. We were both broken and really seeking certain consolation in those that could relate to us. We both understood that deep pain and we were right there for the moment to share our anguish. We both fit but maybe it was meant to be a seasonal relationship instead of a twenty-five year journey only brought forward by circumstances. Or else why has the relationship been super hard to salvage after all the years? It is puzzling. Why so much unrest, and dysfunction for so long?

My husband was by far not ready to experience responsibilities through fatherhood and family life far away from home either. He was not ready to abandon his younger siblings who had depended on him and really looked up to him since he was an adult. Which is part of the reason why he never cleaved fully to me as his wife and family. It was a defensive mechanism effort on his conscience decision because cleaving fully would mean that he would have to give up on his younger siblings who were half orphaned by the loss of their strong leader, their mother. Their mother was the one who did everything for their whole family before she was taken into glory in April of 1993.

I understood that part but his resistance to cleave caused so much hardship in our own young family life because it meant that I had half a husband who was half invested into our marriage.

There were many outside issues that contributed negatively to the whole relationship balance in the marriage too. This, was due to

my mother's higher expectations of me to help out with my family where I came from as an older sibling according to our culture and the same was expected of my husband from his side of the family and siblings culturally. So, when it came to the two of us as man and wife, immaturity and ignorance of the fundamentals of marriage caused us to fail each other time after time.

Therefore, we both were very frustrated every other day because we didn't have each other's back wholly. Then to think of being so far away from home if we migrated to America, would mean that we would have to give up on everything and everyone safe and familiar we knew in our Lilongwe environment. This was what raised many individual internal fears within us. We had no idea of foreign rules and regulations mainly when we thought of our constant bouts of turmoil against each other and the unpredictability of our relationship as a whole. We were both terrified, more him, that I was to go and live in a foreign land with countless strict rules and regulations unknown to us at the time. We knew that such a country as America would probably hold tough rules for foreigners to adhere to.

Sadly, my husband was in no way ahead of our marital issues. I on the other hand thought that we were over our problems by moving away. Off course I was in love, stupid and naive. He on the other hand was bitter and prideful. He had not fully forgiven me yet. He never looked at himself as the reason why I slept with someone else whilst married to him out of frustrations and exhaustion from feeling like I was in the marriage alone.

Adultery is not a simple sin I reckon that. And it is something that has ended marriages for good for centuries and I am by no means taking of it lightly but come on now! Life must carry on! I had chosen openly to share the struggle with him. Yet, I was still in the dark about his shenanigans simply because I wasn't in any position to catch him. He had the privilege to disappear and go far away, come back home and deny everything! Where is justice in this world when the log is in someone's eye?

He for some reason, failed to realize that he was often gone for no reason and I always felt second best. He failed to study me as his wife to know that I was no longer on the timeline of

Malawian lifestyle like I had been for a few years in the past when I chose him over my family. I had abandoned whatever little comfort I knew in my life to join him as my spouse, wholeheartedly in his humble abode. I cleaved to him and started to live with him whilst he was not whole himself because I found him drunk and I felt that my love alone could change him from any path of destruction he was on. I had faith in him, in us, that the future would be bright so long as we were together. I believed that we could come out great in whatever state we were living in no matter what side of the world we would live in. That's how much I loved him. He didn't know how much faith I had in us and he still doesn't know to this day, whoa, sad to say.

Before our arrival in America, he had finally moved in from our little place in his parents' compound and joined us at the place where my grandmother's and mother's house was on their compound. I meant it when I said that I was not going back to his compound.

I would be trapped there and forfeit my American destiny. America was patiently waiting for me. I would leave for America from my elder's compound. That's where we all moved in. For a moment as we started preparing to sell stuff for airfare to America, my marital life seemed good. I noticed that from time to time though, he would ask me questions about how having sex with another guy, besides him felt like. I knew right there that no matter what, I would never be able to shake off the other guy "the elephant in the room" in our marital intimacy. Soul ties and meandering elephants would be, an every other day kind of thing. I wasn't pleased to know that the elephant of the jungles of Africa would never leave my marital bedroom issues in regard to his ways of thinking!

Ladies, use wisdom. I hadn't! Throwing my hands up right now! Sigh!

It was a crowded love affair, no matter how much I thought that the other guy was over, and long gone with, dead and buried, out of sight, out of mind for life. Who was I kidding? My life with this man that I dearly loved more than anything on planet earth was on regurgitation.

As a matter of fact, it was obvious that the other guy was very much alive in our marriage. I found out the hard way clearly when

we arrived in Philadelphia. We left Malawi to bury all of our trials and tribulations to start marital bliss on a different time zone, in a faraway land a few oceans away.

Right, that was what I thought!

Lo and behold every problem that welcomed us in Philadelphia was nothing new. It was a different environment indeed but the mindset of people in the new place was very much the same, unchanged. It turned out that everything that came at us, according to my husband, it was my fault. The horrendous names I thought I would never hear again associated with me as a mother of his precious children he claims to love became the norm in our household.

Bitch, whore! Just to name a few.

I got blamed for bringing him here without correct information on how the country treats people like us who were immigrants at that time without any legal papers to work in the country. Mind you, he was 30 years of age and intact in his intellect when he kissed American soil, hello!

Like I have said, it was the blind leading the blind. I, being such a constant inhabitant of the fantasy world from time to time, brought my family to America on merit and evidence derived from watching American movies. Call me meshuga! I can take it!

BLAME IT ON THE MOVIES

In the movies there is no such thing as a work permit or a green card for a foreigner alright unless one is watching The Green Card movie. I had no idea that part of life is a necessary reality in America, big time! And remember this that the people who were already here in America from other countries who are immigrants don't dare to tell their loved ones the details lest the family members won't believe them.

Usually family members have a way of saying such things as, "Please who is she kidding? This is only her evil way of saying no. She is trying to put us off about trying to catch up with her. Oh, she doesn't want you to be as successful as she is!" Geesh.

So why even bother to shed a light on the immigration issues of America with family members abroad over telephone calls?! Instead, people let their extended family members to witness these difficulties first hand, when they land on American soil. Besides, family members do not celebrate negative information on what they really wish for so well. Everybody I have come to know outside America, in my life, wishes to come to America to visit or to experience their journey somehow here. It's America, is there such another country on planet Earth? Well, nobody tells their family members over the telephone about social security numbers on a card or a work permit or how to get it when you get to America. You pretty much learn about everything once you get here and normally when someone asks for it from you. It has been my experience. A bombshell that's what!

The subject is off limits. Why even bother. Most relatives aren't even interested. Their interest is big on obtaining a visa to America. It usually ends there. Then they get over the oceans. Wham! They begin to understand. Surprise! You almost wanna scream out just to cheer up the mood whenever the epiphany takes place. Seriously. After all the plans and dreaming that took place, it's very easy to feel discouraged and see your balloon diminish itself right there and then. I want to say, brace yourself. You haven't seen nothing yet!

There are a number of misconceptions when communicating over the telephone with loved ones that, when they do get the visitor's visa, they will get into the country and start working right away. Wrong!

I had no idea to ask why my sister, Abiti Bula had opted to be a nanny over a sales representative in any shop in America, every time she telephoned me in Malawi. I knew of her personality that she was better off working as a salesperson in comparison to being a nanny. In life, there are always questions to be asked about things in general and opportunities are always there for the taking to do so. That is the opportunity when the hidden things can be revealed. I knew to ask my sister who was never into kids except with my daughter when she was in her early baby stages, why she preferred to be a nanny far away from home for a living.

So why was she a full-time nanny not a sales lady? The time of our telephone conversations was the moment I could have asked such questions and found out some truth to why. I just never bothered to. Maybe I didn't want to know lest I would have to deal with the truth. And I don't believe that I could have handled the truth at that time before coming to America. I didn't want to know, honestly speaking.

The reality was that any misinformation we had gathered on our way here became a shocker once we landed.

NEWARK NOT NEW YORK

We had finally landed in America three days before Christmas Day in 1997 and settled in Philadelphia. We were received by my sister, her beau and our cousin, Preshe related through my mother's father's side of the family. Our first American home would be in Wynnefield. Late Boutrous B and my sister had picked us up from Newark New Jersey after wasting so much time waiting for us at another famous international Airport known as JFK International Airport.

It was the wrong airport for us. They had gone to JFK because we had misinformed them about our destination way before we landed in America. When the flights from Africa had landed according to our flight arrival time, date, numbers, they realized that we were not in any of the flights via customer services of Kenya Airways arrival center in New York. We were at Newark International Airport instead where they eventually found us. Who said that there was only one international airport on the east coast of America?

Not that I even knew that America had east or west coast or there was a difference between JFK International Airport and Newark International Airport. It's really good to travel. One can never be too educated.

On arrival, Keneilwe, our two children and I checked in with immigration offices to get our entry time allocated to us for our visit. They stamped in our passports 6 months each from the day of arrival although we had claimed that we were visiting the country

for two weeks for the Christmas and New Year's festivities. We were so clueless to the process and we were holding onto our breaths, frightened to death that immigration officers may hold us in one of their offices to inquire of why we were all travelling to America as a whole family in spite of the Christmas season at hand.

You must understand that by this time, we had heard of the horrible stories on how people with genuine legit reasons to come to America for this or the other had been denied visas whilst in their countries to begin with. Yet, we were granted our visitors' visas and the motive to begin with was shady from the start. Then we were also aware that immigration officers do sometimes keep couples or tourists for hours in holding cells right there at the airport before they release them to go on with the American visit or deny them entry at other times. Immigration officers had held my sister and her beau at JFK international Airport when they arrived earlier that year on Valentine's Day. So, we knew that this could also happen to us.

The fact that we were not held back nor given any hardships on entry into the country was a shocker especially when the whole journey from the American Embassy in Malawi then to immigration offices at checkpoint Newark was a walk through the park. We were too young to understand the power of Destiny. What I have come to understand now over the years after a personal encounter with God is that, what God has for you, you best believe, is for you! No clichés. Just believe it. I totally get it now.

You can only imagine what everyone was feeling when Boutrous B and his girlfriend, my sister, Abiti Bula found us at the time, waiting for them at the airport, in the international arrivals section.

You cannot understand the indisputable joy we had! My God, it was awesome. Kissing and hugging. My sister was so amazed at how much the children had grown. Marvel had been 2 years old and 6 months by the time my sister left home for Philadelphia and my son Avedi had been 3 months old.

It had only been 10 months, but it seemed like it had been 20 years! We were all talking to one another non-stop all way to our new home in Wynnefield. I noticed that we were indeed in another

big and advanced country from the moment we left the airport in New Jersey all the way to Philadelphia.

AMERICANS KNOW
HOW TO DO CHRISTMAS

I mean I had experienced Christmas in Malawi, also before that, in Pretoria in the Republic of South Africa when my father was a diplomat in the 6 years we lived there. This was epic! Christmas in America was on a higher and exquisite level. American Christmas decorations were the bomb!

I had never seen such huge, beautiful bloated Frosty the snowman or Santa Claus and Rudolf The Rednosed Reindeer on people's front yards in such large numbers. Christmas lights and decorations covering up entire houses and the houses were huge. Christmas decorations were even on public street lights and poles and on many, many homes. I momentarily found myself deeply thinking about their electric bills because I was a true African at heart. My Lord! People here had money, I couldn't help to think it! Just think of Christmas town, that's how everything was everywhere I looked.

As a child, I grew up decorating my parents' house with Christmas ornaments and indoor decors but never outdoors because of how expensive it would have been for my parents as well as easy bait for thieves in the neighborhood to steal if they happen to pass by and nobody was looking.

What my young family and I were witnessing on our first day and evening in America on our way to our new home in Philadelphia after the airport was absolutely magical! It was a joy ride! We had arrived.

I had arrived, I thought to myself.

This was what I wanted for my children and family to experience. Finally, we were in America and Christmas was in the air!

Yes, America, the promised land on earth to anybody who wants to believe and hope again that life can become whatever you envision it to be!

America is where you decide how your life will unfold. You hold the cards that you have been dealt. You have the power to change how you tell your story, if you don't like what you are handed. The way your story begins, does not necessarily have to end the same way it begun if you don't like the way it started. You get to pick. You get to decide. The ball is always in your hands no matter what life looks like. Roll your dice. Roll it at your convenience. Roll it at your own risk!

If you hold your breath long enough, you will die. But if you decide to breathe a little, you may just smell a few roses of hope around you. Hope. Inhale and Exhale it.

Please believe me when I say that life pretty much becomes how you want it to be no matter what is going on inside of you or around you. The truth of the matter is, there is always someone out there who is worse off than you, surely. Never doubt that. The trick to life is deciding what to do with what you got left to deal with in your hands. Every single time! No matter how bad life gets.

THE BIBLE IS MY COMPASS

You will always have something left in your hands to work with till your dying day as long as the earth remains according to Genesis 8:22 or God will be a liar. God cannot lie according to His Word in the Bible in the Book of Numbers 23:19. I believe that the Bible has everything you need to know about life and its daily issues. The Bible has become my compass by the way.

As long as you are alive, God will provide for you and for your life, that is if you are young enough remembering that He is a FATHER to the fatherless in Psalm 68:5 and He gives a seed to the sower. That is if you are old enough to care for yourself while on planet earth according 2 Corinthians 9:10!

Why would He say that? If He didn't put a gift in you for your own benefit and other people around you to benefit from

and for you to use the gift (s) for survival on earth? But If you haven't experienced life yet in its fullness, you would not know many things that sometimes only experience can teach you and can only come out of you because of that particular experience. So, take heart in knowing that your journey is very necessary for your tailor-made purpose and tailor-made destiny. I have come to know this for myself.

I didn't always know what I know today. That every individual's life has a purpose. That every person is born with a gift or more gifts. The gift(s) are there for each person to use to survive on, to strengthen themselves, and others around them as resources. For many years, I didn't have God as my compass the way I have Him now since I really found Him for myself in the year 2000. He is truly the only One who holds everyone's Destiny in His hands. So, I guess if you are going somewhere know this, that God is anywhere and everywhere, according to the Bible, in Jeremiah 23:24. He has the map and directions of where you are going. You only get there fast enough and accomplish anything and everything if He is in the agenda and on the compass of your journey. Whatever that maybe to you according to your personality and gifting. Know this, all this intellect and realization have taken me over half of my life to figure out.

Sometimes, I want to cry at the countless hours I wasted on battles and all the energy spent on empty results because I fought on my own strength and as a result, they zapped out almost all my being and had always placed me at the end of the line exhausted to begin the class of knowledge and understanding all over again.

It is best to do everything with God's strength and input, I have reckoned. You can never fail. Because it's not in your strength doing it. It's a higher power doing it. And, no, it's not witchcraft or white magic. Faith in Someone Unseen above all creatures and things. How do I know this, you may say?

Experience is the best teacher all day anytime, and information from the Bible. That was not my take when we first arrived here in America. I didn't study the Bible. I was either narrow minded at times or clueless half of the time to the Truth. God.

Nevertheless, we had arrived to our temporary home in the apartment buildings across from the famous Wynnefield Food Produce Junction where they sell fruits, vegetables and flowers.

The apartment was and still stands to this day. Not so bad for first time renters in America far away from home, Mama Africa.

OUR FIRST AMERICAN HOME

The apartment was a long rectangular block. It stood at the bottom section of two other floors above it. The bottom floor was where we lived, I suspect because we had toddlers. The entrance was where the main door was located, and it stood facing Bryn Mawr Avenue. Directly from that entrance was a large living room which was empty that sometimes my children used as an indoor playground. Adjacent to it was the largest bedroom in the house. It was our large bedroom that hosted a queen bedroom set for my husband and I and a small single bed for our daughter and son. It had a large closet for our clothes. We didn't have many clothes. We had brought one suitcase that held four people's prized possessions and $190.00 to our name. The next room to our bedroom was a large full bathroom and toilet. Next to the bathroom was Boutrous B and my sister's bedroom.

Right after it was a small TV room which we all frequented day and night. This living room led to the kitchen. Within the kitchen was another door that lead to another full bedroom. My cousin lived in that bedroom. She was also a nanny. And stretching from the TV room to the front of the house where the big living room was, a very long hallway. It was meant for the entrance to the apartment from the big living room and passing by all the rooms to the small TV room where we often gathered. Everyone at the apartment was fond of using the kitchen door though to go in and out of the building. The building sat on a slope. Everyone would drive up to the apartment and its allocated parking on the kitchen side.

The location for the building was not the ghetto. And it was not the suburbs. It was just right. It was very decent and very clean.

It was a few dollars short of a thousand dollars for monthly upkeep minus the utility bills because my sister had calculated that with 5 grown-ups living together to split rent, food and utility bills, the idea was easily feasible.

My sister explained to me that they had rented this particular apartment because the location was great and safe for raising our children. The public school was nearby. There was a train station within walking distance to transport us back and forth into the city of Philadelphia and all around. Bus number 40 was nearby to transport us between Pathmark where we would buy a variety of other types of food and downtown for entertainment. The apartment building was also located a few miles away from the Mainline. There were rich families there, that employed immigrants as nannies and housekeepers for their homes.

The two job categories were the types of jobs that employed people from other countries who didn't have their work permits or green cards like myself, my husband, the cousin, my sister, my sister's boyfriend, Boutrous B.

My sister then explained to me that My husband, kids and I would eventually end up being illegal immigrants in six months-time, because we did not have money to extend our tickets for returning home within the 6 months of time. The other individuals in the house were already illegals anyhow. The news was not music to our ears at all. What!

I came to find out that, this was the reason why my sister was a nanny not a salesperson for a living! What about my husband whom I thought would just continue to be a banker like he was one successful worker in our Malawi? Well another surprise was in the works for the taking.

It turned out that he would be needing either a work permit or a green card to do anything business like or office like. Oh My God! How does one find these so called items, was our next question.

The blind leading the blind was quite the trend in our lifestyles among the people from Malawi at the time. It was quite interesting because nobody wished to get informed correctly whenever there

was a need to get acquainted with something new or someone new that we had heard of but had never necessarily come across.

We tended to rush to do something by following suit with someone who had done whatever the thing at hand was without proper measures or understanding that not everything is for everyone. There was lack of understanding in acknowledging that what may come easily for one person may not always be so for another.

For instance, if someone was employed without proper working papers somewhere, it didn't mean that it will be so for everyone else who wished to follow the pattern. Then for me to go ahead and suggest for someone else in the same position to try for the same exact job just because I know what is happening there. It can be misleading to others.

The way Africans, including myself, may think sometimes causes us to get stuck in one bad place and not soar for whatever else is out there for the taking.

I have observed that fear is the common denominator in many people from Africa. We are afraid to try new things and new ways of living. We are afraid of failure.

You Can't Take Africa Out Of An African

*E*specially *Africans in the southern hemisphere. We tend to be our own enemies in life.*

One of the cultural habits for an African person like myself, is the assumption that what works for someone else, may be the case for me. That is a simple lie.

And at other times, it is also very common for an African fellow I have witnessed to misinform another about an opportunity they are in by consciously leaving out some information. The partaker does not want the other person to know about that opportunity they are involved in for fear that the other person may steal it from them or may outshine them. Yet, it's my belief that there are enough opportunities on planet earth for everyone. What's meant

for me shall be for me. We all have our individual paths and destinies. Of course, one must always use caution and wisdom in helping others but definitely not selfishness. Selfishness constraints one's own society. Getting ahead in life is always teamwork.

It is very typical for African people to withhold information from one another. If one is looking for a recipe to something successful for example, we among ourselves tend to give parts of the recipe but not the whole recipe. I have found this to be wicked and annoying. This can be about information to do with food, purchase of a thing or property, education or travel or just anything in general. Lame ain't it?

If an African fellow doesn't want you to get in on anything, they will tell you some truth about it and hold some information back, so you get frustrated and quit altogether or suffer while you are trying your best to accomplish whatever that thing is. The notion is that if they struggled for it then why should you get the result so quickly and so easily. Besides, you may just get too big headed. I mean, who cares? Just give them the information already! If you have it, give it, you lose nothing. Besides it pays to be nice. Giving is always an investment that pays back at the least time from the least of persons. Who knows? The next time it may be you looking for something in return. What goes around does come around indeed.

The sad thing about holding back some information from among ourselves in us black folks in general is that we hold one another back by not uplifting and upgrading one another. We hold the community behind. Knowledge is powerful especially the right kind of knowledge. When we don't elevate one another, we may think that we are hurting that one person, but truly we are hurting our own race. That formula is a self- defeating mechanism. The old-adage doesn't lie. It does take a village to raise a child. That village is the whole community wherever you may be together moving ahead towards the mark but sometimes it may take one person at a time.

My destiny is tailor made for me no matter who does what.

If I stay focused. I will get there. I have come to find out that success is predictable if I stay focused, work hard and be consistent. Whether I am an illegal immigrant in America or legal resident elsewhere.

OTHER RACES & CULTURES

I have so much admiration and respect for the Jewish, the Korean people not forgetting Indian cultures so far, based on close up connections here in America. They build one another up. Community is everything to them. They are some of the few true and living examples of how any race or tribe should function to live fully to its potential in my opinion.

They still contribute their different giftings towards a common good/goal for family member's special occasion or memorable events. At times they even reach out to those who aren't directly related to them but are in their communities.

One of the classic examples, was my experience with a Korean lady. She had shared a story joyfully with me about a venue of a wedding she and her family paid to use for her niece's wedding. It was at a castle. I liked the story and idea very much and everything she was telling me about her whole family's experience there. I then turned around to learn more about the contacts, so I could pass the information to my cousin who was also looking for a wedding venue.

If the same scenario was presented between two African women in my own culture, usually it would have been a headache just to get the location and contacts to that castle. Why you may ask? Because everybody wants to be the only ones at the top. The only ones in the limelight. No chance to share the glitz or the glamor. Sadly.

Yet everyone has their own destiny no matter how much energy we spend in holding others behind.

They get there regardless of the bumps and hurdles along the way if God is for them!

I know that it feels good to be nice. And it doesn't cost anything. It is an investment that matures itself and rewards the giver in payback at the least of times and from the least of places, from the least of strangers.

Giving, I have come to find, in most cases for most part is a great investment. This I have learned, and I am still learning and seeing the rewards.

....

GET THE RIGHT
KIND OF INFORMATION

I t sure didn't feel nice to learn everything all at once and in a strange land with no options. I say this to say that, my sister and her boyfriend should have known most of the information about America once they got here from the people before them and in return educate us the new comers to the country about it so that we were not expecting miracles and chasing rainbows from the start.

So, coming to America and learning about some things at the last minute of our arrival on things that were imperative for the journey and our stay in the country while "visiting" was pretty much nerve wracking and very much common among my culture and its people. I will say this with due respect to my race. Black people, we can do better towards one another. Charity begins at home.

I pray that my story will bring an awareness to this bad habit of sabotaging our own growth and future collectively as a culture. Africans, let us unite in building one another up, one step at a time, one person at a time. If one knows something for the benefit of another, please don't hold back. Share it.

For as long as America stands, there's always gonna be an immigrant lurking somewhere in its corners. Its reality for real. Keeping in mind that there's the right and wrong way of living. If you hold back information essential for another one of your kind, even for another race or culture, you have just added one more problem to your community and in the end, you have to deal with it in your society. It is nobody else's fault but yours. Become your brother's keeper in doing good like God expects us in Genesis 4:9. For real y'all.

What you don't deal with doesn't go away. It just gets deeper and wider until the day you have to finally stand bold to deal with it straight on. The issue of immigrants from all over the world is unavoidable. Everybody who has heard about the promises of America wants to come here if they can. This is in every race and in every culture. Don't be notorious and known for being the very one culture or

race that hates on itself! Be different. Set an example. Lead by example. Be known for embracing one another as well as every race and culture on earth that you come across and living in America, because it's just a matter of time before you do. America is a melting pot for all races, all colors, all creeds, all cultures. You will always come across another race in your lifetime, I can guarantee you that!

Love goes a mighty long way, if you pay attention, one person a time.

Please be famous for always getting caught up with your hands ever stretching to others to help out, no matter what race or culture you are caught up with. Give from whatever you have.

We all have something positive or good to give to another at any given time. It does not have to cost a thing. Sometimes it can be just a simple smile, some cash that jingles, a hug or even a sandwich. You will find out that it's the smallest things in life that make a difference in another person's life.

I have learned all this because since 1998, I have been down many times. Most of the time, money or things didn't matter but a person who stopped by and gave a listening ear and made a difference with their time, allowed me to understand that there's nothing compared to one's presence and their time. It is here in America where I have learned to appreciate a person's time in my life. Whatever they gave on top of their precious time to me engraved a spot in my heart forever. Their time meant more to me than their treasures. There has been The Middlemans, Joe Stevenson, S. Eckstein, and my darling friend, late Gloria Bianco Munsell who recently went to be with The Lord. May her soul continue to rest in God's peace. These people have been very outstanding in my life thus far, just to mention a few.

I have had a few people who were sent in my life just to stop me in the tracks of loneliness and demise. It was some of those people that gave my heart another urge, to beat again due to their kindness when life got rough. It made me understand that there's always someone out there who cares, no matter how far away from home you may find yourself. You are never far gone. Citizenship or illegal immigrant. You are never alone.

If you didn't reach out to others in your country of origin, I hope that you will learn to reach out while you are in America, for your own sake. Chances are that you will be the one needing to receive from others at many times in your lifetime here. Without a doubt!

But, you can't expect to receive from anybody if you haven't given either. So, get into the act of giving of yourself to others in healthy ways. I will tell you this one thing also, Networking was created for America.

It is where giving makes a big deal and knowing the right people in return can tremendously change your life for the better!

Since America is a melting pot of a people, nobody should be an island here. It will not help anyone to deny themselves this fact and reality at all. I can almost say that everyone in America is born of an immigrant who came from somewhere somehow for one reason or another except the native Indians of the country. But even them too, I believe that they originated from somewhere else.

Take away the country, there's no immigrant to go anywhere. Leave America to stand and thrive, there will be floods of immigrants, everywhere, always. Somehow!

America was built by immigrants. Three quarters of Americans came from somewhere, some country out there. Go figure that one out. We are all enroute from somewhere.

If anybody goes nowhere except here, they die an immigrant deep down yonder unless they return back to their original home country.

One thing that is not fun for an immigrant is coming out to America and only discovering crucial and necessary information once they are here. Especially if they deserve to know beforehand! Leave the choice to know up to them if they are old enough. But please don't hold back any necessary information. It makes all the difference. What you don't know in America can indirectly destroy you!

Talk about stroke and heart attack! I had no idea. All stress related diseases are here in America. Get information, the right kind of knowledge. God is aware of this in Hosea 4:6. I beg to be different especially if I can help it! Now that I know.

Hear me when I say this, that I personally went straight to the school of hard knocks in America. It was not cool that we learned of the work permits and green cards properly once we got here. Although it was nobody else's fault but our own in this particular case, so long we came into the country when we were of age. We were definitely of age. The blame was on my husband, Keneilwe and myself.

In hindsight, the way I wanted to run away from my country due to personal issues, I am convinced that nothing would have changed my decision to come to America anyway. Destiny was waiting!

AMERICA WAS MY FATE

I knew that I was set for America, whether or not I had a working plan in motion, a green card, Social Security number or a work permit. My mind was set for America. Nothing was going to change that.

But how does one get those imperative items to be able to work in America if they are foreigners or immigrants? My goodness.

We had to learn things pretty fast! What to do?

Let me just say in short, that we obviously did not have those papers and we definitely at that time did not qualify for the work permit or green card. One of the reasons why we didn't qualify for an extension to our days of visiting the country beyond the 6 months allocated to us in our passports, was because we had overstayed our B1/B2 visitor visa and we had not requested an extension in due season which also costs money to do. We didn't have the money to do the applications by end of June 1998.

However, my husband was fortunate to obtain a non-workers social security number on a card as a tourist to be able to drive a vehicle while in the country within his six months visiting days so long he was still in status.

I tried to do the same thing of obtaining the social security number by taking the same learner's permit test he did at Penndot downtown Philadelphia when it was on Market Street, but I had

failed and did not receive the number. The six months were almost over and that disqualified me to continue to try taking the test. Which meant that I could not qualify to go for a driver's license later on after another learner's permit trial and process. But if I had passed the test, I could have gotten the social security number eventually for the purposes of identification and more while living in the United States.

I remember feeling very sad and defeated because I had flunked the test. I definitely had missed out on a big chance for that number on a card! It would have opened up many doors for me in the 19 years that I had lived here without it.

But how could I have passed the learner's permit test? I had never driven anything in Malawi nor in America for that matter.

But I had to give it a try!

I knew to take an opportunity at anything when the chance presented itself and learn properly along the way.

Alas, It would take me three learner's permit examinations altogether almost 20 years later for me to pass and earn it.

The next many years would be very hard to go through life without an American government identification card. I was lacking a social security number because I had tried and failed and run out of time. Our children were not qualified for a social security number either. O Life in America. People outside the country just don't know.

A hurdle nobody wants to openly warn others on their way to America who have no idea of what a social security card is.

It sounds like a name one would give to a card that is used for getting into a social or a nightclub for social events of some sort or luxury lifestyle. Right? Ugh.

Come to think of it, it is a luxury to have a social security number, big time. Although you are very much non-existent without it.

Anyhow. Maybe this card should have been called a mandatory personal information number on a card.

Too long and it doesn't sound inviting, so I see why social security number has a nice ring to it. Pretty much this card tells of the individual's private information if logged into a special computer systems

data. I guess, our two children and myself were nonexistent from that point on, according to the issue of this card, the social security card.

For 20 years, I depended on my husband's social security number for securing our household utility bills and for renting an apartment for accommodation once we had separated living space with our family friend and member Boutrous B.

HOME AWAY FROM HOME

*H*is *younger sister, Phoebella, had helped us secure our first apartment in America. She even put some of the down payment cash for us to be able to rent the apartment. The apartment was on the third floor of the 800 Block on Wynnewood Road. It was where my $250.00 weekly pay held down 4 people in a household for a whole week's needs and took care of utility bills each week. We had less, we were alright, and I felt at home living out my American dream with the 3 people I cherished the most in the whole world.*

This was where we held out cookouts and barbecues with a few friends we had acquired from our own small and youthful Malawian community here in Philadelphia.

Usually all the men drunk whenever they met. They used to drink cases of some Heinekens, Bud light, Coors light and Budweiser. While the women drank Mike's hard lemonade. I know that because that used to be one of my favorite drinks at those gatherings. We ate a lot of home cooked meals and eating out was a foreign thing. If ever we afforded it, once in a while we went to drive throughs by the aid of our friends who had cars.

We would hang out till late at night.

I realize now that we were living a satisfying lifestyle at the time in comparison to the latter years when we eventually fell away from those traditions of gatherings. Our gatherings were on a consistent basis and it was expected from one another to meet. It didn't leave too much room for depression even though those meetings were sporadic but set. There was some sort of depression in many of the young people in the circle although very concurrent but

not so severe. It was mild that if you didn't know what depression looked like, you couldn't tell.

But it was there. In almost all of us. We didn't know what to call it. Or what to do with it if ever there was any chance at all to talk about it. It is not like we had heard of it in Malawi or seen It? One can only deal with what they know. One can only change what they know.

Most of our inner circle knew best to hang around together in our home as functional friends. At times during the warm seasons, we would hang outside downstairs on the shared porch to the apartment on Wynnewood Road for our convenience because of our children. It was easier and cheaper for us to stay at home or keep our children home with us during entertainment than travel to other fellows' apartments. None of us owned a house at that time, due to expenses or legal status. Besides, most apartments rented by our Malawian fellows were convenient but not so big to accommodate busy toddlers.

Everything happy with our fellow Malawians dissipated when Boutrous B left us for good in May 1999. And so, the depression, anxiety, bitterness and buried issues within my spouse and I rose to the surface again. We didn't grieve together. The inner circle we had come to know fell apart too. Life seemed suddenly lonelier.

FIRST SEPARATION IN AMERICA

By early 2000 I wanted out of my marriage. This was due to absolutely no respect left between my spouse and I towards each other. The blame game was much too much. Nothing that we did for each other worked to appease our hearts or feelings for one another. Love, life altogether got harder. Our kids were becoming victimized by hearing rated, uncensored profanities flying around the house instigated by their own two parents who are supposed to protect them from any unforeseen insanity, yet every other day, there they were at each other unpredictably throwing terror at each other non-stop! Things often times, flew in motion at the parents'

direction one unto another in fury. It was a living nightmare on a weekly basis.

It was a no brainer when a need inside of me erupted to move out and go on my own into an apartment within the same neighborhood of Overbrook nearby because of our children's school. By this time, my tax identification number on a card came in handy.

My sister Abiti Bula was back in my life after her loss and the tragedy of May in 1999. During our good moments together, my sister had educated me on how to obtain tax identification numbers on cards for the children and myself from the offices of Internal Revenue Services. I guess I also did the application for the identification numbers with the intentions of doing business transactions someday in the future, in case I wanted to do so as a foreigner.

The truth is, I didn't use it for commerce. Instead, I used it for acquiring a few utility bills that were able to use my tax identification number on a card to create an account with that particular company for as long as I was able to. My family was also able to use the tax identification numbers for filing taxes for over a period of 10 years before we eventually became legal residents.

But there was one troublesome issue with tax identification numbers. I couldn't use the tax identification numbers for extensive necessities like securing my social security funds from the funds I had earned in one of the jobs I had served as a nanny for 10 years at one point. Whatever weekly, monthly to yearly deductions I had on my paycheck paid to the government of the United States of America via that tax identification number, I couldn't claim those earnings for the sake of my financial retirement at a later stage in life but had to obtain a security number to transfer past years' earnings which is what I eventually did.

I will say this about the tax identification number though, it got me the things I needed done and I am truly grateful that my children and I had one for each person for as long as we needed it.

Fast forward to ten years after that sad, tragic and fateful 911 day in America, so much has changed. For security reasons, the IRS no longer issues tax identification numbers on cards to just anybody. Nobody could any longer obtain a tax identification

number unless they are legal residents of the United States doing business in America or via the government of United States of America under intense scrutiny.

If you are a foreigner, you do not qualify to obtain the social security number through a learner's permit to use for any kind of need or reason because you are visiting. Most of the privileges and loopholes that the country had for foreigners were taken away or closed completely due to the horror and tragedy that took place on American soil in September of 2001. I totally stand in agreement.

I mean, anyone shouldn't have a problem with that. Prevention is better than cure. If the government has to wait for something bad to happen again as it was then in that tragic September incident, it would be beyond devastating to go through that again. Therefore, extreme preventive measures had to be implemented right away for the sake of all mankind especially the citizens of the country from all corners and within.

Imagine how hard everything became to obtain from the government from that point on if government documentation was not in line with government protocol and system of doing things. Any essential information for any foreigners to use for the purposes of living in America through the government of the United States became harder. What was already hard to acquire whenever repercussions occur for many people who are just working to survive, to make a simple living, became even more harder. Imagine if the person in need is an illegal immigrant. A thousand times harder. Yes.

Luckily, my tax identification number helped me to obtain an apartment and a few utility bills. I did so for the first time in the year 2000 during my first marital separation from my husband on American soil so far away from home, two years into the country.

That in reality was my second time to separate from him in regards to our marriage. Sigh. Again?! I know, you are saying, what?

Yes, our first breakup in America was for four months. We had physically separated in two different directions from August to December of year 2000.

Let me backup for a few minutes, if you will allow me. Oh Well, this is America for you.

Or should I say that American issues and Malawian issues got to us and the sudden loss of Boutrous B who had become part of us triggered everything stressful and negative within us that was docile for a while up until the day my spouse and I could no longer take any courteous conduct towards each other.

Let me remind you once again that America will either break you or make you.

Don't pout! If you are an illegal immigrant or a legal resident but you haven't settled down yet and feel so lost and alone here, truly I can relate. I can almost imagine your face right now, pouting.

I know, all these trials are very discouraging. Sigh and fly away on your inner, imaginary wings to a faraway island in you.

And take a deep breath. Things do get better or we die. Such, also is Life! Life on planet Earth, is rather trying. Exhale! Come back to me. You can only go through to come through. Don't get stuck in there, come out. But I know you can do this. I know that you are still here. Strive!

Have you ever heard of such a saying that a new environment doesn't make a new mindset in a person? Yep, one has to want to change the whole mindset for anything to change inwardly and outwardly simultaneously plus a lot of effort on many levels of life. Then perhaps everything else around and outwardly may catch up with the mindset in a timely fashion and order. If not, be certain that chaos is around the corners of your heart and your total being.

Be conscious to succeed. For success is obtained by a conscious effort towards it and it is not accidental. In almost if not in every case, success is predictable. So, imagine that, we had finally made it in America, but the hurdles of life continued on a more intense level. Why? It was because the mindset was very much unchanged! We were still functioning with a redundant mindset, filled with unstable consciousness, bittersweet and we were self-sabotaging our own selves without even knowing it. In our hearts, yet expecting new, progressive and pleasant results. Ugh!

Two grown and responsible bodies on the surface had arrived on American soil, indeed. Two outwardly functional adults had lived in America for two years physically to hide away from their

inner misery perhaps a superficial getaway from all the familiarity and maybe the drama but in actual sense they were on the run from themselves. Their biggest battle that needed to be dealt with was in the inside of their bodies, in their minds not the outside of it.

The inner self was going nowhere. As a matter of fact, the inner self was very much stuck and stagnant. It was two adults and "responsible" bodies that were filled with all kinds of negative feelings of bitterness, regret, abuse, immorality, ungratefulness and a dysfunctional incline towards each other restlessly wrecking the atmosphere of their very livelihood by the day! The only different factor at that time, was location. Nothing else had changed. Sad ain't it!?

Looking back in January of 1998, immediately after our first Christmas and New Year's celebrations excitement had subsidized, the discovery of our work limitations dampened my spouse's mood and even my own. The discovered limitations and boundaries due to lack of imperative knowledge on top of lack of money or any outstanding qualifications to extend our visit in the country was a shocker!

With those boundaries along came regrets and a series of physical, mental, verbal abuse exchanged between my spouse and me.

A RELATIONSHIP DISEASE

Depression came to stay. It was made comfortable in our home. And the constant verbal reminders of what we had become to each other as lesser people with blemishes of adultery to seal the deal of incompetence at any or whatever form of success life would present to us individually.

Indeed, he was frustrated and so was I. We had left Malawi without a tangible plan, and without enough money. We had abandoned good and self- sufficient lives to live dependent lifestyles on people who had no idea of what it was like to care for a group of people financially based on their meager weekly income. Let alone no other ways of familiar financial breakthroughs to help fend for

others like in communities everyone in this regard was accustomed to, such as motherland, Malawi, a few thousand miles away.

As I go back in my head to that January of 1998, I remember that after two weeks of our arrival in a small town known as Wynnefield near Philadelphia, things had drastically changed in the household where we had arrived. Keneilwe, our two toddlers and myself would become Boutrous B's sole responsibility to fend for at The Bryn Mawr Road apartment directly across from Produce Junction which still stands to this day. The sudden change was due to a terrible fall out between my sister and her beau.

On that one unsuspecting horrible wintery evening, my sister, Abiti Bula, had packed up with my cousin Preshe, who had lived in the third room of the apartment. The two young ladies, left us behind and started a whole new life apart from everyone who lived with them in that apartment. Yes!

It turned out that the dysfunctional love affair that existed between my sister and her boyfriend became even more contorted. It was so bad that she counted us out and moved away from us in a heartbeat. She never looked back, and it would be 17 months down the road for us to reunite again due a tragedy.

I just want to encourage anyone out there reading this, who has come to America all caught up and invested in relationships that seem unbreakable.

Honey, here in America, I have come to understand this painful truth, nothing on Earth lasts forever literally! Nothing on earth is perfect! Nothing on earth is eternal. Nothing on earth is unbreakable. Even the very relationships you thought were impregnable. Here, they become fragile and very much pregnable.

Especially if God is not in it as the foundation and the balancer, then whatever that thing is, the days of it are very much numbered or rendered restless.

I have witnessed this several times in my lifetime by now. Anything, without the true meaning and essence of love which is the True God Himself is redundantly frustrating. You can't have the real love without the real Person of love in it. God is Agape Love according to John 3:16, which is very rare in people. A love one unto another in people without any conditions and other

limitations is very hard to find. Yet, if we love people without truly understanding the meaning of that type of love then when the ones we deem to love hurt us, we fail to recover quickly from the hurt because the love was based on conditions.

I know so because I have loved with conditions. I probably had Agape Love for my spouse in the first years of our marriage but that type of love shifted to other types of love as soon as things got rough and the same goes with my family members. Isn't this sad?

I feel that this far, I have loved my children and grandparents with Agape Love probably because I consciously made that choice earlier on in my life.

I feel that I love everyone that I have this far, but it is all under the other types of love a notch away from Agape. This is the reason why I may be still struggling to take in any misuse of my being by anyone doing so to me. As for my spouse, when the love shifted gears over the years, I chose to no longer love him unconditionally because I have counted all the hurt, since most of it has been cutting very deeply which has made it hard for me to forget and risk my heart continuously and it has left me a horrible after taste in my mouth that doesn't seem to go away, and makes it hard for us to continue to be together as conventional husband and wife. I truly want to experience true love in my life before God shall take His breath out of me. This time around, the way a man truly loves a woman the biblical way! It is my wish.

I will be the first one to admit. Perhaps, it is possible that I haven't really loved fully yet, according to these conditions I have set in my mind. Total strangers can become the best of rescuers in one's life. I believe this because we don't hold any standards against them.

Strangers can make the best of sisterhood, brotherhood, motherhood, fatherhood and the best of friendships.

So, it's possible to open-up to someone who is taking up an obligation of a family member and receive their kindness so much deeply when we don't expect it or hold it against them. This is all due to expectation. Sometimes, one you least expect from holds less power in the heart to cause probable wounds. Sometimes, we

may hold our loved ones so highly even when they don't deserve to be.

The fact that I came from Africa made this reality worse.

I realized quickly that loved ones aren't perfect either. The one who had let me down in a foreign country to my shock, was my sister, who had once loved me fully! How can any of this be happening? I, still in my foreign culture's mindset was expecting big and certain things from her without fail. Surely, I was well seasoned for a schooling.

This is the reason why I got badly wounded in my heart from the events that transpired after our first Christmas and New Year season in America. Everything that happened from that moment onwards would mark the beginning of a very long teaching of life's lessons for our family as well as a very trying period in my own personal journey. I had no idea that family ties can be severed. The only time family ties got severed in my opinion was when a family member died.

I was wrong once again!

Everything that took place from the beginning of 1998, was as if the awesome two weeks in a new country, America were just a dream!

AN AWAKENING

Suddenly, we all had to wake up to a nightmare! A time of love, giving, peace and harmony suddenly inverted into a time of uncertainty, shock and quickening of one's inner strength to survive.

Whatever hope that had existed and remained in the few weeks of that Christmas season, and that entrance of a new era of 1998, proved to be nothing but a short momentum and simply dwindled to nothing and a feeling of sinking came to stay.

It was too much to handle all around me!

There would be no relationship between my sister and every-one she had left on that day for a very long while. If any relation-ship at all, would be unstable and tumultuous for years to come.

It was sad and very painful to watch unravel right underneath our eyes.

The only explanation that I could come up with was that my sister according to me personally grew overwhelmed overnight about financially caring for a bunch of people. She had been living with her boyfriend and our distant cousin. Each of the three people worked and fended for themselves independently. When bills came along, they all moved together in agreement and took care of the bills at hand silently and systematically. The reality of having to care for four other people became surreal overnight. Whatever reason that transpired to ignite an exit door, I saw my sister run toward it for dear life!

Yes, my 21 year- old sister had abandoned us by early 1998 a few weeks later after our wonderful arrival in America! Hard to believe. Right? I, only after many years, can forgive my sister, in regards to, her abandoning us from that time on. As I sit here right now sharing my story, I watch my son who is 21 this year. He is attending college, I couldn't see him fend for a burdensome of four other family members. It is a lot to bear. I do understand how my sister reacted although I may not agree with the intensity of how she did it.

But then again, at that time, would I have understood? I don't think so because I expected family ties to carry so much more weight than they were capable of. It is a culture thing. It is only now that I understand my sister's dilemma in 1998. This is so after I have lived and experienced life with all its challenges and endeavours this far.

My sister was a baby herself ready to take on two adults and two innocent children. That is one of her costs she didn't prepare for in agreement to having us over in America. It was easy and foolish from afar to jump in and offer financial responsibility but once we finally joined her, it became a reality and too much to bear. The struggle became real.

I and my family should never have been my sister's responsibility nor her boyfriend's. The way my African culture systematically does things on the account of another without their full consent or in-put first, can bring trouble in a person's life. I didn't

see it then, but I couldn't do the same now without my conscience conflicting me from within. It was crazy what we did. I had no idea until now. I am thankful for my sister and her beau for receiving us like they did when they did. After everything I know now, I don't think that I can do what they did. They were bold and courageous! It pays to be naive sometimes.

In 1998 during the turmoil, I comprehended nothing. At that moment, I concluded that my sister must be the devil himself or his daughter. Nobody could tell me otherwise. I was so caught up in the memories and phone calls by her outbursts when she cried for us and yearned for her family to join her in America, the unforgettable arrival with Christmas in the air and then the abandonment. I couldn't understand my sister. Not even if she tried. But the problem was that she didn't even try. She was moving on with her life and from a distance it looked like she was doing well and carrying on happily. She had left behind a very angry people. A bunch of people!

It was a very confusing time, when everything was unfolding before us.

There was something very emotionally disturbing about her attitude towards us between Malawi and Christmas, New Year period, in America to the day she decided to up and go.

She had left us to halt into oblivion after being filled with an excitable welcoming moment of sheer joy which quickly subsidized without a warning into a moment of extreme panic. And everything else that would be the beginning of our share of hell on American soil at the expense of love and loved ones. Imagine? Leaving a home country, you have known your whole life, to reunite with another you love, your bloodline in another strange land. A few weeks in, you are left with that loved one's memories not because they died but simply because they have chosen to abandon you for whatever reason they themselves saw fit to do so. In a heat of a moment.

Absolutely coldness!

Anybody would be expecting some kind of explanation. Right? There was none. It was not in a letter or in any other form of communication to make the one abandoned understand better what

had just happened. Except that a girl and a boy literally excuse the actual ages at that time, had a fall out.

Everyone else that had depended on the two lovebirds within their apartment were then dumped in the lap of one of the lovebirds. The boyfriend became the one to deal with the heavy burden. He, in hindsight, eventually entered a series of depression himself, unknown to all. Only to be understood better by those around him many years later after his untimely death.

America is not an easy place for most people. At countless times, living in America can cause you to be prone to stress.

What may start as a small issue can eventually grow big if not addressed. America can become a very small and uncomfortable place sometimes when one is in trouble, it may even feel as though that person is all alone, even with others around. This is one of the only biggest places I have ever felt alone yet surrounded by others. It can get that lonely.

I have no doubt that Boutrous B had depression, my sister has had a battle with depression, my spouse is still depressed I have watched in sadness and I was in depression for many years if not for over 10 years of my stay in America. But I choose to fight against it with The Word of God!

The worst part at that time, was that no one could help the other person in need and we were all in what seemed like an endless emotional mess, so stuck far away from our comfort zone, Malawi. Unaware of the terrible depressing ride that we would have to ride individually for years to come. It is so prolific but surreal to find out how one person's sudden decision can affect everyone attached to them forever! It can either take a great turn of their life's events or make a downfall of a lifetime. I had no idea how much effectiveness is linked to certain key people in one's human life.

There are people in everyone's life who are placed to divert one's life for the best turn and outcome and there is another group of people placed in one's path to divert a certain person outcome to a worst turn or unpleasant outcome for good. The choice is for each individual to make for the taking. I had no idea until life taught and showed me.

SCHOOL OF ATTITUDE

B e encouraged that no matter where you are, life is simply a journey with a small, amount of things you cannot control and a bigger portion of things you can. The choice is really yours for those things to deter you from or plunge you into your destiny for your proper end result. Many people do not know that they have the power to change their own environment, attitude and outcome of many things that may not seem to be in their favor. They have the power within themselves to change their destiny for the better. The future is within you. It's all about your attitude within you.

Because Malawi did not get a chance to teach me this one lesson on attitude, well let's just say that America had a 101 schooling for me in the many years to come through housekeeping job and childcare job opportunities covered up in humility.

I will never forget my first work experience in America. It was in early of the year 1998, I worked for an Arab-American family, the Shadits. They had a big beautiful house along Montgomery avenue in the neighboring suburbs of the Mainline in Ardmore. Phobebella, Boutrous B's younger sister was the one who had helped me place this particular housekeeping job. She loved her older brother so much that when the responsibility was dumped on him to fend for my family and financial situations got to be too heavy for him to bear in his household, she would often times do whatever it took to make a situation better.

She, somewhat, had become the big sister to all of us. I am about a few years older than her but truthfully speaking, age in this particular issue was just a number because she was able to stand in the unfortunate gap and help her brother and my family afloat financially without sinking low in such a big, foreign pond far away from home when money got funny. She was only 19 years old.

She was so mature beyond her age and precarious in the ways she handled her personal issues. Most of all, she was troubled when others she knew were in need. She is still the same way 20 years later. So immediately after the time my family and I had landed in Philadelphia, Phoebella had resorted to reading The Main Line Times job section to place me a job. When she had found one

....

111

vacancy for me to call, I immediately did so. It was a part time cleaning job.

She even coached me on what to say and what not to say in a job interview for me to land the job. She became my reference. Lying had become the new normal in America for survival. It was either that or stay home and watch everyone crumble financially. Boutros B was barely making a weekly income.

Although my first job would only offer me 3 hours of work for $28.00, I understood earlier on, that a credible reference in America for everything meant a person's very own survival and future chances of opened opportunities.

In Africa, it was mainly connections with very important people in that particular field you needed assistance with and perhaps a little experience, at other times hard work to be able to get ahead. But in America, a good reference first, then experience and skill spoke volumes of a person's conduct long before landing the job.

I had never in my entire life worked so intensely for 3 straight hours in any household on housework for only $28.00, never will I, again!

My first American employers were doctors who also taught as professors at different colleges in downtown Philadelphia. Once a week on Wednesday evenings around 6 p.m., Dr. Mrs. Shadits would pick me up from Bryn Mawr Avenue, in front of our apartment building to go to her house in Ardmore about 5 miles away, to thoroughly scrub her household: kitchen, toilets, bathrooms and change two bedrooms and the linen to the bedrooms and do laundry for their teenage daughter in what seemed like the fastest 3 hours of my life not forgetting the fact that the workload was the heaviest, most strenuous to be done by one single person. My reimbursement was so meager!

Every night when I was done working in that house, after a shower back at the apartment, in my sleep, I would groan and moan sleeplessly due to body aches that seemed to come along in my body with an after smell from that unforgettable strong, awful, languishing fumes that some of the cleaning products carry.

I still do not know what to make of the Dr. Mrs. Shadits each time she gave me an additional compensation for my hard work, a small container that carried curried, cooked Basmati rice. The only best part of the time I was in her house. It was that delicious aromatic flavor of rice I had no idea existed on this side of heaven in comparison to the other precooked rice I was fed up with by January 1998.

I knew that she didn't pay me anywhere equivalent to the workload in the hours I served in her household or near the immaculate results I gave her after each workload each Wednesday. I don't know if she gave me the small container of cooked rice to make up for the difference or whatever? I just know that it was probably for her than it was for me. Along the years, I have come to find out that people know when they are taking advantage of someone. They have their own funny ways of extra unnecessary actions to appease their guilty conscience. When I think about that constant container of cooked rice, it has always appeared to me that it was her own way of washing away guilty stains from her hands for not paying me what I was really deserving each time. America has a way of showing you people's true, heart colors in a jiff than anywhere else I have been, in my life!

Such kind of a confusing behaviour by that employer over my naivety, vulnerability and delicately imposition made my young heart get filled with a lingering dampness because life was proving to be less beautiful and more loaded with difficulty. The only sure thing was the obvious stressful promises lodged at the threshold of my family's dreams and my very own. The new lifestyle that was unfolding in front of our eyes in general no longer made us feel as though we were finally in America! Life would become a series of dampened sadness.

Particularly, that very first job was the beginning of a very difficult era I had not mentally prepared for in any way, whatsoever. The struggle was all for the sake of making ends meet for my family.

Although, I was a young person, my body felt like I was a rundown maid after each Wednesday night I worked in that doctor's house. My body continued to ache, and it silently cried in anguish

because I, the owner of it, was focused in cascaded sweet dreams of Beautiful America and didn't want to back down, give in and confess that coming to America was a mistake to anybody, after all! I knew that I would have to work while living in America, to earn a living but I didn't quite imagine it would be this hard.

It was one of the worst jobs I ever worked in since my American arrival and journey. But, indeed, I needed the reference attached to my name besides my Malawian connections. I can't remember however, what my family did with the $28.00 each Wednesday night I got paid but I know that my health was screaming out loudly, "enough!"

My health was definitely taking a beating and showing warning signs from the way I worked in the 3 hours each time when I did. The strong fumes I was exposing my body to when I cleaned their house was becoming too much to bear. I needed to do something else but clearly, I was not sure of what yet. I had never thought of caring for other people's children because I felt like I was deserting my own kids who were at home with their father each time I went out to work.

My kid's father on the other hand, as an illegal immigrant by this time in 1998, couldn't get a job. It was more challenging for illegal immigrant men in the late 90s to find a job if they did not have their work permits. Now almost 20 years later looking back, it is almost impossible for an illegal immigrant man to find work today.

In 1997, late Boutrous B before he died, had worked at an oriental rug place for part time and that place didn't and couldn't employ many illegals because it is a government risk to do so.

They only employed him to work there for only a few hours. The money that he and I made together before we parted ways alternatively was not enough to do much besides buying a bit of food to eat for that week.

I knew that there was decent work out there not like the type of work load I had experienced in my first American household job.

Phoebella, as usual, had gone on to answer to another job advertisement in the Main Line Times on my behalf. The job was

located near Lower Merion High school. It was a walking distance from my first Job in America. This second job was one that would test many things about me, I didn't know that I had.

I knew that I could easily clean and I had basic knowledge in cleaning but the fumes that would erupt and provoke my airwaves from the first household job from most of the cleaning products I was using were not worth my health. I didn't have medical insurance or been to a doctor's office then although I had a case of asthma here and there. Therefore, cleaning other people's households for a living was becoming problematic and hazardous for my health. What I had resorted to doing in America for the sake of making ends meet by cleaning other people's homes using those strong chemicals was a quick way to kick the bucket.

I had to rethink my job scope and change it for my own sake. What I had resorted to would prove to be even more of a challenge.

Thus, the birth of my Nanny years! Middle of 1998, there I was, taking care of another person's children while my own were home. The only consolation for me was that their father was the one that babysat them.

But in my African culture and thought pattern, it always had been women who took care of children not men, so I still had so much trouble letting go of my children to my husband completely in the first years although I didn't have any options. He was a dad. He was kind but too kind. A spoiler of kids. He had sound judgement but if the kids were hanging on the chandelier not that there were any in our humble apartment but use your imagination here, if there was one and the kids were hanging on it, like monkey bars for fun, it did not faze him. The kids were having fun and so long nobody got hurt! You got the idea. Good.

I mean, there were beans stuck up in our son's nose at one time and my husband was never in any panic about it whatsoever! A deep skin cut to the lower chin of our son's face. No biggie there either! Life goes on. What to do? He is known as "Mr. Slow Guy" in his workplace but I feel like proper justice would call him" Mr. Nonchalant! Nothing seems to faze him to a fault, I will tell you that. I got super frustrated over the years. A frustrated wife is like a fungus that spreads over time and it itches. That kind of an itch

that only stops for a second when scratched and comes back to stay for good!

In my case, it didn't take much time to see that I had to quickly take matters into my own hands when it came to resources in our home.

I would become the breadwinner of my family. O God! This was not part of the plan! My plan? Ugh!

Clearly everything had shifted. I was gone to work to care for other people's children, and I had missed my own children each long hour I spent away from them. The new job and my second American job near Lower Merion High School required that I supervised homework for two pre-teens of the household and babysat their 3 year-old toddler boy, exactly the same age as my first child and daughter at home.

Einstein was his name. He was very brilliant and of high maintenance. I would walk him to his synagogue pre-k a block away and I would pick him up from there at 1 pm and do the same routine for 4 and half days a week.

Everyday there, I would spend teaching the little boy whatever he hadn't grasped yet in regards to everything a four year old must know by that age and beyond. Then I would play with him all kinds of age appropriate board games, pretend games, hide and seek games. It was exhausting!

I had resentment in my heart. My heart felt some kind of betrayal to my own kids as I had no energy to play with them each time I got back home by 6 pm because I was burnt out. I knew in my heart, I was becoming secretively bitter that it was I who had to work long hours, instead of my husband.

He was at home all day long. And if he worked part time here and there at an oriental rug company nearby for a few hours in a week, his priorities were alcohol, cigarettes and watching a daily 2 pm tumultuous, filled with a drama upbeat of a television show called Very Sprinkler. And to top it all, he always made sure to have money to buy himself cigarettes and his Budweiser and he never could really tell me how much money he made whenever he worked which was very little hours but was that how a man should

rule his nest? Hiding his pay? It was very frustrating to deal with each other when finances were concerned.

He really didn't have a social life, so when he had one with other Malawian fellows from our small community, he just drank some more alcohol, came back home to tell me exactly how he felt about me from the past issues until that time he felt to release the knot in his throat about coming to America as well. The frustrated leading the frustrated. What a ride!

He would always blame me for bringing him to America. Before I realised it, I started making life easy for him. It was my obligation to make sure that I pay him back in full in any ways I could come up with for his sufferings in America.

I became the fall to his livelihood. I had become his downfall. The load was too heavy for me to carry. I began to feel much more depressed. I was in a zone of my own, nobody around me could understand. What a load I carried for years. I didn't know that I had just given him a free pass and independence to a wild world manipulation into my own world. I didn't know it then like I know it now.

I paid for believing that I was the reason for his depression in America for coming and living here with us as if it were a favor he was doing me and his children. I never considered that he had operated from his free will by coming along and choosing to remain in the country since the day we arrived.

When my sister had abandoned us in early 1998, now look-ing back, I understand that my sister had to be removed from my life so that I could grow up side by side with this man away from anybody else who was an influence to our relationship. I had to see for myself without others interfering for real who my husband had become. Usually, and generally in life, if any person is crowded, chances of seeing things or people clearer for who or what they really are, can be very slim or crowded. But my sister walked out of my life a few weeks after our arrival, truly, I believe that the weird fallout partly happened so that I could be able to learn of who my husband really was as a man and a human being to his family alto-gether, all around the seasons of life. Not just in good times, but in bad times too!

Anything and anybody else would have intervened and inter-rupted with what I needed to see for myself about him and what he needed to see about me in return.

By the time, I obtained the second job, our marital life was so stressful and so was the job to the point that I found myself resorting to excessive eating and to psychic hotlines to console my anxieties. Hell on earth was that time for me! Yes, psychics.

I have come to find out that desperate people do all kinds of desperate things. There's a very thin line between understanding what is real that works and the difference to understanding what is not real and that which doesn't work. Here I was, struggling to make ends meet, working like a dog in this house for many long tedious hours and spending my money on psychics just trying to find out about my future. Emptiness at its best! When will my life ever get better? When will I breathe again? I often wondered.

When I would go home, I would receive firebombs from my husband for bringing him to hell to suffer and whenever frustra-tion took its toll, the man I slept with out of wedlock back in Salima beaches of Malawi, would be back again in our bedroom, coming out of the mouth of the man who is supposed to cover my shame by his acceptance of my wrong when he took me back in spite of! The elephant from the jungles of Africa never left our bedroom shenanigans.

There were names I endured fit for a harlot flying across the house each time things got rough.

Some people get happy when their spouses are tipsy. I dreaded those moments because at least at that time he was so brazen enough to call me whatever names he saw fit. Soberly he would not do so as much. But with drunkenness, often that did the trick all the time. And he drunk all the time.

He still does as I speak. Alcohol became his escapade, therapy, best friend, confidant, girlfriend, companion, spouse and passion since we landed on American soil. He claims it's the African way of men doing things.

I guess it didn't matter whether we had relocated to a new land or not. It was all about self-love and self-seeking and loads of immediate gratification. My lonely journey intensified. It felt

more, lonely when I would wake up so early in the morning to go to the suburbs and help the preteens of the stressful real full time job, I had obtained for the first time in America. I was there to help, supervise and get ready the older children with their mornings before their school day besides the little boy, Einstein.

Then I would straighten up their bedrooms and do their laundry and whatever needed my attention once the 3 year old was in school for 3 hours. I felt like a walking zombie.

I was miserable. I believe it was the beginning of my depression, intensified with deep anxiety that showcased itself in my weight gain. I had never felt so ugly inside like I felt from that moment on. I didn't love myself. I became shameful inwardly. I felt defeated. I felt hopeless, but I couldn't share out loudly my pain. I began to blame myself for everything negative that had transpired in my loved ones lives within our home. I silently took the blame. I was the one who wanted to come to America! I was the one who pushed and pushed until it happened.

It was a very heavy burden to bear. Sometimes when I think about it, I get teary just to look at what I had allowed to put myself through. It was not my fault. It was part of our journey to America.

It took me this long to understand that everything negative happening in my life and happening to those around me is not always my fault.

There would be a series of many things that began to happen even during our stay in America when we landed in Wynnefield that I didn't cause, and I was not responsible for but somehow, I ended up to carry the blame like a child does with a blankie.

The Bryn Mawr avenue apartment building across from the Produce Junction was our temporary home for a little over 3 months, then we were evicted.

Boutros B was barely making a weekly pay. I wasn't making much money to be able to pay monthly rent on time and in full. We couldn't afford a $1000.00 apartment based on the money we made on part time work basis.

Shortly after that, we endured an encounter with another landlord, he was rather a slumlord who took a large sum amount of deposit to an apartment on the corners of street junction near to Overbrook

High School on the Wynnefield side of town and never delivered a place for us to live in.

It Takes Time To
Settle In America

We eventually landed our first apartment to encompass a family of 4 people, on Wynnewood Road in Overbrook Heights, on the third floor of a building by mid 1998. Boutros B went to live near Snyder Avenue in South Philadelphia where we frequently visited him.

Phoebella was very much the force that propelled the engine of our finances any time we could not afford a necessity. She was there to help us. Until eventually when we were all able to do many if not everything on our own. This was when I landed that second and stressful but real full time babysitting and housekeeping job. It was 10 hours a day for 4 days a week.

Even if I had plenty of money, I could not afford to thank Phoebella for what she did for my family during the darkest hours of my family's lives here in Philadelphia. I will forever thank God for her. If she complained about it when she helped us, I will say that I didn't hear of it.

The goodness of her heart did not stop there. One of the other crucial things that she helped me with was when she opened up my eyes in some of the ways household employers dealt with their employees in their homes without employee's consent or knowledge.

It was a phone tap that the male employer at the time had placed to record every conversation that went through the household over the phone conversations while I was there in their home.

Because of Phoebella, I was able to experience one of the best epiphanies in my life on an unsuspecting day. It was also the very last time I would use my work phone to call her and everybody I would call for personal reasons carelessly. That evening I overheard myself converse with her on the house phone a repetition of what

was already said in the morning but on a tape recorder. A deja vu right under my nose. My eyes were opened!

Meshuga for real! I will never forget it. That event changed my conduct in every household that I went and worked in from that point on. It was a blessing in disguise. This is why I never went in any house thinking that I was ever alone, again. I learned about big brother long before big brother was clearly visible on every street corner to the eye.

One would wonder why that particular employer did such a thing to me? Well, the answer to that at the time would be my response to a particular job advertisement I had spotted in the paper while I was working for him. It had caused a commotion in my employer's family. I had secretly answered to a babysitting job advertisement placed by a woman in another household on the Main Line in close relationship to the man of the house I was a baby sister for. Small world ain't it?!

I tell you, it was his sister looking for a babysitter, they also had placed their need in the Main Line Times. I had responded without knowing that the lady was the sister to the man I worked for. Yep! I was barely a year into America.

What did I know? How many Brenda's were in Philadelphia from Malawi looking for a babysitting gig on the Main Line Area?! How many?

Come on. The joke was on me. It was a no brainer! The sister and brother had confirmed among themselves and then had resorted to taping my calls behind my back. Boy, did I like talking on that phone whenever I was left alone in the man's household as I thoroughly cleaned that big old house as soon as all their kids were in school before I found out about the tape recorder.

I would beep Phoebella on her beeper, and no she wasn't a doctor but that's how she knew who needed a rescue, come to think of it, she was a doctor to those of us who needed her help and expertise! She always delivered too.

Anyhow, once she saw who beeped her, she would call back and this time around, she did just that for the last time while I was working in that house! And we talked, we talked about everything happening. My God, thank God it is no longer like that. I mean the time and energy we spent talking about everything, everyone

....

we knew and yet our lives just remained the same. It was frustration at its best! But those talks kept us going without going insane. We made it through year after year doing difficult jobs, dealing with difficult bosses, sometimes dealing with unruly kids, difficult situations that we thought we couldn't get over, but the long talks chimed us out before cell phones or job scopes were defined.

So, on this particular afternoon, I overheard myself talking on the phone only that what I was hearing was what had already taken place in the morning. What in the world was happening?!

It was creepy when I heard my own chichewa voice talking to Phoebella over a recording being replayed downstairs on my way to pick up one of the household's kids, an ice cream.

I paused in shock and in disbelief. But the man had no idea that I was eavesdropping on him. He thought I was upstairs playing board games with his kids.

The house was huge. Their garage and basement were his afternoon office and a man-cave. In it was also another smaller section that had a huge size food pantry for the children. The family also kept book supplies, arts and crafts and deep freezers for cold snacks during after school activities before their dinners.

He must have forgotten to shut himself in his room to listen in to the tape recorder.

You see, I never heard of anybody besides the FBI to ever record other people's conversation in movies that I had watched. It was never in a regular household but office like setting. I was in shock.

Well, I was in for an education of my own! A rude awakening. My outlook on employers from that day forth changed for the better. I never went into any household I would work in thinking that I was alone. I tell you, from that evening, I begun to look for another job elsewhere immediately for a babysitting gig because I knew that my privacy had been violated in that house. My days in that house were very numbered. For the remainder of my time there, I worked with a sense of uneasiness that clearly told me to always watch my back. I couldn't take that anymore. It was time to hit the road! The stress was high.

Those emotions from that job experience left me always looking at every household's telephone everywhere I went with a sense of indifference and uneasiness. I did lose an appetite for talking on the telephone with anybody if the setting was not in my own home. Of course, I have to remind everybody reading this story that I am talking about the days before portable phones. I eventually obtained my very first portable phone. Before that, the best of us used ground phones. Imagine life without cell phones! We survived it beautifully too, I will say.

The beginning of portable phones ushered with it, an intensified Big Brother security camera on street corners not forgetting those notorious nanny cam in most households that inhabit children for secure relations with their caregivers. Some caregivers over the years have done some damage to trust and the children that were left in their care. As a result of that now every other house with children that have a nanny has to deal with big brother or nanny cam watching that nanny in the household of work every moment they are in that household. Ugh!

The nanny cam watches the caregivers for the consolation of the parents while the parents are away from home.

Meshuga!

I know, my American Dream did not look very promising at all. Nothing I was going through, looked promising. The place of my destiny seemed deader to me whenever I tried to make something out of everything I dared to touch. But you know what?

I was not ready to give up on my destiny yet. I was glad I could work. Hidden Cameras or not. Quitting was not an option either in that household without plan B. I had 3 other people to care for. I couldn't let them down.

Besides, Phoebella was too young to keep on bailing my family out of financial strain. We weren't even her responsibility, so I was determined not to disappoint her or anyone at all. Dreamers don't quit. Too many lives were at stake.

So, I landed on my feet again.

My 3rd job was in Merion Park near a certain middle school. This one job taught me a good, quick lesson that a worker should never mentally cleave to any household job permanently because

nannies and housekeepers are easily dispensable and disposable by their employers. At least, that's what I learned from that household. It was crazy!

Bonny would be my next female boss. I hardly saw her husband, I wouldn't even remember him if I saw him on the street today. They had two sons. I only remember the baby, Lucke. He was the reason for my weekly visits to their house. This woman worked me like a slave! And she fired me by sending her husband and her older son to my apartment on Christmas eve to tell me never to come to her house for work again.

Let's just say that she had a case of multi-tasking me to doing 3 things all at once!

Every now and again I would accidentally shrink her cashmere baby gear. That would send her into ballistic blabbering mouth. She was reddish blonde if that makes sense. I think her real hair color was carrot. And a beautiful face full of freckles.

She had a temper that was gonna get me out of there straight to the moon, any day. It was one of my shortest American household jobs. Frankly, I was relieved. Sigh.

I had tried working as a full-time babysitter in those two particular homes from Mondays through Thursdays of the week by this time, and I figured out something. Long term job commitment for me maybe quite a challenge. So, I began to shy away from babysitting jobs that required long term commitment and resorted to housekeeping jobs again. There's a huge difference between housekeeping in Malawi and housekeeping in America. Aaah yeah, huge difference? Dear Lord!

And to make matters worse, I grew up in my mother's home surrounded by household helpers for 20 years straight. And within those 20 years, I was also once a diplomat's child. At one time we had a housekeeper, a cook, a gardener and a school bus driver for the Malawian embassy community when my dad worked as a diplomat in RSA. So, you get the idea of how much housekeeping I knew.

But I had to experiment on someone and on something really well. O yes, brace yourself or take cover.

My next and 4th household job where I was hired to thoroughly clean a beautiful house in 2 consecutive days of the week totaling 16 hours would be the unsuspecting mansion by Saint Charles seminary development near City Line Avenue across from Philadelphia. It was an experiment on my part waiting to happen.

The family believed my fake references that I had ample experience in this department. Nope!

Somebody had long taught me that you pick up a job if you get an offer and you do your best to learn as you go because if you say no, you may just miss out on a great opportunity that could propel you ahead in life. I adhered to that advice.

There I was in the suburbs of Wynnewood area about 25 to 30 minutes-walk a bit over 2 miles from where we lived. I was ready to show this lady what I knew about housekeeping.

Mind you, we had been in America for less than 2 years by this time. So, these were still the early days of our American journey. The Suburbs of Wynnewood has huge beautiful mansions behind the seminary in a hidden secluded setting. The lady that I was visiting for work was substantially rich. The house was surrounded by beautifully manicured gardens within their large yard of land as well as a pool. I think that for me, she was the most angelic looking being and woman I had ever seen since I came to America.

Everything on her body was how it should be if you can understand what my imagination is trying to say. She was perfect. Her hair was blond. She was about 5"9 inches tall. A super angelic model.

Her husband was a very successful businessman. He was a pharmacist and owned his own pharmacy. He was dark and handsome but nothing strikingly outstanding. His grocery shop was located at Broad and Susquehanna. It was there that my husband worked for very minimal hours a week. My spouse and I both did odd jobs to try to bring in whatever cash we could for food and a roof over our head, our personal apartment in America. We would alternate in taking care of our children. Whoever didn't work in my household on that particular day or week was home with our two toddlers.

Boy, this was the first house I ever walked in anybody's house and everything there looked so heavenly white. It was a hidden paradise somewhere in Wynnewood.

This woman resembled biblical story time female angels. Her house was immaculate. Everything in there and outside of the home was immaculate. I had become consumed with bleach by the time I had left her house. I had not fully understood the power it had on all fabric as well as any surface, a few days into the job.

My goodness! I couldn't get anything stained white enough. I had no idea that not everything was to be bleached. I seriously damaged quite a few things just trying to satisfy her taste. Everything turned into damaged oblivion. How could I know without proper education that everything has the right cleaner, stain remover or polisher. Maybe if I had told the truth, I would have gotten the job and stayed in it too for a while. Now we will never know. I took matters in my own hands and went crazy with that old bleach!

Talk about gentleness! That woman was angelic even in the way that she fired me. It was a simple thank you. But your services are no longer needed.

I suppose I was everywhere for a reason, a season and a purpose. I was in that job to connect my husband to work at the lady's husband's grocery store. This place was another outlet for my husband. There he could feel a sense of being besides babysitting our children day in and day out. He ended up making friends with a young Tunde there and a brilliant Korean student girl. That gave him a sense of purpose besides diapers and prepping lunch meats for our toddlers for that era in time.

Each time I learned a bit of my purpose to a level in a particular household, for a particular season, I moved on to the next lesson for my elevation.

EACH STAGE IN
LIFE IS NECESSARY

I will tell you this, all the years I was travelling along my American journey, I had no idea that each stage was a dotted timeline and very necessary for my making for me to get to where I am today.

There is no skipping stages on this path called life for me and the same goes for everyone on earth out there living life on a limb.

This life is here for you to live it. Purposely and fully. Go for it!

Everyday lessons are imperative for every soul and where one is going to get to their destiny. I had to go through everything for my own good. Sometimes I thought it was the devil hurting me, but it was life churning me into the level of gold that was buried deep inside of me and what my naked eyes could not see at the time to bring out the gold in me, effortlessly.

One could say that we move in life from glory to glory according to how fast one adheres to the lessons life offers us, daily.

I will say this, though. I do believe that the devil gets too much credit for things in this earth that are caused by our own doing. Sometimes, those things are also a necessary evil to get us to where we need to be for our elevation in general. Nothing much really comes out of your comfort zone. No growth there.

Some of the training and pruning is by The Creator Himself to bring out of us the very best for the purpose which He created us for, even through pain. I can testify because when unpleasant things happen to us it hurts so badly. What can make it even harder at times is when we don't see clearly or even begin to understand that some of the issues we may go through in life are very necessary for where we are meant to end up, Destiny. Which is where everyone alive today should be reaching for. Everyone was created to fulfill their purpose and destiny in the Earth!

Sometimes pain and heartache may be the only way to get us on that path, depending on the type of personality the individual may have.

The old me, the type of personality that I had, only the most painful moments and most painful experiences could plunge me into becoming the very best that I could ever be. Although I don't wish for pain anymore for me to beckon. I am no longer that stubborn when it comes to God and me. Nothing in my life that is great has come out of my complacency. I hate to admit to you that it was pain or heartache in most times if not at every point that brought out of me, the very best of what I had in me all along. Yet, I had no knowledge that it was there. Those painful moments though if not channeled right can also be a downfall to someone who may not be strong enough to stand or fight. I only survived because I cried out to God. In most times though I thought that I was going to die while going through some of my issues.

The truth be told, everyone needs problems and difficult situations sometimes just to direct us or place us on the right path.

Especially if you have a stubborn and difficult character that has a resistant soul to receive, accept and make the eminent, necessary changes. Difficult times are imperative. They may sometimes help a person make and take that leap of faith. I have seen it. I am only speaking from my own experiences. Looking back today, I now understand. Don't fight change too much. It is necessary for one's growth.

Back then, I had no clue and therefore I resorted to a lot of lonely pity parties and bitterness that came to stay for a very long time in my American living because I faced every struggle and fought it as if it were a person and didn't leave room enough to see anything positive about it. Which affected the speed I traveled on towards any goals I eventually set for myself. A negative mind is a sure slow ride to anybody's destiny.

I had to go through some things!

JUST LIKE JONAH,
GOD WILL FIND YOU

God was not the biggest part of my life until it was necessary for me to make Him so. I strongly believe that I had to go through such pain for me to turn to God. Nothing else was getting my attention. From birth till 1988, I lived my life in Malawi with my parents sheltered and provided for. By 1988 until February 1993 my mother and father took extreme care of me in Pretoria probably the best 6 years of my whole life because I was old enough to savour every moment.

From February 1993 until February 1994 I had my mother to worry about. It was one of the saddest seasons of my life because I saw my mother struggle for the first time whilst she grieved my dad. Right there and then, I swore to myself that I would never depend on a man or husband for everything. Sadly, that vow came to pass. I had no idea about making vows so carelessly. I have learnt from that. No more ungodly vows.

Then from February 1994 to December 21st, 1997, my married life took off in Malawi. From December 1997 until 2017, my life was intertwined in a tumultuous marriage that was very necessary for my future and everything I needed to learn for the next chapter of my life beyond my midlife crisis. I am not through learning about life yet. I am not through learning about my purpose, my destiny and I am definitely not through learning about my God. I promise you that nothing has been a mistake. I must confess though, that in my mid-twenties, until mid-thirties in my old mindset, God was simply my Santa Claus and a mere figurehead.

I went through the motions of life like most people do pretty much on a yearly routine. I went to church as a weekly ritual composed of a superficial consciousness for the purposes of gratifying myself. Moreover, it was a loud statement to everyone else who saw that I was a church goer. Everything I did about God was for others to see and for affirmation from the world.

I had no real grasp of who I really was as a person or better yet Who God really is in His Totality to all mankind and His creation.

I had no intimate relationship with Him. So, I really didn't know Him.

I don't think that I even cared about God deeply before coming to America except when I needed something from Him.

My life was testifying for itself by the way I was doing everything and reacting to everything all around me. My workmanship of a facade I would put on and off was nothing, but a waste of time and a futile one man show with no spectators. Therefore, the way I had handled the stressful jobs by my fourth one, was chaotic. The unstable friendships, the emptiness in my marriage were some of the obvious signs that I was in trouble and I lacked wisdom that always guarantees peace. Wisdom, peace, joy and understanding are facts that can only come from God.

I definitely knew very little of Him or His attributes and personality and I didn't hold a standard to everything He expects from everyone who calls Him their Father. I did call Him my Father from time to time. I was very unstable in my claims which often resulted into obvious frustration.

DESPERATION COSTS

The frustration often left me very angry and gasping for answers and always pressed me to investigate about my life, its past, present, its future. Thus, when fortune tellers entered into my habits. They were from all over the city of Philadelphia and sometimes my sister, Abiti Bula and I would go to Atlantic City, in New Jersey to find answers through fortune tellers.

I did spend a lot of money paying fortune tellers to tell me what the future held for me. I was very desperate for answers as my housekeeping and babysitting day jobs got longer and more complex by each year.

I tell you this, if you don't have a solid faith foundation, a solid support system in your life or community, you will look for any and every kind of solution in anything and anybody, everywhere all around you without sensibility and considering consequences. And the worst part is when God is not in the solution then your

life just continues to spiral in empty thoughts and actions filled with insanity in repetitive results no matter how much energy you put in your efforts.

SUICIDE IS NOT THE ANSWER/ DON'T KILL YOUR FUTURE

There is a sense of an ever-present deep and sad feeling of uncontrolled emptiness. Life just passes by daily, monthly, year after year regressing and never fulfilling the potential in you, of what could be and the purpose for your creation therefore forfeited.

I remember feeling so lonely so often that I would take the available bus in the middle of the night from 66th and Malvern Avenue in my neighborhood headed to the last terminal where I would catch the train a few miles away, near where my family and I lived. I would ride the train to go all the way to its east end. The intention was to throw myself somewhere along the train tracks any chance I would get so that the oncoming train from the opposite direction could run me over, dead on the spot. My mind was heavily burdened and filled with darkness I was beyond sadness. I was really in the dumps I couldn't see my way out. Depression can be fatal.

I could not seem to shake off suicidal thoughts in my heart or mind for quite a number of years. I often did those suicidal attempts several occasions. It was always very late at random nights in my lonely state of mind. Usually my two babies were always tucked away asleep at the apartment in their room. Their father hardly noticed I was gone because he was often times intoxicated. He was there but not really there. It was really depressing to watch. Every suicidal attempt was always voided.

There was always a voice deep inside of me. I thank God for that silent voice.

The voice deep in my gut, I came to realise that it was the voice of My Creator, God. He often spoke to me gently about how

my two children would feel after I had left them with a sense of my unworthiness and to them who knew me as someone very special and necessary in their life. What would become of me in their mind to the news of my demise? At that thought, their images would flash in my head of happy times and sad times together right before my eyes. Just like that, I would wipe away the silent tears gushing from the corners of my eyes falling down on my face in sheer anguish and then get off the train to catch the bus that headed back towards the direction of my home feeling so sad and so hopeless very early morning hours before the streets were live again. Was America all about this? I would wonder to myself.

But I did have hope. I just didn't know it yet, at that time. I know this now because My Creator would always use my children as my stepping stone into that hope that I was longing to feel so badly. But Jesus was always my innermost hope. When I look back now, I know. I didn't know much about God except very basic factors about Him. I had gone through suicidal thoughts for a very long time. I couldn't exactly say how long I suffered from depression but I can remember a series of long events that would send me quickly into deep sadness that didn't want to go away. I had no idea that suicidal thoughts would someday leave me, hopefully for good. I thank God that I am still here today.

But whenever I went deep into depression, I could not see past any difficulties that were in front of me. I wondered how long I was going to live life like that.

Job after job. House after house with not much relationship or stability to count on. Just working to make money to pay off monthly bills, food to eat and nothing left for a savings or for fun. Life became a depressing trend year after year. Everything costs money in America. Everything.

The kind of pay we were receiving and making was often finished before the weekend had even started. I could not understand the American dream. Where was the American dream I had heard of? How was my family going to get there on the greener side?

Were we really in America, the land of Milk and Honey? Or was all this just a hoax, a chasing after the wind and a nightmare? Hoping to wake up from it soon. Where were we?

....

Yes indeed, we were in America! Two years in and I had never experienced such hardship and uncertainty anywhere else in my life before America. There I was with family suffering together, whenever there was household lack, individually at times suffering from working like a donkey for the sake of my family as a unit.

AMERICA WILL BOND
YOU OR BREAK YOU

*I*f you and your loved ones have never bonded during the times of trouble in your life and you live on earth especially in America, then I don't believe that anyone or anything can bring you closer together with your friends or family elsewhere in the world.*

This is the place where you make it, or you break it that is if it doesn't break you first mentally, physically, financially and spiritually.

This was the first place I ever saw a person walk while having a conversation with themselves before even hands-free cell phones and hands-free technology was invented.

I had laughed at the ones I had seen yet I didn't know that I would one day if not many days to come will also begin to ponder out loudly to myself because I either had no one who could understand my inner battles or better yet, they plainly would cast me aside as crazy.

It was easy to go out and walk around talking to myself and coming into agreement with whatever was eating me up from inside, all by myself. Help me Lord! I had become crazy too!

For a moment.

I do believe that American life has a way of changing a person especially if that person is here with a lot of unsolved issues. I was one ready candidate overly qualified in many levels of dysfunction. I had a lot of unsolved issues. I was carrying a whole young family that was loaded with issues. Some issues were generational. Some issues were pretty brand new. Spoken ones and unspoken ones. I had no mentor. I had no stable relations. I had no outlet that replenished my troubled soul after pouring out for others.

The only man that I had ever loved, had shown me a side to him that said I deserved everything miserable America were to dish out.

The first two years of our stay in America were horrible and lonely. My spouse and I often had fist fights with each other within the four corners of our apartment on Wynnewood Road.

It didn't matter who was around us or what had triggered the verbal and abusive arguments at each particular time to cause a raucous towards each other in the presence of our two innocent children. Imagine?

And the crazy side to our cycle was that we would go back to sex and everyday life after each, and every abusive altercation that had transpired, year in and year out, season in and season after as if everything was alright without properly patching up or fixing the many potholes at hand. We were experts in dysfunction on all levels, I now reckon. Meshuga!

We had money problems big time! Keep in mind that from December 1997, my husband, our two children and I had travelled to America with only $190.00 to our name. I could almost believe that this acknowledgement to my husband and I turned us into having a $190.00 mindset. So financially at the time, it seemed as if our brains were only operating on a mechanical level of meagre. And whatever we were trying to do individually for our family was working against each other. We just couldn't see eye to eye on how to manage our finances or better our home financially in general.

Our marriage has never been harmonious except for the year into our marriage or a little over a year. We couldn't agree on basic family ways of governing our children. Or our home issues besides how we looked at money whether we were buying food, clothes, paying bills, playing the lottery or transportation on a daily basis. Often times, we spent time and energy on frustrating each other and sabotaging each other. We never played as a team. We had no plan in place for profitable ways of governing our marriage or future.

There were no boundaries within or outside our marriage when it came to covering each other's back. It was like we were in a dog eat dog world. One person would easily throw the other under

the bus and each time it felt like a marathon to proving to others who the better person was between the two of us and yet it takes two to tangle to make the dance work.

No one person was entirely right every time which in this situation it was I who was ever wrong according to him. I suppose that our children were the only one thing we did right together. But only God gets the glory in that, I mean that with all my heart.

The children are certainly one of the few best blessings in our lives together. Sometimes, I still feel that even in their welfare on many levels, we couldn't and still do not agree on the best ways of raising them. The way to discipline them or the ways of teaching them on how to survive years down the road, that too is a constant fight. Our Marital journey and parental journey has been very challenging on every level and sometimes much more challenging than the marriage next door so to speak.

It is as if everything that had happened all around my marriage, was a sheer sign that we would end up splitting in two. Never in harmony except during intimacy, sporadically. Everything else that we did was either done divided or individually. There has never been any sense of togetherness as one unit in a marriage.

We dealt with each other as if we didn't count on each other to be together to the end. We tiptoed towards our marital issues and we were always on the verge of breaking up. So much so that after the sudden loss of Boutrous B in 1999, our household went into a depression and our low demeanors were a crushing reality that met us face to face. Head on collision!

A tragedy came on board of our already sunken lives. A sudden shocking death was at our door! Our beloved brother was no more! He had given up on hope and resorted to throwing in the towel. This was one of the most confusing times in my life. Everybody involved was an emotional mess. I had been separated from my sister for almost 2 years at that time. Communication had gone cold.

And Boutrous B became part of my close-knit family from Malawi to the end of his life.

He had fallen into a deep depression from the moment my sister left him. No one knew the impact it rooted deeply within him

until the day he gave up on life. One year of emotional solitude, rejection, depression and sorrow was much too much to bear. Just like that, we had come to the end of his chapter. It was sorrowful.

And his afflictions were a remnant in my sister's psych. Thoughts of guilt. Thoughts of shame. Thoughts of anxiety triggered by seasonal insanity around each Mayhem when it approaches. Thoughts of numbness and disbelief that this indeed happened. A pain that was not identical to all but very much deeply shared and felt for years to come in everyone's heart who had once loved him.

Boutros B would be a memory.

Sadly, at his demise, as fate would have it, there was nothing else to do but to reunite once again as one family. Pain and sorrow has a way of doing that to those that are stricken by it. It is how humanity survives the harshness of life's hard SEASONS. In Togetherness. In Community. In Empathy. We held together for a bit.

SOMETIMES LIFE DOESN'T MAKE SENSE

That was the first hardest most difficult chapters of America by 1999. One and a half years into The American journey. The situation was deep, complex and emotions were so mixed. It was the first-time life showed me that I don't have to understand or justify anything and everything to have an answer to the very challenge or thing that presents itself in front of me. I understood then that life had many things to teach me as well as dish out for me. And some of the things life would dish out for me were in fact things I didn't ask for or even qualify to handle according to my take.

Yet, there I was. To do everything and anything life commanded me to. Instead of yelling at my sister for abandoning my family for a bit over a year before returning back to us under duress on her part because she was in trouble and at that very moment, she was in need of me to help her out. Yikes!

When I looked deeply into her situation, I was able to find a soft place in my heart towards her. It was imminent. I felt pity towards her and a deeper turmoil simultaneously. It was indeed one of the most confusing moments in my life. I am sure the others in our community felt that same way too.

I had regained my sister but Boutros B was no more. He would be missed by everyone who had loved him. He had been part of my family since 1996. Just like that, he was gone. Too soon. It was sour love gone super bitter. Nothing good came out of that relationship except that my sister and my family ended up here in America through their dysfunctional relationship. A lifelong blessing that at one point, turned into an unforgotten tragedy.

I have a lot of mixed feelings each time I think of their journey, Boutrous B and my sister Abiti Bula. I catch myself teary sometimes. I have always fought tears in my eyes in their regards. A tragedy. I ask myself rhetorical questions about love. And everything to do with love. Why did it have to end so badly?

How can everything that was once so full of life, vigour, positivity, promises and fun get so twisted, so sad in a very short period of time? How can something such as love that brings people together in harmony end up in turmoil, negativity and in a quick moment be forever so vanished?

I had all these questions that no one else could answer especially when my own life was filled with turmoil, uncertainty, anger, fear, insecurities. As a result of his sudden death, for a very long time, I carried guilt in my heart for not knowing that our inner circle Boutrous B was deeply hurting the whole time we were with him. I knew for sure that everyone in our inner circle was too busy nursing their own wounded young hearts during the entire tumultuous season of 1998 to 1999 to spot another one who was bleeding among us. Nobody in our inner circle was healthy enough spiritually or mentally to reach out to anyone, until it was too late.

It was one of the deepest and saddest moments in the lives of everyone who knew him in this world, nearer or far, let alone in America and to those that surrounded themselves with him. Boutrous B was a people's person especially those that had become family to him in Philadelphia. I could not explain the anguish

everyone felt for the years to come. I still tear up just to think of him.

I believe that from that May of 1999, until mid-2000, everyone who secretly grieved the shocking news of his premature death was secretly melting down internally. I for one went through it. I was so sad. I had never known loneliness that deep. I was so sorrowful I didn't know what to do with it or where else to take it to. My spouse and I had never shared our sufferings together as a union. This too proved so in a deeper magnitude.

Everyone outside our home who knew Boutrous B was grieving also but everyone grieved silently, in solitude. We at that time in our community among ourselves avoided one another because nobody knew how to deal with the grief in a collective setting. Nobody was showing or sharing their sentiments. And everyone tried to pick up and move on as if nothing terrible had happened and yet inwardly everyone involved was screaming in total grief.

Truthfully speaking, America doesn't give a person enough time to grieve, especially if that person has constant bills to pay. Unless they are rich and money is not a problem. Almost immediately the person grieving often must return to work. My breaking point was when I had decided to move away once again from my husband into Lotus Villa building apartments nearby without the one I had loved.

Whatever, we had shared up until that moment of the year 2000 was not enough to hold us together. The sex was no longer the thing to focus on to keep us glued together as one. The money was far from being enough to keep us together. But money had never been our motive or focus for our love to begin with. Keneilwe and I had begun our journey together from scratch. We were together because we loved each other and nothing else. Everything else we had accumulated was the result of our love together and our fellowship together.

Yet, in the midst of it all, our kids, our stuff, our looks, our age, our backgrounds were not able to keep us together. Nothing was good enough to keep us together anymore. Something so big and so necessary was missing. I didn't know what it was at that time. But I know it now. God!

HISTORY REPEATED ITSELF

At that time, I did not really know what it was but I felt like running away again! Can you imagine that? Once again, I was not mature enough to face life. I felt that running away would be the answer to restart life all over again. This time somewhere away from my spouse. I thought that if I be on my own, that would fix the problems I was facing in my home. So in August of 2000, I rented and moved into a two bedroom apartment at Lotus Villa near Overbrook Farms with our six year old daughter, Marvel and our four year old Avedi. Two children and my 27 years of age, self. I was determined. Keneilwe and I would share the children on weekends.

It was tough. Emotionally and physically as well as financially tough and draining. I was super determined though. Living in a loveless, dysfunctional lifestyle and marriage was no longer cutting it for me.

I tell you, America has dug up some things from inside of me I had no idea I had deeply embedded in me. I didn't know my own strength, but trouble gave me no other choice. I was a frustrated and a restless 27 year-old woman when I moved into my first rental apartment building.

Fate would have it, that on my way out to be on my own, before I was fully out of my marriage during our separation, I had met a man. Talk about history repeating itself. Yes, the devil knew exactly what I liked. He sent his bait. I fell for it too. Again, shamefully.

I know, I couldn't believe it too but where I was then spiritually, I felt justified. My dark side had me bound again. 12620 miles away from Malawi, this time around. Same old Shenanigans again. Caught and stuck. Ugh damn you dark side!

Clearly, I hadn't understood the repercussions I was dealing with since 1997 about Mr. Do-Me. Just like that, in August 2000, I went ahead and repeated history. Again! I know, hey, you can feel my frustration. Defeated! Breathe. Inhale and exhale!

I felt that I was worthless anyway, so it didn't matter who was marking me down as the devil or counting any of my evil and wicked ways this time around. However dirty I was made to feel,

I couldn't feel any dirtier. At the rate my life was going, it didn't matter what I was doing. I also didn't know that what you believe about yourself is what counts no matter what others think of you.

I get mad at myself for not knowing that fact sooner.

I had no idea that I was the one who had given permission to allow anyone that told me anything different about me whether it was true or false, pleasant or not! The choice was mine to receive and believe it, or reject it. I had given permission to my husband to trash me and I had received and believed everything he had said about me to me. I wish I knew then what I know now. I could have saved myself many sleepless nights. The beginning of my insomnia and sleeping pills. May God Help me!

For the longest early seasons of my married life and my children's early days, I often felt that there was something very significant missing in my household and in my young family's life altogether. But I didn't quite know what it was. I had two hearts about many things that were meaningful to me.

AECST TO THE RESCUE

I felt that I needed a close walk with God and I wanted the same for our children. So that's why I, with my two kids on one Sunday morning had attended and joined the church family nearby. The First African Episcopal Church of Saint Thomas. It is located in Overbrook Farms about 10 minute-walk from the apartment building where we rented.

I was compelled to join this church denomination because it is an American version of the African Anglican church in which my father and mother raised their children until the time my family and I, left Africa. My African family and American family is still part of this denomination to this day. I am the only one who is now Pentecostal. I was part of the First African Church of Saint Thomas congregation from the end year of 2000 until 2010.

I became Pentecostal under Jesus Miracle Center in North Philadelphia, somewhere along the year of 2010. I knew all about the Bible and what it says about adultery.

Here I was with this man, who was not my husband, in another chapter of my life yet again clearly committing adultery on the other side of the Atlantic Ocean. Regardless of my emotional state of mind or my reasoning of why I felt justified to do everything I was doing. I felt very convicted. I felt lost. I was a hypocrite. I was in deep sin. I was just an emotional mess within my heart.

I was very lonely, but I was in desperate need of love.

SOMETIMES AGE MATTERS

I had no idea of what I was supposed to be doing as a mother with my two children. I was someone dealing with a deep longing for someone to walk life aside me where matters of the heart were concerned but everything about me emotionally had no idea exactly of who was best for my life and its future. I had no idea that another man was not part of the solution. I was very hormonal and at a sexual peak of my young adult years too. Please don't judge!

27/28 was a high peak in my life! I was athletic, I was gorgeous. I was hormonal, I was rowdy. I was fiery and I was hot on fire waiting for a fireman to extinguish the lust.

The timing of this young man's encounter could not have come at a more wrong time in my life. Geesh!

He certainly caused more wildfires in me than he was supposed to put out! I had met him as I got off the bus number 65 in Overbrook Hills. He, on the other hand got off the bus number 31, just a few yards away from the corner of 66th and Lansdowne Avenue. It was fate and some kind of a dark setup. I know this for sure several years later as I look back now. It was a setup that wasn't from divine realms. It was a trap and a detour I got caught in and got detained on, I am convinced.

I didn't think of it negatively when it happened. I felt like it was supposed to be. Weird part is, how something you think you may need has a way of popping up at times when your reasoning and circumstances are in desperate need of that thing you think you are in need of but when you really think about it, and actually go through it, you realize that you didn't need that thing or person

after all especially when and if your blinders were off. You realize how terrible or destructive that thing maybe and turn out to be, later on, a few steps ahead.

But hey, this is why I am here sharing my mistakes and life lessons. I needed this guy to shed a light on my intimacy with an American guy apart from all the infatuation I had set aside without real tangible information and experience of my own. I needed this guy for the lessons he would teach me. Boy, did he teach me a few of life's lessons or what? In case you are wondering if I had thoughts of my green card in mind when I met this guy. The answer is yes! Do you blame me? If you ever been an illegal immigrant at one point in your life anywhere on the Earth and have experienced the anxieties that an illegal immigrant goes through, you would understand why an American citizen is precious portal to citizenship. Sadly, to admit that as an illegal immigrant at that time, I saw this American man as my ticket to citizenship and I had talked about it too with him. Yes, in that short 3/4 months? Yep, that was the old silly me.

Listen, it is not fun to be an illegal alien in America! I couldn't sugarcoat that fact even if I tried! If you are a reject anywhere, you would understand this concept, easily. It's that simple.

It has not been a comfortable feeling to be an illegal immigrant in America in the last, almost 20 years. If I could speak for another, about immigration laws, I am convinced that things are getting worse by the time you read my story. Being an illegal immigrant in itself has erupted such intense anxiety in people, blood pressure is one of the most common issues stealing life and joy from an illegal immigrant's very own existence, right here in America, constantly. You just don't know!

This man, "Donald" had too many sides to him, when I dated him in those few months that my heart was glad when the fantasy had come to an end. He definitely was never gonna be my portal to my green card. No sir! I would have been in more hell than I had already experienced by the time I was done being his "wife." No thank you.

One of the lessons in life is to think, really think before actions. And seek advice for everything and anything from mentors who

have been there before and it's even better if the mentors do walk with God. They know something you don't. It's all about teamwork, network, community and the greater good. God.

Less unwise people on planet earth, make less frustrated people to work with in communities, resulting in a happier and better environment. We all affect one another wherever we are! You best believe it. At that time. I had no idea that my choices to entertain what I had felt about this guy would leave me even more depleted about myself and love altogether. He came just when I needed him the most.

What a foolish notion!

GOD USES OUR FAILURES

He, I felt, in my naivety, was just the right medicine I needed to take to make my pain go away in that Autumn and Winter season! He was more of the propelling reason why I ended up motioning my cries unto God by the time I was done with him. Remembering that it was after the eros relationship failed, that I had with him, when I really drew very close to an Agape God for the first time ever in my life. We all have the reason why we ended up at the feet of God in desperation at one point or another in our lives. Mine was after two carnal failed relationships. Please don't judge!

So, even though I was seeking to walk close with God at the same time, when this man came around, I didn't. Our chance meeting momentarily took over all the attention I had for God and everything else important I could have been doing with my time, besides spending quality time with my children. I was taken by this man's different appearance altogether. He was and is a born American citizen but he didn't look like every guy I had crossed paths with since my arrival in the United States of America. He was not gorgeous per say but he was definitely attractive. Something in him made my heart skip a bit.

He, to me, I would say, looked like a linebacker of a football team. He was tall. Maybe about 5 foot 11. Dark and handsome.

His skin had a beautiful smooth tone and shade of black almost like the way Blair Underwood looks, but much taller, a slightly protruding belly and a charm to him that spelled, "come hither!" His smile was infectious and alluring. He walked with a swag and his tone to his voice sounded like someone who had definitely been in school. I could tell that he had been well educated or around some people who were educated. He was well spoken. I could tell that he knew what a polished life is about. He didn't wear his pants hanging down below his underwear! It was refreshing to see.

It was very intriguing to see this on a man for once who looked like they were rough around the edges but also carried themselves around as if they were a Mr. Denzel Washington!

When he looked at me and said hello, I thought that I had melted into gold right there on 66th and Lansdowne Avenues and streets of Philadelphia. It was lust at first sight!

I didn't even recognize this inside of me until now that I know God.

He was smitten by me and so was I by him. It was magical. It was a devilish setup. And the mad lust picked up from there for 3/4 spicy shady months! Yes, short and sour. It was another trap. I fell flat for it.

He always called me on my house phone before he could come to sleep overnight by my place. He would sneak out very early in the mornings. I can't remember if he had a cellphone because he only called me from random numbers. Ladies, right there was a big red flag! Telltale signs were screaming out loudly everywhere! But denial is not bliss. But lust is blind!

Have you ever been so lonely, stupid and giving yourself answers to what you already know and finding yourself doing it anyway? Sad ain't it? Ugh!

I had been an African girl all of my life. Still am. Lol! I had never been in a normal relationship except with my husband when we dated from April 1992 until February 1994 when we got married. I was no longer capable of thinking things over in a relationship beyond my marriage that was erotic even when the truth was staring me right in front of my face. I told myself that it wasn't what it actually was! Hehehe! Denial. Do you blame me?

I had no idea what life in America was like among the unmarried folks who were in the dating game.

Golly! I had never heard of a booty call either. That's all I really was to this man. To this day, I still don't know his full name. He gave me his" representative's" name, "Donald". My kids called him Uncle Donald. Yes, I was that stupid and gullible. Everything he told me was a lie. Sigh.

I took everything he told me and ate it all up. He was one of the best con artists I have ever met. He too, was going through a separation. Now don't ask me how I have come to believe that from him. That is one of his declarations. Probably the pictures of kids in his wallet were his, not his nephew's like he had claimed them to be. Inhaling and exhaling right now. Seventeen years later, I still feel very stupid about his lies that I believed.

During his 3/4 months with me, he was able to introduce me to the Hard Rock Cafe downtown Philadelphia on my birthday in September of 2000. Then he showed me another side of Philadelphia I had no idea existed before just less than 9 miles away from my apartment. It was simply breathtaking to me! The place is known as Wissahickon Valley Park, we visited its beautiful forestry, creeks and trails in the Autumn. We had one of the best times ever although the relationship was phony and short-lived. I was able to do those shenanigans with him in the weekends. I had the children during the week for school days and they went to their father on 56th and Vine Street in Philadelphia where he was residing at the time.

The "representative" that I had met in Donald had the best qualities that I was yearning for in a man, a husband. I am reminded today that always most wolves come in sheep clothing. I didn't have that revelation yet. He was not very educated as college level educated but he had an ambition to write and that was one of our common grounds. We talked about writing a lot too. There is this book that he had given me to read for writers for the purposes of guiding me into how to write, edit, publish my own literature if I ever wished to write one day. I never read that book because I guess I felt that he was a phony and so was everything that reminded me of him.

....

But what he was promising me at the time we met was exactly the type of romance I had been longing for and was what and why I was attracted to him. We had a lot of things we liked that we talked about on an intellectual level. You see, the devil knows exactly what to send. I had no insight or antennas at the time to ascertain.

My sister Abiti Bula often laughs at me each time we look back and talk about our bloopers in life this far. She couldn't believe that I had believed every lie this guy had told me in a relationship that should have never been.

Here, I was once again, with a man as confused as I was lusting and doing everything I knew was wrong and sinful. I had a battle in my head. An ongoing battle, every time, I was seeing the guy during the affair. I got conflicted. The tough thing about it was that I was loving every moment I spent with him. Sin can be super sweet but it's consequences aren't so sweet. I was good at running away from my issues outwardly. Yet, they were never apart from me no matter how far I tried to go! My mind was an ongoing tumultuous and chaotic battlefield.

When the second and fourth month into the affair progressed, I begun to get worse a few months in, my constant expectations of needing to have him around more during the weekends and night time behind my kid's back in the next bedroom door became overwhelming to him. My adamant vocal opinions of "our relationship" became a nuisance to him.

I was bombarded with feelings of vulnerabilities, so much so that he begun to find me very "needy." I had no idea that the relationship was only about sex to him and nothing more. I was so naive and so sad that when I discovered that I was the only one invested in the one-sided relationship I wanted to be done with him. Vulnerabilities aren't an asset. But they are liabilities and a downfall!

One Sunday night with him before the wee morning hours on his way out, I had asked him for a Transpass fees for my weekly bus transportation to be able to get me to work which was less than $20.00 at the time. He had no money on him. He had no money period.

He had asked me why I felt that he should leave me the money for my transportation card on that morning. I said to him that because he had been coming to my house, he was always eating my food, drinking my juice and wine and besides I gave him sex. He plainly said to me that we were both benefiting from the sex, so nobody was paying anybody. I felt emotionally and physically robbed, especially being a born African woman. Suddenly! Just like that, my eyes were widely opened! I told him never to come to my door again. In a heartbeat, the affair was over. And I was left behind with cheap and embarrassing memories.

MORE ELEPHANTS IN THE ROOM

B y thanksgiving season of the year 2000, "Donald" had exited my door forever and Keneilwe came back to beg for another chance hardly less than 4 months after our separation. He came inside my new place and apartment for the first time to pick up the kids for that weekend and he didn't want to leave. He wanted me back. And just like in the past, I did. When He returned to reunite with me, along came his utility bill debts from his apartment because he was not paying anything on time. So, in 4 months nothing had changed!

To make matters worse, I had two elephants by this time on my back each time he looked at me. The Malawian "Mr. Do-Me" and The American uncle "Donald". Never mind his sexual excursions with many other women aside from me during his journey with me along the years. And aside from me during our separations. To him, it was always my elephants that stood bigger in the room where he and I were. Never his. What a hypocrite!

I didn't bother to talk about his women because to me that was self-defeating on my end and defeating for our relationship. I was either going to live with him and block that knowledge and acknowledgement of other women in our lives out of my mind and pursue a marriage with him and a relationship with him for the sake of love and our children together. I didn't see any good coming out of talking about things we did in shame and in darkness now

that we were together. I did not see what good any of that negativity would do for us now that we had chosen to stick together as husband and wife. I was there with him. Therefore, it meant that I was forsaking of the past and starting afresh. Again!

I guess I am a woman. So, it was my easy way of moving on. He didn't. He was stuck. He still is stuck to this day. Sadly.

He on the other hand kept on digging up any information he had found out of this "Donald" guy and then he would bring the information to me as life unfolded in our union.

That is how and when I discovered that this guy I had been sleeping with was not and had not been a "Donald" as he had introduced himself to me, but he was in actual sense a "Tie-Something". He was also carrying and washing rugs in Pennsylvania at some company that meets up and does business with the company where Keneilwe works. Ain't life funny? A very small world indeed.

So, life kept on proving itself that this world can really be too small. What you think you will never know or discover right here in this life is usually and presently circulating in your hood under your nose for the taking.

There's indeed no secret under the Sun according to Ecclesiastes 1:9. That everything done in secret shall come to light at any given day according to Luke 8:17. It is just a matter of time!

I was feeling guilty and shame because I had exposed my children to this man who was not in my life for eternity but for a season. Less than 4 months. 3 months to be exact. Ugh!

Three months ladies, is the time frame, I have now come to find out that should be the time allocated in a friendship headed for a relationship with any sensible person towards something good and tangible. Three months should be used to spend on collecting data and studying that person in regards, to a prospective future with them for you to know if you are on the same track with them or not. Three months is not the time to jump straight into bed with them like I did! That relationship was simply a sexual relationship. But I had no idea. There I was. If you could just see me, right there and then I was disappointed with myself. Throwing my hands up in sheer exasperation and surrender, for I had failed once again. Silly me, I thought.

This lover-boy stunt of a guy was sent to me for one purpose, one purpose alone. To try me out! For my next elevation in this journey called life as a woman. Then he somehow was also used to get me closer to my Maker too. I was in so much anguish. In life, everyone is on a path to serve their inborn purpose for their greater destiny. On a daily basis, everyone receives a series of tests in order to build, try and make a person qualified to be elevated to a level towards a personalized destiny for their life. Some others spend a lifetime on one level until death therefore not reaching their potential destiny. Some others pass their trials and tribulations, right away. I wasn't one of them that pass right away. I failed twice.

This man was a perfect example of temptation in my life. I fell for it. I failed the test of denying myself temporary pleasures and gratifications. His job was to try me out by presenting whatever he was offering me that he should not have been offering me in the first place to begin with, for he too was not available financially, physically, mentally and emotionally to be with me. He offered me eros love and I took it. In the process I failed my destiny test at the time because I was having sexual love with this man who was not my husband regardless of what was going on with my real husband and I, during the separation time frame. When this man got what he could get out of me, which was free sex, he was made to take his exit. I was left feeling even worse off than he had found me. Depleted. An empty void that ran deeper!

At this time, I had not known yet about SEASONS of life. I had a habit of making everything permanent. I didn't know that some things and some people are seasonal like the snow or the rain. I didn't know when or how to discern the difference about people or things for the season I was in. Today, I realise that when a person is so empty within, and has no wisdom to carry them through the storms of life therefore everything and everyone is game. Anything goes! In my 20s, I had not acquired much wisdom to withstand the chains of time, whatsoever.

By age 27/28, I had failed with loud colors!

I was one of those people that learns through trial and error. I would be silly not to thank God in my knowledge now. I am defi-nitely much better now than I was then, I will admit that. I am still

learning about life. I will keep on learning till the day I die. I am definitely much better now than I was a decade ago.

It took time and experience for life to show me all that I know now that not everyone in everybody's life is for a lifetime. And that not everything that happens to everyone in life in general is a punishment, some things are great for the making in a person to become whatever the Creator had originally intended for their purpose on planet Earth.

I had no idea about many things in life except that I had to wait it out and proceed as life was processing me. I had become my own guinea pig. It would be a crime to tell my story and not share with you one of the most crucial factors of life in general especially in my own life. One that affects everyone's walk with Christ as well as any faith or creed out there. Attitude.

A POSITIVE
ATTITUDE IS ELEVATING

ATTITUDE is a key factor for all walks of life and creed. Attitude plays a major key in living life in general. Your attitude can either let life crush you or let you live life to the best of your potential and allow you to crush out anything that seemed impossible.

One of the most unavoidable realities is that we all wake up each morning with an attitude no matter who controls your life.

Everyone goes to sleep each night with an attitude. The question I am asking you today is what kind of attitude do you wake up with on each passing day? Exactly what kind of attitude is encompassed by any purpose driven people or better yet all successful people? What kind of attitude gets things done? What kind of attitude makes things happen? What kind of attitude changes the atmosphere?

You guessed right. A positive one.

Especially if you add a touch of happiness, gratefulness and endurance to that positive attitude, you, my friend, will become the

envy of town wherever you will go if you have a vision, a purpose, and a destiny on planet earth. Nothing but death can stop you.

Your destiny depends on your attitude. Your attitude is one of your propellers, big time.

On the other hand if you have a nasty attitude, the journey to your Purpose and Destiny to fulfill your Vision takes much longer time to accomplish it if you ever accomplish the mission at all, to begin with. This is all because most people pretty much everyone hates to deal with a person whose attitude they can't stand. It's a no brainer.

In every VISION, if you have any, WHICH everyone living must have. There is teamwork involved for it to get done. Your Purpose and Your Destiny may be tailored specifically for you by Your Creator, but your Vision/Mission to go with your Purpose and Destiny needs other people to get it accomplished. I absolutely had no idea.

Attitude has been the biggest hurdle in my own life's journey. I didn't know that my attitude to everything that had happened in my life up until today determined how long I was going to be in a dungeon or my trials.

My attitude in everything determines my life's promotions or demotions. It is so refreshing to understand this simple and single reality now after all these years because I was so frustrated for so long. I was my own enemy to my Destiny. I can be effective, infectious or destructive to my own well-being. It is a conscious choice. It is no longer someone else's fault. It all depends on how I channel my attitude towards everything or everyone that has been challenging in my life this far.

I had no idea that nobody was responsible for my attitude. I alone am in charge of how I chose to see and tackle every day or any situation for each passing day for as long as I live with others on planet earth no matter what is happening in the world all around me. There comes a time in life when one must take a look inside and start taking blame for what is reflecting in the mirror dead on. Every blame can no longer be every other person's fault.

It has been quite a long journey I must say. And it may very well be so because everybody is different. Some people are teachable quickly and some need a bit of help getting the lessons through.

I do often take time in learning things. I have found peace in knowing that. Unfortunately, not many people have come to a meeting with themselves about their attitude and why they feel compelled to believe that their happiness is controlled by others behavior towards them or circumstances they are in.

You, my friend, are to blame for each outcome of your day even on your worst day. Yes, even if you are an illegal immigrant in America. Nobody owes you. Changing your attitude will speedily redeem your joy no matter what legal status you are in. Believe me, I know.

In the past few years, I learned that if you change your attitude and become happy by choosing to be so somehow against all odds, life can't help but shift its gears all around you and towards you and begin to adhere to your inner and positive feelings and emotions.

You set the atmosphere.

Not any creatures, animals around you or nature out there. Only you have dominion over everything in the earth according to God's Word in Genesis 1:28 of early chapters of the Holy Bible. It's meant to be. It's all biblical.

RIGHT KNOWLEDGE IS A WEAPON

Your attitude changes the atmosphere. There is no verse in the Bible though that has convicted my heart in so much in-depth, that my life could no longer be the same altogether after the revelation that The Holy Spirit showed me in Hosea 4:6 in KJV reads in its entirety that "My people(God's people) are destroyed for lack of knowledge: because thou hast rejected knowledge, I will also reject thee, that thou shalt be no priest to me: seeing thou hast forgotten the law of thy God, I will also forget thy children." What you don't know can really hurt you. Every child that grows up to be a powerful force to reckon with should and must know this verse, adhere to it and they must understand it with such force,

conviction and clarity to be able to become everything they were created to be by God, The Creator! Nescience is by all means, a form of mental death and in this case, spiritual death too.

I wish that earthly parents and guardians of children and every generation to come could instill the verse in the children and get to practice the old adage, that says that Charity begins at home. It really does. Home is responsible for teaching us that Hosea 4:6 before the world out there starts teaching us all the other deeper stuff of this world, generally.

Although this acknowledgement is a crucial reality in life. Sometimes, it is that not all children get to learn from their parents or guardians the most basic necessary information such as attitude management at home to get the best results out of life or even to get the children grow up to arrive at their God Ordained Destiny.

The way of an individual's upbringing affects an individual's makeup in their thinking. Attitude comes from the major part of thinking. If the individual has not been taught to keep a good positive attitude towards life's trials and tribulations, life is such a great challenge to maneuver through for that individual much more than the average person who might be a bit more relaxed about many issues in life no matter how bad the situation in front of them maybe.

How to carry and hold a positive attitude is crucial in life for successful daily results in all that a person does or goes through.

I was not taught much on attitude if anything at all or the importance of having a positive attitude towards people or circumstances in spite of, any situation I may find myself in. African parents or guardians because of their cultures, stress strongly on how to teach each generation on how to carry good manners always especially directed towards our superiors and even strangers but attitude generates from life's experiences and I had no idea that it is a choice the way an individual decides to be towards anything and anybody no matter the circumstances they may find themselves in. Carrying a positive attitude is a decision, a choice and a learned act that comes from training oneself to be so, anytime, anyplace, always, in spite of everything happening all around the individual.

I tell you, when I received that epiphany, I was mad at myself and all the years I spent concentrated on life's events with such a negative attitude. Ugh!

I had a fairy good upbringing growing up, so that might have been what had shielded me in such a way that many things were done and taken care of so that I didn't have to worry about anything, yet real life out there is not like that. To experience real life, one must actually part take in it at the forefront, daily. No one can live your life, either.

Therefore, the muscle that should have been growing and being strengthened within me from a child's age didn't grow and when I became a grown up and trouble stepped into my door, the miserable attitude in me built a comfort zone for pretty much towards everything that didn't go in my favor or anything that was not happening as per plans.

I had no idea that even trouble or pain only last for a while. It is not there to stay. And sometimes a little trouble is necessary for building resistance in a human heart as well as for building resilient muscles for one's necessary survival. And a positive attitude while going through life's situations makes time pass by quicker than if one is wallowing in their issues of life, relentlessly. Time can seem to drag on and on forever if one has a negative attitude.

Oh, how I wish I knew then what I know now! I could have saved myself them countless lonely pity parties in the last 20 challenging years of my life. Sigh.

And the countless nights I've cried in secret and precious TIME I can never regain because I had no idea that my attitude was the one holding me behind to what was mine all along this journey we call life. All because I carried such a negative attitude which resurfaced in pretty much every area that was important in my life simply because I thought that someone out there owed me happiness and to get my point across to them or any situation I didn't agree with, I would have to use force, be mean and nasty all the time to get my way. Yet, the same thing could have been achieved much more easily in peace, harmony and with a great attitude. At the same time, life wouldn't be so painful. And now I know, that everyone who has come my way by this time, was there

to challenge me and teach me on how to carry a positive attitude all along, no matter what, no matter where.

I get it now. I may not be a hundred percent there yet carrying on a great positive attitude 24/7 today, but I can tell you that I am definitely far from where I used to be 20 years ago. Jeremiah! Jeremiah! It had to take me that long.

My mother's house taught me to have good manners and the benefits of good manners but they didn't teach me on how to have or keep a good positive attitude towards others and life in general, no matter what was going on in my life all around me. I had to learn the hard way through life's trials and tribulations all by myself. It hasn't been easy. It hasn't been fun.

ATTITUDE AND EXPERIENCE

Life and its experiences have been a great teacher on how to seek and keep a good attitude opposed to a negative one even far away from home. Especially far from home which is mama Africa. I think that my upbringing is a reason to blame for my naivety. Although am truly grateful for my parents. They taught me everything they themselves knew. That's how far everyone can teach anyone else out there, only from what they know. Today, I have been graced with the dispensation to one secret of holding on to a positive attitude because of my personal walk without it for a long time. I went through life and took lessons that were tailor made specifically for me for a purpose such as this. To encourage others out there to continue on with life consciously choosing to keep a good positive attitude no matter how difficult the challenges of life maybe. Living my life in America, away from my African community of a family has taught me a lot of things I may never have learned shielded like I was then.

From 1994 when I became independent of my mother and of my immediate family and had moved into my own household and marriage until now, nothing in life had previously prepared me for anything that I have experienced this far in a foreign land without permission to dwell in the land. Never in a million years did I ever

think that a positive attitude has anything to do with the destiny I am walking out right now. Keeping a positive attitude is a quick way to arriving at your God Given success and prosperity in all levels of life!

Off course, in my past, for a very long period of time, I was greatly failing in the love department and the attitude towards the relationships with men in my life. The love relationships controlled most of my livelihood because I thought that to live fully I had to have a man who adored me. I was holding men at a high esteem without the men proving themselves to me first like my dad did by providing, producing, protecting, and loving me as his child. I immediately expected so much from other men that didn't know my worth or understood of my worth at all.

Within my attitude, I saw men as providers, I saw men as protectors, I saw men as leaders, I saw men as loving their women and their job was to do exceedingly towards their women. My men relationships were something I didn't ever think I would be dealing with or even be talking about as problematic.

Simply because I had a great example of a father as a male leader and figure in my youth. My father was by far not perfect, but I thought that my marriage would be like my parent's and that all men were like my father! That all husbands were like my father. Ignorance is idiocy!

Before I was even 4 years into my marriage, I felt like I had become the type of wife or woman you read in the news about or the one you watch in movies or watch on Lifetime channel. A psychotic one! I had a terrible attitude towards my husband, men and life in general. This was so because life was showing me what I hadn't envisioned. Hardships.

But you know what? Life happens and It was happening to me and I was a mess.

And sometimes, when God has a purpose for your life, He allows you to get into your mess in order for you to get out of your comfort zone so that you can find Him and land on your calling for His glory and satisfaction for why He created you in the first place which is success according to Jeremiah 29:11.

When you get with God You can't help but find the calling for your life and the reason why He created you before your LIFE is taken out of here, from planet Earth.

It may take some time for you to find your calling but once you do, you really want to live life to the fullest each day you have and nothing else but death can stop you.

Before I found out what my calling was, I had no idea of my purpose. So, everything I was frustrated about ruled the way I carried myself towards others, things and events. I had such a negative ATTITUDE for this and that.

Men oh men became the type of mess that held power over my attitude, sadly. I was in for the longest haul. For almost a decade, I didn't know that I was in charge of the way I chose to feel no matter who did what to me or no matter who didn't choose to treat me right or love me. This was about me, my husband and other men who were to come after him. During the turmoil, all I saw was hell and nothing about God in my issues.

I was looking for answers, a hiding place and happiness in mortal men, silly me. Whatever was lacking in me, I was looking to find it in other human beings around me and I felt like that would fix the negative attitude I carried towards others once I found true love. Yes, this was true in parts but the whole truth was that God was all the man that had the true Agape love, I was fantasizing about. The Unconditional love I was yearning for.

I felt like the idea of the type of true love I would find would be perfected once the solution was found and I believed that it dwelt in a mere mortal like me. And once there, my ATTITUDE would change for the better. Yet, the solution was never in a man but in Jesus The Son of God and nothing else. But that was my journey for me to take and my only way to find out. Boy, was I in for a ride?! The revelation did not come to me in a quick or short manner. The revelation took time. A very long time! Close to 20 years. The same amount of time I was fighting my illegal immigrant issues.

A God Of Consequences

God is patient. God is very gentle. He gives us humans a free will. He gives us a free will to choose what we want in life and out of life. I have seen Him allow me to run around like a chicken without its head and get busy with whatever it is I have found important against His Will for my life according to everything that the Bible has taught me along the way, as His child, to emulate. Whenever I get stuck because of sin, He knows that I will beckon to Him. If I do, He steps right in to fish me out but always I have paid with consequences. He forgives me completely. He forgets completely. But for my own good I have paid in consequences along the way. Consequences are a quick teacher and checker that I don't repeat the deed again. On the other hand, for everything good I do in God, there's a reward too and Apostle of God, Paul, speaks of this in Romans 2:6. I believe some rewards are experienced in this life before we die. And there are rewards where God is and will be as the Bible promises. The opposite is true if I go against God. The repercussions and consequences go along in miserable and sometimes costly payments on so many different levels and in so many aspects of life in the earth and I believe beyond this planet and life. 2 Samuel 24:11-17 Is one Biblical example that already took place apart from my very own personal journey.

After all, I believe that God created me. Therefore, He is in charge of me. He has a whole book about the pros and cons on the way I choose to live my life. But there's always a way out, if and when, I do decide to beckon on Him during trouble.

That's exactly what I did, every time I found myself in trouble.

I found out that whatever I was doing and had done by this far was not working out for my good or the good of my young children who were tagging right along my men attitude and my men shenanigans. The children were and still are a gift from God to me. There I was creating intense confusion in them because of my personal issues. These children never chose to be born but I had made a clear and conscious choice to have them. There I was, dragging them alongside me with a contorted attitude I had towards men as

my way out of trouble and the contorted attitude was meanwhile, destroying my life, my future.

But God is so good. Sigh.

He had the children be the only positive individuals and reality I begun to focus on in the midst of what seemed like a relentless turmoil.

Naturally, I am the type of person that cares a lot about my children. I knew that my life was crazy, and I didn't want my children to follow and take this restless path that I was modelling in front of them, eventually after all had been said and done in their own life's paths. The laws of nature say that children become what they see. It is common sense. I wanted Godly children. I, myself, was nowhere near Godliness.

How else was I going to obtain that in them if I was so lost and so confused about my own identity and lifestyle.

I once again resorted to a positive resolution because my children were the motive behind the decision. They were the motive for coming to America for a better future to begin with. Once again, they were the motive I had to cry out to God for something better than the life I was leading. The men drama and my lost identity through them.

But Our Creator is wonderful! Looking at Marvel and Avedi 23 years and 21 years later consecutively, you couldn't tell looking from the outside if they had a bit of hell growing up at the hands of their parents in the type of environment that they were raised in. They may have emotional scars, but it is my prayer that God sees them through whatever invisible scars are within them at the expense of their parents. I will be the first one to tell you that, we didn't raise our children well. God did. He was the driving force behind our children and their success. Still is.

Talking about God, He is Real!

As you may know, many people come to know Him during trouble. You already know that's how I ended up at His Throne of Mercy and Grace. After name calling and fist fighting in my household, from December of 1997 until August 2000, I indeed, had resorted to life separated from my spouse.

I CAME TO KNOW
MY OWN STRENGTH

I didn't think that I could live without my husband. He had become my everything and I thought I would die without him by my side. I had never loved anybody on Earth the way I had loved this man. It was a feeling I could never express in simple words and I still don't understand to this day, the level of love I had for him. I didn't think that I was capable of loving another man the way I did this guy. Even when I was with "Mr. Do-Me" in Malawi in 1997 or "Uncle Donald" of America in the year of 2000, it was my husband who I always wished I was with. The men even knew to tell me so. I couldn't hide how deeply gone I was with this man. I didn't know that in actual sense, I had made him, my idol. It was dangerous, and it was ungodly.

During our first separation in America, in the year of 2000, it was a time I would become aware of the other side of me. I discovered that I was courageous. I struggled a little at first, but the world did not come to an end because I was alone with my two kids as their adult.

My yearning to live away from my husband in peace proved to me that I could make it away from him. But I had a desperate inner need to be loved by a good loving man. I was in desperate need of real love. The sad part about that, is that I had no idea of the type of man to qualify for that real love. I had no proper plans or goals about the type of man that would be a friend, lover, husband and a teammate to help me raise my kids with, who also, would satisfy all that I thought I needed in a man. I had no idea of the lifestyle or future that I wished for. One thing I was sure of though was that financial security was of utmost importance because since my father had passed away in February of 1993, I was made aware of financial struggles.

One of the issues I had was that I had such a negative attitude towards my husband who didn't have the drive or ambition to provide for his children and me his wife for the years we had been in America together by year 2000 and I was definitely no longer

willing to fend for him or any other lazy man out-there for that matter.

I didn't wish for another broke man. Although finding a man to love me at that time besides the husband I had walked away from, would be like looking for a needle in a haystack, the financially secure husband that is, I mean. There are men out there with money but even them have their own issues with others looking in for a handout. Besides nothing is free in life. Not if Jesus hasn't paid for it. Jesus was not and didn't pay so that I could get a free pass to adultery. I was a lonesome confused dove, I tell you.

Who knew that financial security in a man or woman was so important? Or why else bother with all the man-woman drama! I was a bondswoman, anyways. I was not supposed to be gawking for a man at all. But there I was doing whatever I felt my heart yearned for although I was not free to do so. I felt done and free in my heart. Or at least that's what I wanted to believe. It is so dangerous to operate on feelings and emotions that change all the time.

But I was far gone, deep into sin. I was now more focused on a man to fish me out of my financial dilemmas. At least that would compensate my constant financial struggles. Lame.

Money is the answer to all things according to Ecclesiastes 10:19. I knew this at a very young age. And my whole life, I heard that money had a mouth, if it talks. But the lack of it in my case was for sure the root of all evil. In true sense, that was not the reason why I was in the sad situation of loneliness away from my husband that I was in, although I continued anyway, to reason with my intellect. I didn't break away to look for money, but it sure would have been nice to have someone that loved me and provided for me also. But it didn't happen in the way that I had hoped for in my carnal mind.

It was just that all the reasons why I wanted to spend my life forever with someone I was in love with no longer held any hope. My husband was not emotionally available. At that point in my life I saw money as a pacifier from the next guy who wished to be with me. I took the plunge when the opportunity of another guy who looked like a promise, when that promise presented itself to me without even thinking ahead. I was hoping that if he had

money, that would be my only consolation prize. I ended up empty handed! The joke was on me.

In my late 20s, from the year of 2000 until 2005, I did many things with shallow motives and I had no plans on how to get out of the damps. Neither did I even know if there was a way out. But when I look back now with Christ in mind, there's always a way out no matter how bad the situation is. I had no idea then. But now I know.

All the crazy stuff that I had conditioned my life to go through were not alright and necessary.

I had accepted every struggle that I had experienced. I had allowed struggle become part of me and struggle had become part of my identity. Moreover, I couldn't see anything positive beyond it or achieve anything easily. Therefore, automatically whatever I did or went through was subconsciously sabotaged unintentionally. Life had become so redundant, I could almost tell how anything was going to end, and it always ended negatively.

It's A choice To Control Your Mind

Being in a negative state of immigration status made life and rela- tionships even harder to maintain alongside my sour attitude.

Whether it was a job relationship or a friendship with another person, I could almost end up in tears feeling rejected or unwanted by the time the relations came to some ending. Sometimes I would feel unworthy of anything good and lasting happening to me. I kept on believing that not having a green card made others see me as of less value or less of a person no matter how hard I invested my heart and my work ethic in things, in people, still people let me down and things just wouldn't work out like I had hoped. I had no idea that not everything was meant to last forever.

My negative attitude therefore had a free pass to act in dysfunction mode most of the time. It always determined and

predicted the direction of how my days, months, years and even future would take if I changed nothing.

Lack of work permits, green card or citizenship made me think that I had to act like a loser all the time and my attitude simply expressed my inner emotions outwardly towards others.

I had no idea that I was letting things and everything I had lacked control me. I didn't know that the very same mind-set had rendered me powerless. I, in fact had no power because I had handed and surrendered it all freely to everything that got me wound up and everyone who got me all worked up. I thought that if I exerted power and authority on everyone and everything whenever I felt like I had to, which I felt like it, always. To me it meant that I was the one in control. Yet The opposite was true. I had it all twisted!

So, I was in a school of learning. I still am. I had no idea that I was looking for comfort and answers from wrong sources once again. The second affair in America had ended in shame once again. History really repeats itself until the chains are broken.

What I needed in August of 2000 was alone time to learn to love myself, I needed time to reflect within myself about who I had become and what I really needed to have in my life for survival on day to day basis regarding money and love. But most importantly, I needed a higher power to consume me and carry me through that difficult period of my life, spiritually! I needed God's Power and Word to carry me through not a mere soul like me to fill the void. I tell you, life can be super lonely sometimes. I had nothing else and no one else in sight or out of sight to call on and rescue me.

I do believe in God and I did believe in God at least at that moment. I had no one else to understand my pain. But I knew that God understood my pain in spite of how far deeply stuck I had gotten myself and how hard I had worked on avoiding any chance to get close to Him. God understood. As I harken to Him, He also motioned close to me.

I was in no doubt of that. I had no idea that He had been there for me the whole time. He missed nothing that I had thought of, done, anything that I had tried to do or wished for in my heart. I didn't acknowledge Him or even bother to consider that He was

all that omnipresent, omnipotent omniscient of everything and everyone on planet earth and beyond prior to this! To me He was Someone I went to get and get and nothing else.

I had not grown yet. I was immature. I had not come to that stage yet. God is very gentle, Glory to Him for that!

He walks with us side by side gently at the measure of our faith. But He is FULLY there! The insight is measured by personal choice.

It took me two rejections by two men for me to wake up and harken to the voice of God. At first, I had been rejected by my husband and then a stunt of a promise "Uncle Donald" all within that millennium year. On Top of that, I had a broken home filled with confusion, a tumultuous lifestyle, a life in a foreign land without work authorization or authorization to live in the land and a fear to raise kids without the Mighty Hand of God or His ways. Any other option out there had nothing better left to offer me but a lonely sinking heart. All others had failed me.

I cried out to God. He answered me.

That Lotus Villa is unforgettable for that!

GOD STEPPED ON BOARD

After the 3–4 months affair, I had no heart's desire for another being besides God. It was now time for God! I couldn't undo what had already happened in my two "love" lives. I was feeling guilty and if shame were money I would be rich today because of it. I took blame and turned on myself. I started to believe everything negative I had heard about myself thus far.

I wanted to give up. I wanted to give in. But I was in deep need of a rescuing power, fast. Someone extraordinary! A Higher Power! I knew God could see. I sang it in Sunday school days. "He's got the whole world in His Hands". So I knew that God had the globe in His Hands. He was aware of everyone in the earth and everything that happened in the earth. It was fascinating in church attendances to sing about and believe of such a Powerful God. I needed Him now. I had to beckon for His aid. It was now or never.

I had to do something so deep. Something I had never done before. Something from deep inside of me I didn't even know was there all along. A cry. From a place within I had no idea was there.

This was about God and me. It was personal. The time was now. I couldn't survive another day. That night, I felt that I would die in my sleep from anguish. At least that's how I felt. I had heard about a heart breaking. I didn't know that it felt so awful and hopeless. The depression was getting so intense! I am so glad I didn't implode. I felt like I was going to. My heart, the way it beat so fast was scaring me. This, all that I felt within me was the yearning for Him that had seemed quite a distance from me because I had made Him so.

But now, everything was real, near and very personal. He really had finally gotten my attention this time. I had nowhere to run to.

Everyone that I could count on was no longer available for one reason or another. I didn't know that loneliness and pain could make a person's body shake and shudder so much until that night when I really knew what it is like to be lonely. I had my face dripping wet in tears and mucus all over my nose and parts of my face all over my pillow. I didn't care what I looked like, but I cried as if I were a 5-year old child again. Alone in my room.

I cried as if I would never ever cry again. Sobbing and groaning. I couldn't call on my mother, she was in Africa. I couldn't call on my dad, he was six feet under. I couldn't call on any one of my siblings. They were too far emotionally and too detached to help. There I was, in desperate need of a loving hand at the center of my bedroom on the edges of my bed clinging for dear life like a little girl. That was the very first time God became real to me, in my bedroom. He was there. He found me. The Mighty Gentle Hand of God. Right there was where I had found myself surrendering my all to Christ. That day in November of 2000, I had become an adopted child of God through His Son Jesus Christ, willingly.

I called on Jesus and declared Him as my Lord and Savior! There were no fireworks in the bedroom. There were no spectators in the room. There was no lightning or thunder going off anywhere near where I was. Not even an earthquake or anything falling off the walls. There was no choir singing Go tell it on the mountain

either. Nothing and no-one but I and my Lord, God! It was quiet and refreshing.

Just like that, I had become brand new. I was with an army of God from that day forth. I felt like a page of my life had been laid in front of me to start life all over again. For real!

I didn't know the impact of my decision on that night from that night and until a few years ago. People often mistake being saved and becoming a child of God through Jesus Christ as a pass to an easy life. They have no idea that, this may just increase their radar as a Christ follower in a world that can be so cold to Him.

And no, I will be the first one to declare this. Problems don't dissipate from a believer's life either, the problems just get intensified because now the believer has become not of this world but he or she is traveling through this world which becomes more foreign as he or she begins to get deeper in their individual spirituality. At that fine line changing-decision you become a tourist on earth passing through with a heaven bound mindset. And anyone or anything that is not like you becomes an enemy. The best part of your life is that you are no longer yours and therefore Christ becomes your defender and your army for the rest of your life in the Earth. And if you are knowledgeable of this truth, then you become very powerful, strategic and careful about how you conduct your life and everything about your life because your life becomes about Jesus.

And everything you do on earth is on borrowed time and you can't get too comfortable living on earth because even this earth, you will leave it behind. Anything that is not permanent should not keep you bound to earth.

THE SIMPLICITY OF MAN TO MY UNDERSTANDING

The body is visible and tangible to the naked eye but temporary on planet Earth. Your body hosts an invisible and eternal you, in the form of your soul and spirit. Your soul and spirit are inside of your tangible outer shell, the body. The spirit in you is The Breath

of God which cannot live on earth without a soul(character) and a body. The soul holds your emotions, will and intellect which all of these sum up as your character. But character is also eternal. To express one's character is done through a body to define and showcase itself through a visible you or the outer shell of you that is a body which also decays because the breath or the Spirit of God is taken out of you by Himself when He does so. The body was only created for planet Earth when God created the first Earthly man-Adam from dirt, according to The Word of God in Genesis 2:7. The soul or character comes alive with the breath of God, but it must function on the Earth via a body or human-being. The soul and the spirit are illegal to dwell in the Earth without a body. That's how you and I are living beings. We are the only creatures on earth formed and made in God's image according to the living compass. The Living Word of God=JESUS=The Wisdom of God in The Form Of The Tangible Bible with reference found particularly in Genesis 1:27, once again. We have a body, a character and the breath of God in us to qualify us as living beings. Your character is the main personality of your soul which governs you and is also eternal because that's how you get judged by in both worlds, Earth on your day to day lifestyle, activities and in Heaven—on judgement day according to 1 Corinthians 3:13. Matthew 13:49, just to mention a few Bible verses. And If you received your salvation through Jesus Christ as your Lord and Savior in Romans 8:16 then according to Matthew 25:46, you shall proceed into eternity. The same character is also what God uses to judge you into your FINAL destination depending on how you lived in your body on earth whether good or bad according to 2 Corinthians 5:10.

Many things by God I found to be common sense. At least, the ones I do understand clearly make sense to me this far. I have not articulated yet into perfection or near the standards by God's expected end for my life, but I guess someday I will know and I hope to be a good servant that gets a well done when I transcend into God's glory in regards to Matthew 25:23.

I used to think that the moral story of "you reap whatever you sow" is just a myth. It is not a myth. It is plain common sense but even God Himself declared so in His Word. It is not mythical. It's

biblical according to the Word of God in the book of Galatians 6:7.

NOBODY GETS A FREE PASS
TO LIFE'S TROUBLES

I have come to understand that to go through this world, everyone especially a believer must go through some things too. The only difference is that with Christ there's always teamwork involved. One is no longer alone according to Bible verse in the book of Hebrews 13:5-6. With Christ, everything a believer goes through in this life or does is all about teamwork for the glory of God and to the satisfaction of God for the purposes He created Spirit-man. According to His Word in the Bible books of Romans 11:36 and Isaiah 43:6 and 7 just to mention a few Bible verses. Man was created to give God His glory and satisfaction by praising Him, worshipping Him and living life in fulfilment with His Will and Plan for man's life. Furthermore, in Ecclesiastes 12:13 KJV, it reads, Let us hear the conclusion of the whole matter: Fear God, and keep His commandments: For this is the whole duty of man.

In case you are wondering if I had gotten this revelation then. The answer is no. If I knew this then, I would not have candid bloopers for almost 20 years to share with you except my probably straight forward journey into my destiny which is here in America without all the foolishness that have developed me into the person that I am today. You see, I needed my bloopers in order to put me on the right track once I got tired of them.

I strongly believe that if I were spiritually steady from Malawi to here Philadelphia, then my American struggles with finances, family, my husband, my kids, friends or work and relationships could not have tried me so badly and left me immensely frustrated like I was before I saw the light.

During all of these problems, life's issues and any situation I was in until now, I felt as if I were alone, and I thought that what I didn't have was the reason for my struggles. Yet that was not true

but because of my personality, I needed every struggle that would bring me to my expected end by God just like in the biblical verse where He says that and we "know that all things work together for good to them that love God, to them who are called according to his purpose" found in Romans 8:28.

Living with Christ makes it easier to carry life's issues, but it doesn't guarantee a free pass to life's issues. I am still struggling with many of life's issues on a daily basis but they are not controlling me as much as they did me before I made Christ as my Lord and Savior! Therefore, I already know that whatever happens in my life, Jesus Christ is with me, every step of the way until He calls me into eternity. And the best thing about now is that if I do not give all of my struggles and troubles to God, then it is my conscious choice because I know very well what the Bible has taught me about God the Father, God the Son, and God the Holy Spirit. They ALL are with me every day, everywhere all year long each day of my life. And whatever still frustrates me, are issues I haven't willed to surrender totally unto God.

Everything in life I reckon is a process. Life has to process you to get you from one appointed timeline on your lifespan to another until your purpose on planet earth is done, then you die and transition to your FINAL destination which is not the gravesite but beyond.

Since I am still here, I am continuously getting processed for my refinement into glory. I pray that when I do die it will be heaven I will end up in because I feel that I have seen much of hell already on earth. I do not find it hospitable by any means.

JESUS IS MY SPIRITUAL EYE-OPENER

Living in my country showed me a bit of hell on a smaller level because I had my extended family to chip in whenever trouble arose from wherever trouble came from. Then I came to America with the intention of staying and working in America for 5

months, do any labor work, make some money and go back to my country. Do the same thing all over again until there was a better way of lifestyle I had come to start in 1997. I indeed stayed with my immediate family and this I will admit is where I have experienced real life with real life's issues so far. A hell of challenges. I had to learn to die to self by assuming and carrying the load of my family. Then I discovered that only Jesus can carry the load. It was so liberating!

My only guarantee without a shadow of doubt in my mind for staying sane through it all has been God. His one particular assignment on my life has been to refine me into whatever He wants me to be for His glory and for His Sole purpose over my life on earth in the end before I continue into heaven where eternity is one of the awesome features in God's existence. I had to come to America. This is where I have been a real mess but with a message. This is where I should be.

I had to come to the Mother of The World! No other place in the world could have raised me up to become the person that I have come to be. If America with its trials and tribulations does not kill you people, believe me when I tell you this, it will make you stronger. I didn't die, Thank God! So strength of God in me has to be one of the strongest attributes I made it out this far.

I am still imperfect based on what another may want for me to be. The reason is because I can't be perfect for everyone even the perfect Son of God was not welcomed by everyone who knew of Him or heard of Him according to John 1:11. As for me, I am still getting processed. I am very much with Christ but Christ will never impose Himself, His ideas, His ethics, His personality, His Character or His beliefs on me if am not yielded fully.

So, for me, it has been an uphill battle. It still is a daily walk and trial. I am not there yet completely but am definitely far from where I used to be.

November 2000 came and went. Jesus Christ never left my heart but, honey, when I say to you that three quarters of my flesh had been battling clubbing in places I had no business being for the earliest years of my being as a follower and believer of Christ after that year of 2000 when I had invited Him as my Lord and Savior. I

went places with people I had no business with. I cussed and fussed at any given moment I had. I watched provocative things I had no business watching. I sang to and listened to anything that Jesus Christ Himself would not. All the while, I felt miserable inside as a person throughout those years. I was conflicted in my heart and I didn't understand what was happening. Outwards, I would do as I pleased but inwardly my heart knew what was right and what was wrong. At night, or by myself, I would feel very convicted. I had become worse than I felt when I didn't know Christ.

When I didn't know Christ I felt bad anyways for a moment but I didn't know any better. After I had known Christ, I was convicted and afflicted within myself for continuing to do as I pleased in things I knew better not to be doing. I became miserable inside my heart and around others.

I had issues in my home with everyone because I didn't understand their ways. I had carried my family's heavy load for almost 20 years until the same people began to brand me a mental case. That's when I started to learn on ways on how I could start loving myself by putting boundaries, limitations on how much I could take from others or how much I could offer to others. I changed on who could get to me and who couldn't. I had to protect myself. This was a job I assumed was for others who loved me to do for me. I began to guard my mouth. An art I hadn't mastered before. Still not perfected it.

OUT OF THE
ABUNDANCE OF THE HEART

I had a sharp tongue and a busy mouth that I used to the best of my knowledge for tearing down others whenever I felt the need to retaliate. I had a knack of saying some stuff based on how I felt at any given time without thinking about what God says in the Bible Book of Matthew 12:36. The Words say that "But I say unto you, That every idle word that men shall speak, they shall render an account of it in judgment day." And I know that was a big issue

in my life and I had to repent unto God and change the way I had dealt with others in regards to my mouth. I was a mess before that realization took place in my heart.

I felt like I always had to defend myself all the time because I was really convinced that no one appreciated my deeds no matter how hard I tried. I was an emotional basket case. I had been living in an abusive and chaotic environment for so long, defense mode became the only mode I flowed in. Wounded people wound others.

I read in the Bible about Simon-Peter and the Roman soldier's knife in the Garden of Gethsemane in the Bible verse of John 18:10 just before Jesus was arrested by the soldiers to go through the crucifixion. I understood Peter. I could relate to Peter! I was one like that. I will admit to that, sadly. I wouldn't have known it if I didn't read the Bible. There is every one of us in the Bible at one point or another. It was put there for our redemption.

I knew that I was weird but not completely hopeless. I could become better. For as long as I continued to get deeper into other stuff that were not like Christ, I got sadder and farther away from what I desired privately in my life. I wanted to resemble Christ, but it wasn't happening fast enough.

I was feeling horrible by each passing day. But the Grace and Mercy of God! I had no idea that's what kept me in spite of what I deserved for staying on a path of destruction. I still struggle from time to time because The Spirit in me, which is the breath of God is clean and saved from the time I accepted Jesus Christ as my Lord and Savior but the breath of God lives in my soul and body where things do get hectic by my daily choices and then my soul can at times store up things that in return cause a battle that never seems to end in my spirit, in my soul, and in my body. My mind and mouth are constantly in a debate. Only the SPIRIT of God can fix them together for good.

When I made the decision to reunite with my husband by December 2000, I took that as a Christlike step and personality I had been longing for to thrive on it as a new person in Christ.

But what resulted from our reunion afterwards in the years from 2000 until 2004 was much more difficult for me in comparison to the years before I had encountered without Christ as my

Lord and Savior. Once again walking with Christ does not mean a life without problems, it just simply means that Christ is now responsible to fight your battles and carry the load with you as a team! And no, I didn't immediately welcome that fact at the time I was really going through it. I was still trying to manhandle my issues by quick fixes. I was in denial that Jesus has to be the center of all parties involved as well as the issues at hand.

SPLIT NUMBER THREE

By 2004, we ended up splitting, third time in all but second time in America far away from motherland, Malawi. The separation was due to several trust issues, money issues and just plain lack of respect for each other, mind you that this was 10 years later into the marriage. The separation was much longer than the 4 months of the year 2000. During this separation, we both lived within the same neighborhood so that we could raise our children nearer to each other. I had chosen consciously to stay celibate. I wanted to look within and really find out what was actually wrong with me.

I became stronger in knowing how to take care of myself and the children financially and I became much more independent. But I still was not strong enough or independent enough physically, psychologically as well as sexually. Sexually, I didn't want to sleep around. I was still very young, in my early thirties and very much hormonal and yearning for sex each day I lived without it.

Let's face it, it's very difficult to stay celibate anywhere under 40 years of age once one becomes sexually active, I have reckoned.

SOMETIMES SEX IS NOT THE ANSWER

So one night I ended up saying yes over the telephone to having sex with Keneilwe. He had asked if he could have sex with me once more, one night after I had lasted for 11 months without it and he on the other hand got fed up with his bachelor days free-lancing lifestyle filled with empty nights with all sorts of different women in sexual soul ties.

....

I was getting to know God a little more by 2004 but I was still struggling openly as a believer and follower of Christ. As you can plainly tell.

One great reality that I took from receiving Christ when I did in my bedroom at Lotus Villa was this one request that I had given my husband when we reunited after the 11 months of separation in 2004. I had one specific condition. We would all be praying together. I had read somewhere that a family that prays together stays together. Therefore, we had picked up much more on our time for prayer and our church attendance from where we had slacked in the year of 2001, after the whole family had openly become members of the church family of The First African Episcopal Church of Saint Thomas in our neighbourhood.

When trouble prolonged in our household this time around before the 2004 separation, we had resorted to our family church through the interim Pastor to help us sort out our marital issues. They had a marriage ministry. The interim Priest, Father Menengichian from Nairobi, Kenya headed that marriage ministry. He was our close family friend. He came to our rescue. He put aside his to do list and immersed himself fully to help us.

He was phenomenal!

He would meet us some evenings in the weekdays, once a week. He would give us little assignments to do for each other to help us get back to each other again before we would meet him again for counseling. One of the things I learned from him and I still remember to this day was what he said to us about lovemaking.

He said to us that sex or "love making" starts from the moment a couple wakes up in the morning not by the act itself, but by the way the two people in a marriage converse with each other throughout the day until the moment they decide to have sex or "make love" whenever they decide to at their encounter. Which leaves out no room for ill feelings because the couple had been good and loving towards each other all day anyways leaving no room for animosity. It is easy to have quality sex or "make love" with a spouse that is in tune with his or her mate and if there is enough conversation there is room to air out all if not most concerns, to make the marriage bed easy for sex or "love making." He

always recommended to always make time to reconcile with each other on time each day. Because sex or "lovemaking" is a language and a dance. It is mostly a form of worship unto God but also a way of showing gratification unto each other's true feelings in physicality.

Nobody had ever told me how to converse in love throughout the day for the sake of each other in a marriage especially about this particular love language.

What he picked up from my marriage was that there was no love language. The sexual act started at the necessary time and ended as soon as the act was done which led to feelings of ungratefulness, animosity, anger, bitterness and estrangement in my marriage.

By 2004 so much had happened, each passing day led my husband and I further apart. To others the longer the couple is together the better the couple strengthens like fine wine. I wish I could tell you that him and I were getting better by 2004. Sigh. I know hey.

I guess my husband and I didn't reciprocate or even begin to understand what the priest was telling us about real functional love and how it operates in lovers and couples. He told us that love was a conscious decision that each person makes towards the other. What he came out with from our meeting sessions after a few interviews for a few weeks of his efforts to help salvage whatever was left of our marriage was irrevocable. Sadly.

Some of the resistance came from deep issues that had occurred in us towards each other from 2000 until 2004. A lot of it was too deeply rooted from things that were too painful to bear. This was especially on my end. My spouse never admitted to his part in one particular sensitive event that he put me through emotionally in 2004 and for years to come. To this day, it has been the elephant on his part in our room. He never took ownership to what he did wrong. It had been very difficult since then. This was the main reason I have never been the same to this day towards my husband. I lacked trust and confidence I needed from his end.

This was the reason why I had made the conscious decision to walk away from him in 2004. It was also the main reason we went to see the priest for counseling. Him and I by that time had

destroyed each other's trust deeply. There was absolutely no respect and whatever good that was left in the both of us towards each other was out of the window. There was so much hurt, we both just continued to dig each other's wounds deeper by not confronting what was real in accepting our wrongs, by making the effort to fix the issues instead we kept on heaping the pain in our actions towards each other by the day. Nothing got sorted out. And being together would be even more painful. I was deeply wounded. This time, I felt much more betrayed than the other stuff we had done to each other in the past. And Sex was no longer the answer.

So instead of moving on separately forever, we were always back and forth together. Broken up and back together again and again. The only main reason we got back together again all the time wasn't what we were telling each other, "our children", but it was about sex and a bad relation system of doing things and a strong negative soul tie. And the many soul ties we each had previously altogether brought into our matrimonial bed. I suspect is the reason why we have never been the same since our Malawi sexual shenanigans as well as American sexual exploits. Outside soul ties are dangerous to every couple. Trust me, I can grudgingly testify.

I on my hand had to break away from any efforts or habits of sleeping around with anybody I was not in Godly covenants with especially the losers I would fall for since my marriage and outside of it. I didn't know that I was in way too deep by committing adultery.

For sure in 2004, I was still very convicted in my thoughts of sex outside a marriage covenant. I was very sure that even if I tried to cheat on myself again, I would end up with either losers or liars who were also going through a rough time in their own marital affairs that I would fall for. I was terrified to repeat my luck in men. So I resorted to the devil I knew at that time than anyone else in the likes of my husband who was more confused than I was. He didn't know who he was, I doubt it if he does at the present time. Sadly.

LACK OF GOALS BECKON
CONTORTED MOTIVES

He knows that he is here in America, but I don't believe that he really knows why he is here. I have never heard him say about where he wants to be a year or further down the road from anytime the question is raised. He has never told me or anyone I know of what he wants out of life except win a jackpot via The State lottery and return home to Malawi to drink and spend his winnings and time on the beaches of Malawi while relaxing away.

He has never said what he wanted for his wife or his children or the whole family in general, really. It has been the blind leading the blind all the way. It has been super frustrating being married to my husband, I hate to admit. I truly wish that it wasn't so especially now that I know Jesus Christ as my Savior and Mediator.

Since 2004 until now, our household has been on a tumultuous battlefield with all kinds of good and bad things happening.

GOD IS OUR
CHILDREN'S TEACHER

The positive factor in our household from the time we lived in Malawi our home country, to the time we arrived in Philadelphia our new home until the present time, has been our CHILDREN. They have been the positive influence and motivators since they were born. I have come to realize that it is God who raises up children in homes, no matter how many servants or money or lack of it may take the credit for their welfare. A guardian or parent can do many things for a child, but it is the Mighty Hand of God that cares and makes things happen for that child through and through.

I had no idea until I walked this journey of my own as a parent and guardian for my kids together with their father here in America to know what it really means to be a parent of a child. You can only imagine raising children up in a foreign land with

no authorization for everyone in the family to live and stay in the country.

Let's say that, their father and I had the Mercy and Grace of God without us even knowing what really was going on for the longest part of our lives here. In our ignorance and journey, we both made sure to keep their home "safe," somewhat, with food on the table and paid rent on time so we were not found homeless. Life in general, felt like we carried a constant chip on our shoulders with hidden emblem that spelled fear of immigration services. But there were a lot of things that the Mighty Hand of God Himself took charge of and still does without our aid.

It is not like God needs our help. By far, He has done many outstanding things in our lives for the sake of our children using us, the two dysfunctional parents.

But God uses people to get things done. I guess He used us to show Himself Mighty in our children. I, personally, couldn't take credit for the incredible success of my household's offspring even if I tried.

Private schools for instance, is one of the outstanding ways that God showed up in our children's lives and household in general as illegal immigrants.

My God, talk about GOD answering a prayer! Dare to ask God anything! You best believe, He will bring it to pass!

I say this because one of my innermost wishes as a young mother in Malawi came to pass in America. I had prayed for my children to have the best of education because I too had the best of the best of education growing up in my father's household as a child. This is so because of my earthly dad and the way he had run his household. Without a doubt, education was of utmost importance.

I had one of the best fathers on planet Earth! My dad, Ted Edward Jacob, may God continue to rest his soul in God's heavenly peace.

My dad was a real father! He was a provider, a protector, a father every daughter deserves, a teacher literally, a great example to emulate. When my mother confided in me about my father's flaws due to his early and untimely death, I couldn't believe her.

....

It was hard for me to believe because everything he did with us at home and in our presence before his children and the whole family qualified him as a perfect household and all-time father.

So, when I think about my earthly father, all these wonderful thoughts come alive! I am able to tell you my story today because of my father. As a habit, and a punishment to most of my mischiefs during my years growing up in his house, his choice of punishment would be my confessing about my evil actions on paper. I was required to write a letter to my parents, Dad especially. In there, I would write about the whys and the lessons learned from my mischievous actions. I hated it then. But now I am truly thankful for my father's choice of punishment unto me.

Not only was he an intellectual person naturally and via education but he was also a diplomat even in his conduct with others in his lifetime. It was befitting for my father to be selected to become a representative of his country to another southern country of The Republic of South Africa in 1988 as a diplomat via his government tenure and duties at the Offices of The President and Cabinet under the leadership and presidency of the Honorable, His Excellency Dr. Hastings Kamuzu Banda (deceased) of Malawi. May his soul continue to rest in peace. Under his excellent leadership, my earthly father was commissioned to Pretoria, for a period of 5 years. Those 5 years in Pretoria were the best 5 years that any family could ever ask from God!

When the 5 years were cut short in February of the year 1993 due to the untimely death of my father, the cut was so traumatic after what had seemed like 3 months of serious illness. His death was so traumatic that I felt as though at the time, a part of me had died also. He was gone before we could really nurse him as his family and loved ones. When he was gone, I had no idea that his spirit would live on in us and all the memories, teachings he embedded in his children were forever in us.

I know now that an education is very important to a child's welfare as well as confidence because my father embedded that powerful knowledge in his children. Especially in me.

When I started having children of my own in 1994, I had secretly wished in my heart to give my children what I was able

to have because of my father. It was a long shot though living in Malawi. If we were to fulfil the dream that I secretly had in Malawi, it would mean a lifetime of loans from my job and from the job of the children's father to give our kids, the two kids we had at that time, the best of the best.

Yet, God saw what was in my heart! All along.

Destiny was calling in Philadelphia! That is where God had my children's future and education in mind. Imagine that! Isn't God Epic?

America, had us on her agenda! God is musically good and tantalizingly awesome!

To all immigrants here in America, right now, who have come from elsewhere outside America, know this. America is really capable of producing sound results in your life and know that America can make your dreams and child's dream come true! Hard work, persistence and God if you are fortunate enough to read between the lines. Matthew 19:26 declares that Everything is possible with God! And I can testify.

I say this because our American experience in my family's life speaks for itself on our behalf. Marvel and Avedi came here at the age of 3 and 1 years of age respectively. One of the things that Keneilwe their father and I did right together was their education. From the beginning, we both knew and silently agreed that if the children would benefit anything at all from living life in America, education would be it. The best part of education was that no child was left behind by the government and school systems via an executive order that was enforced by President George Bush II by 1999.

All legal and illegal immigrant children and every American child under the ages of 18, were expected to be in school learning during school hours and school seasons no exceptions unless homeschooled. This executive order took a load of anxiety off of our shoulders, when it came to enrolling our children in public schools. All that the schools needed from us were their birth certificates and proof of residency in Philadelphia.

Fast forward to days beyond the year of 2017, I am certain that many things pertaining to registering any child in public schools

may need a bit much more of information from enrollees. No child left behind policy was and is still an awesome policy and still in action. Children are our future. But just think to what would have become of our children then if illegal immigrants' children did not qualify to attend any school in America? What would have become of our two children then? I pray that for as long as America stands, every child will deserve to have an education, or the country will be in trouble and suffering from an influx of illiteracy.

Another great factor was that my family and I had come to America at a time when public schools' quality of education was excellent. Some public schools' quality of education is still excellent, since 20 years ago, today.

Keneilwe for the most part of the first two years in America was home with the kids because he was mostly on part time basis for work. It used to be very hard for an illegal immigrant man to obtain work in America, I don't know about nowadays. With our recent President, President Trump, chances of an illegal immigrant man obtaining work may be getting slimmer by the day. I have been watching the news lately on immigration, and it hasn't been good so far.

So, in 1998 and 1999, I was the one who provided as a breadwinner through housekeeping and nanny jobs for our family. For the longest time, I worked for other families in their households while he worked at home with our two children until he secured a job at an oriental rug cleaning place in Philadelphia.

Then the children were full time in school and aftercare. At that point in time Keneilwe and I would alternate our chances to pick them up from the after-school care which was also the daycare, nearby.

UNDERSTANDINGS
OTHER'S STRENGTHS

We had agreed to divide household chores between the two of us. He would do school work each end day with the children. I would worry about the other house chores and necessities on to do list that I was able to handle. I knew from the get go, that I am not a teacher of school work so that department has forever been my children's father.

One of the things, I was able to discern about myself quickly earlier on in life was my ability to gauge what I had the tenacity, skills, gifting for at any given time especially once we had settled down in Philadelphia. When reality hit me in December of 1997 after our arrival here in America, that everything about our two kids, was on the shoulders of my spouse and I, alone. It was a shocker that I would become the servant I was able to hire back home and the comfort I was endowed with in my household in Kawale 1 back in Africa. Those privileges would be gone for years. There I was now, a household servant at a job for the purposes of bringing in cash to afford a roof over my family's heads in rent money, then food, utility bills and everything else in between. The reality of life in front of me meant that I would have to work around the clock.

That type of acknowledgement and reality was oftentimes overwhelming! Whoa.

Let us not forget the fact that I was a wife too. Life in America had taken us higher to another level of thinking and doing everything else other than what we had known to do in Malawi. And nothing had prepared my husband and I for everything that was unraveling before us in America.

It was do or die.

My spouse and I worked very well together to the point that the children were the best of the best in their classes, school overall on elementary level, middle school level and high school level resulting in great universities so far. In spite of their parents'

dysfunctional characters and dysfunctional marital bond. I say, God was doing the marvelous! Listen, I have no doubt.

Candid. That I have always been towards our children about their father's and mother's jobs to make a living! If they did not want to be laborers and struggle for cash like we did then education was their only option. The children harkened to that very clearly.

IT TAKES A VILLAGE TO RAISE A CHILD

It so happened that Marvel and Avedi, our two children by the year 2000, were attending our neighborhood public elementary school here in Overbrook Hills known as Lewis Cassidy for a short period of time from 1st to 5th grade, and 1st to 4th grade consecutively. But while at the public school there, the public system of education had put in place a program for gifted children in the school curriculum. In this gifted program, were children that excelled above others in every subject in the regular classes. Those particular children needed more academic challenges while they were in school during the school season. It was in this program that had ushered the students and prompted them to join an outside educative program known as the steppingstone scholars program which worked with minority students in public schools all over the United States of America.

In this Stepping Scholars program, the organization put the chosen few students under a strenuous academic training, taking place during the student's weekends in 5th grade and all vacation time of that students 5th grade. This was all in preparation for a more higher learning system of education in selected independent private schools in the neighboring suburbs nearby where the students were selected to attend school from middle school, high school then college. The program was super extensive that at times, I couldn't help but feel a bit sad for my 10-year old girl.

Steppingstone scholars' program was phenomenal in the life of my family's education for our kids especially in Marvel's life.

It is true what they say about children. It takes a village to raise a child. Steppingstone Scholars Program and its crew was our academic village far away from homeland, Malawi all the way in America!

Lewis Cassidy school, the Stepping Stone Scholars program and my daughter's hard work, her tenacity and persistence in her education, not forgetting God, ushered her into a high end private school known as The Baldwin School for Thinking Girls on an almost full scholarship ride. We are speaking of thousands of United States dollars in yearly tuition for 7 years straight. Somebody Scream," God!"

During her early academic years there, the school also afforded her private piano lessons with our own small amount of monetary contributions towards each lesson taught by one of the phenomenal school teachers there Ms. Jennifer. After some time, my daughter began to rebel against her school work load and everything else that she had to do in the name of education. On her mouth, she began to compare her life story to that of the legendary King of Pop, Mr. Michael Jackson (deceased). May his soul continue to rest in peace. He had once complained in a TV interview that he had no childhood growing up. No childhood, whatsoever! My daughter had adamantly complained.

She had felt this way due to stress that had stemmed from her strenuous academic and athletic schedule as well as any extra school/educational stuff she had to do at school. As a result, she ended up forfeiting the piano studies to alleviate her stress. I wasn't too thrilled.

But my daughter was overwhelmed, and she had to take it a bit easier however way she had to do it. Her education and achievements were about her, I have grown to let go as an African parent. Along the way, towards her end of high school years, she was selected as class vice-president, probably a first black class/grade president since the school was opened in 1888. It was a huge accomplishment. Say out loud," God!"

She went on to co-wrote and rearranged the lyrics to one of the class of 2012 farewell grade songs in her final year of high school. She matriculated high school with honors and was on her

way to Rhode Island School of Design for an industrial design degree which was postponed in August of 2012 and was derailed for mechanical engineering degree instead starting from August 2013 at Temple University. We thank God for His Plan B which turned out so much better than where she thought she needed to be.

DACA For Our Kids

After her graduation in June 2012, she had to sit out for a year to wait for her green card which she qualified through her father who at the time was a green card holder. This type of a green card process for a child of legal resident parent takes a while as opposed to an American citizen filing for a child who is not a legal resident yet. If a green card holder parent files for their child, like in Marvel's case, her and her father had to receive the green card after what had seemed like almost two years of waiting and they both had to go to the country of origin in Malawi to pick it up at American Embassy and re-enter America. The wait for her green card was very hard to do, that time was a very emotional time in her life. God had not forgotten about her.

Because in June of 2012 President Barack Obama and his administration established DACA which stands for The Deferred Action for Childhood Arrivals. It is an American immigration policy that allowed some individuals who entered the country as minors at the hands of a legal guardian, and had either entered or remained in the country illegally, to receive a renewable two-year period of deferred action from deportation and to be eligible for a work permit. Both Marvel and Avedi were enrolled in the program created by DACA by end of 2012 until 2013 for Marvel when she received her green card in Malawi of June of 2013. And Avedi received his work permit through DACA program enrollment and had it until 2018 when he qualified for his green card as a child of an American citizen through his father who is now an American citizen. When it comes to Marvel, we all have found out that Temple University was her God destined university for it was there

that she is walking out her destiny as a mechanical engineer. You see, God does not make any mistakes no matter what you may be going through wherever you are! My beautiful daughter graduates in the year 2019. Is anything too hard for GOD?

But if you really look back to year of June 2012, when my daughter graduated high school, lack of green card in her hands made it impossible for her to go to her desired college, Rhode Island School of Design. She needed a green card for her to qualify for some of the loan she needed to dwell on campus far away from home. It was a heartbreak to see my daughter stay home one year behind because of something she wasn't responsible for, when all of her friends had moved on.

Her father and I had brought her to America 15 years earlier so that she can become everything and anything she had dreamed of!

At that moment as her mother, I got even more depressed. I felt hopeless to watch my daughter's dreams of college look like they were fading away because she was an illegal immigrant together with her family. It looked like there was no hope for her college years. The American dream had come to a standstill.

But thank God for Hope! It was hope in Jesus, that kept her going! It was God who had held her together that she didn't go astray during one of her most trying seasons of her life. I am so grateful to God and her that she fought through and made it to where she is today. I didn't implode due to feelings of failure, doubt and shame for feeling like we had failed our hardworking daughter. I kept on looking to God and what would be His next plans in regards to her. I thank God for that!

Today, as I look back over my family's life and hers, I know that Temple University was very much her destiny because every door there that she needed opened for her while attending school there, opened.

PLEASE DON'T TAKE DACA AWAY

As I sit and watch the news regarding DACA- Deferred Action for Childhood Arrivals program today, I get concerned about the children who were and still are under this program, who may not be able to renew their work permits to be able to stay in the country legally anymore and be able to earn money legally to support themselves. Which can lead these children to become depressed and resort to dark measures of financial survival as a result, bringing the country down morally, physically, mentally, spiritually and financially. Let me tell you something, that program helped both my children to move on financially here in America on the levels I couldn't articulate with words. Marvel was able to work at a sports and goods shop and earn money to help her with a startup savings account she was able to use when she went to college after she had gotten her green card. Apart from being a babysitter, her world of employment due to the DACA program had gotten wider because the program granted her a work permit. This DACA program gave my hardworking children hope again to know that they were thought of and cared for as the children of illegal immigrants who had nothing to do with coming to the country in the first place. The program pushed my children to work harder towards their individual education, dreams and future goals.

Since the arrival of Marvel's green card, she has continued to flourish and do awesome things once she got to her studies of Engineering School as well as outside The Engineers Fields here on the East Coast of The United States of America. She has experienced paid internships with some of the best Engineering Companies out there today! As I share my story, I see her future looking really, brighter by the day. But it was not always easy. For a small period of her life, it had seemed like all the hard work would never pay off for a moment. But it is as we speak!

The same goes for her brother Avedi. He left Lewis Cassidy school in our neighborhood when he graduated 3rd grade. His story was different. Although he too was just as gifted but in different ways to his sister, as it should be. He too while at Lewis Cassidy School was in the gifted class. The reason why he didn't go

....

to his private school, through the same leeway as his older sister, was because we had decided to send him directly to the Shipley School by fourth grade on our own without him undergoing an extra academic program. It was a beautiful blessing to watch the two children go to school side by side and both excelled in all that they did there. My family was made aware of the Shipley school by the same interim priest from our church in 2004 who was our marriage counsellor who also had continuously encouraged us to look into the Shipley private school because of their great packages they were offering to minority families of students who go there. We followed what the Priest had advised us and here we are 13 years later! You should know by now that God will have His way in your life or loved one's life for His glory and satisfaction. I have seen Him do it!

I personally thank God for that Father and priest from our motherland Africa, Kenya particularly, who God sent personally to nourish and uplift my family. He and his wife and their daughter at the time were very close to us as a family and he always recommended and insisted on sharing with us whatever good was out there for the taking. He was a Godsend.

The Shipley High school was tailored for Avedi. It was his destiny. His first Teacher and 4th grade Teacher, the late Mrs. Hen (may her soul rest in eternal peace). She had adored him mightily. She was the reason why Avedi's transition was easy and swift. My family will never forget her. The teachers from each grade of his studies there throughout his academic journey were fond of him. And even beyond his study years there. While at The Shipley school, he was famous for his drum playing among his peers and throughout the school years, but he has always remained humble. He originally started playing the drums out of The Philadelphia Clef Club on Broad Street since he was 7 years of age. Eventually, his middle school teacher at The Shipley school Mr. Dan. Another phenomenal musician took him on. The drum lessons there were paid by the school trust fund and we did a bit of co-pay towards our share of payments for as long as the drum lessons went on. He was the drummer in the jazz ensemble in the school while he continued to maintain an honor roll academic performance during

the 9 years he attended school there! He also loved to play varsity soccer with school peers. Avedi's many achievements next to his sisters made us aware that coming to America was one of the best decisions we had made no matter how hard life has been on many aspects of life while living here.

In June 2015, he had an opportunity to go Princeton University or University of Pennsylvania but he ended up here in Philadelphia through an early decision acceptance into the University, with a GPA of over 4–5 grade average where he is still pursuing his studies!

Isn't God, Great?

My family is truly grateful to God for the two private schools namely The Shipley School and The Baldwin School that stand next to each other in the suburbs of Bryn Mawr. I am forever thankful to God for everyone who partook in helping my children's lives evolve in such a way to where they are today, in spite of what they didn't have as legal residents of the country when they did. Don't ever let a status of any kind hinder you from becoming everything you can become on planet Earth!

Once again, a village raises up a child. I can testify. God, teachers, the kid's father and I all did it for the betterment of Marvel and Avedi far away from motherland, Malawi! Teamwork goes a mighty long way.

Their teachers respectively have played a great part in ushering two unsuspecting African children into priceless assets that they are today in our society in the Western hemisphere and beyond.

I look forward to Marvel's and Avedi's contributions to society in giving back because that's what it all comes down to. After all they have been through, my children's best way of expressing their gratitude in the places of education where the odds said impossible, but God said possible, is to give back. My children will and must give back with glee when the time to do so shall come because it took everybody for them to reach where they are! May God always help my children to never forget how they got to the top. God through People, did it!

People Who Helped
Our Children

S omebody gave generously to my children for their higher learning in their education in their consecutive private schools concerning finances, concerning their physical needs such as books,
uniforms, time, counsel, such as mentorship and emotional support when things got tough. Those who gave money, gave hope
and encouragement in believing that my children were and are
worth their attention and investments. The type of education and
the amount of money it costed to get things done is simply surreal.
And everyone else out there who played any part or paved a way
that ushered my children to their individual and collective suc-
cesses to date, I commend you greatly. Among the people, a few
have remained close and have become part of us. To everyone out
there who stopped and helped my family in any way along the 20
years, I want to say to you, thank you!

I have lived in America long enough to hold to a high standard anybody who stopped their time, at times took their time, to
pour it into my life and or into my family's life especially when
there was nothing for them to gain.

I say this with due respect. Anybody, who has ever given into
your life, especially here in America, if you can never reciprocate
the good deed I beseech you to stop and thank God for them and
bless God for them because of the times we are living in. We are
living in the times of what's in for me and everybody living for
themselves era. I hate to admit.

Yet one of the best things you can do for anybody and yourself
is to GIVE.

There is healing, in the gift of giving. The gift of giving is
always best at any time, any day throughout the year. You may say
why? Acts 20:35 in The Bible commands us so. It says that it is
more blessed to give than to receive. Giving is an investment that
keeps maturing in relentless returns at times that are unpredictable
and unstoppable not only or necessarily from the one that you gave

to but also from others that are givers and continue to give just like you.

Giving is more powerful when it is reciprocated and the chain of giving left unbroken! Giving is very empowering if you wish to feel good about yourself.

I have no doubt that my children will continue to give back extensively. Without a doubt, the two schools are now part of our family and our family's American legacy.

An American dream coming true right in front of our eyes! Isn't this why we dared to come to America and forfeit all that we knew for the sake of the unknown, far away from home? I don't know what your sacrifices maybe, but for my family, God has paid us with an overjoy for our sacrifices. With God, all things are indeed possible.

DELINQUENT PARENTS

I wish I could say that all this was a walk through the park when it was happening. It was not. I would tell you that financially on what was expected of us to pay by the two private schools collectively to make things happen for our children was not easy.

I remember at one point, my family lived from advance loan to another, from week to week just to be able to afford the little bit of couple thousands of United States dollars that was the small amount allotted for my family to pay to the two schools. The amounts were very small in comparison to each individual child's yearly tuition in total. There were many times, we left our small amount of school fees get blown up into a bigger amount in arrears and interest because we were not always on time and on point with our finances in general.

But how can one maintain a steady financial standing with so much to be done and so little money to do it with?

With God's help, through people it was done. Our children indeed started at 6th grade and 4th grade level in the private schools, remained there during school years and finished high school at the top of their classes in the schools standing side by

side. After all, God originally used the two of them, for me to have a desperate need for their better life and future here in America. That desire for them led us to the entry borders of America, to obtain the American dream. We did get the American dream. We are living it out.

But you must know that it costs to be successful in America. And yes, everything in America costs.

Finances is where, most of the trials and tribulations during our arrival on American soil begun. The financial issues stayed and continued to stay within our family for many years if not for all the 20 years we had lived here.

My God! The Children and my American Dream for them, everything looked impossible from a distance and without God.

Everything needed money in so many ways.

Let's go back to work issues. Nobody shows it in television shows or American movies, I will tell you that about money in America and how hard it is to earn the American dollar. It is not a walk through the park, like I had thought of it to be before we got here. The limited job opportunities for an illegal immigrant while living in America financially is another reason why I was prompted to share my life's story in America all the way from Malawi, my home.

Whatever anybody decides to do to survive in America, money is at the root of that survival mode. The Bible says that money is the answer to all things in The Bible Book of Ecclesiastes 10:19 by King Solomon. The writer was not kidding.

I had a dream about my children and my family in America but our money to make it all happen was very funny in comparison to the size of that dream that I had.

At that realization, I felt like blowing air straight out of my mouth each frustrating moment which I was often in. Sighing.

The dreams have always been bigger than me, the person. I will admit that. This caused me to live in fear, anxiety, doubt, stress and defeat oftentimes.

I think I spent about 14 years of my 20 years of life in America being afraid, nervous, defeated and wondering what would become

of some of the dreams that I had carried in my belly that seemed like they were never gonna get birthed out.

One of them was about this one dream I had for my children. I wondered about their education after high school life. So, what, they were "A" students! But what would become of their lives after high school? After all the certificates they had accumulated. What would be next with everyone in my family living in the country under illegal immigrant status? Rhetorical unanswered questions are a sure easy way to self-defeat. I was secretly defeated.

Insecurities are a quick self- disqualification to one's potential success. I was sinking in by each unanswered question I presented to myself in front of me.

For a very long time I did just that. But I didn't know it then that it was crazy and wrong. I just thought that it was alright to carry on this way; a crazy lunatic with ongoing speeches to self. So, I had to stop for my own good.

It was not healthy for my mental being or anybody else around me for that matter.

IT IS GOD WHO APPOINTS LEADERS

But Thank God for His Mighty Hand in selecting every president of the United states of America, I will tell you. That I have come to understand with the help of Bible Book of Daniel 2:21. Obama was finally in The White House y'all! The Beacon Lighthouse of The World! Hello Somebody! He had fixed the issue that had caused migraines in my house about my children being able to go to college by the leeway of that DACA program.

That was one sweet sensational executive order that I was screaming out for joy when he did. There he was!

I will tell you this. Many people remember where they were on November 4th of 2008 when Senator Barack Hussein Obama II was elected the 44th president of the United States of America, defeating the Republican nominee John McCain. Senator McCain who continued his role in the Senate until 2017 but recently passed away due to illness. He was a family man, a patriot, a veteran, a

hero, and is now an American legend. May his soul continue to rest in peace. On January 20th of 2009 at 42 years of age, Barack H. Obama II was sworn in and became the President of The United States of America, changing history as we knew it! He was the first black commander in chief to lead America and the world.

That fateful year would prove to be a divine set up for my family when God approved his candidacy for presidency. His administration by 2009 had already issued some changes in the way some things were to be governed in The United States of America during his future leadership and administration by the time he was in office. January 20th, 2009, ushered in the administrative reign of President Barack Obama in full throttle. It was Epic! His legacy was bittersweet to my family but mostly sweet.

Check it out. When Inauguration day had arrived! I saw Mr. President, his lovely wife Madam President, Michelle and their beautiful daughters on that podium in Washington D.C. Let me tell you what was happening on that incredible day on my end. My location to witness the impossible was Bala Cynwyd. In a mansion.

By this time, I had worked as a nanny, babysitter, housekeeper/household manager for a wealthy family for 3 years. I am not naming names, so I will just call them, the Peas Residence. I had a fabulous relationship with my employers, the madam especially.

You see, as I sat in their living room on their best reclining chair in the whole living room next to my madam Peas, I was with my African American twin boys in my belly exactly 20 days before their birth and arrival on American soil.

I will never forget the joy that I felt rushing through my veins as my lady boss and I, watched with unspeakable joy that inauguration ceremony via television. And the rest of the world was watching too from all over the world I am sure. It was epic to see history unfold right underneath our eyes.

I was carrying history in my own belly for my family's lineage as I was witnessing America change forever!

In my mind, at that very moment President Barack H. Obama II was my family's hope. But at that hour, I had no idea that Obama was also my family's major immigration issue. Here is why and how!

ROUNDHOUSE AND ICE

O n one unsuspecting late hour of the 7th of June 2008, on a
Saturday, my husband had been picked up by police officers
on the road while he drove drunk. At the time, I was in Soho, NYC
where my Malawian colleague had to house sit her day job for that
weekend, feeding the cats of the house while the owners were on
vacation in another country. I was there for the weekend which
was from that Friday till Sunday to regroup from life's stresses in
Philadelphia.

While I was there in Soho, NYC I had a habit of calling
Keneilwe twice a day to check in. I remember that before I went to
bed that Saturday night, at 11 pm, I called him via my cell phone
to check off for the day and learn of our children and their day.
Everything was on schedule. Our daughter's best friend NaeJa was
over for a sleepover to visit Marvel. Our son had been dropped off
by my husband on time at a school friend's house for a birthday
bash and sleepover to be picked up the following Sunday morning
by 9 am.

But before that Saturday night was over, just after my husband had talked to me on the phone when he already sounded
tipsy, he had secretly decided in his heart to get more drunk. He
was on his way to Third World Nightclub on Baltimore Pike in
West Philadelphia when the Philadelphia police car stopped him.
Right there begun a scaffolding to what seemed like a relentless
nightmare!

The police took him to the Roundhouse here in center city due
to my husband's driving under the influence of alcohol. There, they
kept him from that moment to sober up and fine him on criminal
charges of his case by the following day. On Sunday morning when
he got a chance to call home, he did but our daughter looking at
the house phone caller id with no adults in the house, did not
really know whether to pick up the phone call or not. In the end
she opted not to.

By 10 am, the parents of the birthday boy, where our son was,
began to call our home over and over again until Marvel finally

picked up the phone. Our daughter gave them my cell phone number. My cell phone was then ringing off the hook.

I picked up a frantic phone call from her asking me when was the last time I had spoken to her father!? My world begun to spin. Why? Had something awful happened to her? "Oh no!" She said. "His bed looked like nobody had slept in it," she had answered me.

But the boy's parents from the sleepover birthday bash desperately needed Marvel's father to pick up her brother from their house as they were on their way out to some island abroad on vacation. Wait a minute!

I asked her to hurry up and go to look elsewhere for a clue about where her father's whereabouts might be. The phone history on the caller id as well as the voicemail which she did.

She called out a strange number that I eventually traced back to the number of the Roundhouse downtown Philadelphia via their voicemail which alerts you that someone you may know is in correctional facility. I immediately told her to calm down. I asked her to ask her friend's mother to come and pick her friend up from our house without showing any alarm.

I then told her to stay put to wait for her brother when the family drops him off which was my next move to make the phone call to them via the number my daughter had given me. I would call the family and ask them to do me another huge favor by dropping my son off. Of Course, I made sure to apologize for the inconvenience. But my heart was in disarray.

After I had hung up the phone, I called the family and did just what I had promised my daughter.

The family was on their way to my home, to the apartment building which was on Lotus Villa, a few miles from the family's suburban home.

Then I called my daughter back again to assure her that I had spoken to the family, her brother would be home soon. I told her that I would board the next Chinatown Bus and return to Philadelphia right away. She wanted to know if her father was alright. I said yes without really knowing if her father was dead or alive. I was certain that whether dead or alive, the police knew exactly where he was. I was so sure that he was somehow in jail. But why? Had

196

he gotten in jail by beating up someone? Was he in jail because he was drinking and driving? Oh my Lord, he left the children alone!

I had all these questions and furious thoughts arising in my head and my brain was spinning out of control with all kinds of negative thoughts.

Oh, my goodness, who will now bail him out?

By June 2008, we didn't have many people that we could confide in or depend on to do such a thing for him. Or better yet, everyone we knew was either an illegal immigrant or in the process of filing their immigration papers. Oh, my HEAVENS, what were we going to do?

I have heard of adrenalin power surge in people's analogies. I had no idea what it felt like until that day.

I was under the spell of adrenaline. I was functioning completely under the rush of it in my veins. It was really The Holy Spirit in me, but the truth be told, I didn't know it right away in that season. It would take years later for me to understand in fairness the truth of everything that was happening at that time. As well as the reality of who took over my body, for me to function the way I did without losing my mind.

I had been to NYC in Brooklyn to see this particular friend from Malawi who lives there many times before this incident. That was the most rushed uneasy goodbye I ever said to her or anyone in my life since then. I pray, I never had to do that again.

The bus ride back to Philadelphia seemed to take forever no matter how recklessly fast that Chinaman was stepping on that driving pedal.

While I was on the bus, I quickly called my day job on the mainline and explained to my bosses that I may not be coming into work on the next day which was Monday because my house was not in order. Something terrible had happened to Keneilwe but I didn't really know exactly what it was.

From the vague looks of things on my house caller ID and my gut instinct of Keneilwe being in jail at the roundhouse was all I could build the circumstances on. I couldn't tell exactly what to make of the situation at hand except sit by my house phone once I would get home or keep diligent watch on my cell phone

for another call to learn on how best we were going to help my husband get out of his present unforeseeable bind. I still had heard nothing from him by the time I arrived home that noon. Then the dreaded call came in!

It was him. In a very dejected, subdued voice and am sure with his tail between his legs too from wherever he was! He said a defeated hello.

I said Keneilwe where are you?! In a panic. At the roundhouse in jail was his simple answer. "Why?" Was my question in fury. He continued to say that he was caught drunk and driving on his way to Third World Nightclub right after he had spoken to me via the cell phone late that Saturday night.

His consolation over the phone was for me not to worry so much because he had to wait for the Judge to pass judgement on him and set bail before he could come home. According to his intellect he figured that it was his first offense therefore the judge would be lenient. And for me not to worry because he would be coming home he said the next day on Monday after hearing his judgement that Sunday evening. At that moment, I was relieved.

On my end, I don't think that he knew exactly what was going on in my head, like how badly I wanted to cuss him out for being so selfish, so irresponsible, so neglectful of our children's need for supervision and chaperoning besides his need for immediate gratification at the wrong time. But I kept my cool except start wondering about the next move of who I would have to ask to bail him out.

That became my next move on my to do list on that Sunday afternoon. But all that was cut short by his second phone call from the roundhouse shortly after 3 p.m.

He was on the phone again. It turned out that he was no longer at liberty to return home the next day which was Monday like he thought.

Instead, Immigration and Customs Enforcement also widely known as I.C.E, a department of the United States of America Homeland Security had his number and were taking his sorry behind to one of the two deportation camps in York, Pennsylvania or New York to serve time for his air ticket back to motherland,

Africa. He would be on deportation proceedings and that we would know more of his next destination in details by Monday!

I said What?! "Come again?"

Yes, his subdued behind was being sent to a Deportation Camp. Then back to Malawi where he came from in December of 1997.

By June 2008, one of President Obama's policies was that every illegal immigrant had an open arrest warrant for being in the country illegally and that if and when found committing a crime of any sort in any one of the American States, that person would be put in deportation proceedings.

Such was my husband's case. Our family's immigration issues had come to the surface, suddenly. My Lord. We were no longer unknown, or under the radar to the Immigration and Customs Enforcement, like we had hoped to be for another 10 years. I had to tell somebody, this news was going to knock me out. Oh my God!

"What would become of me and the children now?" I silently wondered. We had become an open target to the Immigration and Customs Enforcement in Philadelphia. Now the children and I, would be hunted down. I had heard stories of immigration officers raiding on illegals in their communities. I knew for sure that our apartment would next. Oh God! I couldn't explain what I was feeling at that moment.

I had to do something. Once I got the message from my sorry husband. I encouraged him to pray to His God like never before for a miracle. I told him that I loved him. Then I hanged up the phone with a feeling like I would throw up in my mouth and pee in my pants simultaneously.

I quickly called my boss in tears violently sobbing. Professor Peas and His Wife were eagerly awaiting my call from the previous hours' information. Immediately they picked up my phone call and they comforted me in the best way they knew how. They then quickly advised me to call their neighbor and immigration lawyer Jonathan who would know exactly what to advise me in regards to this situation at hand. That's what I did next.

Well, if anyone knows Jonathan. He is not very good at sugar-coating any immigration issue at hand. He gave me the worst-case scenario and I don't blame him at all, to this date. According to him in regard to my husband's matter at hand, the way things seemed, my husband was indeed between a heavy hard rock and a tight place. My husband had committed two different crimes, and nothing was looking good for him. It all boiled down to one solution. By the end of everything no matter what, he would be on his way home to Africa.

Jonathan continued to advise me to say goodbye to my husband, the next time he had another chance to call me from The Roundhouse. He asked me to focus on that because there was only a 0% to 5% chance that officers from Immigration and Customs Enforcement agency would let him go back home to us to remain in the country once he was done at The Roundhouse with the Philadelphia Police.

The truth of the matter in regards to issues dealing with The United States Homeland Security Department in my husband's case by 2008, I don't know about now a few years later, but at that time was that if he were to end up at any deportation camp, my children and I would never be able to visit him due to our immigration status. And eventually, If he ended up in Malawi, then we would see him there, which according to my household was a far off reality and uncertain financially, if ever possible! My world was spinning.

In very rare cases, The United States Immigration and Customs Enforcement Agency may consider a deportee current assets in America. These specific assets at times maybe able to be used to fish the person in question out of the impending dilemma.

But when it came to my husband, it is not like he had an American child or children to return to his apartment to if they decided to let him return home at that hour. None of his family members were in any kind of predicament of any psychological or chronic health issues that had need for him to fend for them or that held him back in the country to care for their needs. He had no American assets whatsoever. He had no issues whatsoever that rendered him another opportunity at a living in America.

....

Except that he had been found driving under the influence of alcohol, and had become a deportee in the process of getting arrested by The Philadelphia Police. Now he was in big trouble. After managing to stay out of trouble for almost 10 years of his stay in America. The only best part of his story was that he was a religious taxpayer since the year of 2000 until that year of his dilemma in 2008.

Since things didn't look too good for him. I immediately realized that my husband had no options to help him qualify to remain in the country for another chance at life with Immigration.

In my mind, I began to hear a spiritual song that played around me many times before but didn't hold any meaning in my life up until that moment. If you are like me, I often hear songs in my head for each season that I go through. Psalmist Smokie Norful began to play,

Not a second, or another minute, not an hour, not a day.
But at this moment with my arms outstretched,
I need You to make a way
As You have done so many times before
Through an open door
I stretch my hands to Thee
Come rescue me.
I need You right away.
I need You now!
Lord, I need You right now!

Believe me, I could taste the pain and the desperation in those lyrics word for word! That was my issue, my plea, my case.

Meanwhile, my bosses, The Peas since the moment I had laid out my husband's immigration issues from previous hours, they went ahead and had contacted Jonathan the lawyer to hear of the logistics of things about my husband. And again, they contacted another lawyer from downtown center Philadelphia to compare notes. Two different top notch lawyers from two different top notch law firms were checking in on my husband's case on his behalf by Monday morning, the day of Deportation camp proceedings. Both lawyers came down to the same probable conclusion in his regard, that when he was done at the Roundhouse with the Philadelphia

Police, the answer was the same, deportation camp would be next. The two lawyers concluded that there was only 0% to 5% chance of him returning home to us.

I thank God that those two top-notch lawyers were very frank with me the very evening I found out from my husband that his sorry behind was on his way back home to Africa.

Thanks to them, I called his family back home to go into the throne room of God to intercede on his behalf. I called our family therapist at that time Cassie, another powerful praying woman of God who had spent the 2 previous years in counselling our family in hopes of putting the broken puzzles together to help us see the bigger picture. Love.

The only reason why we had stopped the therapy sessions was because Keneilwe saw nothing wrong with his drinking until this night when he really was found out to be a careless alcoholic and in desperate need of prayers. I called a few people in my Malawian community to pray for him. This was also the time I learned personally about who was with my family even through the fire. Some people I had held up high in esteem fell off because, they didn't want to have anything to do with us in our most time of need. I am not mad at them. I am actually grateful for their rejection. Tough times show you who is really for you. So, if anything at all, I now have eyes wide open.

Even that last conversation with him had me more prayerful than I had known of myself to be and instead, I gathered enough strength within myself to encourage him and I made sure to remind him to seek God, so that he could repent for everything he knew he had done wrong as well as everything he couldn't remember up until that night in a jail cell and ask God for a second chance.

AS YOU TURN, GOD TURNS

I will never forget one of the major sins that he and I committed together. It was the major sin of abortion. God hates abortion! Life starts way before one is born according to Psalm 139 from

verses 13, 14, 15, 16 with emphasis in verse 16. I with my husband's approval did abortions a couple of times.

But our main reason for the abortions was what would we do with an extra child in a foreign land? In God, on Earth, there are no extra people. So, I found out, although it took me a few years later after the repentance of the abortions happened. If you are here, God means for you to be here for a specific reason only you can. No matter what foreign country you are in, or your circumstances.

By 2008, our life of turmoil, and trials were much too many it just seemed hard to get by in many ways with a third baby in our home. It was hard enough to contain bills, food, now there was a chance that my husband would need a criminal lawyer, criminal fines for driving under the influence of alcohol then not forgetting an immigration lawyer in this new battle if ever he was in the 5% chance to return home!

By this time, I couldn't tell anybody any good thing about my marriage and the couple in it. The evidence was too obvious and he and I had bad habits we practiced and did together and sometimes apart from each other in spite of the union we had. Or better yet, our matrimonial issues couldn't embody another innocent soul. The thought or idea was just unimaginable! It felt impossible to do.

So, I went before God knowingly that I had power in me to seek The Lord for a miracle on behalf of the father of my children. At least if not for him or me, I owed it to our 2 children at the time of his Roundhouse deportation day. Those two innocent children we had dragged to the United States of America in search of the golden American dream would now have to live life in this America without one of their parents! I could not imagine. The thought was too much for me to bear. I needed God desperately!

As I went in before the Throne of God, I started off to repent fully for everything I knew we had done together as a couple knowingly and unknowingly. And for God to forgive us on the sins we didn't remember but needed His forgiveness so that my husband and I could stand a second chance together from God, in America.

People, be careful what you pray for! You may just get the prayer answered. You will understand this later on.

I was crying to God for my husband to come back home, because at that hour, I didn't see how I was going to raise a 13 year old girl and a 11 year old boy in private schools by myself without the sensitive information their father used like his social security number for financial aid and all the minor things that seemed large before me as a probable single mother in a foreign land far away from home.

I did have my younger sister Abiti Bula, my mom's younger sister's daughter Navessa, and my youngest sister and sibling, Tazie all living nearby in the hood. Each one of them was very much engrossed in their own world that literally everything that my household ever did or needed, depended solely on my spouse and me. Now, I had such a headache to think of the lonely blurry road I would have to walk if Immigration and Customs Enforcement agents were to send him back home to Malawi.

Oh, Dear God! Africa? It is indeed our home, but it had been 10 years already and we were getting established in America. Going back home unprepared on every level of life was suicidal. Immigration and Customs Enforcement had a way in how they deal with vigilante immigrants sometimes, as I had gathered my information from hearsay by thus far. With so much fear in my mind, I had no choice but to call on my sister Abiti Bula to come and get my children before it got dark that Sunday evening. Drunk as she was but willing and eager to come to my aid. Thank God for family even when they themselves are going through their own issues.

At the time, she lived about 10 minutes-drive within the neighborhood. She came with Navessa in her jalopy and had picked up the children. It was hard to watch my children go and discover how they felt about what was unraveling before them. A nightmare!

I knew that for a moment, they needed to go somewhere else safe besides our apartment where they didn't have to face fear like I did. My children would be safe for the night by her apartment. I was not going to risk immigration officers raid our home in the middle of the night and have that experience traumatize my innocent children on top of their new awareness or knowledge of immigration issues.

They had come to find out that everybody in their family was an illegal immigrant and there was a warrant available out there for their arrest. That was not how I had envisioned my American dream. That night, my plan was to stay behind alone and go before God on behalf of my husband in seclusion.

Honey, when I say that I had not been super desperate for the Mighty Hand of God in my life like I was on that night, I am not kidding you. I didn't know it before. Honey! Honey! Honey! That was one of the most restless times in my life. That night of June 8th, 2008, I was on my knees then on my feet. I was on my back one minute and the next on my tummy. On my side, with hands on my chin. At other times, I was standing up with both of my hands with fingers meeting at the top of my head

I was walking all over the house poking through the kitchen and living room windows then I was looking through the corners of the bedroom windows all awhile in the dark. I continued to do everything in the house while in the dark till the morning light lest Immigration and Customs Enforcement officers were lurking in the courtyard of the buildings or its backyard.

Yet, Jonathan, the lawyer had assured me that Immigration and Customs Enforcement officers would not come into my apartment without a written warrant but you know at that point, I felt like Immigration and Customs Enforcement officers could easily come anyways. To me, they were the big bad wolves of my illegal immigration era. They were afraid of no one. My Lord! Have I ever cried in quiet desperate sobs like that night? Not like that. I had heard of people lying prostrate before The Lord. But I never imagined in my life that I would be next! The bed wasn't comfortable anymore. I suppose a good bed is appreciated when all is well, mentally.

Nothing that night seemed comfortable or well enough. Loneliness was my cup to take once again. Fear was prancing at my door.

Dread had become comfortable in my world I could almost touch it. Self-pity and anxiety I reckon, had ushered themselves into my life, the day I had become an illegal immigrant on American

soil. Only that I didn't vividly register the intensity of the predicament we were in until that night in the pin drop of silence!

Even my heartbeat was too loud for my quiet room and for
my loneliness. My heart had beat so loudly and so fast nothing
could numb my mind from hearing it. I tried to pause my brain
from thinking too much for a second, but my heart was racing at
a speed I couldn't measure in words. As a matter of fact, it was as
if my heart and my brain were working hand in hand headed to
an impending eruption which I was praying to God to relieve me
from, lest my body decided to shut down.

Lord, I just can't die right now not like this! I tried to con-
test in sheer anguish and desperation, murmuring. What about my
children?

What would become of them? Oh God if You can hear me, I
promise I will do things for You!

I continued to make my case before The Lord. I cried with
tears of sorrow falling off my face like dew on leaves early in the
morning time.

Only that this sight wasn't peaceful, pretty and it definitely
was not calm. I started to whisper to God in relentless prayers and
petitions late that midnight hour.

I strongly believe that the next move that I made before God
at that particular hour created a major breakthrough that changed
the course of my family's life and everything that I have ever done
in my entire life as a human being under The Almighty Hand of
God!

From the bottom of my heart, I made that one but wise desperate petition and vow unto God. By me declaring that vow, I
knew for a fact that Heaven had to release my husband from the
dungeons of hell and mouth of that prison cell, he was in from that
day and would never ever visit or stay there again. This was true
also for his children and everyone that is in spiritual and physical
attachment to him, literally.

Just like that, I whispered to God in the darkness of the room.
I said to Him, that I Brenda, no matter what, would never ever
stand for abortion in my life or others knowingly ever again for as

long as God has His breath in me. My declaration and vow, was sincere and specific.

I then repented to God of everything my husband and I did together on his behalf from the beginning to where we were! Have you ever heard of nick of time? Do you understand that God is never late nor early? But He is always on time! When you turn, God turns.

Well! I had to see it to believe it.

Do you know that there are some things in one's life about God that can't be taught or taken seriously on hearsay alone? I had to go through everything thus far to understand everything for myself when it comes to the things of God. The next few things that followed after that specific declaration and vow proved to me personally and undeniably, God to be so real on the Earth as in The Heavens than ever before. When I say God is Real. Y'all best believe it.

That Sunday night into Monday had seemed so long. People who were praying for my husband abroad and near were still praying and hoping for a miracle in spite of what Jonathan, the immigration lawyer and Amy, the other immigration lawyer from another top notch law firm downtown Philadelphia were saying. Their individual insight into this particular immigration issue was sincere and genuine. They were simply telling me what the statics have been in their experiences. They were being typical lawyers.

What they didn't know about this situation was that God in the Midnight hour had stepped on board and He had changed the status of my husband already, beating all odds, and all statistics. I feel like shouting right now! Can you feel the joy that I am feeling right now?

I know that this relief was not felt at home, or the Round-house yet, but it took a few hours to manifest itself. As a matter of fact, it did later on that day. Although, the morning looked like nothing good was going to come out of that day. I remember being on the phone with everyone who had their heart in aiding us from the moment it was dawn on that Monday.

I was talking to the lawyers back and forth from 9 a.m. of that Monday, then my bosses. Then Cassie the therapist and prayer

warrior. Father Bennie the Assistant rector from our family church, The First African Episcopal Church of Saint Thomas. I spent the morning pacing back and forth while I was on the phone. No longer panicky but getting probabilities and transferring the information to everyone at that moment that needed to know what would take place at the Roundhouse and after the Roundhouse that day in regards to my husband.

I had made peace with the fact that God was overseeing the issue and my worrying was not going to do any good.

By noon time, the two lawyers' concern from two different angles of their law firms was to figure out exactly which deportation camp my husband was getting sent to. Was it Upstate New York Deportation Camp or was it going to be York Pennsylvania Deportation Camp?

I suspect you are wondering why the two excellent lawyers had both stepped on board to do one person's job. Let me just say FAVOR. You can only understand this if you have things or people in your life, you know you do not deserve! It is nothing but The Almighty Hand of GOD at work!

And yes, the tension was on, but God does not put anybody through more than they can handle. With God, He always makes a way where there seems like there was no way! He is a God of suddenly! God loves to pleasantly surprise those that He loves, His children.

And suddenly, the verdict was in!

My husband would be heading to York Pennsylvania Deportation Camp. It had been decided.

At that discovery, I was at peace with God's decision. I had left everything in His hands. I was learning to totally trust Him for the first time in my life after everything that I had prayed for.

Meanwhile, at the household where I worked, my bosses, the Peas among themselves had already made a decision to help my husband by paying off the $10,000.00 bonds if need be once he was at York Pennsylvania Deportation Camp.

Sometimes the immigration system can allow deportees to face deportation proceedings and trial from their individual homes until at the end of the process. During the end, the ruler or decision

maker who is the immigration Judge either rules against the illegal immigrant or in favor of the illegal immigrant and renders a criminal forgiveness for the crime the convict had committed. My bosses on their own, out of the goodness of their hearts had decided to take care of whatever Jonathan, the main lawyer who represented my husband during his legal immigration battle to use for the purposes of getting my husband out of his current predicament at the Deportation Camp to await his trial from home. First thing in the morning of that Monday the 9th of June 2008, on D DAY, my bosses broke down the news to me. Honeychild.

Let me try to tell you. I was like boohoo in tears of joy. I promise you, God in His Sovereignty is awesome that He had placed me in this household at such a time as this when that traumatizing event took place and I needed all the right people in the right places to hold me and family down.

You should never underestimate the Mighty Power and Strategy of The Almighty God. He is truly Sovereign. It was not by chance that I was a servant to that household. It was not for fun, not for games or nonchalance altogether! It was all God ordained.

I would like to point out to you that $10,000.00 in 2008 was a large sum amount of money, and it still is by the time you read my story! Hello, somebody. Tell the truth.

Not a day later, but immediately, I begun to see my bosses through a different lens. You are laughing. Right? But I know you would too. Stuff like that has a way of changing a person's perspective.

By June 8th, 2008, I was 3 years into the job and each year before this, I had thought of quitting my job like a thousand times. My bosses had what I would call today a "problem child." Eventually I reasoned that she was really a child with repressed gifts which came out as misplaced outbursts that drove me and everyone around her nuts.

In spite of every shenanigan that the child and I went through by 2008, her parents were willing to sacrifice in cash a sum amount of $10,000.00 for my husband in his desperate time of need and there had been no talk of how I would repay them or if there were any hopes that I would be able to ever pay them back. They were

simply going to do it in faith that it was a necessary but noble thing to do when it happened. Hands down.

That was one of the most beautiful sides to that couple.

It felt great to know that my family was in great company too! Something good was happening. You may say what? Well, how many people get a $10,000.00 offer in that type of situation? Deportation Camps in America are full of deportees who don't have any money to bail themselves out of there or friends who have money to bail them out. Lack of money is the culprit most of the time.

Since we knew for sure by noon what was happening, I had finally decided to reunite with my children, my family members, and friends who had supported us at my sister's apartment a few minutes away within the hood.

I then called Father Bennie who came to pick me up and dropped me by my sister's house. Allow me to make you laugh about this ride my priest and I took. Drama! Before he dropped me off, would you believe what had happened while father Bennie was driving me towards my sister's apartment?

We took much longer to get there for a trip that normally takes less than 10 minutes. Among other crazy things on that afternoon, I saw a James Bond side to my priest. He thought to drive to my sister's in circles that way to lose anybody if they were following us from the immigration office just in case they were hiding nearby my apartment building and were actually following us. When he told me why he was driving in circles, I begun to crack up then suddenly my cell phone rung.

It was Amy! The immigration lawyer from the Law Firm downtown! What possibly could she be calling me about now? I wondered in my heart because everything that I had needed to know at this moment, I already did. Now what?

She asked me if I was somewhere seated. I said yes. Then I asked her Why? She said that there had been a sudden turnaround in my husband's case! Immigration and Customs Enforcement department was sending him back home to us that afternoon instead of York, Pennsylvania Deportation Camp. I said to Father Bennie please stop and park this car. There was exciting news!

What? I felt like shouting! I felt like dancing! Right there where we were. God is great! And greatly to be praised!

Yes, I was hearing correctly. It turned out that once every deportee at that station had been loaded on the deportation bus, enroute for York, Pennsylvania Deportation Camp ready to depart, another Immigration and Customs Enforcement officer run from the Roundhouse building to the bus to fish my husband out of the bus in the nick of time.

My husband was not going to serve time and await his deportation trial at a Deportation Camp before finally being sent to his home country from there, anymore. He was returning home to us.

He was in shackles when he was on the deportation bus. They had to unshackle him loose. And begin a different process that allowed him to await trial from his apartment. Look at GOD! I said, Look at What God can do in the Knick of Time.

A GOD OF SUDDENLIES & JOY

Father Bennie and I were joyous. We then proceeded to my sister's place, fearless. I bid Father Bennie goodbye outside and thanked him for his prayers, support and for the ride.

The Party had already started at my sister's place. I walked into a happy celebratory atmosphere and a people! It was incredible to see everyone's bright smiley faces from what was filled with fear and anxiety a few moments before. One of the people, I had spoken to on that Monday morning was my sister Abiti Bula who was very worried.

Instead, everyone was laughing and talking about their individual feelings and fears just before the great news had arrived and they continued to share but this time around with joy.

That day, I saw a small community of family and friends cleave together in love with one accord even in what was stressful for a moment! I truly miss that now a few years later. Family and friends are the major force behind the reason why God created this world.

Before we could all be together again that afternoon, my husband had to make a quick pit stop at our apartment. Then he

proceeded to where we all had gathered excitedly awaiting his face by my sister's apartment.

When we all finally got together, my husband revealed to us why he had to go to our apartment first. It was due to The Immigration and Customs Enforcement monitoring bracelet that had been placed and locked onto his uncle. It worked hand in hand with another monitoring gadget that connects to a house phone for his daily curfews. He wore the embarrassing restricting reminder of that gadget for months in the year of 2008. He had to surrender his passport too to the agency.

As we all sat around him, I couldn't help but see the infectious love come alive on everybody's face that was present there.

The evening was spent on hearing of funny jail stories, from the Roundhouse to the deportation bus until he was asked to come off the bus. He too did not understand why he was beckoned to come off the bus and he did not register right away what was unfolding in his own life. Remembering that he was still a bit tipsy and suffering from a severe hangover from Saturday's events even though this was Monday mid hours of the day.

Everyone in my sister's living room begun to exchange with one another their own experiences with anxiety, their own views on immigration fears and immigration shenanigans.

One thing for sure, was that everyone who did not know that there is God at the time became aware of Him. They also understood that His Mighty Wonders and Miracles are for real. They got to know and see what others talk about when it comes to God by the time it was for everyone to disperse! Right there we all understood the meaning of nick of time! We had witnessed it.

We all had just witnessed A God of Many attributes and wonders! He is a God of Teamwork. There was a group of people who worked together for the common good of another when really the signs were not clear if all was gonna be well.

One of the attributes to God is that He is A God of Forgiveness. Clearly someone had forgiven and favored my husband a notch for him to return home to us against all odds.

He was also A God Who Honors Vows! I say this to say that my husband came home from the hands of Immigration and Customs Enforcement officers on Monday 9th of June 2008.

A GOD OF VOWS

B y exactly 8 months later, on February 10th, 2009, he and I had conceived, and birthed out a set of beautiful twin boys. Yaakov and Yehoshua!

Talk about speed. Talk about Abundance and overflow. What about A God of Double blessings for Your troubles. This God I have come to know, is expedient too. My. My. My!

Yes, you got to believe this. That's The God That I have Come To Serve.

The twin boys Yaakov and Yehoshua, God in His Sovereignty has used them to bless us with so much since their birth. Everything we had feared was just really false evidence appearing real.

Our home, however has gained so much more in their birth than when the children were not yet in our lives.

I would take forever to confess of God's goodness from their pregnancy up until today in their 8th year! During the 8 months I carried them, I saw God first hand in people. I had favor at my job. I had favor at church. I had favor on the road from strangers. I had favor of God at home. I had favor of God with the nurses and doctors at Hahnemann hospital where the children were born under the leadership of that handsome Dr. Delvadia and his mighty team of excellent doctors.

I had favor with my personal doula who is now one of the most amazing entourage of godparents to the twin power. I had favor with my older children at home. I had favor with my husband. By mid-2008, I had been through so much but somehow, I had managed to carry on with life as if life hadn't been so cruel. I know it was God in me. He helped me choose to dwell on what was going to rule over my life. His Joy.

A God Of Signs And Wonders

I will share with you a bit about the pregnancy. It was just as fascinating! The favor of God was clearly all around my pregnancy. I couldn't tell anybody enough to justify the sheer joy and anxieties that come along with carrying multiple souls within your belly. During the time I was pregnant, I saw the intimate Funny Side to God. God is hilarious! He will make you aware of things in you and all around you long before you will understand but if you are not with yourself, you can miss it. I wasn't with it until later.

This is how loud God was during my pregnancy. While I worked as a babysitter for the Peas Residence, this is the longest household I have ever worked in, which is also when and where the lifespan of the pregnancy took place. There at my job for the little girl that I watched for many years, during the early- stages of my pregnancy, around August/September, I would oftentimes prepare the little girl's breakfast before her summer camp, and you know what? Each time I cracked an egg to fry, or scramble for her, you would not believe it if I tell you that things were super spooky, each egg was always with twin yolks. She was 8 years old at the time. But If I asked the little girl to crack one, it would be just one yolk. I felt like somebody was playing with my mind. Yes, It was God in His Sovereignty. He was trying to tell me something. But I was not with it to know at the time. That was sign 1.

Then, during the same time around August /September 2008, I had been to Atlantic City with my close friend and my goddaughter, her daughter. We took a picture together. I have a picture on Facebook that I had posted at the time. I wore a pair of white shots and a sleeveless sky-blue blouse in it. A friend of mine who also has a set of twin boys, who lived in Washington D.C. at the time but now lives in Texas, saw the picture and immediately commented under the picture and said to me, are you sure, you are not carrying twins in your belly?

I laughed with her and laughed at her desperate need for me to share in her twinning expeditions! I thought she was crazy! I brushed her off. That was sign number 2.

Then the very final and 3rd sign was something super phenomenal. It was happening in my belly nonstop. I was in church and clearly very uncomfortable, this was when my husband and I were seated side by side in service at The First African Episcopal Church of Saint Thomas in my 20th week. I remembered on that Sunday, I kept on switching my butt by leaning on one side at intervals of 5 minutes at a time. I could no longer sit up for periods over 5 minutes. I had to switch up every often times. He was looking at me strange and wondered if I was alright. No, I wasn't!

Then I remember telling him and whining about the sleepless baby who was very much all over in my belly at that hour, nonstop restlessly.

I began to wonder if I had done something terrible in my previous years to cause the restlessness in the baby to come. I was so troubled within my heart.

Lo and behold it was 2 the whole time and my simple mind could not fathom it!

GOD works in signs all around us! If you pay attention long enough, you would be able to see and hear God all day everyday all around you.

God is Very good like that, all the time.

The day to end the mystery came when the 4 of us arrived at Hahnemann Hospital one great Monday morning to experience a sonogram. The four people in my family who had skipped a few hours of work and school were my husband, myself and our two older children. They were supposed to be at The Baldwin School and The Shipley School respectively but no, they wanted to witness this epic baby moment in all our family's life.

My Lord, they had no idea what they had interrupted their regular schedules to witness. We all had no idea!

Our lives were about to be changed forever in the most beautiful way. I remember looking at my husband and telling him to run and never look back before we found out the sex of the baby. This way he didn't have to worry. Off course I was joking. I was more in love with him at that moment than ever.

Just think about it for a second. There we were in the midst of fire together and yet life was still full of hope and promises. I

knew that I was honoring my matrimonial vows to him right at that moment by sticking with him in the mud and the bleakness of season. Another baby? When our lives together were really going through unforeseen makeover enough to scare anyone in his case or mine.

To him, he still worried about being forced to leave his unborn baby on his way back home to motherland. He was very nervous. But of course, by this time, he had no idea that the deportation process would linger on for years, 2 years to be exact! I didn't know either, but I didn't look at his case. I was looking at God to solve the problem for us.

All my husband saw during that sonogram episode and beyond was what he saw in his mind and there's was no hope. He believed that he would end up being sent home to Africa anytime sooner and he didn't want me to end up raising 3 children alone. I do understand his take but thank God that I have often seen everything he sees the very polar opposite of his take in life.

I will tell you, he was not on Mount Kilimanjaro at that moment. If anything, he was in the valley of it. He was standing there in the room terrified.

When I looked at my oldest son, he was kind of "disgusted" and I choose that word to appropriate his attitude towards the everyday life's situation he often found his parents in and the two kids already on board. To him, we were super irresponsible in having an "extra child" to join our irresponsible unfit family. By this time the lad had seen a lot, so I did get his "kindest attitude" totally towards the whole situation in the room and beyond. The only thing I didn't know was how much damage his father and I his mother had done in him by this time to make him see another child as such a heavy burden to our family especially with his father's bleak future. I mean the boy was right. So much was at stake.

He wondered how else we were going to afford another child when the two parents struggled to afford the two children who were already there. Did I tell you that my children are very vocal and unpretentious too? I was laying there with half of my belly naked in front of my family who were going through a lot of

inaudible rhetorical questions psychologically. And then besides that, I was trying to make of what I would take by watching my daughter's face.

Outstandingly predictable. She was on another level of thinking. But then she wouldn't be my daughter if this weren't so, I will admit that much. She only cared that the baby be a boy! She was 14. She was all about herself. No one else was going to parade on her show but her and her pretty cute self and no one else. I mean not a soul was going to rain on her parade either. None! She made it clear too!

And when I asked the sonographer what sex of the baby she could see through the ultrasound? She surprisingly cut me off quickly in a nice way with her short answer saying, "Wait a moment for me to tell you which one is a boy or a girl!"

"Huh? Hello! What did you say?" Was my question.

Yes! You heard right. There was more than one child in my belly. God was laughing out loud from His Heavenly Throne at that exact moment. He had gotten me out loud. Wham! Bam! How is God, Y'all! Don't play with Him!

By this time, I had made Him, the Commander of my life! He finally had a say about this creation in my life and family's lives. No room for abortion, not even an inkling in me. A promise is a promise. Vows.

All at once, everything to me begun to make sense. Just like that.

I mean, the egg yolks, the Facebook comment from a friend who has twin boys, the restless sitting positions while in church prior to the sonogram. Oh dear God!

He'd really done it this Time! I was speechless! We were all speechless! All the selfish reasons about the gender of the baby were outside the room.

By far, definitely no abortion for me at some clinic ever! A million times, No!

When I said the room was suddenly cold and quiet, Visualize it. Feel it.

There it was. The spirit of shock had settled in the hearts of the people and any signs of joy had disappeared, gone baby gone! I

am sure that God was amazed at our ungrateful, sour reactions. But God is merciful and gracious. Our hearts were inwardly excited but not outwardly so. I probably was the only one in pure tantalizing delight and feeling very honored. God had really heard my vow and my petition. Those were my secret thoughts. How about that? Isn't God great?!

If you know me, you would know that I am a number one person in optimism most of the time. But at that moment, the truth staring right at me was very overwhelming no matter how optimistic I wanted to be.

Suddenly, I begun to see everything in doubles. When I say everything. I mean everything. Then I saw myself, I could only see my future self in exhaustion and exasperation, not to forget, exaggeration! I imagined everyone else in my family feeling the same way. Yikes!

I had been the breadwinner since day one. How would I work as a nanny or house manager for anybody out there with these two children to come? How would we afford the "two extra children" as my son had phrased it? What?

My mind was spinning. I had forgotten about the vow I had made with God. There was a condition I had put on our vow. I vowed never to abort so long God was going to take care of everything the baby would need. Assuming at the time, it would be one child. Now it was two children! Oh Lord! There goes my Life!

The pressure was on now for my husband and me. When the sonographer said it was two boys. The only joyous one was my daughter!

She got her wish alright!

The son on the other hand was mopping emotionally and psychologically for 8 months that followed that meeting and had managed to escape south in his mind the whole entire pregnancy.

We were worried for real. It's not like we could do something about it at the time financially or emotionally, shrink wise. We left it alone.

The father was in fear for 8 months and had no idea how everything would come to pass.

I had to be strong once again. A deal is a deal. I made it with God. So now what?

Let's see God be God!

That, He has never failed to be in my life especially from that point on.

God was awesome the entire 8 dreaded months, pregnancy wise. I worked till 7 months. I was paid in full for 2 and half months. So was my sub during the entire time I was on maternity leave. And God was strong and mighty financially wise, medically wise, immigration wise although the case was still pending.

What was interesting to watch unravel too were the 3 women who individually volunteered to be my unborn children's god-mothers out of the goodness of their hearts. Out of sheer joy along with 2 men. 5 stepped forward voluntarily and 2 more I had to incorporate them as godparents myself. One woman, my doula, a Jewish beautiful dear heart, I had to ask her. She was awesome during my pregnancy. Then the priest from Church, Father Bennie. I had to ask him because I wanted the twins to have spirituality in their lives if their father or I were not implementing it first-hand.

The twins have 7 godparents altogether. 4 women and 3 men. Each godparent has done amazingly to date. Each one has a spe-cific duty from God unto the boys! The very best godparents that never wavered or missed a beat in the twins lives from day one have been V and T Bythewood. My family could never thank them enough! What a difference they make in our kid's life spiritually and financially thus far. Isn't God amazing?

WHAT A SHOWER OF LOVE

It would be sinful not to mention God showing Himself might-ily once more through the people at the incredible and only baby shower I have ever had in my life! A family friend Phoebella had helped me organize it. It was splendid!

I will say this from the baby shower that took place at that church. The people really came out. These were some of our church friends, family and close friends we had come to know by that

season in time. We couldn't invite everyone. But amongst the people that came we collected diapers that lasted for a year. Gift cards that were over $2000.00 in American currency. There were clothes that the children wore for the first two years of their lives. We had strollers and car seats and everything a new mother needs in abundance! Everything we received was in multiples.

I would like to encourage someone out there that when God is involved in your adventure, He is thrilling in every way. Just remember to brace yourself.

We had nothing to worry about only that impending immigration case that lingered over our shoulders. Ugh!

Ain't that something?!

Can life just be smooth sailing?

I guess not, lest you will forget your Maker and think that you are in control of your life.

WAITING FOR A
JUDGMENT IS TORTUOUS

Well, we couldn't forget our Maker! Too much was obvious that God was on board and He was making Himself known whether we wanted to admit it, acknowledge it or not. But that impending notorious Immigration case was still unresolved although there were times my husband went to the courthouse with his lawyer and came back with nothing much but continuing to wait. I guess, it was part of the process. It just seemed like the case would never be over.

The anxiety was becoming a problem. I hated the fact that my husband would be the only one getting his green card of course whenever the judge would make the decision in his favor that is, although we still didn't know for sure which way things were gonna go. His lawyer explained that it would have been unwise for him to include and submit the 2 older children and myself in the removal process with my husband in case the immigration deportation judge would rule against my husband which was unpredictable,

but we had to be wise about the sensitivity of the way this issue was. Which in the end was indeed a wise decision although it was very difficult for me to accept.

But man, it meant that I would have to wait for 5 years before I would qualify to file for my green card through spousal privileges of a permanent legal resident. That was torture for me and I hated the wait.

Having unsure and insecure thoughts about the impending immigration case which could be ruled against my husband was even more uncomfortable. The thoughts were ever at the corners of our minds. We had two American children on board now going through this dilemma with us!

Every day was a trial to go through mentally.

I remember that from June 2008 throughout the year of 2009 was a time of shock of the deportation news, trying to recover from the shock, followed by two more miracles of good news! One was when my husband was sent back home to us instead of the Deportation Camp in York Pennsylvania and then immediately the news of another baby in the family which turned about to be news of twin boys!

For almost a year, my husband had stopped drinking alcohol cold turkey. Then halfway throughout 2009 until to date, he picked up the drink again and became a heavier drinker than he was before. I am blowing air from my mouth right now if you can use your imagination. Argh!

That type of discovery on my part made life for me very difficult emotionally to go through alongside him day in and day out. I kept on wondering what else to do to deal with the situation. He was diseased. But he was in deep denial.

It was not a secret among our friends or family members that he was in deportation removal process due to the alcohol consumption that ushered him in the presence of immigration offices. I couldn't understand him. I was more frustrated than I had ever been with him. I knew that loving him and living with him was starting to become toxic within me. It was getting worse to the point that I got more emotional and became very combative with him in the year of 2010 when I started seeing our twin babies crawl

around cans of beer around the new house where we had moved in for rent a few blocks away from where we finally bought our first house in March of 2011, here in the hood.

I was a basket case of emotions. I had not gotten over the whole trauma of the deportation removal process. The money we were spending on two different lawyers to fish him out of the deep gutters he was legally in, not forgetting the legal fines we paid.

The criminal case and the immigration case were both costly. Then our family got larger in the process of the turmoil. But in him there was NO change. He was still practicing old behaviors and seemed unmoved while I went through a heavy bodily change, an emotional change as well as spiritual change because there was no way I was going to come through this without God!

I kept on feeling short changed in all of the changes that our household went through "supposedly" together. Yes, I will admit that, I was the one who desperately wanted to come to America and so everybody was here for my ambitious drive but man, was this really the price I had to pay alone? Still?

I kept feeling like I was violated in so many ways, but it was still my lonely pill to swallow nobody could walk through my pain and feel what I was feeling.

The only best way I could describe it if ever to anybody listening to me about how I felt regarding his drinking would be like the following analogy. A wife seeing their husband with another woman having sex live. At that moment and from that moment on, he is as guilty as guilty can be! He is momentarily apologetic but not sincere.

A day passes, then he goes back to the same woman and many other women and goes wild with all of them having rampant sex and there seems to be a no end to it! Then when he does it this time around, he is not even sorry or secretive about it. That's how I felt about my husband when he picked up that can of beer or wine bottle again in our home or in secret to this day. It is like a slap in my face that all my tears and his older kid's tears, and hardship during the turmoil he put us through were in vain because of that alcohol/immigration trauma he uninvitingly provoked on our behalf.

....

Would you carry on with that man? He has clearly shown you his behavior and the type of a person he is and even how he desires to spend the rest of his life.

Now, if you have a desire to have longevity in your own life, peace of mind for other things that matter to you like your children or just your sanity. Would you allow that to carry on the way I did constantly troubled by others? Heck No!

The love affair after the deportation day was short lived. Up to September 2010 the day of the reversal of the Deportation Process, my husband and I lived in months of misery and anxiety.

Deportation removal process is not a good experience. Added with other issues in life, is hell on earth!

I believe that it was during this bracket of time that everything that should have brought us forward and closer as a couple, estranged us even more.

HOPE DEFERRED
MAKES A HEART SICK

Secretively, in my heart, I was still trying to be hopeful that my husband would eventually change his behaviour once the Immigration Judge reverses his deportation removal process and ruled in his favor, in spite of everything he was doing. I will admit that I have created and made excuses for my husband's behavior for years, I didn't realise it until later on in life. I thought how would I behave if I was on the chopping board of deportation process?

He was just the type of a person who already in his mind had given up and had packed up. He already was in Africa, just his body was here! The reason why he continued to be self- destructive and unreliable.

One of the most frustrating moments in any couple's life is when two people's bodies are in one place bodily but actually their two minds are scattered all over the place thinking and doing other things which are in actual sense not with one accord and not

beneficial for the union. God in His Word according to Amos 3:3 asks this question "Can two walk together, except they be agreed?" KJV.

Whatever thing in question to do with the two when asked among the two, the answer or result has two different answers that have nothing to do with each other, or their life or future together yet the result is supposed to be the bedrock of the union! It doesn't work.

We lived in one house with different seasons of times all at once. Impossible!

We started becoming uncomfortable with each other.

It was more uncomfortable when I realized that after all that we had been through together in the most crucial 24 months of our lives in regards to the deportation process, and then the family had grown bigger with 4 children and all, and an almost homeless situation that happened at the mercy of a landlady that managed to foreclose the property we rented from her, our first accommodation in a house setting. Somehow, she had forgotten to share with us about the legal and financial status her property had been in.

My husband still had not taken leadership reigns. I was the one who run around again to different kinds of lawyers once again, who this time around, enabled to secure our current rental housing for us to remain in the property for 10 months without pay in spite of its pending foreclosure. That was how we were able to secure and buy our own house nearby for our four children. God provided through His mighty direction in me for I was the one running around to make sure that we didn't end up homeless with four children on the streets of Philadelphia far away from motherland, Africa. After I had fasted and prayed for days, God showed me on the computer this house we bought and live in at the present time since March 2011. I could not count how many ways I have seen God move on my family's behalf here in America! Whew! You just don't know.

Sometimes I well up with joy inside of me.

Then I was discouraged when I had asked him about his future plans in case the judge ruled in his favor and granted him a green card. He told me plainly that he had none. I was sad in my

heart. Thirteen years in America, and this man had no plans for his life, nor vision for his family. After all we had been through!

To make it worse, by the 24th month of this miserable reversal of deportation process, the physical abuse towards each other had been much too much, along with the emotional and substance abuse, we found ourselves no longer sleeping with each other.

He had told me to earn the sex from him. It was devastating!

I strongly believe in my gut that at this moment in time he had an affair with someone he had met on the train that he took every week day to work. So much was happening between us it was too much to grasp.

This was the first time he spoke to me about earning sex. Then he referenced to me and my weight as fatty ass in his bouts of verbal justification from time to time.

The most abuse came out of his mouth during his drinking bouts which were often. His drinking to me has been a constant slap in the face!

It's where and when the deportation case comes alive over and over again each time he sips his cans or bottles of alcohol. It's like my struggles and nightmares due to the alcohol were after all, in vain.

The whole family had been traumatized because of it.

A few things should have changed by this time, drinking was no longer a privilege or an option. He now had 4 kids to think about, feed and fend for, in regards to their needs.

One of the most frustrating factors about his alcohol abuse around the house was being a step forward the toddlers everyday so that they could not experience alcohol from beer cans nonchalantly left behind on the floor around the living room floors or all over the house by their father.

I just couldn't stop feeling resentful. I often asked myself a rhetorical question I sought badly for the man I loved to answer me and see me for once.

Didn't I almost lose my mind due to the trauma of the deportation episode? The criminal fees and fines due to alcohol. What about the immigration fees and anxieties caused from it all?

Let's not forget the older children. They saw nothing between their parents change even after what everybody had been through. The constant squabbles.

I was often angry because he didn't honor, validate or understand my pain. I had given up all my living power and sanity to be controlled by his demeanor and treatment towards me and everyone in our home.

I had no idea that he was telling me all along on how he felt about me, our marriage, our home and our children and our future the whole time he continued to use alcohol as a clutch. He was out, and I was in. Alone, in the relationship! Sadly.

We got colder and colder to the day of the final immigration ruling in September of 2010.

THE AWAITED GREEN CARD

The judge showed my husband mercy, I say it was God who did through the immigration judge. My husband had been granted permanent legal residency, finally! It was absolutely, wonderful to have a member of our household legal in America! You will never really understand this if you are a born American! You are privileged. Yes you!

In our household, this meant car ownership and insurance in our household name. We were able to purchase our own house. And the list goes on and on for all the reasons why a green card is imperative in America for any foreigner in need of one! A green card for one of us meant that at least one of us would drive on the road without fear of running into a police traffic officer. And the green card meant having many countless privileges that come with being a legal resident in general.

A green card for my husband had opened up so many doors in our household and family life.

It was great news for those 2 bright children that were on their way to college. Their college years, green card wise were looking promising because one of their parents had a green light to live legally in the United States of America.

There was so much hope for everyone in his household.

Unfortunately, this seemed wonderful in theory yet in action, regarding the head of our family, nothing in action and in his life-style had changed!

He never changed his first full time job since 1999. He never took in more hours. He refused to take up any class courses of his liking to improve himself education wise to achieve a better carrier than the one he has been in. He didn't want to pick up another job or a second job to upgrade his income.

I was still the breadwinner even after he had obtained the one thing he claimed made his life difficult to acquire or find work in America from the start. Even after he had the green card! Nothing had changed!

At that moment, I begun to realize that God was trying to show me the heart behind the man. My husband had no intentions of upgrading himself for the sake of his family if not for himself. None whatsoever! I was in more duress. I was still feeling very much alone. I won't lie, I had bouts of anger many times and feelings of bitterness towards him for a long time after the green card had arrived.

Here I had fought the battle and put everything I wanted on hold, to help him pay for his criminal lawyer for his DUI case and Immigration lawyer to help reverse the Immigration Deportation case. There he was, doing nothing for himself or the family with the awaited green card.

Unbelievable!

I began to look at him completely differently. I don't know if I respected him anymore, but I became very resentful. It got worse when he became unmoved about our daughter's immigration issue.

It was after 2010 for crying out loud! The immigration case and its misery was over.

The Peas residency had been the place of my employment for 5 years. God had allowed me to have them in my life for so many things by the fifth year. I was very resentful towards my husband that I had to go to my bosses for help once again, in regards to fees for our daughter's green card process.

This was crucial about our daughter's green card. She needed it. The process had to begin immediately if she was going to go to college at all by 2012.

Don't Exhaust Your Employer

By 2010, I am ashamed to admit that I was asking for help from my bosses, day in and day out. I hate to admit this embarrassing fact. My bosses embraced me with a $4500.00 surprise. They paid for "my" daughter's green card filing lawyer fees. But both my daughter and her father will never willingly tell you this about me. Their view and perception of me is that I am a crazy person mentally. I will reject their claim until Jesus Christ, my Lord and Savior comes! Crazy persons DON'T achieve half of the successful things that I have as an illegal immigrant in a foreign land, far away from home. I am definitely crazy about God. That you can plainly see. So I get teary sometimes when I think about every injustice I have endured over the years from the same people I have sacrificed so much for, for us to get here. Confusion is a sin and a sure fast way for anyone caught up in it to get frozen in time with it too. Ungratefulness is a joy snatcher!

My household knew that our daughter was next in line for her green card due to college which was her immediate need by June of 2012, her high school graduation month. Her father's green card arrived at the end of 2010 which was only 2 years in. A child of a green card holder in her case had to go back home, out of the America, and reenter the country with her own green card via the American Embassy in her own country of origin.

So, in 2012 even though she graduated from The Baldwin School for Thinking Girls among the top of her class and was headed to a top notch college where she was accepted to study industrial design at Rhode Island School of Design. She had to forfeit and sit out of college for a year as she waited for her own green card starting all the way from Malawi into America although filing and paperwork was done here in America via our Immigration Lawyer, Jonathan.

Why am I sharing this episode of my daughter's green card journey? You may wonder, why? Well, as I watched life unfold for my husband's green card in our household for the betterment of our household, I also saw so much that I had hoped for my husband to achieve dissipate wherever it was. I was dreaming dreams in my head and hoping for my husband to share the dreams for our family. I was chasing after thin air and rainbows.

I quickly became aware of this each time I wished he dreamed to improve anything to do with his family. What a lonely journey I had been on until I came to a screeching halt.

Before I came to this halt, I watched our 19 years old daughter scrounge for air tickets to Malawi, to pay for her father and herself which she ended up borrowing from her former high school friend's father so that her green card was not forfeited as well. Yes, doesn't that make your heart sink? It did mine for a moment.

Her father knew this from the day he was granted his green card two years prior. He, my husband could have gotten an extra job to save up at least for his part of the air ticket for the necessary trip but no, it never happened. You see, since the day the four of us landed in America, my husband's excuse for not acquiring work or any extra hours on top of his 40 hours per week since mid-1999 has been one alone. He didn't have a work permit or green card.

Well what happened after September 10th of 2010? I quickly found out that it had been all a lie, all along. I was the fool!

In my journey to this country, I have witnessed many illegal alien men over the years work all kinds of jobs and fend for their families as if they had work permits or green cards. It is the heart of a man that drives him to work and fend for his family. Mine did not possess that kind of a heart. Instead, I had to become the man in my household pretty fast, from the get go. I had to put my life on the line, switch hats and become a man. And let me tell you something. Doing so, it almost costed me, my mind! To my family in America and family in Malawi, they claim that I am crazy. To me, I DON'T receive that. Instead, the one crazy thing I did before today was stick around for over 20 years in a dysfunctional relationship to expect a different result by doing the same things over and over again. That was definitely crazy! One thing for sure is that

if they had to walk in my shoes, they would understand the stress levels I had endured in the name of LOVE and THE AMERICAN DREAM, altogether.

God birthed me out as a woman, clearly. But for over 20 years now, I think like a man. I so badly want to reverse that. But I have no clue on how to do that. Life has not yet given me that opportunity to reverse into a mindset that matches my gender. I love being a woman and I seriously wish to feel how a good man treats a woman in simplicity.

From day one in America, I have done what most women who love their husbands and families do. I became the burden carrier for my household. My guilty conscious ushered me into allowing his manhood or whatever drive in men that makes them feel that they are men dwindle into hibernation. He went under as soon as we arrived and has never come back out fully.

Whenever my household needed something desperately, I was the one on the forefront to attain and obtain it for them or whoever needed it within the family.

Everything that I ever dreamed of for my family, I became the hunter for it and brought it back home to them, although my daughter thinks otherwise. She believes that, all the household shenanigans and journey, are all about me, she claims. Whatever she thinks of me in her eyes, I have made peace with my past. In time she will understand how sad it is to want the best of everything for the ones that you love in spite of all the accumulated losses along the way. At the end of the day, you have the same beneficiaries reject you and your efforts. In reality, whose loss is it?

I FELL OUT WITH BOSS ANDY

One of the major losses I experienced because of the love for my family was in 2006. I ended up losing an amicable relationship with a former boss I had worked for 5 years in center city Philadelphia because of his money that had to do with my family. I needed cash fast to pay an outstanding tuition bill that was my

family's portion to pay after the yearly school scholarships had been endowed to the children individually.

The private schools that my children were attending had called me in regards to the smaller portions of money that needed to be paid right away, that was long overdue that semester.

If not paid soon, the kids were going to get kicked out. Well, my husband and I didn't have the money on hand for the part of tuition my household was responsible for. It was not much, but with time and not paying on time, the amount accumulated interest. We needed desperate help with the finances. We couldn't borrow from the bank because we were not documented. We were very much illegal immigrants by year 2006.

I called my former boss, Andy. At this particular time, I had just started a new household job with the Peas residency. I explained my situation to Andy and asked him for a loan. He was all over the world on his yacht at the time.

He agreed to lending me the money with no strings attached. He paid directly from his bank account to the two schools an amount that was over $1500.00 altogether to put my household in clean balances with the schools, our children attended. It was when I failed to pay it all back on time, our relationship ended badly. It was my fault.

I won't lie. It was wrong of me and my family not to pay back in full what I had owed the man who was gracious enough to pay the schools directly from wherever he was, abroad. That's one relationship I regret to have lost due to wanting my children to get the best in life.

And my daughter has no idea of half of the things I went through for her to maintain a top-notch education from The Baldwin School for Thinking Girls.

I say this to say because "my" daughter believes that am not half a good mother I should have been to her when she was growing up. But the burden I had to carry while raising her and her brother up and the household issues we were facing on a daily level, were not so kind. Sometimes the stresses of life in me came out in the shortness of whatever she needed me to do for her that I didn't get to do according to her.

I was often overwhelmed. I feel saddened at times. I just thought at the time that I couldn't help my situation. It is sad now that I look back over my life and what is left are sour memories. It brings me tears sometimes. If only she knew the truth. I was going through a lot of stress all around me and employment issues didn't even end with my dilemma with Andy. They had only begun.

THE DON'TS I DID TO MY EMPLOYER

Right after that episode with him in 2006, I begun to take all my household financial issues from home that my husband and I could not solve together for our household and I resorted to my current job for problem solving. In June 2008, it was the same household that had offered to bail my husband out of the deportation camp by paying an incredible amount of $10,000.00. Fortunately, he was released before going to the camp. That saved everyone from spending large sums of money that was hard to find and I bet hard to return if we had needed it.

This happened to be the same household that payed for my daughter's green card filing and lawyer fees of $4500.00 or more after the year 2010. It was the same household that awarded both of my children in 2012 and in 2015 an amount of $1500.00 individual checks during their high school graduation.

Hear me somebody. Please! Don't do it! Don't ever make your job, your personal emotional, financial or physical clutch. Do not ever bring your household problems to work. It is unprofessional. It is a very, very bad move! I recommend that you never ever do what I did! It is a corrupt mindset which cripples any potential to discovering anything good within oneself to get ahead in life.

Besides, the borrower becomes a slave to the lender is what the Bible says in the book of Proverbs 22:7. Eventually someone in the equation becomes hurt or bitter in the process. I will admit this to you that from 2005 until 2012, I was not knowledgeable of what I know now about money and borrowing money. I had lived on loan advances in my job for 80% of the 10 years I was there at

the Peas Residency from 2005 until 2015. It reached a place where it was becoming very tiring on myself and my bosses, the lenders.

BAD FINANCIAL HABITS & POOR FINANCIAL MANAGEMENT

My husband and I, we were both culprits when it came to money management. He was a failure in my eyes by not stepping up whether the green card was there or not. Then his gambling and drinking. I was a failure in my eyes as well because I saw gambling as a way out. Yet I had labored so hard for the money I used to gamble with. We were fools who were chasing after gold where there was only dirt. This type of foolishness ate away at our joy as well as our marriage.

We had real issues at hand. Most of the issues needed our attention and money especially our household portion of private schools' tuition yearly whether we liked the idea of paying that portion or not. It was our family's yearly obligation. Then the daily necessities for our 4 kids. Not forgetting our rent/mortgage, monthly utility bills, transportation and food which were always a must to this day! But with addictions to the plate, it all became too much as time went by.

Misery became our invited and honorable guest and our children paid the price of heated money arguments each time the arguments flared up.

The American dream was seemingly getting dimmer as time went by. But, in spite of what everything was looking like within the family affairs, some things were not going to cave in.

The children were not going to quit private schools. That was never an option! Their tuitions together was over tons of United States dollars each year in scholarships from 2005 until 2012 when our daughter graduated from The Baldwin School but the portion my family was responsible to pay for both of the children yearly, altogether was less than $6000.00. Then our son graduated in 2015 when that became bittersweet history.

Since 2005 until 2015 we had spent all our yearly tax returns in tuition fees at these private schools. But, if and when we allowed interest to accrue for not paying on time, the amount of our share easily doubled over some time. That was always our case. Looking back, regardless of our immaturity, it was all well worth it.

MONEY ISSUES CAN
BREAK UP A MARRIAGE

MONEY AND SEXUAL SOUL-TIES are two of the major reasons that eventually ended up breaking up our marriage besides the way we treated each other in our household. We did not see eye to eye on how to manage our finances gambling or no gambling. The addictions I feel just evolved with time.

I play the Lottery every day since I arrived in America, sadly to say. I am trying to quit by God's Grace. But I am not yet delivered, not as fast as I wish to be. It is not a kind addiction. It takes a toll on one's relationships as well as pocket book. Maybe, by the time you read my story, I will be totally healed from this addiction. It is my hope and prayer.

Gambling is one of the worst of addictions anyone can have. This is one of the quickest ways anybody can get messed up mentally and financially. I used to tell myself that I would win big and pay off the debts. Well, it is a lie from the pit of hell. Instead, money gets lost, followed by misery and edginess mixed with fear takes over. You have a good image how that can look like, right? It is NOT the American way to a dream.

My husband on the other hand, thinks that he will win and return to motherland and spend the winnings. Chances of winning in any lottery are very slim. Besides, two gamblers any day in a household financially, is a quick route to a man-made sink zone. And the financial arguments are a no zone for any child bearing, whatsoever.

That type of stress added with extra marital sexual soul ties led him and I to succumbing to a lifestyle of roommates for the

sake of raising our children together. Even in this arrangement, it has proven to be more toxic for everyone especially to the innocent children we lovingly brought together in this world.

KENEILWE IS NOT TO BLAME

I am in NO way blaming Keneilwe for all my misfortunes to date. I will tell you this though that the type of partner you choose in life will help usher you into your destiny in a wholesome state or in a butchered state. The choice is usually yours to make and take.

I have come to know the importance of asking God daily for Spiritual Discernment, His Direction, His Grace, His Wisdom, His Will for my life, His Knowledge of His Laws and Revelation for everything in life, before embarking and immersing myself fully with a specific other or thing. I have learnt that God wants me to take time and investigate people or matters more in order to see the real heart in people or things for my own sake all around. Some unnecessary bloopers in life can be avoided.

I didn't know this then. I would have been able to facilitate through life a bit better and less bruised.

I am nowadays spending my time recovering from everything that has transpired in my life between Keneilwe and I since the day him and I became one in marriage. From the day we left Lilongwe to the day we got to the point of no reversal in Philadelphia, so far away from home. It is not like there is not an answer to this predicament him and I were in. In life, according to the Bible there is an answer to everything. But how can two people walk together, except they be agreed? That Bible verse comes from the Book of Amos 3:3. Once again! Therefore, him and I got to the end of our marriage road.

MY DESTINY NEEDED
MY MISFORTUNES

I have realised that, Keneilwe and I becoming together as husband and wife in our home town in February of 1994 was not an accident. He had our children in him. I needed to incubate the children and bring them forth for the glory of God and satisfaction according to each child's individual's purpose and destiny. The children were encased in the urge and the need for us especially in me to run to America, My Destiny, for a hopeful future for everyone in my family and beyond. God creates No mistakes! In this regard, our children are a certainty that God is very good even when we may not deserve His goodness.

In the matrimonial journey, there had been many issues that took place,that had happened to me personally whether I had a hand in them to happen to me or not. But some of the issues needed to happen to me to mold me into what I needed to become, to usher me into my very own destiny. That was a way tailor made for me specifically. That was the only crucial way I would have answered to my Destiny calling which was not in my homeland of Malawi but in America where I would have to go through so much turmoil to arrive at it, but all for the glory and satisfaction of my Creator, God. I can't help to understand and relate to Job 23:10 Bible verse. God needed my state of mind to become pure gold so that he could trust me to carry more of His glory for His purpose for my life and my destiny. Life had to get that way!

Keep in mind that my husband went through the fear of deportation which to me was traumatic and I too because of that particular experience dealt with my own trauma alongside him. But that same season caused me to get closer to God, yet the same impact of this particular event, did not have the same effect towards him and his Maker. Different personalities, different attitudes, different behaviour patterns, different outcomes, different callings and different purposes and destinies.

God knows how to get you when He calls You! He got me!

Whatever needed to happen to me in my motherland of Africa to get me to America where I needed to be, had to happen. Maybe if my husband was faithful and dutifully satisfying in his role, I would have seen no need to come to another land because I would have no need to run from anything. My life would have been void of chaos that is if he were a protector and a provider for me when we landed in America. I would also have never known the strength that was in me all along let alone the creativeness God embed in me. This was the place where God would make me laugh and show Himself creative through me. You are not following? Yes, I understand.

THE BIRTH OF MY INVENTIONS

You see, after being in my job for 8 years at the Peas by 2013, job life was becoming redundant. I went into work and the satisfying feeling was no longer there. I thank God that even during the beginning of the recession in 2008, my job had need of me and had the money to pay me too.

But living on loan advances was no longer satisfying me. Please do not get me wrong, the family paid me good money over the table using my tax identification number. It was not so much about the money.

It was what was inside of me. I didn't know that it was there but it needed to come out. It had been lying dormant and had rendered me restless until a dog came into my life. I found out when the Peas family bought a beautiful show dog pedigree for their little girl who was 8 in 2008.

My life was going to turn surprisingly interesting. The dog at first was a disaster and a nuisance for me. He was my responsibility to train and walk. Yet, a dog in my upbringing had been my brother's responsibility so I had no idea on how to handle a dog 101. I will confess that at one point I had found myself shedding tears as I cleaned the dog's diarrhea and throw up all at once during the dog's early days at their house.

I am a very emotional human being, so I cry easily. Boy, did I cry during those dog housebreaking days with that handsome dog or what? I was caught sobbing a lot. I had become confused about my life at that point in time. God, what was happening? I knew that I had graduated high school from one of the best of schools on Planet Earth! Although I wasn't the smartest of graduates. But Lord! Was dog training and dog poop picking part of the plan? Ugh. I had felt so defeated!

But God was laughing in Love in His Heavenly abode.

Yes, He was laughing because this very dog was what God was going to use to bring about ideas in me He Himself had placed in me that I once thought were foolish. 1 Corinthians 1:27 explains my sentiments.

It was when walking this very dog in the outdoors, that I was inspired to create a special bag I call the "POOCHPOOPOUCH" that would carry and hide the dog poop I would pick up and clean up after it. The walks in the outdoors were twice a day. I got super irritated to carry or clutch unto my hand the waste bag for long periods of time before I would toss it in the next available trash can. On these walks, I would also bring with me other items such as house keys which I would hook onto the bag, my water bottle onto another hook and my cell phone for talking into another pocket on the bag, dog treats into another pocket. The plastic waste bag of dog poop was always hidden away separately, until trash-can time. Out In the suburbs, public trash cans were scarce and sporadic. In case my fellow African natives from motherland, Malawi are wondering why I am making such a big deal about tossing dog poop or any trash in the trash can. It is because Littering in Pennsylvania comes with a $300 to $1,000 penalty and at other times the penalty comes with jail time.

It was sweet when I found out from my patent lawyer Eric LaMorte, that the feature of the hidden pouch on bags had never been done before. I would be the first inventor to protect its use legally for the next 20 years. So, in July of 2015, I received a certificate to my first patent. It was there where I became alert and begun to take seriously all the other ideas that God has placed in my spirit, for retail.

....

I have many other ideas that are tantalizing and exciting that should be out into the marketplace for the betterment of mankind on a daily level,one of these days.

I wish I could tell you that my journey to my first Utility Patent was smooth. A thousand times, Nope!

All these peculiar discoveries and improvements in my life became a conscious nuisance to the people who didn't think much of me but due to circumstances had to be around me or me vice versa.

BE CELEBRATED NOT TOLERATED

My job, for instance, started to show a side to them towards me that I didn't know existed. On The morning of July 14th of 2015, I was fired after 10 years of service as a full time babysitter, house manager via a mobile phone text message because I was afraid to show up for work for 2 days. Their "problem child" on several manic bouts of her issues had previously thrown sharp stuff at me. Then the knives and all the sharp things in their house were hidden with nobody sitting me down to explain to me what was really happening besides other problems we had encountered by that time of the year. I was offended because I would spend 8 hours with their child. If anything, I needed to know what I was dealing with so that if I could prevent anything I could do, accordingly. After all, It was their word against mine in a moment of trouble with the police. I was, and I am black in a white neighborhood. By 2015, I was still an illegal immigrant. Whew! Help me Jesus! And everyone who knew me was in disbelief at the news of my loss of employment. I had never spoken ill of this job until July 14th of 2015! Yep.

It had been 10 years since that written and signed contract between the Peas and me. In my naive and comfortable days, I had misplaced it and never thought that I would need it to prove their promises of a severance pay. Gone baby Gone! Just like that! My 10 years at that job were dissolved into nothing but turmoil. Well, at least that's what I thought in anger for a year because the Peas

had resorted to defaming my name and babysitting conduct into oblivion.

I spent 5 months looking for a nanny job until a family told me never to use the Peas as my job reference. The Peas would tell the families I would interview for that I was beating up their 15 year- old daughter whom I had spent 10 years with. My world became a challenge to live in from July of 2015 until July 2016. I was so defamed that even the job I tried to acquire for 4 months in Gladwyne, hired me on purpose after knowing everything from the Peas with the intention to abuse me on the job as I took care of their 8 month-old daughter, Skye. They in turn fired me the morning I had picked up my son Avedi, from a hospital stay because I was not at work on time, without a severance pay, once again.

They too got their Regional and Local Police where they stay to scare me off. I have recorded and detailed proof. It was sad to watch and crazy that all this nightmare was happening once again. Yet, all I wanted to do was make a decent living for my household. The wealthy families used their connections, their power to destroy the little I was trying to achieve for my family. I didn't resort to violence or crime in any way in return. I went inside my little shell and prayed for God to be The Vindicator. I sought God out for forgiveness so that I could continue my personal journey to receive and be able to walk into my Destiny which is the reason why I am still here in my right mind, sharing my journey.

All I needed was another chance to work in a person's household remembering that a utility patent is always better executed if the owner is in the United States of America with a Green Card under their belt and money. Well, I had not gotten there yet. There was no Green Card yet. Money was scarce that is why I could not give up on life and abort my God given dreams. I still had to strive for work, the Green Card, all my inventions and the American dream for my family and for myself.

Those two work experiences prompted me to share with you the reader the need for a job contract. Yes, even if you are an illegal immigrant. Especially if you are an illegal immigrant because to the government or anyone you have no say. But when something is written then it is spoken first before it is written, that in itself

has power. Power to help you do what you pledged to do in the job scope and get compensated for the work you have rendered in peace. You can go separate ways without either party in the agreement feeling violated or taken advantage of. You are an illegal immigrant but that does not make you a slave or a NOBODY.

Those two unfortunate work experiences taught me that it is a hard challenge for the lesser guy to try to make something out of their life from whatever little resources they have. It is seen as an okay thing whenever a lesser guy struggles. People are fine so long you are not trying to make anything good for yourself. It was not comfortable that I as a small person, illegal immigrant and all, was shielded from becoming all that I could be, by trying the only best way I knew to do, in the only best job that circumstances had me in. I was not trying to get out of the job scope, but I was using the very job scope to make room for something else out there that was calling my name. America, my destiny!

I thought that the people of power, authority and connections I was around would celebrate my efforts of trying to get up in life and make this American dream come true. I had no idea that they would be the very ones who were in my path to sabotage any hopes of getting my dreams come to pass. It was disheartening.

THE ROAD TO SUCCESS IS LONELY

And a few Facebook frenemies started to make fun of me by texting me inboxes that undermined what I was claiming as an idea never done before until I claimed it. I did lose some friends there too. Isn't it sad that the road to success is super trying and lonely?! To those that have been there and are still there know what I am saying.

It was even harder to feel the love at home when I was not bringing in the cash for bills after that July 14th, 2015. My husband was not pleased at all.

I feel like God gave me 1 year of financial struggles with no sure way of where next the money was coming from to really ZERO in on my loved ones' true characters which I was able to see

for real one by one. It was very difficult while I went through it but it brought me enough clarity on how I needed to do things even in my own life so that I did not end up there where it hurt so bad ever again, at the mercy of anybody but God alone.

In July 2015 until August 2016 I had no income. This was when our house almost went into foreclosure. It was saved by a few family members, family friends and three Jewish families that reached out to my family to help us.

I don't think that you understand how much love and respect I have towards Jewish people. They to me, have done for me more than a kinsman. They remind me of what Jesus said to His Disciples about family in Matthew 12:50. Anybody who does the Will of God is Jesus' mother, father or brother. I felt the love of God on me when the families all worked together to help us to avoid that foreclosure because it truly was unfortunate that I had lost my job.

God was still in control in my life. Just like in Romans 8:28. All things were working together for good, to them that love God, to them who are called according to His purpose. I had the evidence that God had not left me yet. I continued to feel His Mighty Hand over my life.

It was rough, but God was still showing Himself Strong in my life no matter what was happening all around me just like He said in Isaiah 43:2. It was hard when my family members begun to show me some of their tried out but hidden characters. Lordie!

Who is she trying to be? They sneered behind me when I began to chase after these ideas God had endowed me with while broke.

Keneilwe once spat on me towards the end of the year in 2015 when life and money in our household was proven scarce. Most Philadelphians remember when Pope Francis was in Philadelphia and traveling from downtown Philadelphia to Wynnewood where Saint Charles Borromeo seminary stands about 6 minute-drive from our home. Everywhere, the streets were closed. We were all on lockdown. Nobody could go anywhere. Money was funny in our home at that particular time, as it was usually when it came to mortgage. He instead was sending money and a suitcase full of new clothes for his siblings to Africa through a family member

who had come from our home country through the Roman Catholic church for the Pope's visit representing our homage religious sector. When I contested to his thoughts of sending money instead of paying for the roof above his family. He was vexed with me.

It was in the afternoon, I was laying on the love couch in our home. Our daughter was home from her apartment visiting her baby brothers, seated in the living room by the house desktop computer chair behind the love couch, and on either side of her were her twin brothers looking at something on her laptop when their father and I continued to verbally fight in their presence.

At one moment during the argument, fury caused Keneilwe to get up from where he was sitting by chair to the door whilst everyone was trying to watch the motorcade travelling on City Line Avenue via live TV enroute to the seminary and suddenly he walked over to me, stood above me, and he disturbingly and unapologetically spat on me.

He did this to me to show me how disgusted he felt about me because he was convinced that my choices and efforts in life to put money in my "stupid ideas" were just plain stupid and amounting to nothing. And at that particular time, he was not going to let anybody tell him what to do with his money. When I say that he said the words with a devilish emphasis. He meant every word of it too. I knew at that point and understood clearly that what he was feeling and expressing in my presence and that of his children was violent and dangerous and deeper than my eyes could see.

And you must believe me when I tell you that we were not behind in mortgage this time around during Pope Francis visit to Philadelphia, solely because of me alone. Ugh.

SOMETIMES IT'S ALRIGHT
TO WALK AWAY

For years, I had taken the blame for every one of his failures! So, I came to a screeching halt one day and made a decision to stop the lie from carrying on. I was no longer going to allow myself

to feeling like I had brought him to America against his will, he'll always find himself blameless if I carried myself like that. I could never pay him back enough for however he made himself believe all the things he wished to believe about me. Then I in my world at that very moment had decided that it was time to bury the hatchet and try to live, move on and continue alone on this journey of my destiny. I became driven to investigate more on and entertain the ideas/inventions that God in His Sovereignty placed in my spirit. At least I should try to pursue these ideas first before I give up. The ideas are intertwined with the ultimate purpose and destiny for my life. If I am with the wrong person or people, I could easily abort my destiny which is in my purpose, which I have no doubt in my mind that both include my journey to America. I have learned to walk away from whosoever is a threat to the reason why I was specifically created by God for Him. I owe Keneilwe, the father of my children respect due to the years shared and the precious most beautiful children we have together. I owe him brotherly love for the sake of peace amongst the family. And the Bible requires that everyone is obligated to love one unto another in the book of Romans 13:8.

I strongly believe that America is my destiny. It's where I need to be, come rain or shine! I have no regrets.

God has use of me and these ideas He put in me. I can use the resources from these ideas to help enlarge His kingdom on earth for His Glory. I really believe that!

Therefore, consciously, I am taking careful measures that avoid any future love partner that may be a stumbling block on all aspects of life. If and when I am not careful with my choices, the result could hinder me from fulfilling any of my God given purposes for my destiny.

So, letting go of my husband emotionally, physically and legally recently, on the basis of our marriage by submitting to a consent divorce, was a very difficult decision in spite of our issues, overall. For a long time, we had disagreed on everything. Amos 3:3 always reaffirms clearly that it's impossible for two people to walk together when they disagree so much especially on the essentials of the very fundamentals that build up a healthy and functional

lifestyle such as a marriage. Especially when all this occurs after marriage counseling, 4 separations within the house and outside of matrimonial home.

GOD BECAME MY FIRST LOVE AGAIN

One of the easiest things in those years of my journey for me to do was making God My First Love again! It is God's desire in the book of Revelation 2:4 that we never forsake His love. That was easy for me to fix because I had realized that I was in distress because I had perverted and reversed the order in which real LOVE should always be in my life. Matthew 6:33 is a compass to an everlasting joy and a rewarding lifestyle forever!

God was not lying when He said that no one comes before Him and He shares His glory with no one in Isaiah 42:8. I have seen first-hand evidence in my own life, the consequences of making other worldly things and worldly people take up the place of God whether you are a citizen, an illegal immigrant or legal immigrant of wherever you may call home.

After examining my journey, I discovered that all of my human efforts in 25 years, I tried to make, to win overs Keneilwe's heart, were never good enough living in Malawi nor America. I could not win him over even if I tried some more. I exhausted everything I thought I knew to do to make him see that I was originally doing all that I did for us for a better future and better living conditions for our family.

I have no doubt that he has never agreed with my motives or the intent of why I have made my choices and entertained them thus far. I have since made peace with it. He made my turning point seasons very easy for me. Spitting on me on several occasions was a real deal sealer, along the years. I forgave him, for each time he did so but I completely begun to put boundaries all around me so that he and nobody else will be able to do unto me negative things that can be avoided. There are things in me that I can change for a better tomorrow. That's for sure!

....

I have talked to God and made peace with the situation of the father of my kids and me.

I second to the bible verse that says that in all things give thanks unto The Lord for this is the perfect will of God in Christ Jesus concerning you in 1 Thessalonians 5:18!

Thanking God for the difficult moments in my life was one of the challenges I had to overcome! I hope that you too, will become thankful in your daily life and maybe, you will also become closer to God no matter the circumstances in your life whether you are here in America as a citizen, or a legal resident like me. Not forgetting that I too was once an illegal immigrant. Wherever you are on planet Earth, WHATEVER you aspire to be, consider yourself a special human-being, becoming whoever God intentionally created you to be.

I truly BELIEVE that we are not really home on Planet Earth but immigrants of some sort and therefore can never really get loose here until Heaven calls us back!

For now, if anything, remember to keep the laws (principles) of the country wherever you are as well as God's laws (principles) found in the Bible. You are Guaranteed Success in your individual giftings, callings, purposes and destinies no matter what. Whatsoever you decide to do in your life, I beseech you, not to become a victim of that Bible verse of Hosea 4:6 KJV! Once again it reads, "My people are destroyed for lack of knowledge: because thou hast rejected knowledge, I will also reject thee, that thou shalt be no priest to me: seeing thou hast forgotten the law of thy God, I also forget thy children."

Believe me, I am learning that The Information, Knowledge and Wisdom of God's Word is True and Life Transforming!

But for now, I encourage you to find out your destiny. I found mine. America is my Destiny, 20 years later! I have no doubt, I have no regrets whatsoever. If anything, I am very grateful for everything life has taught me this far, for the glory of God and His satisfaction for the reason why He created me. I am confident that you also now understand HOW AMERICA BECAME MY DESTINY.

SHALOM!

....

ABOUT THE AUTHOR

Brenda **Amanda Mwaya** is a native of Malawi and a Permanent Legal Resident of the United States of America. Brenda is a designer, inventor, and patent holder. She is also a professional nanny. She was compelled to share her story with others—those who long for the American Dream—in the hope of educating them about the difficult realities and hardships of living life in America without proper legal documentation. She desires to share some of the lessons learned, as well as the blunders, heartaches, and pains that could have been avoided in her day-to-day work life and at home.

She deeply believes that the secret to success in America and the surest way to an American destiny is a combination of keeping the laws and principles of the country, having faith and a positive attitude, and being part of a close-knit and supportive community. A sound plan, a good bill of health, and implementing useful information is also essential.

She is confident that the American Dream is still attainable even when faced with difficult odds. She is very sure of this because her life and the life of her family members speaks for itself—twenty years later.

Made in the
USA
Middletown, DE